ISLAM
its
Concepts & History

By

SYED MAHMUDUNNASIR
B.A., LL.B., LL.M. (Alig.)

KITAB BHAVAN
New Delhi-110002

KITAB BHAVAN
Publishers, Distributors, Exporters & Importers
1784, Kalan Mahal, Darya Ganj,
New Delhi - 1100 02 (India)

Phones : (91-11) 23277392/93,23274686, 32906494
Fax : (91-11) 23263383

Website: www.nusratalinasri.com

Email : nasri@vsnl.com
: nusrat@bol.net.in

1st Published in Inida : 1981
4th Edition : 2014

ISBN : 81-7151-051-5
Book Code No. : I000105

Printed & Published in India by
Nusrat Ali Nasri for KITAB BHAVAN
1784, Kalan Mahal, Darya Ganj,
New Delhi - 1100 02 [India]

CONTENTS

PART (1)

Basic Principles of Islam

PART (2)

Outline of Islamic History

PART (3)

The Holy Qur'an

Part (1)

Basic Principles of Islam

CONTAINING

Chapters

1. THE ARTICLES OF FAITH.
2. THE CONCEPT AND SPIRIT OF *TAUHEED*.
3. FINALITY OF PROPHETHOOD.
4. PRACTICES OF ISLAM.

Chapter 1

The Articles of Faith

The word "Islam" is derived from *aslama* meaning to resign oneself. The true religion with Allah is Islam, which signifies not early peace, salvation, resignation of the will of man to God but also a striving after righteousness. Those who profess the religion of Islam are called *Mussalmans* or Muslims.

The six main beliefs to which every good Muslim adheres are :—

(1) Belief in one God (Allah).

(2) Belief in angels, who intercede for men.

(3) Belief in the Holy Qur'an.

(4) Belief in the Prophets of Allah.

(5) Belief in the judgment, paradise and hell.

(6) Belief in the divine decrees.

The leading doctrine of Islam is the belief in one All-Powerful Allah, which Prophet Muhammad (Peace be upon him) firmly established. Salvation is attained by all who submit to Allah, that is live according to His rule as revealed by Prophet Muhammad. The Qur'an has enjoined upon the Muslims to bear credence to the existence of angels. The Prophet has also instructed the believers, to have faith in the angels, only next to Allah. To deny the existence of the angels is *kufr*. The Holy Qur'an is accepted as a direct revelation from Allah to Prophet Muhammad and hence form the basis of all Muslim teaching. The Qur'an admittedly occupies an important position among the great religious books of the world. It has created on all but new phase of human thought and fresh type of character. It is the youngest of the epoch-making works belonging to religious literature. The Prophet used 852 verses to foretell the fateful Day of Judgment when Allah would reward all men with their eternal bliss of punishment. Paradise is pictured as a great garden filled with mountains, rivers, shady trees and a pleasant climate, while Hell is hotter than the most torturous desert which the Arabs might imagine, and abounds in burning wind and scalding water.

In addition to the six main tenets of Islam there are five essential duties which a loyal Muslim must perform. These are called five pillars (*arkan*) of Islam. The cardinal principle in Muslim Creed is the *Shahadat* or the recitation of the confession of faith. There is no God but Allah, and Muhammad is his Prophet. *Shahadat* is normal manifestation of Muslim religious belief (*Iman*) rather than an obligatory duty (*Amal*). The observance of the ritual prayer is repeatedly emphasised as one of the essential religious duties.

Parts of the Muslim Prayers :

The Muslim prayer has three distinct parts :

(*i*) Physical purification ;

(*ii*) Certain movements and gesticulations ; and

(*iii*) Recitals.

As Prophet Muhammad has said Purity is half of the faith, the Muslim prayer is preceded by physical purification by *wadu*. Apart from the adoration of the Lord which is the primary function of *salat* the form of worship in unison, the obedience of *Imam*, the standing of every faithful shoulder to shoulder in the same row without the least distinction of colour or race are some of the additional beauties of prayer which can rightly be emphasised as peculiar glories of Islam. The prayer ground thus became, as Joseph Hell remarks, the first drill ground of Islam. Islam condemns spirit of hoarding and emphasises charity. *Zakat* which has taken the form of this obligatory contribution means purification. In the Holy Qur'an *Zakat* is often associated with the *Salat*. Fasting is the fourth pillar of Islamic faith. The fasting is obligatory on every Muslim who is grown up or physically fit. The month of *Ramadan* is specified for the purpose of fasting. Pilgrimage is the fifth and last pillar of Islam. Once in a lifetime every Muslim of either sex who can afford is supposed to undertake at a stated time of the year a holy visit to Mecca.

Some of the topics have been discussed in greater detail under the heading "Practices of Islam" of this part.

(1) Belief in one God (Allah)

The subject now needs no elaborate arguments in its support, especially when Science accepts it as a verity. A century before, Biology took the universe as a freak of Nature which in her works, as the then atheistic belief what observed no other system. But today the rule of the law has been admitted on all hands. Everything in the world appears to have been enchained by the Law. It follows it implicitly. Nature discloses regularity, punctuality, knowledge, power, command, intellect, preordination, prearrangement, precaution, and several other features that are the possessions of the mind exclusively. In their presence the universe cannot be taken as the outcome of accident. It needs an intelligent design to precede the process of its creation. The word "design" sometimes used to bore minds with sceptic tendencies, but it has become now widened in its connotation. It brings within it so many facts and figures recently discovered by Science that disbelief in God would amount to ignorance. But how wonderful of the Holy Qur'an to anticipate, in its pages, all that Science advances to substantiate her belief in Divine Exercise. It in itself is an extra-cogent reason, firstly, to believe in an Omniscient Being and, secondly, as to the Divine Origin of the Book itself.

The Holy Book, though teeming with reasons on the subject, adopts also another novel but laconic method to explain its verities. It gives us a list of Divine Attributes which in their signification also imply the best of logic needed to prove all Qur'anic tenets.

The word *Al-Rab* includes *Al-Badi*—He who creates out of nothing. *Al-Bari*—He who originates things with various faculties in them. *Al-Batin*—He who knows latent and hidden properties of things. *Al-Zahir*—He who brings things to manifestation. *Al-Wahid*—He who finds and knows the whereabouts of the required things. *Al-Jami*—The collector of things in the place they are needed. *Al-Jabbar*, *Al-Qahar*—He who subjects others to His will and makes them to work according to His wishes to their good. *Al-Khaliq*—He who combines things in a given proportion to create new things. He fixes the said proportion first. *Al-Rashid*—He who puts things on the right path. *Al-Hadi*—He who guides further progress on right lines. *Al-Razzaq*—The Nourisher, *Al-Rahman*—He who prearranges the needful. *Al-Muhsi*—He who comprehends (every necessity). *Al-Basit*—He who expands. *Al-Qabid*—He who contracts. *Al-Mani*—He who guards things against the encroachment of other destroying factors. *Al-Muqit*—The Controller. *Al-Raqib*—He who watches every movement. *Al-Akhir*—He who brings things to their final development.

These attributes refer to various functions of the mind that are observed even in the creation of a single thing.

The Holy Qur'an did a real service to scientific research through Divine Attributes. It facilitated investigation. These names supply us with a sure data, and in the light of their significance we proceed in our research work as the Qur'an itself suggests when it asks us to study Nature. The Chapter 3, Verse 190 of the Holy Qur'an clearly says that in studying things in the universe we have to keep these Attributes of God before our mind. The Muslim scientists put the abovementioned names on their chart as a guide and took no time to discover the laws working in Nature for creation.

Among the heathen Arabs the idea of Godhead varied according to the culture of the individual or of the clan. With some it rose, comparatively speaking to the "divination or deification of Nature, among others it fell to simple fetishism, the adoration of a piece of dough, a stick, or a stone. Some believed in a future life, others had no idea of it whatever. The pre-Islamite Arabs had their groves, their oracle-trees, their priestesses, like the Syro Phroenicians. Phallic worship was not unknown to them, and the generative powers received adoration, like the hosts of heaven, under monuments of stone and wood. The wild denizens of the desert, then as now, could not be impervious to the idea of some unseen hand driving the blasts which swept over the whole tracts, or forming the beautiful visions which rose before the traveller to lure him to destruction. And thus there floated in the Arab world an intangible and unrealised conception of a superior deity, the Lord of all.

The Jews, those great conservators, of the monotheistic idea, as they have been generally regarded in history, probably might have assisted in the formation of this conception. But they themselves showed what strange metamorphoses can take place in the thoughts of a nation when not aided by a historical and rationalistic element in their religious code.

The Jews had entered Arabia at various times, and under the pressure of various circumstances. Naturally, the conception of the different bodies of emigrants, refugees, or colonists would vary much. The ideas of the men driven out by the Assyrians or the Babylonians would be more anthropomorphic, more anthropopathic, than of those who fled before Vespasian, Trajan, or Hadrian. The characteristics which had led the Israelites repeatedly to lapse into idolatry in their original homes, when seers were in their midst to denounce their back-slidings, would hardly preserve them from the heathenism of their Arab brothers. With an idea of "the God of Abraham" they would naturally combine a materialistic conception of the deity, and hence we find them rearing "a statue representing Abraham, with the ram beside him ready for sacrifice" in the interior of the Kaaba.

Amongst the late-comers the Shammaites and the Zealots formed by far the largest proportion. Among them the worship of the law verged upon idolatry, and the Scribes and the Rabbins claimed a respect almost approaching adoration. They believed themselves to be the guardians of the people, the preservers of law and tradition, living exemplars and mirrors, in which the true mode of life, according to the law, was preserved. They looked upon themselves as the "flower of the nation", and they were considered, through their intercourse with God, to possess the gift of prophecy. In fact, by their people as well as by themselves they were regarded as the prime favourites of God.

The veneration of the Jews for Moses went so far, says Josephus, that they reverenced his name next to that of God, and this veneration they transferred to Ezra, the restorer of national life and law under the Kyanian dynasty.

Besides, the mass of the Jews had never, probably, thoroughly abandoned the worship of the Teraphim, a sort of household good made in the shape of human beings, and consulted on all occasions as domestic oracles, or regarded perhaps more as guardian penates. This worship must have been strengthened by contact with the heathen Arabs.

When Jesus made his appearance in Judea, the doctrine of divine unity and of a supreme Personal Will, overshadowing the universe with its might and grace, received acceptance only among one race—the worshippers of Jehovah. And even among them, despite all efforts to the contrary, the conception of the divinity had either deteriorated by contact with heathen nations, or become modified by the influence of pagan philosophies. On the one hand, Ghaldaeo-Magian philosophy had left its fingermark indelibly impressed on the Jewish traditions, on the other, their best minds, whilst introducing among the Greek and the Roman philosophers the conception of a great Primal Cause, had imbibed, in the schools of Alexandria, notions hardly reconcilable with their monotheistic creed.

The Hindus, with their multitudinous hordes of gods and goddesses, the Mago-Zoroastrians, with their two divinities struggling for mastery, the Greeks, the Romans, and the Egyptians, with their pantheons full of deities whose morality was below that of the worshippers—such was the condition of the civilised world when Jesus commenced his preachings. With all his dreams and aspirations, his mind was absolutely exempt from those pretensions which have been fixed on him by his overzealous followers. He never claimed to be a "complement of God" or to be a "hypostasis of the Divinity".

Even modern idealistic Christianity has not been able yet to shake itself free from the old legacy bequeathed by the anthropomorphism of begone ages. Age after age everything human has been eliminated from the history of the great Teacher, until his personality is lost in mass of legends. The New Testament itself, with "its incubation of a century" leaves the revered figure clothed in a mist. And each day the old idea of "an Aeon born in the bosom of eternity", gathers force until the Council of Nice gives it a shape and consistency, and formulates it into a dogma.

Many minds, bewildered by the far-offness of the Universal Father, seek a resting-place midway in a human personality which they call divine. It is this need of a nearer object of adoration which leads modern Christianity to give a name to an ideal, clothe it with flesh and blood, and worship it as a man-God.

The gifted author of the "Defects of Modern Christianity" considers the frequency with which the Nazarene Prophet asserted that he was "the Son of God", and demanded the same worship as God himself, a proof of his Divinity. That Jesus ever maintained he was the Son of God, in the sense in which it has been construed by Christian divine and apologists, we totally deny. Matthew Arnold has shown conclusively that the New Testament records are in many respects wholly unreliable. So far as the divinity of Christ is concerned, one can almost see the legend growing. But assuming that he made use of the expressions attributed to him, do they prove that he claimed to be "the only begotten of the Father". Has the apologist not heard of the Eastern dervish, famous now as al-Hallaj, who claimed to be God Himself. "*An-al-Hakk*", "I am God—I am the Truth", said he, and the *Musulman* divines, like the Jewish Sanhedrin, pronounced him guilty of blasphemy, and condemned him to death. A poor simple heart, kindling with an exalted mysticism, was thus removed from the earth. The Babi still believes that his master, "the Gate" to eternal life, was not killed, but miraculously removed to the heaven. Can it be said that when Abu Maughis al-Hallaj and the Babi called themselves "Truth" and the "Gate to Heaven", they meant to imply that they were part of the Divinity, or, if they did that their "claim" is tantamount to proof ? But, as we said before, we deny that Jesus, whose conceptions, when divested of the Aberglaube of his followers, were singularly free from exaggeration as to his own character or personality, ever used any expression to justify the demand attempt to be fixed upon him. His conception of the "Fatherhood" of God embraced all humanity. All mankind were the children of God, and he was their Teacher sent by the Eternal Father. The Christian had thus a nobler exemplar before him. The teachings of the Prophet of Nazareth should have elevated him to a purer conception of the Deity. But six centuries had surrounded the figure of Jesus with those myths which, in opposition to his own words, resolved him into a manifestation of the Godhead. The "Servant" took the place of the Master in the adoration of the world. The vulgar masses, unable to comprehend or realise this wonderful mixture of Neo-Pythagoreanism, Platonism, Judaeo-Hellenistic philosophy, and the teachings of Jesus, abored him as God incarnate, or reverted to the primitive worship of relics and of a tinselled goddess who represented the pure mother of Jesus. The Collyridians, who were by no means an unimportant sect, went so far as to introduce in the Christian pantheon the Virgin Mary for God, and worship her as such, offering her a sort of twisted cake called collyris, whence the sect had its name.

As the Council of Nice which definitely settled the nature of Jesus, there were men who held that besides "God the Father", there were two other gods—Christ and the Virgin Mary. And the Romanists even now, it is said, call the mother of Jesus the complement of the Trinity.

In the long night of superstition the Christians had wandered far away from the simplicity of the Nazarene teachings. The worship of images, saints and relics had become inseparably blended with the religion of Jesus. The practices which he had denounced, the evils which he had reprehended, were, one by one, incorporated with his faith. The holy ground where the revered Teacher had lived and walked was involved in a cloud of miracles and visions, and "the nerves of the mind were benumbed by the habits of obedience and belief.

Against all the absurdities we have described above, the life-aim of Prophet Muhammad was directed. Addressing, with the voice of truth, inspired by deep communion with the God of the Universe, the fetish-worshippers of the Arabian tribes on one side and the followers of degraded Christianity and Judaism on the other, Muhammad, that "master of speech", as he has been truly called, never travelled out of the province of reason, and made them all blush at the monstrousness of their beliefs. Muhammad, the grand apostle of the unity of God, thus stands forth in history in noble conflict with the retrogressive tendency of man to associate other beings with the Creator of the Universe. Ever and anon in the Qur'an occur passages, fervid and burning, like the following : "Your God is one God", there is no God but He, the Most Merciful. In the creation of the heaven and the earth, and the alteration of night and day, and in the ship which saileth on the sea, laden with what is profitable to mankind, and in the rain-water which God sendeth from heaven, quickening again the dead earth, and the animals of all sorts which cover its surface, and in the change of winds, and the clouds balanced between the heaven and the earth, are signs to people of understanding, yet some men take idols beside God, and love them as with the love due to God". What a depth of sympathy towards those benighed people do these words convey. Again "It is He who causeth the lightning to appear unto you (to strike) fear and (to raise) hope, and formeth the pregnant clouds. The thunder celebrateth His praise, and the angels also...........He launcheth His thunderbolts, and striketh therewith whom He pleaseth while they dispute concerning Him...........It is He who of right ought to be involved, and those (the idols) whom they invoke besides Him shall not respond to them at all, otherwise than as he who stretched forth his hands to the water that it may ascend to his mouth when it cannot ascend (thither). He hath created the heavens and the earth to (manifest His) justice, far be that from Him which they associate with Him. He hath created man............and behold He is a professed disputer. He hath likewise created the cattle for you, and they are a credit unto you when they come trooping home at evening-time, or are led forth to pasture in the morn......And He hath subjected the night and day to your service, and the sun and the moon and the stars are all bound by His laws............It is He who hath subjected the sea unto you, and thou seest the ships ploughing the deep...........and that ye might render thanks."

Shall He therefore who createth ye as he who createth not? Do you not therefore take heed? If ye were to reckon up the blessings of God, ye shall not be able to compute their number, God is surely gracious and merciful. He knoweth that which ye conceal and that which ye publish. But those (the idols) whom ye invoke, besides the Lord, create nothing but are themselves created. They are dead and not living.

"God there is no God He—the Living, the Eternal. No slumber seizeth Him. Whatsoever is in heaven or in earth is His. Who can intercede with Him but by His own permission? He knows what has been before, and what shall be after them, yet nought of His knowledge shall they grasp but He willeth. His Throne reacheth over the heavens and the earth, and the upholding of them both burdeneth Him not........... He throweth the veil of night over the day, pursuing in quickly. He created the sun, the moon, and the stars subjected to laws by His behest. Is not all creation and all empire His? Blessed be the Lord of the Worlds. Say, He alone is God: God the Eternal. He begetteth not, and He is not begotten, there is none like unto Him. Praise be to God, the Lord of the Worlds, the Compassionate, the Merciful, Kind on the Day of Reckoning. Thee only do we worship, and to Thee do we cry for help. Guide us on the straight path, the path of those to whom Thou art gracious, with whom Thou art not angry, such as go not astray...........Against the evil in His creation I betake me to the Lord of the Daybreak". Thou needest not raise thy voice, for Thee knoweth the secret whisper, and what is yet more hidden. Say, Whose is what is in the heavens and the earth? Say God's who has imposed mercy on Himself.

With Him are the keys of the unseen. None know them save He. He knows what is in the land and in the sea, no leaf falleth but He knoweth it, nor is here a grain in the darkness under the earth, nor a thing, green or sere, but it is recorded by itself. He taketh your souls in the night, and knoweth what the work of your day deserveth, then He awaketh you, that the set life-term may be fulfilled, then unto Him shall ye return and then shall He declare unto you what you have wrought. Verily, God it is who cleaves out the grain and the date-stone.

He brings forth the living from the dead, and it is He who brings the dead from the living. There is God. How then can ye be beguiled ?"

It is He who cleaves out the morning, and makes night a repose, and the sun and the moon two reckonings, that is the decree of the Mighty, the Wise.

"There is God for you, your Lord. There is no God but He, the Creator of everything, then worship Him, for He over everything keeps guard."

"Sight perceives Him not, but he perceives men's sights, for He is the Knower of secrets the Aware".

"Say, Verily my prayers and my devotion, and my life and my death, belong to God, the Lord of the worlds".

"Dost thou not perceive that all creatures both in heaven and earth praise God, and the birds also ?"

"Everyone knoweth His prayer and His praise."

"Unto God belongeth the kingdom of heaven and earth, and unto God shall be the return."

"Whose is the kingdom of the heavens and of the earth ? There is no God but He. He maketh alive and killeth......He is the Living One. No God is there but He. Call then upon Him, and offer Him a pure worship. Praise be to God the Lord of the Worlds......My prayers and my worship and my life and my death are unto God, Lord of the Worlds. He hath no associate. It is He who hath brought you forth, and gifted you with hearing and sight and heart, yet how few are grateful......It is He who hath sown you in the earth, and to Him shall ye be gathered......O my Lord, place me not among the ungodly people......He it is who ordaineth the night as a garment and sleep for rest, and ordaineth the day for waking up to life".

"Is not He the more worthy who answereth the oppressed when they cry to Him, and taketh off their ills, and maketh you to succeed your sires on the earth ? God the Almighty, the All-Knowing, Forgiver of Sin, and Receiver of Penitence".

"Shall I seek any other Lord than God, when He is Lord of all things ? No soul shall labour but for itself, and no burdened one shall bear another's burden".

"At last ye shall return to your Lord, and He will declare that to you about which you differ. Knower of the hidden and the manifest, the Great, the Most High......Alike to Him is that person among you who concealeth His words, and he that telleth them abroad, he who hideth him in the night, and he who cometh forth in the day".

"God is the light of the heavens and the earth. His light is as a niche in which is a lamp, and the lamp is in a glass, the glass is as though it were a glittering star, it is lit from a blessed tree, on olive neither of the east nor of the west, the oil of which would well-nigh give light though no fire touched it—light upon life. God guides to His light whom He pleases, and God strikes out parables for men, and God all things doth know."

"In the houses God has permitted to be reared and His name to be mentioned therein, His praises are celebrated therein mornings and evenings."

"Men whom neither merchandise nor selling divert from the remembrance of God, and steadfastness in prayer and giving alms, who fear a day when hearts and eyes shall be upset, that God may recompense them for the best they have done, and give them increase of His grace, for God provides whom He pleases without count".

"But those who misbelieve, their works are like the mirage in a plain, the thirsty counts it water till when he comes to it finds, nothing but he finds that God is with him, and He will pay his account, for God is quick to take account".

"Or like darkness on a deep sea, there covers it a wave, above, which is a wave, above which is a cloud—darkness one above the other—when one puts out his hand he can scarcely see it, for he to whom God has given no light he has no light."

"Has thou seen that God ? All who are in the heavens and the earth celebrate His praises, and the birds, too, spreading out their wings, each one knows its prayer and its praise, and God knows what they do".

"Hast thou not seen that God drives the clouds, and then reunites them, and then accumulates them, and then mayest see the rain coming forth from their midst, and He sends down from the sky mountains with hail therein, and He makes it fall on whom He pleases, and He turns it from whom He pleases, the flashing of His lightning well-nigh goes off with their sight".

"God interchanges the night and the day, verily in that is a lesson to those endowed with sight".

The chapter entitled "The Merciful", which has been well called the Benedicite of Islam, furnishes one of the finest examples of the Prophet's appeal to the testimony of Nature.

"The sun and the moon in their appointed time. The herbs and the trees adore,

And the heavens He raised them, and set the Balance that ye should not be outrageous in the balance,

But weigh ye aright and stint not the measure. And the earth He has set it for living creatures. Therein are fruits, and palms with sheaths, and grain with chaff and frequent shoots.

* * * * *

He created man of crackling clay like the potter's and He created the firmament from the smokeless fire.

* * * * *

The Lord of the two easts and the Lord of the two wests, He has let loose the two seas that meet together, between them is a barrier they cannot pass. He brings forth from each pearls both great and small.

* * * * *

His are the ships which rear aloft in the sea like mountains. Everyone upon it is transient, but the face of the Lord endowed with majesty and honour shall endure. Of Him whosoever is in the heaven and in the earth does beg, every day is He in (some fresh) work. Blessed be the name of thy Lord, possessed of majesty and glory".

"Every man's actions have we hung round his neck and on the Last Day shall be laid before him a wide-opened Book"...... "By a soul, and Him who balanced it, and intimated to it its wickedness and its piety, blest now is he who hath kept it pure, and undone is he who hath corrupted it"......"No defect canst thou see in the creation of the God of Mercy, repeat the gaze, seest thou a single flaw, then twice more repeat"......"He quickeneth the earth when it is dead, so too shall you be brought to life".

"The heavens and the earth stand firm at His bidding hereafter when at once He shall summon you from the earth, forth shall ye come"......"When the sun shall he folded up, and the stars shall fall and when the mountains shall be set in motion, when the she-camels shall be left, and the wild beasts shall be gathered together, when the seas shall boil, and souls be repaired (with their bodies), when the female child that was buried alive shall be asked for what crime she was put to death, when the leaves of the Book shall be unrolled, and the heavens shall be stripped away, and the fire of hell blaze forth, and paradise draw nigh, then shall every soul know wha) it hath done"...... "What knowledge hast thou (Muhammadt of the hour ? Only God knoweth its period. It is for thee only to warn those who fear it"......"What shall teach thee the inevitable ? Thamud and Ad treated the Day of Decision as a lie. They were destroyed with thunderbolts and roaring blasts".

And yet with all His might, His tender care and pity are all-embracing.

"By the noonday brightness, and by the night when it darkeneth, thy Lord hath not forsaken thee, neither hath He been displeased. Surely the future shall be better for thee than the past, and in the end He shall be bounteous to thee, and thou shalt be satisfied. Did He not find thee an orphan, and give thee a home, erring, and guided thee, needy, and enriched thee ? As to the orphan, then, wrong him not, and chide not away him that asketh of thee, and tell abroad the favours of thy Lord". "Did ye think We had made you for sport, and that ye should not be brought back again to Us." "O our God, punish us not if we forget and fall into sin, blot out our sins and forgive us" . "Have mercy, O Lord, of the merciful, Thou art the best". "The heavy laden shall not bear another's load. We never punished till We had sent an apostle." "This clear Book, behold on a blessed night have we sent it down for a warning to mankind." "Not to sadden thee have we sent it thee".

And so on goes this wonderful book, appealing to the nobler feelings of man—his inner consciousness and his moral sense, proving and manifesting the enormity of idolatrous beliefs. Scarcely a chapter but contains some fervid passages on the power, mercy, and unity of God. The Islamic conception of the Almighty has been misunderstood by the Christian writers. The God of *Islam* is commonly represented as "a pitiless tyrant, who plays with humanity as on a chess-board, and works out His game without regard to the sacrifice of the pieces". Let us see if this estimate is correct. The God of *Islam* is the Almighty, the All-Knowing, the All-Just, the Lord of the worlds, the Author of the heavens and the earth, the Creator of life and death, in whose hand is dominion and irresistible power, the great, All-Powerful Lord of the glorious Throne, God is the Mighty, the Strong, the Most High, the Producer, the Maker, the Fashioner, the Wise, the Just, the True the Swift in reckoning, who knoweth every ant's weight of good and of ill that each man hath done, and who suffereth not the reward of the faithful to perish. But the Almighty, the All-Wise, is also the King, the Holy, the Peaceful, the Faithful, the Guardian over His servants, the Shelterer of the orphan, the Guide of the erring, the Deliverer from every affliction, the Friend of the bereaved, the Consoler of the afflicted, in His hand is good, and He is the generous Lord, the Gracious, the Hearer, the Near-at-Hand, the Compassionate, the Merciful, the Very-Forgiving, whose love for man is more tender than that of the mother-bird for her young.

The mercy of the Almighty is one of the grandest themes of the Qur'an. The very name (*Al-Rahman*) with which each chapter opens, and with which He is invoked, expresses a deep, all-penetrating conviction of that love, that divine mercy which enfolds creation.

The moral debasement of the followers of the two previous Dispensations wrings the Teacher's heart, and then burst forth denunciations on the Christians and the Jews for the Superstitious rites they practised in defiance of the warnings of their prophets. The fire of religious zeal, that had burned in the bosoms of Isaiah and Jerekiah, was rekindled in the breast of another and far greater man. He denounces, but above the wail. the cry of agony at the degradation of humanity, is heard the voice of hope.

The Qur'an severely censures the Jews for their "worship of false gods and idols", the teraphim before referred to, and for their exaggerated reverence for the memory of Ezra, the Christians, for their adoration of Jesus and his mother. "Hast thou not seen those to whom a portion of the Scriptures have been given ? They believe in false gods and idols. They say to the unbelievers they are better directed in the right way than those than believe (the Moslems). The Jews say, Ezra is the son of God, the Christians say, al-Masih (Jesus) is the son of God. How infatuated they are. They take their priests and their monks for their lords besides God......They seek to extinguish the light of God with their mouths......"The Jews and the Christians say, we are the children of God, and His beloved". Many of those unto whom the Scriptures have been given desire to render you again unbelievers, after ye have believed......Be constant in prayer, and give alms, and what good ye have sent before you for your souls, ye shall find it with God......"They say, "Verily, none shall enter paradise except those who are Jews or Christians......Say, produce your proof if ye speak the truth. Nay, but he who directeth towards God, and doth that which is right. he shall have his reward with his Lord".

"O ye who have received the Scriptures, exceed not the just bounds in your religion, neither say of God otherwise than the truth. Verily, al-Masih, the son of Mary, is the apostle of God and His word. Believe therefore in God and his apostles, and say not : There are three Gods, forbear this...... al-Masih doth not proudly disdain to be servant unto God". "It beseemeth not a man, that God should give him the Scriptures, and the wisdom, and the gift of prophecy, and that he should say to his followers : "Be ye worshippers of me, as well as of God, since ye know the Scriptures, and have studied deep".

The following passage shows the feeling with which such religious conceptions were regarded : "They say the God of

Mercy hath gotten to himself a son. Now have ye uttered a grievous thing, and it wanted but little that the heaven should be torn open, and that the earth cleave asunder, and the mountains fall down, for that they attribute children unto the Merciful, whereas it is not meet for God to have children. Verily there is none in heaven or on earth but shall approach the Merciful as his servant. He encompasseth them".

But the inspired Preacher whose mission it is to proclaim the Truth does not confound "the good with the bad". "Yet they are not all alike, there are of those who have received the Scriptures, upright people, they meditate on the signs of God in the night season, and worship, they believe in God and the Last Day, and command that which is just, and forbid that which is unjust, and zealously strive to excel in good works, these are of the righteous."

The mutual and burning hatred of Jew and Christian, the savage wars of Nestorian and Monophysite, the meaningless wrangle of the sects, the heartless and heart-rending logomachy of the Byzantine clergy, ever and anon bring down denunciations, like the following :—

"To Jesus and other apostles we gave manifest signs, and if God had pleased, their followers would not have fallen into these disputes. But God doeth what He will." "Mankind was but one people, and God sent them prophets of warning and glad tidings, and the Book of Truth to settle all disputes. Yet none disputed like those to whom the Book had been sent, for they were filled with jealousy of each other". "O people of the Book, why wrangle about Abraham ? Why contend about that whereof ye know nothing".

The primary aim of the new Dispensation was to infuse or revive in the heart of humanity a living perception of truth in the common relations of life. "The moral ideal of the new gospel", to use the phraseology of an eminent writer, "was set in the common sense of duty and the familiar instance of love."

"Verily those people have now passed away, they have the reward of their deeds, and ye shall have the need of yours, of their doings ye shall not be questioned". Every soul shall bear the good and the evil for which it has laboured, and God will burden none beyond its power". "Blessed is he who giveth away his substance that he may become pure, and who offereth not favours to any one for the sake of recompense ..... but only as seeking the approval of his Lord the Most High".

"They are the blest who, though longing for it themselves, bestowed their good on the poor and the orphan and the captive (saying), "We feed you for the sake of God, we seek from you neither recompense nor thanks".

"Worship God alone, be kind to kindred and servants, orphans and the poor, speak righteously to men, pray, and pay alms". "Defer humbly to your parents, with humility and tenderness say, O Lord, be merciful to them, even as they brought me up when I was helpless." "Abandon the old barbarities, blood-vengeance, and child-murder, and be united as one flesh." "Do they alms openly or in secret, for both are well". "Give of that which hath been given you before the day cometh when there shall be no trafficking, nor friendship, nor intercession". "Wouldst thou be taught the step (path). It is ransom the captive, to feed the hungry, the kindred, the orphan, and him whose mouth is in the dust". "Be of those who enjoin steadfastness and compassion on others". "Woe to them that make shows of piety, and refuse help to the needy". "Make not your alms void by reproaches or injury". "Forgiveness and kind speech are better than favour with annoyance". "Abandon usury". "He who spendeth his substance to be seen of men, is like a rock with thin soil over it, whereon the rain falleth and leaveth it hard. But they who expend their substance to please God and establish their souls, are like a garden on a hill, on which the rain falleth and it yieldeth its fruits twofold, and even if the rain doth not fall, yet is there a dew".

"Judge between men with truth, and follow not thy passions, lest they cause thee to err from the way of God". "Covet not another's gifts from God". "There is no piety in turning the face east or west, but in believing in God only and doing good". "Make the best of all things, enjoin justice and avoid the foolish, and if Satan stir thee to evil, take refuge in God". "Touch not the goods of the orphan. Perform your covenant, and walk not proudly on the earth". "The birth of a daughter brings dark shadows on a man's face"………"Kill not your children for fear of want : for them and for you will We provide. Verily the killing them is a great wickedness." "God hath given you wives that ye may put love and tenderness between you".

"Reverence the wombs that bear pou". "Commit not adultery for it is a foul thing and an evil way". "Let the believer restrain his eyes from lust, let women make no display of ornaments, save to their own kindred".

"Know ye that this world's life is a cheat, the multiplying of riches and children is like the plants that spring up after rain, rejoicing the husbandman, the then turn yellow and wither away. In the next life is severe chastisement, or else pardon from God and His peace". "Abandon the semblance of wickedness and wickedness itself. They, verily, whose only acquirement is iniquity, shall be rewarded for what they shall have gained". "Those who abstain from vanities and the indulgence of their passions, give alms, offer prayers, and tend well their trust and their covenants, these shall be the heirs of eternal happiness". "Show kindness to your parents, whether one or both of them attain to old age with thee, and say not to them Fie neither reproach them, but speak to them both with respectful speech and tender affection". "And to him who is of kin render his due, and also to the poor and to the wayfarer, yet waste not wastefully".

"And let not thy hand be tied up to thy neck, nor yet open it with all openness, lest thou sit thee down in rebuke in beggary". "Enjoin my servants to speak in kindly sort". "Turn aside evil with that which is better". "Just balances will we set up for the Day of the Resurrection, neither shall any soul be wronged in aught, though were a work but the weight of a grain of mustard seed, we would bring it forth to be weighed and our reckoning will suffice". "Seek pardon of your Lord and be turned unto Him ; verily, my Lord is merciful, loving". "And your Lord sayeth, Call upon me, I will hearken unto you". "Say O my servants who have transgressed to your own injury, despair not of God's mercy, for all sins doth God forgive. Gracious, merciful is He". "The good word riseth up to Him, and the righteous deed will He exalt".

"Truly my Lord hath forbidden filthy actions, whether open or secret, and iniquity, and unjust violence"

"Call upon your Lord with lowliness and in secret, for He loveth not transgressors. And commit not disorders on the well-ordered earth after it hath been well ordered, and call on Him with fear and longing desire. Verily the mercy of God is nigh unto the righteous". "Moreover, we have enjoined on man to show kindness to his parents. With pain his mother beareth him, with pain she bringeth him forth, and he sayeth, O my Lord stir me up to be grateful for Thy favours wherewith Thou hast favoured me and my parents, and to good works which shall please Thee, and prosper me in my offspring, for to Thee am I turned, and am resigned to Thy will". "For them is a dwelling of peace with their Lord, and in recompense for their works shall He be their protector". "Lost are they who, in their ignorance, have foolishly slain their children, and have forbidden that which God hath given them for good, devising an untruth against God. Now have they erred, and they were not rightly guided".

"The likeness of those who expend their wealth for the cause of God, is that of a grain of corn which produceth seven ears, and in each ear a hundred gains, they who expend their wealth for the cause of God, and never follow what they have laid out with reproaches or harm, shall have their reward with their Lord, no fear shall come upon them, neither shall they be put to grief. A kind speech and forgiveness is better than alms followed by injury".

"God will not burden any soul beyond its power. It shall enjoy the good which it hath acquired, and shall bear the evil for the acquirement of which it laboured"......"O Lord punish us not if we forget, or fall into sin, O our Lord and lay not on us a load like that which Thou hast laid on those who have been before us, O our Lord and lay not on us that for which we have not strength, but blot out our sins and forgive us and have pity on us". "The patient and the truthful, the lowly and the charitable, they who seek pardon at each daybreak"... ..."Who give alms, alike in prosperity and in success, and who master their anger, and forgive others. God loveth the doers of good" (theirs a goodly home with their Lord). "O our Lord forgive us then our sin, and hide away from us our evil deeds, and cause us to die with the righteous"......"And their Lord answereth them, I will not suffer the work of him among you that worketh, whether of male or female, to be lost, the one of you is the issue of the other". "And fear ye God, in whose name ye ask favours of each other—and respect women".

"And marry not women whom your fathers have married for this is a shame, and hateful, and an evil way".

"Covet not the gifts by which God hath raised some of you above others".

"Be good to parents, and to kindred, and to orphans, and to the poor, and to a neighbour, whether kinsman or newcomer, and to a fellow-traveller, and to the wayfarer, and to the slaves whom your right hands hold, verily, God loveth not the proud, the vain boaster"......"He who shall mediate between men for a good purpose shall be the gainer by it. But he who shall mediate with an evil mediation shall reap the fruit of it. And God keepeth watch over everything. "O ye *Moslems*, stand fast to justice, when ye bear witness before God, though it be against yourselves, or your parents or your kindred, whether the party be rich or poor. God is nearer than you to both. Therefore follow not passion, lest ye swerve from truth".

Do the preachings of this desert-born Prophet, addressing a larger world and a more advanced humanity, in the nobility of their love, in their strivings and yearnings for the true, the pure, and the holy, fall short of the warnings of Isaiah or the tender appeals of Jesus.

The poor and the orphan, the humble dweller of the earth with his mouth in the dust, the unfortunate being bereft in early life of parental care, are ever the objects of his tenderest solicitude. Ever and again he announces that the path which leads to God is the helping of the orphan, the relieving of the poor, and the ransoming of the captive. His pity and love were not confined to his fellow-beings, the brute creation shared with them his sympathy and tenderness.

"A man once came to him with a bundle, and said "O Prophet, I passed through a wood and heard the voice of the young of birds, and I took them and put them in my carpet, and their mother came fluttering round my head". And the Prophet said, "Put them down", and when he had put them down the mother joined the young. And the Prophet said, "Do you wonder at the affection of the mother towards her young, I swear by Him who has sent me, Verily, God is more loving to His servants than the mother to these young birds. Return them to the place from which ye took them and let their mother be with them". "Fear God with regard to animals", said Prophet Muhammad, "ride them when they are fit to be ridden, and get off when they are tired. Verily, there are rewards for our doing good to dumb animals, and giving them water to drink".

Concept of God has been further discussed in the Chapter of "*Tauheed*".

2. Belief in the Angels

The Qur'an speaks of angels as sentient beings that move the forces of Nature in creating new things. We cannot deny the existence of some such agencies working in the universe. But to return, for the moment, to the question of our means of nourishment. All these are derived from elements and atoms which automatically unite and reunite to help the process of creation. They are punctual and regular, they follow a prescribed path, they combine with each other in given proportions, to create new things. The whole process shows that knowledge is possessed by them, though they themselves belong to the dumb world which has no consciousness. Their work exhibits mathematical precision and exactitude ; which means that the processes are carried out under the direction of some mind, but they themselves are without mind. God is, without doubt, the First Intelligent Cause, but He seems to work through various agencies. He is All-Powerful, but it pleases Him to work in the human body. They follow implicitly the injunction of the Lord. The Qur'an speaks of three functions of angels. The first, is of moving the power of Nature to perform their respective tasks. The other two have to do with their ministry to man. They inspire us to do good ; and if certain unseen agencies incite us to evil, it must not be forgotten that we in like manner receive urges to do good in an imperceptible way, and such "urges" come from the angels. All this lies within the experience of any average man. If we listen to the angelic voice, they become our guardians, during life and protect us from evil ways and in the end they become subservient to us, if we understand the secrets of Nature and proper use thereof. Science has to a great extent brought the angels of the elements under our rule. They may be termed as Laws of Nature. But Law in itself is lifeless and unconscious. It needs a mind behind it. It is Allah of the Qur'an, Who has appointed angels as functionaries of His Law.

Sayyid Abul Ala Maududi in his book entitled "Towards Understanding Islam" as translated and edited by Mr. Khurshid Ahmad about the angels has observed as follows :

"Muhammad (God's blessings be upon him) has informed us that these imperceptible spiritual beings, whom people believe to be deities or gods or God's children, are really His angels. They have no share in God's divinity ; they are under His command and are so obedient that they cannot deviate from His commands even to the extent of the slightest fraction of an inch. God employs them to administer His Kingdom, and they carry out His orders exactly and accurately. They have no authority to do anything of their own accord ; they cannot present to God any scheme conceived by themselves ; they are not authorised even to intercede with God for any man. To worship them and to solicit their help is degrading [illegible]n's creation, God had made them prostrate before possessed and passing over them bestowed upon Adam can, therefore, be greater for man than prostrating before and soliciting favour of those who had prostrated before him.

Muhammad (God's blessings be upon him) forbade us to worship angels, and to associate them with God in His divinity, but along with it he informed us that they were the chosen creatures of God, free from sin, from their very nature unable to disobey God, and ever engaged in carrying out His orders. Moreover, he informed us that these angels of God surround us from all sides, are attached to us, and are always in our company. They observe and note all our actions, good or bad. They preserve a complete record of every man's life. After death when we shall be brought before God, they will present a full report of our life-work on earth, wherein movement left out, however insignificant and howsoever carefully concealed it may be.

3. Belief in the Holy Qur'an

This topic has been discussed very elaborately in the third part of this book.

4. Belief in the Prophets of Allah

The Holy Qur'an on many places emphasizes that God had sent messengers among every people and that all have brought the same religion as Islam. Maulana Maududi has opined that in this respects all the Messengers of God belong to the same category and stand on a par with each other. If a man belies any one of them, he, as it were, belies all, and if a man confirms and believes in one of them, he must and ought to confirm all. The reason is quite simple, suppose ten men make one and the same statement ; if you admit one of them to be true, you *ipso facto* admit the remaining nine of them as true, and if you belie anyone of them, by implication you belie all of them. It is for this reason that in Islam it is necessary to have implicit faith in all the Prophets of God. One who does not believe in anyone of the Prophets would be a *kafir*, though he might profess faith in all the other Prophets.

Maulana Maududi in his book entitled "Towards Understanding Islam" has further said :

It occurs in traditions that the total number of all the Prophets sent to different peoples at different times is 1,24,000. If you consider the life of the world since it was first inhabited and the number of different peoples and nations that have passed on it, this number will not appear too great. We have to believe positively in those of the Prophets whose names have been mentioned in the Qur'an. Regarding the rest we are instructed to believe that all Prophets sent by God for the guidance of mankind were true. Thus we believe in all the Prophets raised in India, China, Iran, Egypt, Africa, Europe, and other countries of the world, but we are not in a position to be definite about a particular person outside the list of Prophets named in the Qur'an, whether or not he was a Prophet, for we have not been told anything definite about him. Nor are we permitted to say anything against the holy men of other religions. It is quite possible that some of them might have been God's Prophets, and their followers corrupted their teachings after their demise, just as the followers of Moses and Jesus (God's blessings be upon them) have done. Therefore, whenever we express any opinion about them, it would be about the tenets and rituals of their religions ; as for the founders of those religions, we will remain scrupulously silent lest we should become guilty of irreverence towards a Prophet.

The following are the injunctions regarding the Prophet in the Holy Qur'an :—

1. Each and every Messenger who was sent by Us was sent for the sole purpose that he should be obeyed under the sanction of Allah.
2. He it is Who sendeth down clear revelations unto His bondman, that he may bring you forth from darkness into light ; and Lo ! for you, Allah is Full of Pity, Merciful.

3. And We made them Chiefs who guide by Our Command and We inspired in them the doing of good deeds and the right establishment of worship and the giving of alms and they were worshippers of Us (alone).

   The Prophets are, thus, the devoted teachers of the "sacred school of the knowledge of God and of the spiritual life of all mankind". We verily sent Our Messengers with clear proofs and revealed with them the Scripture and the Balance, that mankind may observe right measure.

4. With clear proofs and writings ; and We have revealed unto thee the Remembrance that thou mayst explain to mankind that which hath been revealed for them, and that happy they may reflect.

5. We have revealed the Scripture unto thee only that thou mayst explain unto them that wherein they differ, and (as) a guidance and mercy for a people who believe.

6. Each and every Messenger who was sent by Us was sent for the sole purpose that he should be obeyed under the sanction of God.

It is a good sign that the Sermon is getting the better of the Sacrament. It will to universalism. No religion in the world is without its Sermons. Morality, after all, is a common property.

Most of the Sermons on the Mount is a re-echo of the past. Buddha and others before Jesus gave similar precepts to the world. Many of the parables of Jesus were only renderings of the parables in Buddhistic literature. Jesus, did not owe his enlightenment to Buddhistic lore ; all his knowledge came directly from God. This new development of religious thought in the West will create harmony among religions, for a closer study will enable people to appreciate the Qur'anic truth that no nation was left without a Divine Message and that all the great religions of the world came from God and brought the same message, and that Jesus was one of the Prophets of God. The pedlars in religion and there are so many in the West will have to take themselves and their absurdities from God's earth. A new race of evangelists will appear with minds too elevated to pick holes in others. They will go more after the tenets than after the Teacher. They will respect the Master through his precepts ; and in whichever religion they find the same or a parallel to their tenets, they will not suspect plagiarism, but will accept it as a proof of Divine revelation in that religion. That will be the day for the Glory of God and of Islam. Islam has already created that psychology among its adherents. A Muslim must believe in the Divine origin of every great religion. He must believe that Prophets were given to every nation and that all the Prophets of God were entitled to equal respect, and he must not make any distinctions between them. The position is logically tenable as well. We are composed of body and soul. Both should be equally nourished by our Creator. If in His physical dispensation to minister to our physical needs He has made no difference between man and man, shall He then be partial in His spiritual Providence ? If His Message through Jesus could not reach the four corners of the world—even now there are millions whom it has not reached—would the Sustainer of all the human race suffer those waiting multitudes to starve for lack of spiritual food ? No. He sends His Message to them through other Divine Messengers ; and this it is that explains the existence of so many religions in the world. These Messengers from above brought Divine lore and illuminated the world. They were the Teachers, and the models for the practice of the tenets they inculcated in their people, under Divine guidance. But their contemporaries did not keep full records of the words and deeds of these Masters. Whatever has come down has been merely hearsay, giving such ample occasion for adulteration that within the space of a century each religion had suffered in its purity. Coming generations were given a religion which was never taught by the Master, and in the case of Christianity, I may say, not even imagined by the Founder. This paucity of contemporary records of the various Teachers has led to a further difficulty. None of the old religions possess enough material to meet the needs of the day, and the world in general has been left to its own judgment on many vital matters of life. Christianity is a case in point ; if we leave aside the mystical side of the creed, the sermons and other utterances of Jesus do not come up to our demands. His teachings, as recorded, give a general outline of a religion of Love and Kindliness, and that again in an idealistic way, that hardly suits the practical side of life ; and this is not all, as Arnold Bennett rightly says : The ideals of Jesus tend, rather more than less, to influence the individual towards the life of a recluse. They do not fit in with social or national life. They have no bearing on international relations. There is, moreover, a sort of discrepancy between the various utterances of Jesus and his recorded actions which does not help us in understanding his precepts. They in a way are contrary to his own teachings. The root of all is that his disciples or other contemporaries did not leave us an adequate record of his life. Such has been the case with the other Prophets of God. "Unlike all other Prophets, whose proper likeness is concealed from us in a mist of reverence, Prophet Muhammad is clear historic character, the numberless details of whose conduct and demeanour are recorded for us by his own contemporaries."

Muhammad is the only Prophet who may be called historic in the true sense of the word. From his childhood to his death, most of his life and especially the period of his ministry as a Prophet is on record. I know more of him than I know of my own parents in many respects ; and is it not a wonderful thing that, with all our knowledge of him, he commands our respect and admiration ? I cannot say what would be our estimate of others had we known more of them. The lives of other Prophets are enshrouded in mystery and myth ; we know very little of their daily life, they speak like oracles ; and are tolerable only when considered as subjects of fiction ; but Prophet Muhammad is more definitely historic than any personality in the history. It is indeed wonderful how little his detractors find to use against him in all this mass of evidence.

Herein lies the superiority of the Holy Prophet, and for this, among many other things, we accept him as the Ideal Prophet. The record of his words and deeds is complete, and his precepts and examples stand in complementary relation to each other, as if every need of the human soul has been anticipated and every contingency of human existence provided for the mirror of his life. As a Muslim I cannot say that other Prophets of God did not perfect their mission. I only say that we find very little in their record to help us. They must have done that for which they were sent ; but their historians have not been faithful. In the matter of this dearth of record of the world's Prophets, I am constrained to remark that had it not been for Prophet Muhammad we should not be able to appreciate the Divine institution of Prophethood. If a Prophet comes only to read homilies on morality, while he himself in his life does nothing to raise humanity, but simply reiterates in a different accent the lesson taught by others before him, I fail to understand the necessity of his Divine Mission. We can learn the same from those who did not claim to have been raised up by God.

There is an ancient Indian book in Sanskrit literature called Panchatantra "Words of Wisdom from Birds." The book gives hints for good government and good citizenship. It used to be an essential part of the course prescribed for the training of princes and the children of rulers in the East. All questions of morality, ethics, and polity have been lucidly discussed in the mouths of birds and other dumb creatures. A pigeon gives us a lesson how "a friend in need is a friend indeed," and illustrates the dictum by his personal experience of his friend, a mouse. An owl teaches us stratagems of war ; a crow drives home to us a piece of wisdom, namely, that we should not be deceived by our enemy's apparent insignificance, telling how a lion, for example, was lured to a snare by a fox. Another lesson that a stupid friend is more dangerous than a wise enemy is taught by reference to the story of a monkey who used to be on the watch when his master was asleep. One day some flies were disturbing the sleep of the master ; the monkey killed him when trying to remove the flies with a sword. An interesting book of wisdom, no doubt ; but the modern mind scarcely believes in its utility, seeing that it lacks reality and life-like colours. We cannot be guided by precepts which were never put into action by their own teachers. That is a sound principle, and one that should guide us when selecting our teacher and guide. His actions, rather than his words, should entitle him to our allegiance. In fact, an ethical aphorism written on a wall is as good as in the mouth of a teacher, if he has never been able to put it into practice.

But few act upon this principle, especially in matters of religion. We find any amount of stories of homilies and moral lessons in sacred books. But they are not sufficiently effective, if they are not translated into actions by the teachers. They may even mislead us, since we do not know how to act upon them, if the actions of the teacher are wanting to enlighten us on the subject. Our own ingenuity, then, comes to work, and we do what was perhaps never intended by the teacher. For example, every student of the Gospels knows that there are hopeless contradictions in the teacher. For example, every student of the Gospels knows that there are hopeless contradictions in the teaching of Jesus as to the use of the sword. Had there been some action of Jesus to explain his precepts, the history of Christendoms would have been different. The pulpit, on the other side, has always been subservient to statecraft. The clergy further the ends of the State rather than guard the conscience of the people. They read homilies of war when the State wants war, as did the Bishop of London in 1918 at the Marble Arch, but they lay special stress on the Sermon on the Mount when the time has come for the sword to return to its scabbard. Humility, meekness, forgiveness, and non-resistance to evil are some of the claimed ethics of Christianity, but here history discloses quite a different chapter. There we find heartless, sanguinary persecution of others, want of charity and lack of kindliness. Had there been actions of the Master translating his precepts the love of his followers for him would at least have actuated them to follow his actions.

It should not be forgotten that a potentiality is no proof of actuality. Even negative virtues, especially in teachers of morality, are no virtues at all. They cost them nothing ; neither are they of any assistance to those who need practical illustrations of moral lessons. We may read to others homilies of forgiveness and sermons of meekness, but lip-teaching in itself furnishes no proof that we possess the morals we teach to others.

Words converted into actions alone can show that we possess moral virtues. Moreover, how can we teach others what we have not experienced ourselves ? A man must face the hardest trials of life, like Jesus and Prophet Muhammad, before he attempts to teach others a lesson of patience and forbearance. Jesus however, could not find the proper occasions necessary to mould various other moralities into practical shape like Prophet Muhammad.

Again, we may become struck with the idealistic beauty of some of the teachings of a Prophet ; we may admire them, but our sentimentality should not influence us in accepting them as verities of life, we may only respect them sacred relics of the past. In this respect we make another mistake when judging the character of a person. We accept words for actions. Virtues preached are often believed to be actually owned by their teachers. But it is a mistake. Practically every race has its own ethical literature in which we sometimes find rules of high morality worthy of a Prophet ; but if the contents of books could be accepted as an index of the moral character of their writers, our judgment on the moral side of Lord Verulam should be other than it is. A character, however highly divine its claims may be, should not be accredited with all the moral attributes which it inculcates in others, unless it acts upon them itself. In the case of a Prophet the Muslim attitude is, however, different. If he accepts some person as a Prophet, he must as well believe that anything actually taught by the Prophet to others was either done or would have been done by him had occasion arisen. We are taught that all Prophets charged with the same mission and of the same calibre came to do the duty imposed upon them as such. "All people are a single nation, so Allah raised Prophets as bearers of God's news and as warners, and He revealed with them the book with truth" (Qur'an, II : 213). The English word "truth" in the verse has *haqq* as its Arabic equivalent in the original text. It means that the Message that comes from Above for human guidance is a practicable verity and not a dreamer's ideal ; anything of the latter sort, even if found in the record of a Prophet, is not from God and is a subsequent accretion.

But almost all these Prophets have laboured under two disadvantages. First, they did not pass through various vicissitudes of life like Prophet Muhammad, and had not, therefore, the necessary occasions to give expression to the various phases of true humanity. Had they had such occasions, they would have done the same as a Prophet of God would do. For instance, much of our happiness depends upon observance of true domestic morals. Jesus could have made an ideal husband if he had married, but he had no opportunity of doing so, and we cannot look to him as a guide in the matter. On the other hand, those who perhaps had such chances, and probably acquitted themselves well in the circumstances have left us a very meagre record of their lives, and that record, again, is not the narration of the actual happenings of their lives, but an account of the impression of those around them who wrote their history. They wrote what appealed them. These two factors chiefly disappoint a seeker of light when he tries to find something helpful in the life of the various Prophets of the world. Prophet Muhammad is the only personality among the race of the Prophets whose records and experience satisfy all that could be demanded of a Prophet.

A few prayers and a few curses, or a few sermons and a few miracles, do not make up the whole furniture of a Prophet; much more than this is needed to make a Prophet of a man. A Prophet comes to resuscitate humanity when mental, moral and spiritual death has overtaken it; he comes with high principles; he acts upon them himself, and leads others to do likewise; he thus brings reanimation to his environment. In a word, he comes to evolve humanity, a problem of a very complex nature. Humanity has very many sides physical, emotional, sentimental, social, moral, mental and spiritual. They all are mixed with each other; they are complementary to each other for their existence and growth; they serve each other reciprocally in performing their respective functions. We cannot neglect one for the benefit of another. For instance, we hear much said against our low passions. We are advised to crush them. But that would be unnatural. These passions are in their evolutionary state; they are the bedrock of high morality, and germinate spirituality. A Prophet must have regard to them all. He must evolve a system that may bring every human instinct into proper play, and control every faculty in a way that may raise humanity and enable man to reflect Divine morality.

5. Belief in the Judgment, Paradise and Hell

We shall have to rise again, since we have not passed the stage of the Commanding Spirit, though we did possess a rudimentary knowledge of right and wrong. Our resurrection will bring us face to face at once with the advance of the mind in the form of the Chiding Spirit. And then another trouble awaits us. Here we can avoid the detection of wrong-doing, because wrong-doing is mostly under the cover of the body, but there all our efforts to conceal evil will be of no avail, and our inner self will stand forth naked in the sight of all. All that has been done clandestinely will stand forth as an open secret. Thus the pangs caused by the Chinding Spirit will increase exceedingly. It will be a terrible day, subjecting us to unimaginable pains and torments. Our perceptions will grow more intense, our physical nature weak, and our remorse and sense of shame will reach a fearful pitch. We shall suffer torments in their most acute form on the day when we will be stripped of all our physical parts. This awful day has been called by the Holy Qur'an "the Day of Resurrection." The sacred books have not entered on any campaign of terror, as the Church says, if they appeal to us by their message concerning the Last Day. Its pains cannot be exaggerated, because the Sciptures themselves have not conveyed a hundredth part of the agonies that we shall have to experience on that Day. It is not an inconceivable thing. We can understand it if we only visualise the Chiding Spirit by its zenith and every moral and spiritual wrong in us revealed. Just as the body of a patient suffering from a venereal disease bears sometimes pulpable marks of the scourge, it will be no surprising thing to find our various organs bearing witness to the wrongs we have done in this life. The agonies of the time will be simply unbearable, and we shall naturally long either of return to our past life in order to do better, or to have some purgatorial treatment that may relieve us of the torment. But the Beneficent Lord has anticipated our need and His Providence has created for us a hospital in the form of Hell because we, being in the course of evolution, cannot go back. Hell, in fact, though an evil resort, is the best suited for our progress in the spiritual world. Had we left the world with the Chiding Spirit perfected and the voice of conscience heard in every way, there could have been neither Resurrection nor Hell. We would have been like angels, our souls freed from all earthly passions and none to be reclaimed by the Hell. But since we could not avail ourselves of our opportunities in this life for the required evolution, and abused all the blessings of God which He gave us for this purpose, we must descend into Hell, as a matter of certainty to make up the deficiency at the cost of fightful torments. Hell, for this reason, has been called in the Holy Qur'an a mother or a friend. It will take us in her lap, like a mother who brings her child willingly to a surgical operation to free his body from the wounds from which he is suffering, though the operation will be a most painful one.

Hell and Heaven :

Hell is a natural sequence to our evil actions may, it is a logical necessity, we need it, and cannot avoid it. It has been created to meet the needs to which we will become alive as soon are resurrected. Hidden Truths will then become revealed. They will appear before our eyes, and nothing will remain concealed. Heaven and Hell will become manifest to us, the former as the abode of bliss and happiness and the latter as the place of affliction and chastisement, the only place for that spiritual purification which will be our indispensable need.

We shall not be able to return to earth for our purification, though we may long and even pray for it, because we shall leave behind the material body, as it is necessary only for an earthly sojourn. Heaven, on the other hand, will not receive us in the condition in which we now find ourselves, since it is a place exclusively for purified souls. Besides, if we be not purged of our earthly appetites, then how can we live in regions which provide only spiritual food? Again, if Heaven is the place of light how can we face it if we are of dark substance. Heaven is also the place for the spirit at rest, whereas our minds will surely be full of restlessness. The voice of conscience, which after the Resurrection, will become too strong to be ignored by us, will goad us on to purification. In these circumstances we shall be left with no other alternative than to enter into Hell. We shall also realise the agonies which its denizens will have to experience, and their imagination alone will terrify us, but as there will be no other course open to us, we shall be driven towards it, as if we were dumb and blind, and there will be no injustice in it.

The description of Hell given by the Qur'an is like a hospital established for the treatment of persons suffering from some most painful diseases. There will naturally be the shrieks and cries, weeping and moaning of those suffering and these will not die out until the end of the treatment is reached. Besides our affliction, remorse for wrong doing, would arise from pains analogous to those we feel when taste some bitter medicine, we shall have to drink of a distasteful drink and a very hot one too.

Like those who suffer from a skin disease we shall also need a change of skin if we are to get any relief. We shall have to undergo a sort of surgical operation.

Fire is admittedly the most cleansing of all purifying factors. It is most natural, therefore, that this house of purgatory should be made of burning, purging fire with a pall of smoke over it. It will be fitting that its walls, floor and roof should all be of fire and that sinners be placed on beds of fire also. If sufferers from never-troubles or filthy diseases are ordered by their medical advisers to be placed in a steamed room in a Turkish bath, how can we scoff at the idea of Hell and of us being ordered thither by Nature's relentless surgeons, rough in their methods, perhaps, but bound to do as directed? Metals mixed with alloy are usually put in the melting pot, so that impurities are burnt off and the substance purified, so also we shall have to undergo a similar process to rid ourselves of physical impurities.

The different names given by the Qu'ran to Hell help to explain its nature. *Sair*, *Jahim* and *Jahannam* mean something in the nature of a burning fire. *Laza* explains the nature of its functions meaning anything that stupefies the brain.

But *Hutamah* its sixth name, is very suggestive. It means remorse a feeling of shame and disgrace, because abasement and intense remorse are some of the chastisements administered to the denizens of Hell which they may in no wise escape. It shows that Hell is a mental torture : that its agonies are agonies of the mind. For, otherwise, why else should our physical body share our troubles if to be nothing but an instruments. The body is a lifeless thing unless it comes under the operation of the mind. It is, as it were, an unconsenting party if it joins with us in our wrong-doing. The principle of justice and equity do not punish a party who is forced to give his consent. Moreover, the verse which explains the nature a *Al-Hutamah* decides the question—Speaking of the fire of Hell the Qur'an says that it will come out of our own hearts. Here in this life we are conscious of the same burning of the heart, when a strong desire, unbecoming in its very nature, goads us to do some wrong. The very idea of shame makes our blood hot and we feel as if we were being driven towards a pit of fire.

The Qu'ran makes mention of some seven gates of Hell meant for different classes of sinners. The doors would lead to seven spiritual evils.

It has already been shown that no sooner does our consciousness begin to evolve than we need knowledge of right and wrong, which comes to us either by Revelation or by the requirements of the society in which we live. We find it in its rudimentary form in the Ten Commandments of Moses. They have again been developed into seven principles of good living in the first 10 verses of Chapter 23 of the Qur'an, wherein the Book speaks of the birth of human mind. These principles have been given us so as to build the newly formed mind and to make it fit for heavenly life and they are :—

1. Good beliefs.
2. Humility in prayers.
3. Abstention from vanity and levity.
4. Purification as well as almsgiving.
5. Continence or purity in sexual relations.
6. The keeping of trust and covenants.
7. Remaining always on our guard against anything contrary to the demands of prayers.

What a wonderful and wise improvement we find here on the Ten Commandments of Moses. It would be sheer folly to call it plagiarism, as certain silly minds among the Christian missionaries generally do, who fail to realise that the Fountainhead of these two sets of injunction is one and the same, the One Lord, who sends to humanity from time to time that knowledge of which it stands in urgent need. An evolved social law, like that laid down in the Qur'an, could never have been appreciated by the Israelites of the time of Exodus. Hence the difference. The Qur'an was given to coming generations when they became advanced in their requirements. This is the true explanation of the coincidences otherwise Jesus would seem to have committed the worse type of literary larceny, since most of his sayings and parables can be easily traced to Krishna and Buddha.

These seven principles comprise within their scope all that is needed to constitute the best form of society. The violation of even one of them involves a multitude of sins. Thus the whole course of evils becomes narrowed down to the breach of these seven injunctions, which therefore create the seven gates of Hell.

We read, too of nineteen wardens of Hell. Consciousness, according to some psychologists, is only an assemblage of various passions. The whole generation of passions arises from two root-passions—Desire and Anger. These are, in fact, the mother-passions born of the knowledge which we receive from the external world through our sense or through our food upon which we live. We have five outer senses which give rise to five inner ones—Hearing, Sight, Smell, Touch and Taste are the former. If any of the ten senses does not perform its functions properly, our knowledge will be defective and this will affect the two mother-passions.

But food has a far-reaching influence, indeed, when it turns into ideas and creates anger and desire in their best or worst forms. Ideas are the result of the physical nature nourished by food. Food comes under the action of seven other faculties in the system before it becomes an idea.

1. *Jazibah*—This literally means pulling in, drawing or taking in. In the case of food, it would mean eating and drinking.
2. *Masikah*—The faculty of retaining food in the system.
3. *Hazimah*—The power of digestion.
4. *Dafiah*—The faculty of getting rid of deleterious matter derived from food.
5. *Ghaziah*—The faculty of nutrition.
6. *Namiah*—The faculty of growth.
7. *Muwallidah*—Creative agency.

Food could not perform its function properly if any one of the abovementioned seven faculties were out of order. It would naturally give rise to false ideation.

The seven faculties, combined with the ten senses, instantly create these two passions, which, in their turn, branch away into various passions which control all our actions. Thus these nineteen agencies have direct bearing on our morals. If Hell is a place where we are chastened so that we turn from evil to good, it will be the work of said agencies to subject us to some sort of treatment to remedy our moral defects.

Hell, as it appears from the Qur'an is like only a hospital or purgatory for moral and spiritual cure. How can our mere belief in some intermediary, whether Jesus or another, cure our disease, or act as an antidote in our system ?

Again, Heaven is not a delimited area. The Qur'an says that it brings all the Heavens and the Earth within its circumference. It ought to be so, if it is intended for our minds, because we leave the body here, where we die, and even here the mind when it is free from physical taints, requires a very vast area for its exercise. With the aid of imagination it reaches the corners of the earth. But if we die with a mind which is still fast, and in the snares of our carnal nature, it must gravitate to the earth, seeing that carnal nature is of the earth. The doors of heaven too must remain closed to us, since earthly things cannot live in those regions, we shall hover between the Earth and Heaven, and Hell alone can purge us clean of earthly tendencies. How can the suffering of another for us free us of such a burden ?

Many men jeer at the very idea of Heaven and Hell. But science tells us to believe in the continuity of life, we must also admit the possibility of its happy and miserable aspects, which in the Sacred Books have been named Heaven and Hell. Besides, if the principle of causation is another verity and we must reap what we sow, our various actions here would remain unrequitted. There must be a day of requital at least for such actions as remain unrecompensed in this life. We may not understand the nature of these future conditions, but our inability to do so does not justify our denial of their existence. Even with all our fight of imagination, we often fail here on the earth to picture an earthly thing as it really is. It would not be a matter for surprise, therefore, if we fail to appreciate truly the things of the future life, especially when they are of different substance from those on the earth. It may be said that in a sense, the mind and the spirit are the foundations of Heaven and Hell. The Holy Prophet has simply stated a truth when he quotes our Lord in the following words :

> Allah says : I have prepared for My righteous servants what no eye has seen and no ear has heard and what the heart of man has not conceived.

The Qur'an, however, explains to us these verities in their general character. True, it makes mention of many of the delights of Heaven and calls them by names associated with many things here on earth, such as milk, honey, musk, and fruits of various kinds. But at the same time it warns us against conceiving of them as in their earthly form. They have been described figuratively and in parables as the Book says which goes on to tell us that God has created for us two Heavens, one here and the other in the Hereafter. So it is also in the case of Hell, in order that we may have a foretaste of future conditions, with this difference that only the heaven and hell of earth are but shadows of the things to come. There is also another difference, which is this that here we find those things in earthly allowed form.

If the chiding spirit becomes materialized in the strongest possible manner taking the form of Resurrection, as explained above, the other four stages of Spiritual Evolution will become actualized in their best aspects and will take the form of heaven. It is absolutely inconsistent for a doubting mind laugh at Resurrection of Hell and Heaven because he himself has realized the pangs of conscience here and is eager for the happiness which even falls here to the lot of such blessed ones as have become free from internal struggles and remains satisfied. No one can avert the toils of life, but such men keep their minds unruffled under all circumstances being serenely indifferent to pains and pleasures. If such serenity of mind and happiness of soul are things to be coveted, they will come to us in their fullest excellence in Heaven. Its chief characteristics, as given in the Qur'an, are as follows: In Heaven we shall be free from all troubles and trials and released from every sort of anxiety, fear and grief, we shall listen to no absurd or vain talk, nor shall behold any vanity. Doubtless we shall have some sort of food and drink for our nourishment there but these will never be attended with illness or disease. Our good actions have been compared to fruits in Heaven in the Holy Book. Here also we enjoy the fruits of our labour. If our beliefs in truths here are the seeds of all our righteousness, they will be planted there, as well as seeds in our system. Our actions will water them and transform them into a radiant garden. It is for this reason that wherever the Books speaks of beliefs and good actions, it compares them with gardens watered by perennial streams flowing beneath them. Our actions there will bring these streams to the surface. The streams may be of a water the component elements of which are beyond our comprehension, but they are the transformation of our actions in this life. The Arabic word *Jannat* is very significant. It means primarily something hidden. It also means a garden with trees luxuriant in growth. Every piece of land sown with various seeds is a garden in embryo while all the seeds remain hidden. It is *Jannat* in the first meaning of the word. But, when the seeds come up and trees grow, it becomes *Jannat* in the other sense. Even here, those who do not lead dissolute lives and hold themselves aloof from any sort of dissipation, enjoy a form of heavenly life by reason of their good beliefs and righteous actions. The Heaven to come is but the materialization of these beliefs and actions. It is the garden of our own nature, where all our good faculties will grow and bear fruit a hundredfold.

The Muslim Paradise is not, it must be understood, a garden for the voluptuary, where he may sit in the company of maidens under the shade of trees, with goblets of wine circling continually for the enjoyment of the dissipated. We read, it is true of *Hur* in the Muslim Paradise. We are told that the women of our family will also be with us in Heaven, purified like ourselves. Some commentators of the Qur'an take these *Hurs* to mean our own wives, mothers and sisters, but others regard them as belonging to some heavenly order, where beautiful damsels and boys have been called *Hur* and *Ghilman*. Woman is not a despicable companion to us in our earthly career, though sickly theologians may call them to be the "Gateway of Hell". St. Jerome, St. Cyril, Tertullian and other Christian fathers have made these pious aspersions on those who might have been their better halves, and the like, as they are indeed our better halves. They are our utmost happiness and their company is the choicest of God's blessings. Though when misfortune and ill-luck transfer their affection and love to alien quarters they make the life a hell. But we are assured that these damsels of Heaven will be possessed of a pure and spotless heart, which the very word *Hur* literally means. Their eyes, fascinating as they may be, will not be the bearers of amorous message. They will in no wise ponder to any unworthy feelings. Besides, they will be of no earthly order, nor would they stand in connubial relations to as in the earthly meaning of the word. We shall all be free of physical appetites and there will be no further procreation of the species, which, when all is said and done, is the main object of all matrimonial connections on earth. It may be said that the *Hurs* are not wanted if they are not to play the role of wife as in our earthly sojourn. But those say so only betray the hollowness of their own minds. Even in this life bed is not the best part of our happiness. All earthly tastes lose their attraction for us when we pass a certain age. Intellectual or spiritual pleasures alone captivate us for good. Knowledge, and not the flesh, is our real pleasure.

The Qur'an uses various names to denote the things of the future life. If we take their meanings literally, they all refer to some sort of knowledge, and the place that intervenes between Hell and Heaven also has been called *Araf* which means knowledge.

In short, Heaven is a spiritual experience of the best type whereby all desires will be more than satisfied. Everything will be of an honourable character with no ignoble feature of any kind. The Qur'an suggests this idea in the clearest terms when it gives us the list of those we are entitled to enter into the heavenly abode. Their very characters show that it would not be a place of licentiousness. Here are some of them :

1. Those who hold good beliefs and translate them into actions.
2. Those who lead a pious life or have come under the forgiveness of the Compassionate Lord.
3. Those who possess humility of mind and are penitent in heart and whose minds have become purified of all alloy.
4. Those who on earth kept their promises and fulfilled their covenants.
5. Those who are righteous and not only remain in prayer but translate the demands of their prayers into actions.
6. Those who have become cleansed of all their wrong desires and whose hearts are pure of every error.

In short, good deeds of all kinds—piety, righteousness, patience, chastity, charity, almsgiving, regard for bonds, truthfulness, abstention from absurdity and vanity, giving good advice to others are the chief qualities of those who will enter into the Paradise of the Lord. Again, it has been repeatedly shown that peace will reign supreme there so much so that Heaven has also been named, *Dar-us-Salam*, the House of Peace. All our highest capabilities which have remained latent here, will come to full fruition there. For this reason Heaven has been also named, *Dar-un-Naim*, the House of good gifts.

Evil things which, according to the Qur'an, will carry men to Hell, are guilt, injustice, pride, niggardliness, ungratefulness, rebellion, inordinacy, doubts as to truths, transgressions of limits, the forbidding of good deeds, want of good deeds, disbelief, opposition to God, polytheism.

The abovementioned virtues and vices clearly explain the nature of Heaven and Hell. They exclude all idea of earthly things. All of them appertain to things mental or spiritual. The Qur'an therefore, makes a lucid but true statement of the coming reality. It says that we come here with the highest capabilities, but at the beginning start at the lowest rung of the ladder. We have to work out our own advancement and reach, as best as we can, the highest stage of our growth.

We are on an evolutionary journey and we have been given every kind of guidance to carry us to our destination. We come on the earth to prepare ourselves for future progress. If we can develop our faculties to such an extent as will enable us to enter into a life of future progress, we leave the life of this world successful. But if we cannot do so, we shall have first to become cleansed of our impurities which have stuck to us in our sojourn on earth, and when we are purged thereof we shall begin our journey and ultimately reach the place wherefrom we come at first. We came from Light and to Light shall we ascend.

The Holy Qur'an when speaking of the Heaven, says that it is like the heavens and the earth in the vastness. When the Holy Prophet was speaking about this verse to his companions, there chanced to be present an Ambassador from the Roman Emperor Heraclius, who observed that if Heaven were so extensive, it would hardly leave any room for Hell—a remark very much to the point. But the reply was more than equal to it. "God be glorified" said the Holy Prophet, "where is the night when the day comes ?" This may not be appreciated by those who imagine the universe to be a three-storeyed house, with our earth as middle one. But the Qur'anic verse and the Holy Prophet's comment thereon explains the whole thing on a scientific basis. It is the earthly matter in us which gravitates us towards the planet. The moment we lose such matter we depart from it, as indeed we find in the case of birds. If death consists in the separation of the spirit from the body, the former cannot remain attached to the earth without its physical clothing. But since low passions are a rarefied form of earthly matter, the spirit, if filled with such passions, cannot go beyond certain regions in the adjoining space, and, like a toy balloon filled with gas, cannot ascent beyond a certain height. As long as there are earthly passions in us, we shall have to remain hovering in a place called Hell. The doors of the Heaven will be opened to us only when we are purged of all carnal desires. We may have any substance for our body, it will be much lighter than the clay of which we are now fashioned. That body, indeed, may be of electrons of light itself, as we read in the Qur'an. Supposing we could visualise a species of balloon, made of electrical matter with a man sitting in it whose body itself was made of the same substance with various devices for eating and drinking, but all of the same substance, it would be an easy matter for the person in the balloon to move throughout the whole space of the universe with electric rapidity. A similar description has been given by the Holy Prophet of our movements in the Heaven.

As to the pleasures of Heaven, we may enjoy them in the same way as we enjoy our pleasures on earth. But since our various organs, our tastes, digestion and the rest, will not be the product of earth, the things for our enjoyment in Heaven cannot be of earthly nature. I am neither exaggerating nor inventing when I say that I have known Muslim gentlemen of rare piety who at times used to enjoy the delicious flavour and taste of several fruits without actually eating any. Men of that character sometimes hear the loveliest music, the most bewitching songs when none actually is being played. I know of another friend, who once had a novel experience. He was neither dreaming nor in a trance, but he was quite wide-awake sitting meditating at midnight. He felt as if he was in the company of a woman and appreciated her company. The Qur'an has also referred to this when it says that the inmates of heaven when given a portion of the fruit thereof shall say : "This is what was given to us before ; they shall be given the like of it". The italicised words most eloquently explain that the pleasures of Heaven will be like those we enjoy here, but not of the same nature. There is another similar statement in Chapter 76 which tells of the various pleasures which we shall enjoy in Heaven. Now, for example, camphor, is the best of antiseptics, and the Book, after mentioning the condition of the sinners in Hell, speaks of the righteous who drink of a cup admixture of which is camphor. After patient's bowels have been thoroughly purged, he needs an antiseptic because he has still germs of putrefaction in his system. After he is fully relieved he requires a tonic. Ginger, they say, is one of the finest invigorating medicines, so we read in the same chapter that the inmates of Heaven will be given to drink "a cup the admixture of which shall be of ginger".

We need nourishment wherever we may be, and if we perceive the nourishing value of those fruits, the namesakes of which will be given us in Heaven, it shows that they are invigorating and stimulating especially in cases of heart weakness. If the heart is the seat of the mind then it must have in the heavenly regions similar food like that which is beneficial to it on earth.

The Holy Qur'an thus also explains many other aspects of this subject, nourishment in Heaven and Hell being one of them. Everything is to be nourished, but its nourishment is derived from the same substance as that which gives it its body. If, on our death, we have to leave our bodies behind us, then we cannot naturally assimilate anything of the earth by way of nutrition. But since the mind of the sinner, at his resurrection, will long for earthly things, these hankerings will of themselves place him in torment on account of their absence in those regions. He will feel that he is forbidden the very things which he used to enjoy on earth. On the other hand, he will be interested in the heavenly food, because he will find some of his friends there enjoying it. If he asks them to share their delicacies with him, and if they refuse, it will be all too natural. The verse further explains the stuff of which the food will be prepared. It will be light. Our bodies will be made of light, for otherwise we would not be able to assimilate any articles made of light. This takes us a step further. Charcoal has within it various gems of light, and a stage comes when every piece of coal becomes all light. But before reaching that brilliant state, every particle of soot and smoke must be consumed. It must also go through fire to get the brilliance which is innate in it. It is just the same with us. We come fully from light. That light became denser and denser until, eventually it assumed the form of the earth which brought forth man as its best product. From this condition we enter upon a sort of backward journey for we have to return to the same condition of light, so it is not surprising if a case-hardened mind, full of metaphorical soot and smoke, is thrown into a pit of fire. But he must live on something and that something is, as the Qur'an says, the fruit of tree called *Zaqqum*.

The tree of *Zaqqum* has been mentioned in the Qur'an as growing at the bottom of Hell. Its fruit, it is said, will be the food of the sinful. It will boil in their bellies. They will be thirsty and run for water and they will be given boiling water to drink. The very description show that the fruit would act as a medicine. A Muslim divine, who was also an experienced physician, treated a syphilitic patient with a fruit of the same name which grows in India. The patient felt hot and the physician gave him hot water which caused a violent evacuation of the bowels. Motion after motion came bringing out black deleterious matter from his stomach, and the patient was relieved. The Holy Qur'an suggested the idea to the physician, and he used to apply it in all serious cases. Another similarity found in the Qur'an between hospital and Hell. When a patient is admitted into a hospital he is often accompanied by his friends, but if he is under treatment for some very serious disease, no visitor is allowed to see him. A sort of a wall, a barrier, as it were, is placed between him and those who are in good health. He does not see them again unless and until he is fully cured. His friends may come to enquire after him, but they are not allowed to see him. So we read in the Qur'an, when it speaks of a wall raised between the hypocrite and the believer, separating the two each from the other. The Holy Book speaks also about the duration of Heaven and Hell. Heaven, it says, is an everlasting gift that will never be cut off. It establishes the eternity of Heaven, but, as Hell is only a purifying entity, it cannot exist if there are no impurities of wrong inclinations to be got rid of. It must exist as long as the two things exist, because no one can enter Heaven unless he has a pure spirit. These impurities are no other than the earthly passions in us which, in their uncontrolled condition, are the cause of wrong-doing during our earthly sojourn. We may not have any occasion to do more sins after our death for lack of means, but the inclination to do so will subsist in us as long as these passions survive. They are a kind of barrier between the sinner and the heavenly abode, which, indirectly give rise to Hell. If we commit sin, it is on account of these inclinations which emanate therefrom, and if we continue to feel the said inclination after death, it is for the same reason. These passions, in their uncleansed form, even after death must tend towards earth for their satisfaction. They will exist as long as the earth exists, and will create a hankering in us to return to the terrestrial sphere, but we shall not be able to gratify them for want of a physical body—the necessary wherewithal of earthly life—for the body is left behind on our death and reduced to its elements. This inability will act as a second barrier between our inclinations and the means to satisfy them. A sinner will thus have two barriers, one before him and the other behind him. The struggle between the tendency and the inability to satisfy it will surely create a new hell for a sinner, which must co-exist with the earth and would naturally come to an end if our planet were to be destroyed. We read in the Qur'an of a calamity which will be the end of the earth. The Book speaks of some terrible concussion that will shatter it to pieces, and make the mountains, which were created to keep the earth steady, like unto loosened wool with the men on it scattered like moths in space. The calamity will be in the nature of a collision of the earth with some larger heavenly body, as science also says when discussing the possible fate of our planet. If Hell be co-existent with the earth, it must disappear with it. But we read of a third thing co-existing with Hell. The Book when speaking of sinners in Hell, they will abide therein so long as the heavens and the earth endure. This statement, however, makes no difference to my point of view. The Arabic words *Ard* and *Samawat*, which correspond to the English words the earth and the heavens respectively, do not literally mean the earth and the heavens. Their primary meaning refer rather to the position they occupy in space than the substance of which they are made. *Ard* in Arabic means anything that stands below another thing, while *Sama* means height. The two words are thus relative, so much so that the first of the seven heavens may be called *Ard* of the second heaven. Similarly the second may be termed *Ard* in relation to the third. It shows that though the regions, here called *Samawat*, of the heavens may survive the extinction of the earth, yet they will not be called by their present names. If the demolition of the earth will make an end of Hell, the word *Samawat* will no longer be applied to the regions now so called. There is, however, another word in the verse under discussion which gives rise to a misconception as to the duration of Hell, and that word is *Abad*, which has been wrongly interpreted as eternity. But *abad* has *abab* as its plural, while the idea of eternity cannot admit of plurality. Eternity is one indivisible thing. Therefore, the word *Abad* only means a very long period. The existence of Hell cannot be ascribed to any Divine revenge or to the passion of an "angered deity". The Qur'an absolutely denies any such reason. It says that God is not interested in any way in punishing us. But as we have not used His gifts aright, and therefore remain unfit for further progress, we are sent to Hell for the removal of all that retards our progress in the coming life.

(6) Belief in the Divine Decrees (*Kismet*)

We are often beset with what may be called the riddles of life. We are in a maze but have no notion how we are to get out of it. We want knowledge because the very consciousness of ignorance serves to increase our ignorance. We are sometimes comfortably off and enjoying life, when some sudden and unforeseen mishap upsets all our calculations and changes our prospects completely. These abnormal events, for such they seem to be, need a proper explanation as to their why and wherefore in order to put us on our guard and set us on the true path of happiness. Science is of very little assistance to us for the purpose. It seems to favour Fatalism which is about the worst thing possible. It renders us helpless, and at the same time weakens our sense of responsibility. Men of science hold that since everything in the material world runs on preordained lines, events being already preordained, therefore it must be the same with human affairs. In short, if we need a light to guide us out of the complexities of life, it is here. We must have a clear view of the case. It is not only a matter of religion ; it is a most important factor in all mundane affairs, and no system of theology prior to the coming of Islam has had a word to say on the subject. The Qur'an is the only book that enlightens us. It shows us a clear way and saves us from groping in the dark. Evil often comes to us as if it were an uninvited and most unwelcome guest. Knowledge from God should enable us to deal with it when it comes, for no man-contrived system of philosophy has ever succeeded in evolving a satisfactory solution of the problem. Some refer to *Kismet* an Arabic word used by Orientalists to convey the idea of predestination though its literal meaning is 'division' or 'distribution'. It is thought that good and evil are prearranged entities, and that they have already been allotted by the Lord amongst the people of the world. No effort, therefore, on their part can change their course, while they act as playthings in the hands of Fate. No prophet of God ever taught a tenet as this which could relieve men of all responsibility for their actions. We, however, find a similar doctrine in the Church creed, but it is none of Jesus' teaching. Since the days of Saint Athanasius the doctrine of predestination has been laid down in all Christian creeds as an article of faith. It has taken a practical shape in every Christian home at the birth of babies still-born, or who die before they can be baptised. The poor souls are believed to be condemned by the Lord to eternal perdition, and must be buried in unconsecrated ground. The division of Mankind into "the saved" and "the unsaved" smacks strongly of predestination.

The Qur'an gives us a sailing direction, as it were, by the aid of which we may steer a safe course through the troubled waters. First of all, we have been warned that we are under the governance of the Law. All laws are unchangeable and admit of no infringement. Their breach is sin, which entails unavoidable penalty. We must therefore respect the laws if we wish to keep ourselves immune from trouble. In this connection, the Book makes special mention of certain laws, which regulate our lives. These we must always keep before our eyes if we are to avoid disappointment and disaster.

The laws of Causation and Requital work together under certain circumstances. But any confusion of ideas with regard to them opens the door to an infinity of trouble. We must know that events occur under a course prescribed by God, and that everything has got its cause, as a result of which it inevitably appears. Similarly no action remains without its required under Divine Decree. God has, therefore, been described as the cause of all things. We create circumstances, that develop under Divine Ordinance, to produce a result. We touch the cord and the instrument begins to sound automatically in accordance with His Laws. For example vegetables. God made them to bring things to fruition wherever or by whomsoever they are grown. In this way God is the producer of the harvest, but its first cause is the person who planted the seed. If we sow wild oats they will produce an evil harvest under His Laws, but we shall have to reap the crop which we have sown.

We often commit wrong under the impression that we shall evade detection or escape the consequences. We have, therefore, been clearly told in the Holy Qur'an that we are under the eye of a Supervisor Who reads all that is hidden even in the innermost recesses of our hearts and, knows everything that is concealed. As to the consequence, we are warned that these must inevitably ensure under the working of the laws concerned. The truth is perhaps best expressed by the principle that God brings forth good and evil consequences as they arise under His Laws. And in this respect three things have been told us.

That all responsibility lies on our shoulders. Thus says the Qur'an :

> "Allah does not impose upon any soul a duty beyond the extent of his ability ; for it is (the benefit of) what it has earned, and upon it (the evil of) what it has wrought."
>
> Again "Whoever goes aright, for his own soul does he go aright, and whoever goes astray, to his detriment only does he go astray."
>
> "It may be that your Lord will have mercy on you, and if you again return (to disobedience), We too will return to punishment."
>
> "Surely, Allah does not change the condition of people until they change their own condition."

That no one will bear our burden. The incidence of our action will fall on us.

That no one will intercede with the Lord on our behalf but under His previous and special permission.

Divine Economy has created very few things, but has put them to many uses. These work under different measures and in different ways to serve different purposes. But if we change the measures and ways which have been fixed by the Divine Law harm must result. These measures, in themselves, are not conducive to any evil, but the harm is endangered when we do not apply them as they should be applied. These measures and ways have been called in the Qur'an the "Bounds of God" and he who trespasses against them, is punished as an evil-doer. We, therefore, have been exhorted to acquire knowledge of these bounds. We are never punished unless we are given that knowledge beforehand. The Book recommends the following three ways by which it may be acquired :—

(*a*) The first way is through observation. We have been given all possible means of information ; we possess various senses and we have been advised to use them.

(*b*) We must not behave like animals in the use of our eyes and ears, but we must make intelligent deductions and inferences from the knowledge we receive, otherwise through our ignorance we shall court disaster.

(*c*) But there are things which call for minute observation which is not within every man's capacity ; and consequences, moreover, are very slow in coming especially in the case of moral delinquencies.

This delayed action leads us to disregard moral laws. Sometimes we remain unaware of their very existence. Revelation from God, therefore, comes to enlighten us on these things.

Vicissitudes of life occur for our instruction and often come in the guise of hardship, leaving an indelible impression on the tablet of our mind to be our guide for the future.

Whenever we go against the knowledge thus gained we are straightway punished ; but since our actions are judged by the All-Knowing Lord, He knows the extent of the knowledge we have received, and judges us accordingly. He makes every concession on this score, for punishment never comes unless we have received guidance beforehand and have ignored it. But we cannot plead ignorance before Him, as He knows all that is manifest or hidden. But He is not a judge Who is out to administer the extreme penalties of the law in every case. In judging between two parties, He acts as justice demands, but in dealing with our wrongs, He is not so strict as an average judge. For this reason the Book styles Him as "the Owner of Requitable." He may award punishment to an offender or He may remit it, but he never makes an arbitrary use of His discretion. The three redeeming factors which invite His forgiveness are our forgetfulness, our mistakes and our inability to meet the requirements of the case. If some wrong is done under circumstances which are beyond the control of the doer he is not punished. Every case is decided on its own merits and God deals graciously with cases which deserve His consideration. Punishment is seldom eternal. Sometimes it takes such a form as venereal diseases, that punish from within the man who vitiates his blood through misconduct. The punishment of the Lord is of the same nature. He does not take delight in seeing us punished. He has given us various gifts, but if we abuse them the very fact in itself becomes punishment. The Qur'an calls it a thing acquired. We read of Divine discretion in the matter of punishment and forgiveness, but it works only in cases where our actions deserve some punishment. It never comes undeservedly, but when a punishable wrong is committed. He may exercise His discretion of forgiveness. But if the remission of punishment would only confirm the offender in wrong doing, the law will take its course. As long as He finds any redeeming feature in our conduct His mercy outweighs His anger ; but when men are surrounded with sin and crime on all sides, punishment becomes inevitable and is meted out in proportion to the measure of the evil done. Good actions receive plentiful rewards, but misdeeds invite corresponding punishment.

Freewill is the best gift granted to us by the Lord. No other creature in the world besides man has been endowed with freedom of action. Other creatures work as machines. But the Lord has given to Man, His vicegerent, the power of discretion. He wants us to be as sound in our judgment as He is Himself. Every latitude has been given us to perfect the exercise of the gift, and it is His wish that we should always take the right course but not under compulsion. We needed three things and we have them :

(*a*) **True Knowledge of Things :** We have been given all necessary information, and have also been told how to acquire it so that it may guide us in the exercise of right judgment.

(*b*) **Own Choice :** Nothing should come in our way to interfere with our judgment. We are, therefore, allowed to pursue the course which we choose for ourselves. Equal facilities are given to the righteous and the wicked in this respect, and the Book speaks of it in the following words :

> "All do We aid these as well as those out of the bounty of your Lord and the bounty of your Lord is not confined".

Everything has been left to our choice. Whatever course we elect to adopt we find no one to check it. All things come to us if we exert ourselves, whether we make a right use of them or not. Men enjoy all the amenities of life which makes them forgetful of the actual situation. They commit sin after sin as if unnoticed, until the Law of Recompense moves and they are brought to naught.

(*c*) **Chastisement :** This is most essential as a disciplinary measure. We should be punished and should suffer the evil consequences of wrong judgment, otherwise, we shall not realize the effects of wrong discretion. If it be God's will that we should cultivate soundness of judgment. He will chasten us.

Guidance and Misguidance :

Misconception of this principle has given rise to various false notions. Had it been left to the wishes of the Lord, He would have put all of us on the right path but in that case we should have been mere automations. To start with He sets us all on the right path, and then leaves us to our discretion. We abuse it often and come near destruction, and in this connection the Qur'an speaks of the Divine discretion, that is used always to our benefit. He may practise it to correct us or He may leave us to our own desires according to our past conduct. If He sees that we respect words of guidance we receive, He helps us ; but if He finds that we do not seek it, He leaves us to misguidance, when a person passes it and there is no hope of his reclamation, God decrees him to be misguided in which case no one can put him on the right path. This fact has been disclosed to us as a warning, but is often taken as a piece of fatalism. This is what the Qur'an says plainly, but it has been misread by many.

The Sun is the source of all light, but if we close the windows of our room, it will become dark, and if we choose to remain in it for a considerable time our eyesight will suffer The misfortune occur to us under the working of the Divine Laws, but we ourselves are the real cause. In order to emphasize the case the Qur'an says that God works out mishaps. The Book first speaks of the various evil courses adopted by sinners and then says :

> "Their parable is like the parable of one who kindled a fire but when it had illumined all around him Allah took away their light and left them in utter darkness they do not see".

The Prophet in the words of the Qur'an kindles the fire to expel the darkness from his neighbourhood, but there are people who would not care to listen to his words, and depart from him. They will reach the place where they will find no light. Words of advice fall on them as though on deaf ears. Thus they become dumb and deaf and blind for the purposes of guidance. It should not be forgotten that this stage of sinfulness comes only to man after a life of iniquity and unrightcousness.

Chapter 2

The Concept and Spirit of "Tauheed"

Faith in the Unity of God is the most fundamental and the most basic teachings of the Holy Prophet Muhammad. This is expressed in the first *Kalima* (there is no deity but Allah). It is the route of all the teachings of Islam. Muslims are essentially required to offer five times' formal prayer (*Salat*) daily and in each prayer they repeatedly say before their God :—

> "Thee alone do we worship and Thee alone do we ask for help".

In *Surah An-Nihal* it has been said :—

> "And We did raise among every people a Messenger to preach to worship Allah (God Almighty alone) and shun the evil one".

The meanings of the *Kalima* (*La ilaha illallah*) shall be very helpful in understanding the true impact of the ideology of *Tauheed* that is onenses of God. Maulana Maududi explains the *Kalima* as follows :—

In the Arabic language the word *ilah* means "one who is worshipped", *i.e.*, a being which on account of its greatness and power be considered worthy to be worshipped, to be bowed to in humility and submission. Anything or any being possessing power too great to be comprehended by man is also called *ilah*. The conception of *ilah* also includes the possession of infinite powers : powers that may astonish others. It also conveys the sense that others are dependent upon *ilah* and that he is not dependent upon anyone else. The word *ilah* also carries a sense of concealment and mystery, that is, *ilah* would be a being unseen and unperceptible. The word *khuda* in Persian, *deva* in Hindi, and *god* in English bear, more or less similar meanings and significance. Other languages of the world also contain words with a like sense.

The word Allah, on the other hand, is the essential personal name of God. *La ilaha illallah* would literally mean "There is no *ilah* other than the one Great Being known by the name Allah. It means that in the whole of the universe, there is absolutely no being worthy to be worshipped other than Allah, that it is only to Him that heads should bow in submission and adoration, that He is the only Being possessing all powers, that all are in need of His favour, and that all are obliged to solicit His help. He is concealed from our sense, and our intellect fails to perceive what He is.

Regarding *Tauheed* Maulana Maududi has opined in his book "Towards Understanding Islam" that *Tauheed* is the highest conception of Godhead, the knowledge of which God has sent to mankind in all ages through His Prophet. It was this knowledge with which, in the beginning, Adam had been sent down to the earth, it was the same knowledge that had been revealed to Noah, Abraham, Moses and Jesus (God's blessings be upon them all). It was this very knowledge which Muhammad (God's blessings be upon him) brought to mankind. It is the knowledge, pure and absoulte, without the least shade of ignorance. Man became guilty of *shirk*, idol-worship and *kufr*, only because he turned away from the teachings of the Prophets and depended upon his own faulty reasoning, false perceptions, or biased interpretations. *Tauheed* dispels all the clouds of ignorance and illumines the horizon with the light of reality. Let us see with significant realities this concept of *Tauheed*. This little phrase : *La ilaha Illallah* points out : what truth it conveys and what beliefs it fosters. This we can grasp if we ponder over the following points :

First of all we are faced with the question of divinity, we are face to face with a grand, limitless universe. Man's mind fails to discern its beginning and visualise its end. It is moving on in its chartered course from time immemorial and is continuing its journey in the vast vista of the future. Creatures beyond number have appeared in it and go on appearing every day. The phenomena are so bewildering that a thinking mind finds itself aghast and wonderstruck. Man is unable to understand and grasp the reality by his unaided vision. He cannot believe that all this has appeared just by chance or accident. The universe is not a fortuitous mass of matter. It is not a combination of unco-ordinated objects. It is not a conglomeration of things chaotic and meaningless. All this cannot be without a Creator, a Designer, a Controller, a Governor. But who can create and control this majestic universe. Only He can do so Who is master of all, Who is infininte and eternal, Who is all-powerful, all-wise, omnipotent, and omniscient, Who is all-knowing and all-seeing. He must have supreme authority over all that exists in the universe. He must possess limitless powers, must be the Lord of the Universe and all that it contains, must be free from every flaw and weakness and none may have the power to interfere with His work. Only such a Being can be the Creator, the Controller and the Governor of the universe.

Secondly, it is essential that all these divine attributes and powers must vest in one Being—it is virtually impossible for two or more personalities having all the powers and attributes equally to co-exist. They are bound to collide. Therefore there must be one and only one Supreme Being having control over all others. You cannot think of two governors for the same province or two supreme commanders of the same army. Similarly, the distribution of these powers among different deities, for instance, that one of them is all knowledge, the other all providence and still another life-giver—and each having independent domain in his own field—is also unthinkable. The universe is an indivisible whole and each one of such deities will be dependent upon others in the execution of his task. Lack of co-ordination is bound to occur. And if this happens, the world is destined to go to pieces. These attributes are also untransferable. It is not possible that a certain attribute might be present in a certain deity at one time and at another time it be found in another deity. A divine being who is incapable of remaining alike himself cannot give life to others. The one who cannot protect his own divine power is definitely unsuited to govern the vast limitless universe. Thus the greater you reflect upon the problem, the firmer would be your conviction that all these divine powers and attributes must exist in one and the same Being alone. Thus polytheism is a form of ignorance and cannot stand rational scrutiny. It is practical impossibility. The facts of life and nature do not fit into that explanation. They automatically bring man to Reality, *i.e.*, *Tauheed* (the Unity of God).

Now keeping in view this correct and perfect conception of God, cast a searching glance at this vast universe. Exert yourself to the utmost and say if you find among all the objects that you see, among all the things that you perceive, among all that you can think, feel or imagine—all that your knowledge can comprehend—anyone possessing these attributes. The sun, the moon, man or a group of men—does any of them possess these attributes ? Certainly none. For everything in the universe is created, is controlled and regulated, is dependent on others, is mortal and transitory, is not self-acting and self-propelling its slightest movements are controlled by an inexorable law and it cannot deviate from that law. Their helpless condition proves that the attire of divinity cannot fit their body. They do not possess the slightest trace of divinity and have absolutely nothing to do with it. They are simply without the godly powers and it is a travesty of truth and a folly of the highest magnitude to attribute to them the divine status. This is the meaning of "*La Ilaha*", *i.e.*, there is no God, no human and material object possesses the divine power and authority deserving worship and obedience.

Chapter 3

Finality of the Prophethood

The concept of the Finality of the Prophethood is the basic principle and the fundamental of Islam. It has given a deep imprint on the outlook, behaviour and feelings of the Muslims. If we go through the Old Testament and the New Testament, we find that every Prophet Muhammad (peace be upon him) foretold the advent of new Messenger. But we do not find such a reference in the Holy Book Qur'an on the other hand in the Qur'anic verses it is quite clear that the work of sending messages is over. The following verses are hereby quoted as a proof of the Finality of the Prophet :

> "This day have I perfected your religion for you and completed My favour unto you and have chosen for you a Code of life—al-Islam".
>
> "Muhammad (peace be upon him) is not the father of any of your men, but he is the Apostle of God and the last of the Prophets".
>
> "Say (O Muhammad) O Mankind ! Lo ! I am the Messenger of Allah to you all (the Messenger) of Him unto whom belongeth the Sovereignty of the heavens and the earth".

We also find the same view narrated in *Ahadith*. The following *Ahadith* are cited below as quoted by Mr. Abdul Hamid Siddiqi in his book "Prophethood in Islam" :—

There were the Apostles who led the sons of Israel to the path of righteousness. Whenever any Prophet dies, he was succeeded by another. But no prophet would come after me. This function would be performed by the Caliphs.

"My relation to the (long chain of) prophets (can be understood by) the parable of a palace, the palace was most beautifully built, superb and fine. There was left, however, the space of a brick. The people went round the palace and asked in amazement, Why is that this space was not filled up ? I have filled in this gap and I am the last of the prophets".

Abd al-Rehman ibn Jubayer said, "I heard Abd Allah bin Amr ibn al-Az saying this : One day the Holy Prophet came to us. The expression of his face indicated as if he was going to depart from us and said, I am Prophet Muhammad who can neither read nor write (he repeated these words three times) and there is no prophet after me".

> "There is no prophet after me and there is no *ummah* after my *ummah*".

There are a few versions quoted by Maulana Maududi in his book "Tafheem al-Qur'an" about the great Islamic Jurists. Imam Abu Hanifa, a great jurist of Islamic Law has remarked :

> "Anyone who would demand from him any proof (of his Prophethood) would become *Kafir* since the Prophet Muhammad has emphatically said : No prophet will come after me".

Alghazali has observed as follows :—

There is complete agreement in the whole of the *ummah* on this injunction (there is no prophethood after me). It signifies the fact that no prophet is to be raised after Prophet Muhammad. This injunction is so clear and unequivocal that it leaves no scope—not the least for any other interpretation. Anyone who interprets it in any other way, is an unbeliever, his writing is nonsensical and his interpretation is fit to be called a heresy and its writer a *Kafir* : since he is falsifying that very fundamental on which there is consensus in the *ummah* :

The opinion of Qadi Iyad as cited by the learned Author of the book '"Prophethood in Islam" by Mr. Abdul Hamid Siddiqi :—

"Anyone who claimed to be a shareholder in the Prophethood of Muhammad, either in his own lifetime or after him, is an apostate".

Imam Shafi has said as follows :—

Allah decided to send Muhammad to lead man out of chaotic condition. This was not a novelty, for since mankind was but one people. God sent Prophets to announce glad tidings and to warn people. The mission with which Prophet Muhammad was charged was a part of that carried on by the prophetic chain although it came to be the last link of it.

"Allah charged Prophet Muhammad with His Mission because he was the noblest and the most perfect of His creation. Prophet Muhammad was to inaugurate His mercifulness and to seal prophethood. He was to transmit Allah's word and to show man the way to the right path. The word which Prophet Muhammad received and transmitted was the genuine word. It was free from human modifications and univeralisation of all that Allah had revealed previously".

The Finality of the Prophethood can also be found in the following verses either directly or indirectly :—

1. "Verily in the Messenger of Allah ye have a good example for him who looketh unto Allah and the Last Day, and remembereth Allah very much".
2. "Whoso obeys the Messenger, obeys Allah. Lo ! Those who swear allegiance unto thee (Muhammad) swear allegiance only unto Allah. The Hand of Allah is above their hands. So, whosoever breaketh his oath, breaketh it only to his soul's hurt : while whosoever keepeth his covenant with Allah, on him will He bestow immense reward".
3. The saying of (all true) believers when they appeal unto Allah and His Messenger to judge between them is only that they say : we hear and we obey, and such are successful. He who obeyeth Allah and His Messenger, and feareth Allah and keepeth duty (up to Him) : such indeed are the victorious".
4. "But may, by the Lord, they will not believe until they make thee judge of what is in dispute between them and find within themselves no dislike of that which you decide and submit with full submission".
5. "It does not become a Muslim man or Muslim woman when Allah and His Messenger have decided an affair (for them) that they should (after that) claim any say in their affair : and whoso is rebellious to Allah and His Messenger, he verily goes away in error manifest".
6. "And they say : We believe in Allah and the Messenger and we obey them after that faction of them turn away. Such are not believers".
7. "Say (O Muhammad to mankind) : If ye love Allah follow me, Allah will love you and forgive your sins. Allah is Forgiving and Merciful".
8. "Say : If your fathers, and your sons, and your brethren, and your wives and your tribe and the wealth you have acquired, and merchandise for which ye fear that there will be slump and dwellings ye desire are dearer to you than Allah and His Messenger and striving in His way, then wait till Allah bringeth His Command to pass".

In short the following factors show that Islam has given last and perfect ideology :—

1. Islam emphasises on the unity of God, His person as well as in His attributes. In Islam even the Prophet Muhammad who is considered to be the greatest

amongst the human beings for all the times is but one of the created human beings and a servant of His Lord.

2. The teachings of all the past prophets have reached their perfection in the teachings of the Prophet Muhammad (peace be upon him). This is quite clear from the following verse of *Surah Al-Maida* :—

   "This day have I perfected for you your religion and completed My favour to you and chosen for you Islam as the religion".

3. The teaching of the Holy Prophet has been assured to be preserved for the guidance of mankind till the end of the world. The following verse supports the version :—

   "Surely We have revealed the Reminder, and surely, We are its Guardian".

4. In *Surah Al-Anbiya* it has been said that the Prophet was sent for the guidance of the whole mankind till the Last Day. It is quoted as follows :—

   "And We have not sent you (O Prophet) but a mercy to all the nations".

   There is also the same depiction in *Surah Al-Saba* which runs as follows :—

   "And We have not sent you but a Bearer of Good News and Warner to all mankind".

5. The Prophet was sent as the last. This is said in *Surah Al-Ahzab* which is cited below :—

   "Muhammad is not the father of any of you men, but (he is) the Messenger of Allah and he is the Seal upon Prophets (*i.e.*, the institution of Prophethood was sealed after him).

Moreover the Holy Prophet himself announced that there will be no prophet after him.

Maulana Maududi in his book "Prophethood" cited the following three conditions which are necessary for the advent of a new Pophet :—

1. That the teachings of the earlier Prophets have been interpolated or corrupted or they have died and their revival is needed. In such a case a new prophet is raised so that he may purge the impurities from the lives of the people and restore religion to its pristine form and purity, or

2. That the teachings of a Prophet who has passed away were incomplete and it is necessary to amend them, improve upon them, or add something to them, when a new prophet is sent to effect these improvements.

3. That the earlier prophet was raised particularly for a certain nation or territory and a prophet for another nation, people, or country be required.

If we study the present conditions we find no such state exists. The teaching of the last Prophet Muhammad (peace be on him) are alive, and have been preserved and made immortal.

———

Chapter 4

Practices of Islam

Islam has attached to its precepts certain practical duties. Some of them most important are discussed below :—

1. Prayer (*Namaz*):

Man's consciousness of a supreme, all-prevading Power, his helplessness in the eternal conflict of Nature, his sense of benefaction, all lead him to pour out the overflowing sentiments of his heart in words of gratitude and love, or repentance and solicitation, to one who is ever-wakeful and merciful. Prayers are only the utterance of the sentiments which full the human heart. All these emotions, however, are the result of a superior development. The savage, if supplications do not answer his purpose, resorts to the castigation of his fetish. But every religious system possessing any organic element has recognised, in some shape the efficacy of prayer.

The early Hindu worship consisted of two sets of acts—oblations and sacrifice accompanied with invocations. In the infancy of religious thought the gods are supposed to possess the same appetites and passions as human beings and thus whilst man needs material benefits, the gods required offerings and propitiation. This idea often finds expression in the old hymns of the Rig Veda. With the development of religious conceptions, it is probable that, among at least the more advanced or thoughtful minds, the significance attached to oblations and sacrifice underwent considerable modification. But as the hold of the priestly caste, which claimed the possession of a "secret virtue" transmissible only through the blood, strengthened on the minds of the masses, Brahmanism crystallised into a literally sacrificial cult. The sacrifice could be performed only by the priest according to rigid and unalterable formula, whilst he recited the *mantras* and went through the enthusiasm, the worshipper stood by a passive spectator of the worship which was performed on his behalf. The smallest mistake undid the efficacy of the observances. The devotional spirit, however, could not have been entirely wanting, or the Bhagavad Gita could not have been composed. But for the people as a whole, their worship had become a vast system of sacrifice, the value of which depended not so much upon the moral conduct of the individual worshipper as upon the qualification of the officiating priest. The former had only to believe in the efficacy of the rite and be in a state of legal purity at the time.

The Mago-Zoroastrian and the Sabaean lived in an atmosphere of prayer. The Zoroastrian prayed when he sneezed, when he cut his nails or hair, while preparing meals, day and night, at the lighting of lamps, etc. Ormuzd was first invoked, and then not only heaven, earth, the elements and stars, but trees, especially the moon-plant, and beasts. The formulae were often to be repeated as many as twelve hundred times. The moral ideal, however pure with the few, would be perfectly eliminated from the minds of the common people. But even the sort of spiritual life enjoyed by exceptional minds was monopolised by the ministers of religion. The barriers of special holiness which divided the priesthood from the deity, shut out the latter from all spiritual enjoyments of a nobler type. The Magians, like the Ophici, had two forms of worship, one esoteric, especially reserved for the priestly classes, the other exoteric, in which alone the vulgar could participate.

The Mosaic Law contained no ordinances respecting prayers, only on the payment of tithes to the priests, and the domestic solemnity of the presentation of the firstlings, was there a prescribed formula of a prayer and acknowledgement, when the father of the house, on the strength of his having obediently performed the behests of the law, supplicated blessings from Jehovah on Israel "even as He had sworn unto their fathers". But with the rise of a more spiritual idea of the Deity among the people and the teachers, and the decline of an uncompromedium anthropomorphism, the real nature of prayer, as the medium of inter-communication between God and man, began to be understood. Tradition and custom, in default of any express regulation by the law, made the Jews at last, as Dollinger says, a people of prayer. Three hours daily were consecrated to devotional exercises, *viz.*, nine, twelve, and three o'clock. The necessity, however, for the service of priests, combined with the absence of any positive precedent coming down from the Law-giver himself, tended to make prayer, in the majority of cases, merely mechanical. Phylacteries were in use in the time of Jesus, and the Qur'an reproaches the Jews in bitter terms for "selling the signs of God".

The teachings of Jesus, representing a later development of the religious faculty in man, recognised the true character of prayer. He consecrated the practice by his own example. The early disciples, in the spirit of their Master, laid great stress on the habit of devotion and thanksgiving to God. But the want of some definite rule for the guidance of the masses, in process of time, left them completely adrift in all regarded the practice of devotion, and under subjection to the priests, who monopolised the office of regulating the number, length, and the terminology of prayers. Hence missals, liturgies, councils, and convocations to settle articles of faith and matters of conscience, hence also, the mechanical worship of droning monks, and the hebdomadal flocking into churches and chapels on one day in the week to make up for the deficiency of spiritual food during the other six, hence also the "presbyter" who merely a "servant" at first came to regard himself as "the Lord of the spiritual heritage" bequeathed by Jesus.

All these evils had culminated to a point in the Seventh Century, when the Prophet of Arabia began to preach a reformed religion. In instituting prayers, Prophet Muhammad recognised the yearning of the human soul to pour out its love and gratitude to God, and by making the practice of devotion periodic, he impressed that disciplinary character on the observance of prayer which keeps the thoughts from wandering into the regions of the material. The formula, consecrated by his example and practice, whilst sparing the Islamic world the evils of contests regarding liturgies, leave to the individual worshipper the amplest scope for the most heart-felt outpouring of devotion and humility before the Almighty Presence.

The value of prayer as the means of moral elevation and the purification of the heart, has been clearly set forth in the Qur'an.

Rehearse that which hath been revealed unto thee of the Book, and be constant at prayer, for prayer preserveth from crimes and from that which is blameable, and the remembering of God is surely a most sacred duty.

The forms of the supplicatory hymns, consecrated by the example of the Prophet, evince the beauty of the moral element in the teachings of Islam.

"O Lord ! I supplicate Thee for firmness in faith and direction towards rectitude, and to assist me in being grateful to Thee, and in adoring Thee in every good way, and I supplicate Thee for an innocent heart, which shall not incline to wickedness, and I supplicate Thee for a true tongue, and for that virtue which Thou knowest, and I pray Thee to defend me from the vice which Thou knowest, and for forgiveness of those faults which Thou knowest. O my Defender ! assist me in remembering Thee and being grateful to Thee, and in worshipping Thee with the excess of my strength. O Lord ! I have injured my own soul, and no one can pardon the faults of Thy servants but Thou, forgive me out of Thy loving-kindness, and have mercy on me, for verily Thou art the forgiver of offences and the bestower of blessings on Thy servants".

Another traditional prayer, called the prayer of David, runs thus. "O Lord ! grant to me the love of Thee, grant that I may love those that love Thee, grant that I may do the deeds that may win Thy love, make Thy love to be dearer to me than self, family or than wealth".

The following are the injunctions regarding the prayer in the Holy Qur'an :—

1. Successful indeed are the believers who are humble in their prayers.
2. "Come to prayer come to success".
3. Thee do we serve and of Thee do we seek help, guide us on the right path.
4. And glorify thy Lord by praising Him before the rising of the sun and before its setting and glorify him also during the hours of night and during parts of the day that you may be well-pleased. And enjoin prayer upon those dependent on thee and steadily adhere to it thyself.
5. Recite that which has been revealed to thee of the Book, and keep up prayer. Truly prayer keeps one away from obscenity and evil and the greatest felicitation is the remembrance of God.
6. Woe to the worshippers who are unmindful of their prayers.
7. Dost thou not see that Allah is He whom do glorify all those who are in the heavens and the earth—the very birds with outstretched wings. He knows the prayer of each one, and its glorification and Allah is cognizant of what they do.
8. And whatever creation that is in the heavens and that is in the earth makes obeisance to Allah only and the very angels adore Him free from pride.
9. Prostrate thyself and draw near.
10. Say to my servants who believe that they should keep up prayer.
11. Be of those who turn to Him and be mindful of your duty to Him and keep up prayer and be not of those who associate others with God.
12. And they were not enjoined anything except that they should serve Allah, being sincere to Him in obedience, and be upright and keep up prayer and pay the poor-rate and that is the right religion.

13. Say : my Lord has enjoined justice. Set upright your face at every time of prayer and call on Him being sincere to Him in obedience.

14. And ask assistance through patience and prayer and most surely it is a hard thing except for the humble ones who know that they shall meet their Lord and that they shall return to Him.

15. O, ye who believe ! Seek assistance through patience and prayer. Surely Allah is with the patient.

16. Therefore pray to your Lord and offer sacrifice.

17. Say : Surely the guidance of Allah, that is the true guidance and we are commanded that we should submit to the Lord of the world and that we should keep up prayer and be careful of our duty to Him. And He it is to whom we shall be gathered.

18. O, ye who believe ! Remember Allah with frequent remembrance and glorify Him morning and evening.

The Qur'anic verse is clear on the point that all Muslims should turn their faces towards the direction of *Kaaba* in token promise given by God to Ibrahim.

We shall surely turn thee to a *Qibla* which thou shalt like. Turn then thy face towards the sacred mosque and wherever you are (O Muslims) turn your faces towards it.

The followings are the versions of the Holy Qur'an regarding the necessity of prayer :—

1. He indeed shall be successful who himself purifies and magnifies the name of his Lord and prays.
2. O, ye who believe ! Bow down and prostrate yourselves and serve your Lord and do good that you may be successful (xxii : 7).
3. Recite that which has been revealed to thee of the Book and keep up prayer. Surely prayer keeps one away from obscenity and evil and certainly the greatest felicitation is the remembrance of Allah, and Allah knows what you do.
4. Warn only those who fear their Lord in secret and keep up prayer and whoever purifies himself, he purifies himself only for the good of his ownself and to Allah is the eventual returning (xxxv : 8).

The following are the verses in which the Holy Qur'an has shown the importance of the prayer :—

1. Surely they who recite the Book of Allah and keep up prayer and spend out of what We have given them

secretly and openly, hope for a gain which shall not perish (xxxv : 29).

2. Surely man is created to a hasty temperament being greatly grieved when evil afflicts him and niggardly when good befalls him except those who pray, those who are constant at their prayers (xx : 19-23).

3. Successful indeed are the believers who are humble in their prayer and those who pay heed to their prayers. These are they who are the heirs to inherit Paradise—therein shall they abide (xxiii : 1-2-9-11).

4. This light is in those houses which Allah has permitted to be exalted and that His name may be remembered in them. Glorify Him therein in the mornings and the evenings men whom neither merchandise nor selling beguileth them from the remembrance of Allah and their constancy in prayer and the giving to the poor their due, who fear a day in which the hearts and eyes shall be overturned (xxiv : 36-37).

5. This Book—a guidance and good news for the believers who keep up prayer and pay the poor-rate and of the hereafter they are sure (vii : 2-3).

6. Those whose hearts tremble when Allah is mentioned and those who are patient under that which afflicts them and those who keep up prayer and spend benevolently out of what We have given them (xxii : 35).

7. And for those who hold fast the Book and keep up prayer surely We do not waste the reward of those who reform themselves (vii : 170).

8. Muhammad is the Apostle of Allah and those with him are hard against unbelievers, compassionate among themselves, you will see them bowing down, prostrating themselves, seeking Grace from Allah and His acceptance, their marks are on their forehead as the effect of their prostration (xviii : 29).

The following are the conditions laid down in Qur'an under which a person should perform his prayers :—

1. O, ye who believe ! Do not go near prayer when you are in a state of intoxication until you know well what you recite, nor when you are under the obligation to perform a bath unless you are travelling on the road—until you have washed yourselves. And if you are ill or on a journey or one of you has come from the privy or touched women, and you cannot find water,

betake yourselves to clean earth, then wipe your faces and your hands. Surely Allah is Pardoning, Forgiving (iv : 43).

2. O, ye who believe ! When you rise up to prayer, wash your faces and your hands as far as your elbows and wipe your heads and wash your feet to the ankles, and if you are under the obligation to perform a bath then go through complete wash and if you are sick or on a journey or one of you come from the privy or you have touched women, and you cannot find water, betake yourselves to clean earth and wipe your faces and your hands therewith—Allah does not desire to put you into difficulties but He wishes to purify you and that He may complete His favour on you so that you may be grateful (v : 6).
3. O, children of Adam ! Attend to your embellishments at every time of worship and eat and drink and be not extravagant. Surely Allah does not like the extravagant (vii : 31).
4. O, thou that art clothed ! Arise and warn, and thy Lord do glorify and thy garment do purify, and uncleanliness do shun. (xxiv : 1-3).
5. Surely Allah loves those who turn much to Him and He loves those who purify themselves (ii : 222).

The prayer timings have been fixed. As regards the position of the timings it is for the five times considered as obligatory prayers. As regards for the fixation of the timings for prayers the Qur'anic injunction runs as follows :—

1. Surely prayer is ordained for believers to be performed at fixed times (iv : 103).
2. O, ye who believe ! Remember Allah with frequent remembrance and glorify Him morning and evening. (xxxiii : 41-42).
3. And keep up prayer on the two extremities of the day (*i.e., Fajar* and *Maghrib*) and in the first hours of the night (*i.e., Isha*) (xi : 119).
4. Keep up prayer from the declining of the sun till the darkness of the night and observe the morning recitation of the Qur'an (xvii : 78).
5. Therefore glory be to Him when you enter upon the time of the evening (*i.e., Maghrib*) and when you enter upon the time of the morning (*i.e., Fajar*) and to Him belongs praise in the heavens and the earth, in the afternoon (*i.e., Asar*) and when you are at mid-day (*i.e., Zuhar*) (xxx : 17-18).

7. Glorify your Lord by the praising of His before the rising of the sun (*i.e., Fajar*) and before its setting (*i.e., Asar*) and during hours of the night do also glorify Him (*i.e., Isha*) and during parts of the day (*i.e., Zuhar*) that you may be well pleased (xx : 130).

Ameer Ali says that the Islam of Prophet Muhammad recognises no caste of priesthood, allows no monopoly of spiritual knowledge or special holiness to intervene between man and his God. Each soul rises to its Creator without the intervention of priest or hierophant. No sacrifice, no ceremonial, invented by vested interests, is needed to bring the anxious neart hearer to its Comforter. Each human being is his own priest, in the Islam of Prophet Muhammad no one man is higher than the other.

European rationalists have complained of the complex character of the Moslem prayers, but the ritual of the Qur'an is astonishing in its simplicity and soberness. It includes the necessary acts of faith, the recital of the creed, prayer, almsgiving, fasting, and pilgrimage, but lays down scarcely any rules as to how they are to be performed. "Observe the prayers and the mid-day prayer, and stand ye attent before God, seek aid from patience and prayer. Verily, God is with the patient, but nothing is said regarding the manner in which the prayers should be offered. "When ye journey about the earth", says the Qur'an, "it is no crime to you that ye come short in prayer if ye fear that those that disbelieve will set upon you. God pardons everything except associating aught with Him".

The practice of the Prophet has, however, attached certain rites and ceremonies to the due observance of prayers. At the same time it is pointed out in unmistakable terms that it is to the devotional state of the mind the Searcher of the spirit looks, "it is not the flesh or the blood of that which ye sacrifice which is acceptable your piety which is acceptable to the Lord". "It is not righteousness", continues the Qur'an, "that ye turn your faces in prayer towards the east or the west, but righteousness is of him who believeth in God......who giveth money for God's sake unto his kindred, and unto orphans, and the needy, and the stranger, and those who ask, and for the redemption of captives, who is constant at prayers and giveth alms, and of those who perform their covenant, when they have covenanted, and two behave themselves patiently in hardship and adversity, and in times of violence these are they who are true".

It was declared that prayer without "the presence of the heart" was of no avail, and that God's words which were addressed to all mankind and not to one people, should be studied with the heart and lips in absoulte accord. And the Caliph Hazart Ali held that devotion offered without understanding was useless and brought no blessing. The celebrated

Imam al-Ghazzali has pronounced that in reading the Sacred Book by heart and intelligence must work together, the lips only utter meaning, the heart, in paying obedience to the dictates of duty. "It is not a sixth nor a tenth of a man's devotion", said the Prophet "which is acceptable to God, but only such portion thereof as he offers with understanding and true devotional spirit".

The practice of baptism in the Christian Church, even the lustrations, which the Egyptians, the Jews or the hierophants of the heathen religions in the East and the West, required as preliminary to the performance of devotional or religious exercises, show the peculiar sanctity which was attached to external purifications. Muhammad, by this example, consecrated this ancient and beneficent custom. He required cleanliness as a necessary preliminary to the worship and adoration of God. At the same time, he especially inculcated that mere external, or rather physical, purity does not imply true devotion. He distinctly laid down that the Almighty can only be approached in purity and humility of spirit. Imam al-Ghazzali expressly says, as against those who are only solicitous about external purifications, and have their hearts full of pride and hypocrisy, that the Prophet of God declared the most important purification to be the cleansing of the heart from all blameable inclinations and frailties, and the mind from all vicious ideas, and from all thoughts which distract attention from God.

In order to keep alive in the Muslim world the memory of the birthplace of Islam, Prophet Muhammad directed that during prayers the Muslim should turn his face towards Mecca, as the glorious centre which saw the first glimmerings of the light of regenerated truth. With the true instinct of a prophet he perceived the consolidating effect of fixing a central spot around which, through all time, should gather the religious feelings of his followers and accordingly ordained that everywhere throughout the world the Muslim should pray looking towards the *Kaaba*. Mecca is to the Muslim what Jerusalem is to the Jew. It bears with it all the influence of centuries of associations. It carries the Muslim back to the cradle of his faith, the childhood of his Prophet, it reminds him of the struggle between the old faith and the new, of the overthrow of the idols, and the establishment of the worship of the one God, and most of all, it bids him remember that all his brother Muslims are worshipping towards the same sacred spot, that he is one of a great company of believers, united by one faith, filled with the same hopes, reverencing the same things, worshipping the same God, Prophet Muhammad showed his knowledge of the religious emotions in man when he preserved the sanctity of the temple of Islam. But that this rule is not an essential requisite for devotion, is evident from the passage of the Qur'an quoted above.

2. Fasting (*Rozaa*) :

The institution of fasting has existed more or less among all nations. But it may be said that throughout the ancient world the idea attached to it was, without exception more of penitence than of abstinence. Even in Judaism the notion of fasting as an exercise of self-castigation or self-abnegation was of later growth. The Essenians (from their connection with the Pythagoreans, and, through them with the asceticism of the further East) were the first among the Jews to grasp this moral element in the principle of fasting and Jesus probably derived this idea, like other conceptions, from them.

The example of Jesus consecrated the custom in the Church. But the predominating idea in Christianity, with respect to fasts generally, is one of penitence or expiation, and partially, of precedent. Voluntary corporal mortifications have been as frequent in Christian Church as in other Churches, but the tendency of such mortifications has invariably been the destruction of mental and bodily energies and the fasterling of a morbid asceticism. The institution of fasting in Islam, on the contrary, has the legitimate object of restraining the passions, by abstinence for a limited and definite period, from all the gratifications of the senses, and directing the overflow of the animal spirits into a healthy channel. Useless and unnecessary mortification of the flesh is discountenanced, nay, condemned. Fasting is prescribed to the able-bodied and the strong, as a means of chastening the spirit by imposing a restraint on the body. For the weak, the sickly, the traveller, the student (who is engaged in the pursuit of knowledge—the *Jihad-ul-Akbar*) the soldier doing God's battle against the assailants of the faith, and women in their ailments it is disallowed. Those who bear in mind the gluttony of the Greeks, the Romans, the Persians, and their excesses in their pleasures as well as their vices. will appreciate the value of the regulation, and comprehend how wonderfully adapted it is for keeping in check the animal propensities of man, especially among semi-civilised races.

Mark the wisdom of the rule as given in the Qur'an "O ye that have believed, a fast is ordained to you...... that ye may practise piety, a fast of a computed number of days. But he among you who shall be ailing, or on a journey (shall fast) an equal number of other days, and they that are able to keep it (and do not) shall make atonement by maintaining a poor man .... But if ye fast, it will be better for you.

This rule of abstinence is restricted to the day, in the night, in the intervals of prayer and devotion, the Muslim is allowed, perhaps indeed, is bound, to refresh the system by partaking in moderation of food and drink, and otherwise enjoying himself lawfully. In the true spirit of the Teacher, the legists invariably laid down the rule that, during the fast, abstinence of mind from all based thoughts is as incumbent as the abstinence of the body.

No religion of the world prior to Islam had consecrated charity, the support of the widow, the orphan, and the helpless poor, by enrolling its principles among the positive enactments of the system.

The main object of fasting is to make a spiritual, moral, and physical discipline. The Holy Qur'an enjoins :

> O ye who believe ! Fasting as prescribed for you as it was prescribed for the followers of the prophets before you that haply you may able to guard yourselves against evil (ii : 183).

Ramzan brings the human being near to God. The Holy Qur'an says :—

> *Ramzan* is the month in which the Qur'an was revealed, a guidance to men, containing such clear instructions which would lead men to the right path and a criterion of good and evil. Whoever of you comes across this month shall fast therein and when My servants ask you concerning Me, then verily I am very near, I answer the prayer of the supplicant when he calls on Me, so they should answer My call (by fasting) and believe in Me that they may find the way (to Me) (ii : 185-86).

The following verses of the Holy Qur'an refer to the spiritual, moral and physical aspects of the observation of the fast :—

1. O, ye who believe ! Fasting is prescribed for you as it was prescribed for the followers of the Prophets before you that haply you may be able to guard yourselves against evil. For a certain number of days (you shall fast) but whoever among you is ill or on a journey, then he shall fast a like number of other days, and those who may find it hard to do so may effect a redemption by feeding a poor man, and if he of his own accord does more good, it is better for him. But fasting will be more for your own good if you can understand. *Ramzan* is the month in which the Qur'an was revealed, a guidance to men containing clear instructions to lead men on the straight path and a criterion of good and evil, therefore whoever of you comes across this month, he shall fast therein, and whoever is ill or on a journey, then he should fast a like number of other days, Allah desireth ease for you and He doth not desire hardship for you and He

desireth that you should complete the period, that you should glorify Allah for His having guided you and that you may give thanks (ii : 183-85).

2. It is made lawful to you to go unto your wives on the nights of the fast, they are a garment for you and you are a garment for them. Allah knows you acted unfaithfully towards yourselves (in the month) so He has turned to you mercifully and removed from you this burden; so now you may hold intercourse with them and seek what Allah hath ordained for you and eat and drink until the white streak of the day become distinct from the black streak of the night at early dawn, then observe the fast till night fall. Have no intercourse with your wives while you keep yourselves secluded in the mosques, these are the limits of Allah, so do not cross them, thus doth Allah expound His commands for men that they may guard against evil (ii : 187).

3. Fasting men and fasting women—Allah has prepared for them forgiveness and a mighty reward (xxxiii : 35).

3. Giving of Alms (*Zakat*) :

By the laws of Islam every individual is bound to contribute a certain part of his substance towards the help and assistance of his poorer neighbours. This portion is usually one part of forty, or 2½ per cent. on the value of all goods, chattels, emblements, on profits of trade, mercantile business, etc. But alms are due only when the property amounts to a certain value and has been in the possession of a person for one whole year, nor are any due from cattle employed in agriculture or in the carrying of burdens. Besides, at the end of the month of *Ramzan* (the month of fasting), and on the day of the *Id-al-Fitr*, the festival which celebrates the close of the Muslem Lent, each head of a family has to give away in alms, for himself and for every member of his household, and for each guest who breaks his fast and sleeps in his house during the month a measure of wheat, barley, dates, raisins, rice or any other grain, or the value of the same.

The rightful of the alms, as pointed out by the practice of Prophet Muhammad and his disciples, are : (1) the poor and the indigent, (2) those who help in the collection and distribution of the obligatory alms, (3) slaves, who wish to buy their freedom and have not the means for so doing, (4) debtors, who cannot pay their debts, (5) travellers and strangers. General charity is inculcated by the Qur'an in the most forcible terms. But the glory of Islam consists in having embodied the beautiful sentiment of Jesus into definite laws.

The following verses of the Holy Qur'an show the importance of the institution of *Zakat* :—

1. This Book (the Qur'an) there is no doubt in it—shows the way to live straight in the world to those who (wish to) guard themselves against evil, those who believe in the unseen and keep up prayer and spend benevolently out what We have given them (ii : 2-3).

2. And keep up prayer and pay the *Zakat* and bow down with those who bow down (ii : 43).

3. It is not righteousness that you turn your faces to the East and the West but righteous is he who believeth in Allah and the Last Day and the Angels and the Book and the Prophets and giveth his wealth out of love for Him to his kinsfolk and the orphan and the needy and the wayfarer and the beggar and for setting the captives free and observeth prayer and payeth *Zakat* (ii : 177).

4. But if they repent and keep up prayer and pay the *Zakat*, then they are your brethren in faith (ix : 11).

5. Those who, if We give them power in the land, will keep up prayer and pay the *Zakat* and enjoin good and forbid evil, and the end of all affairs is in the hands of Allah (xxii : 41).

6. And the believers, both men and women, are protectors one of another, they enjoin good and forbid evil and keep up prayer and pay the *Zakat* and obey Allah and His Apostle, Allah will show mercy to them, surely Allah is Mighty, Wise (ix : 71).

7. By no means shall you attain to righteousness until you spend (in the way of Allah) out of that which you cherish most (iii : 91).

8. And those who are saved from their own greed shall be the successful (xiv : 91).

9. And let not those of you who possess grace and ease swear against giving to the near of kin and to the needy and to the fugitives in Allah's way, and let them forgive and shows indulgence. Yearn ye not that Allah may forgive you ? And Allah is Forgiving, Merciful (xxiv : 22).

10. And they give food out of love for Him to the needy, the orphan and the captive (saying) we feed you for Allah's sake. We wish neither recompense nor thanks from you (xxvi : 9-9).

11. O, you who believe ! Spend benevolently of the good things which you have earned and of that which We have brought forth for you out of the earth, and seek not the bad (with intent) to spend (in charity) while you would not take it save with disdain and know that Allah is Self-Sufficient, Praiseworthy (ii : 267).
12. And hasten to forgiveness from your Lord and for a Paradise as wide as are the heavens and the earth prepared for those who guard against evil, those who spend benevolently in ease and in adversity (iii: 132-33).
13. Whatever good things you spend, it is for your own good, and you should spend only to seek the pleasure of Allah (ii : 272).
14. O, you who believe ! Let not your wealth nor your children distract you from the remembrance of Allah. Those who do so are themselves the losers (xiii : 9).

The *Zakat* has been dealt with in greater detail in Volume III of this Book.

4. Pilgrimage (*Hajj*):

The word *Hajj* means literally as "the intention of a person wishing to pay a visit to a sacred place". Therefore the visit from all the places of the world to the Kaaba at Mecca is known as *Hajj*.

The institution of *Hajj* was originated from the time of the Prophet Abraham. When he was born and came to age of manhood he found all around him the idol worshippers. He started the mission of preaching in the unity of God. He faced many difficulties and the people became inimical to him. The monarch of the time persecuted and ill-treated him so much so that he had to leave his native land, and wander about in Syria, Palestine, Egypt and Arabia. Then he was tested by God for the sacrifice of his only son Ismail. He was taken up in high esteem by God. He has such a known leadership amongst the Prophets that the people of the world—the Jews, the Christians and the Muslims owe their allegiance and recognise him as their patriarch. The Qur'an enjoins as follows :—

> And (remember) when His Lord tried Abraham with His commands and he carried them out most faithfully, He said, "Surely I have appointed thee a leader of men". (Abraham) said : "And what of my off-spring (will there be leaders among them ?)". God replied. "My covenant does not include the wrong-doers" (ii : 124).

Now the mission of the proposition of Islam was taken up by the two sons, Ishaque and Ismail and by the nephew,

Prophet Lot. Both Ismail and Ibrahim made a centre of their mission as *Kaaba*. This can be well understood by going through the following verses of the Holy Qur'an :—

1. Most surely, the first sanctuary appointed for men is the one at Bekka, a blessed place and a source of guidance to the nations, wherein are plain memorials (of Allah's guidance) the place where Ibrahim stood up to pray, and whosoever entereth it receiveth peace and security (iii : 95).

2. Have they not seen that We have appointed a sanctuary immune (from violence) while men are ravaged all around it (xxix : 67).

3. And We made the House (at Mecca) a resort for men and a sanctuary and appointed for you a place of prayer on the spot where Ibrahim stood up to pray, and We imposed a duty on Ibrahim and Ismail (saying) "Purify My House for those who visit it, and those who abide in it, for devotion, and those who bow down and prostrate". And when Ibrahim prayed : "My Lord ! Make this a region of security and provide its people with fruits, such of them as believe in Allah and the Last Day". He answered : "And whoever disbelieves, I will leave him in contentment for a short while, then will drive him to the chastisement of the fire—an evil destination.

   And when Ibrahim and Ismail were raising the foundations of the house (Ibrahim) prayed "Our Lord, Accept from us (this duty) surely Thou, only Thou art the Hearing, the Knowing. Our Lord, and make us both submissive to Thee and raise from our seed a nation submissive unto Thee and show us our ways of devotion and turn to us mercifully, surely Thou art the Oft-returning (to mercy), the Merciful. Our Lord, and raise up in their midst an Apostle from among them who shall recite to them Thy revelations and teach them the Book and wisdom and purify them, surely Thou art the Mighty, the Wise (ii : 125-29).

4. And when Ibrahim prayed, My Lord ! Make this city secure and preserve me and my children from serving idols. My Lord ! Surely they have led many men astray. But whoso followeth me, he is surely of me, and whoso disobeyeth me—still Thou art Forgiving, Merciful. O our Lord ! Surely I have settled a part of my offspring in an uncultivated valley near Thy Sacred House, Our Lord, that they may keep up prayer, therefore make the hearts of people yearn towards them and

provide Thou them with fruits, haply they may be thankful (xiv : 35-37).

5. And (remember) when We assigned to Abrahim the site of the House (saying), Do not associate with Me aught and purify My House for those who make the circuit and those who stand to pray, and bow and prostrate themselves, and proclaim among men the pilgrimage. They will come to thee on foot, and on every lean camel, coming from every remote place, that they may witness things that are of benefit to them and mention the name of Allah during stated days over what He has given them of the cattle, then eat of them and feed the distressed one, the needy (xxii : 26).

This institution of *Hajj* was revived by the advent of Prophet Muhammad. The Holy Qur'an recognises and declares the pilgrimage (*Hajj*) in the following words :—

> And pilgrimage (*Hajj*) to the House is incumbent upon me as a duty they owe to Allah, upon those who can afford the journey to it, and whoever refuses, to pay heed to it, then Allah is Self-Sufficient, above any need of the word (iii : 196).

The following are the other verses on the *Hajj* in the Holy Qur'an :—

1. Celebrate the praises of Allah near the holy monument and remember Him as He has directed you, though before that you were certainly of those who had gone astray (ii : 197).
2. Whoever undertakes the duty of performing the *Hajj*, let him remember that there shall he no lewdness nor abuse nor dispute during the pilgrimage (ii : 197).

The sprinkling of the blood and scattering the meat of the sacrificed animals on the walls of *Kaaba* has been prohibited by the following verses of the Holy Qur'an :—

1. There does not reach Allah their flesh nor their blood but to Him reacheth your devotion and your piety (xxii : 37).
2. Say (to them O Prophet) : Who has prohibited the adornment (*i.e.*, the wearing apparel) of Allah which He has brought forth for His servants and the good provisions (of life) (vii : 32).
3. Say (O Prophet) : Surely Allah does not enjoin lewdness (vii : 28).

4. O children of Adam ! Wear your good apparel at every time and place of worship (vii : 131).

The wisdom which incorporated into Islam the time-honoured custom of annual pilgrimage to Mecca and to the shrine of the *Kaaba*, has breathed into Prophet Muhammad's religion a free masonry and brotherhood of faith in spite of sectarian divisions. The eyes of the whole Muslim world fixed on that central spot keep alive in the bosom of each some spark of the celestial fire which lighted up the earth in that century of darkness. Here, again the wisdom of the inspired Law-giver shines forth in the negative part of the enactment, in the conditions necessary to make the injunction obligatory : (1) ripeness of intelligence and discernment, (2) perfect freedom and liberty, (3) possession of the means of transport and subsistence during the journey, (4) possession of means sufficient to support the pilgrim's family during his absence, (5) the possibility and practicability of the voyage.

Part (2)
Outline of Islamic History

CONTAINING

Chapters :

1. THE HOLY PROPHET OF ISLAM—
   - ★ Perfect Personality.
   - ★ Main Events of His Life.
   - ★ Conception of *Sunnah*.
2. THE PERIOD OF KHULFA-I-RASHIDEEN.
3. THE PERIOD OF UMAYYADS.
4. THE PERIOD OF ABBASSIDS.
5. MUSLIMS IN SPAIN AND NORTH AFRICA.
6. POST-MONGOL-MUSLIM PERIOD.
7. ISLAM IN THE 19TH AND 20TH CENTURIES.
8. THE WORLD OF ISLAM TODAY.

Chapter 1

The Holy Prophet of Islam

The main sources for the life of Prophet Muhammad are firstly the Qur'an or record of the revelations which he received from God, and secondly historical works by writers of the third and fourth centuries of Muslim era. In the second group the works accessible to us are :

1. The *Sirah* or Life of Prophet Muhammad by Ibn Hashim.
2. The section of the *Annals* of at-Tabari dealing with the life of Prophet Muhammad.
3. The *Maghazi* or History of Prophet Muhammad's Campaigns by al-Waqidi.
4. The *Tabaqat* of Ibn Sa'd the secretary of al-Waqidi.

Mention should also be made of the Collections of Traditions (or anecdotes about the sayings and doings of Prophet Muhammad) such as the *Sahih* of al-Bukhari and that of Muslim and the *Masnad* of Ahmad b. Hanbal, *Usd al-Ghabah* by Ibn al-Athir and *Isabah* by Ibn Hajar. There are later Muslim biographers of Prophet Muhammad but none appears to have had access to any important sources other than those used by the abovementioned writers.

Prophet Muhammad's Ancestry :

The Arabs of Hijaz and Yemen made themselves famous in the Middle Ages. The principal tribe among the former was that of Quraish. The Quraish were descended from Fihr, who lived in his third century of Christian era. He was descended from Maad, son of Adnan, a descendant of Ismael, son of Prophet Abraham. In the fifth century, Qusayy, a descendant Fihr, became the ruler of Mecca. He was entrusted the guardianship of the *Kaaba* an office of highest honour in Arabia. His first step was to bring together the Quraish, who had previously been dispersed over a wide area, into the Mecca valley. He built a house of Assembly where matters affecting the common were discussed by the elders of the tribe. He also instituted and centered in himself a number of dignities in connection with the Government of the *Kaaba* and the administration of the Pilgrimage, besides others of a political and military character.

Qusayy died in 480 A.D. and succeeded by his son Abd Dar. Upon Abd Dar's death a dispute broke out among the grandsons and the sons of his brother Abd Mannaf about the succession to the rulership of Mecca. This dispute was, however, settled by a division of authority. The administration of the water supply of Mecca and the raising of taxes were entrusted to Abd Shams, a son of Abd Mannaf, whilst the guardianship of *Kaaba* of the Council-chamber, and of the Military standard, was given to the grandsons of Abd Dar. Abd Shams a quiet and unassuming man and he transferred his authority to his brother Hashim, a leading merchant of Mecca. But Abd Shams' son Umayyah was a very assertive person. He became a rival of his uncle Hashim. It was not long before the families of these two grew into clans. They were called Bani Hashim and Bani Umayyah. The Bani Umayyah took to commerce and taking advantage of the trade route through Hijaz, became quite prominent leaders of the commercial group. The Bani Hashim leaned either towards piety and towards the manly sports of hunting, archery, or swordsmanship. Whatever was the relative importance and prosperity of the two, the comparatively early death of Hashim weakened his descendants and their associates. Hashim's brother, al-Muttalib, was now head of the whole group, but it does not seem to have any prominence in Meccan affairs until Hashim's son, Abd al-Muttalib, who had been brought up in Medina with his mother was brought to Mecca by his uncle "al-Muttalib".

Abd al-Muttalib became the chief of the Bani Hashim. With Abd al-Muttalib the position of the clan appears to have improved once more. He was respected by all. The leader of Bani Umayyah was Abu Sufiyan son of Umayyah. "He was a prominent Meccan, an astute old man, wise in his ways, and shrewd in his judgment. "But in spite of this, the high character of Abd al-Muttalib, and the veneration in which he was held by all the Quraish, enabled him to rule Mecca for nearly fifty-nine years". Abd al-Muttalib had many sons and daughters. Among the sons four are famous in the history, viz., Hamza, Abu Talib, Abbas and Abdullah. Hamza was a great hunter and a mighty warrior. Abu Talib and Abbas were sober men of affairs with good judgment and cool heads. "Another son was Abu Lahab, who is referred to in the Qur'an as a persecutor of Islam". Abdullah was the youngest son. Abdullah was married to Amina, daughter of Wahb-bin-Abd-i-Mannaf, of the Zuhra family. "The pair stood eminent, not only in respect of the nobility of their families, but for what stood for greater distinction in that age of darkness and corruption, they were both possessed of a pure and sublime character".

Birth and Early Life :

Muhammad, the Prophet of Allah (peace of Allah be on him), was born, a posthumous child in the "Year of Elephants",—the year of Abrahah's unsuccessful expedition against Mecca. This is usually held to be about 570 A.D. (12th *Rabi-ul-Awwal*). It was a custom among the Arab gentry and nobility that the mothers did not nurse their children, they were on the contrary sent out to be reared in the country. At his birth the infant Prophet Muhammad was first nursed by his mother. After this he was entrusted to Halima, of the tribe of Banu Sa'd. He remained in the charge of Halima till the age of six, when he was returned to his mother Amina. At this time, his mother desiring to pay a visit to the tomb of her husband, undertook a journey to Medina where he was buried, taking the child along with her. On the way, however, the orphan child was deprived also of his mother, who passed away at a place called Abwa. Thus he was bereaved at the tender age of six, both of his father and mother.

The charge of the child now fell to his grandfather, Abd al-Muttalib. Barely two years had elapsed, however, when his patronage was also snatched away from him by the hands of death. Thus he was eight years old when his guardianship passed to his uncle, Abu Talib. Whosoever came in contact with him, even at that early age, was impressed with his ways and manners. Sweet and gentle of disposition, he was much loved by all. Abu Talib always kept him in his own company, took him out with himself wherever he went, and even at night had him in his own bed. His early life was not free from the burden of labour, for Abu Talib was not rich like his ancestors, and the younger members of the family had to take their turn in tending the flocks and herds. When he was twelve years of age, Abu Talib undertook a mercantile journey to Syria. Prophet Muhammad travelled twice into Syria with his uncle, and there notice the misery of the people, and their evil ways, their wranglings and strife. The Syrian journey added a new experience to the life of the Prophet and the life of Syrian monks must have impressed on his mind the usefulness of mediation for attaining the truth.

At the age of twenty, the Prophet took part in the battle between the Quraish and the Qais which goes under the name of Harbul-Fijar. After that, he organised the alliance known as the Hilful-Fuzul formed to vindicate the rights of the weak and the oppressed against tyranny. Thus his early inclination to render help to the distressed go to show that human sympathy was implanted in his very nature.

Marriage with Khadijah :

Khadijah bint Khuwaylid bin Asad was a highplaced widow of Mecca. "She had acquired in pre-Islamic days, by her virtue and righteousness, the title of *Tahra* (the virtuous)". When Khadijah heard of the honesty, trustworthiness, and high moral character of Prophet Muhammad she invited him to set as her agent on a caravan journey to Syria. Prophet Muhammad accepted the proposal and went to Syria on trade journey. Khadijah was so pleased with the results of Prophet Muhammad's stewardship and so impressed by his personality that she made an offer of marriage to him. Abu Talib agreed and the two were married. She is said to have been forty at this time and Prophet Muhammad twenty-five. Khadijah gave birth to three sons and four daughters. All the sons died in infancy, but the daughters lived to see the great events of their father's life. The youngest, Fatima was married to Ali, the son of Abu Talib.

Prophet Muhammad's marriage with Khadijah was a turning point in the early part of his career. He was devoted heart and soul to Khadijah for her moral excellence. Khadijah never rejected his recommendation for spending her riches on charitable purposes. "He was of a religious frame of mind and this marriage must have provided him with an opportunity to prepare for the great task that lay ahead". At this early age, the Prophet's integrity had already won household fame in the town of Mecca. His gentle disposition and the severe purity of his life, his unflinching faithfulness and stern sense of duty, won for him during this period, from his fellow citizens, the title of *Al-Amin*, the "Trustworthy". This epithet does not imply honesty in money matters alone but is all-comprehensive, denoting righteousness in every aspect.

It was about this time that the necessity arose for the reconstruction of the sacred house of *Kaaba*. In the course of construction a serious dispute took place for laying the sacred Black Stone. Each tribe wanted to avail of the honour. This might have resulted in the outbreak of inter-tribal feuds. Then an elderly man suggested that let the first man to enter the sanctuary next morning be the umpire in the dispute. The proposal was unanimously agreed to. The first to come was the Prophet. Here is *Al-Amin* ! Here is *Al-Amin*, all shouted in one voice. Taking a sheet of cloth he placed the Black Stone thereon with his own hands. Prophet Muhammad thus averted what might have developed into a terrible conflagration of internecine warfare.

Call to Prophethood :

When Prophet Muhammad attained to the age of forty, he began to take himself more frequently to solitary meditation. Retiring to a cave on Mount Hira, near Mecca, he would give himself up to Divine contemplation for days. One night in the month of *Ramadan*, the angel Gabriel appeared to him and said, "Read". The Prophet replied, I am no reader. Three times the angel repeated the request to read, as many times the Prophet pleaded his inability to do so. Then the angel recited the following verses :—

"Read in the name of thy Lord who created,
Who created Man of blood coagulated,
Read. Thy Lord is the most beneficent,
Who taught by the pen,
Taught that which they knew not unto men".

On hearing these words Prophet Muhammad returned, trembling, to Khadijah and cried, "wrap me up, wrap me up" and remained covered until the terror passed away from him. At this juncture Khadijah reassured him of the great mission. She encouraged him with the inspiring words that God would never desert him and that he would succeed in his mission. Waraqa Ibn Naufal, a cousin of Khadijah and who had knowledge of old religious scriptures, proved very much helpful. When Khadijah related everything to Waraqa he at once recalled similar experiences of Prophet like Moses and assured Khadijah that he was the Prophet of Allah.

For some time he received no further revelation. This is known as the period of *fatratul-wahy* or the cessation of revelation. After a lapse of time, he saw the angel seated on a throne between earth and heaven. Again he asked Khadijah, now less awe-stricken than before, to wrap him up. This time the following verses were revealed :—

O thou that hast wrapped thyself up.
Arise and prophesy.
And thy Lord magnify.
And thy raiment purify.
And the abomination fly.

"Prophet Muhammad no longer doubted that he had a divinely ordained mission to preach in public".

Perfect Personality

The greatness of a man does not consist in the working of miracles or the doing of wonders, neither does it lie in the preaching of sermons or the formulating of theories. These are but passing phenomena. The greatness of a man lies in the possession of a mighty personality. Personality is one of the wonders of the world, and......personalities can and do the marvels of the world. It is of everlasting value for those who are immediately around it, and for those also, who come after. It conciliates opposition and inspires respect and imitation, which result, in the long run, in implicit obedience. It inspires others with its own spirit and dyes them in its own colour. It changes ideas and revolutionizes the thoughts, the habits and the customs of its contemporaries. It creates a new basis for the beliefs and actions of generation after generation of the races of mankind. In a word, it creates new heaven and a new earth. Prophet Muhammad was such a personality, and, as such, was unique. There have been other personalities in the world. We may clothe them with attributes they never possessed, we may attribute to them virtues and ethics that they never owned or taught. We crucify Saviours or transfer them from the human to the divine on Mounts of Transfiguration. But all this is an afterthought that seeks to defy or magnify a unit of humanity. On the other hand, the light of personality shines like the sun, instantly opposition shrivels into nothing before its fiery ardour and unconquerable soul. Our judgment as to a person believed to possess personality must, therefore, be based on the opinion and action of his own contemporaries. If the test of a great man's inspiration is the reverence which his words inspire in those who acknowledge their divine origin, as is remarked in the editorial columns of the Daily Express of November 10, then Prophet Muhammad must be numbered among the greatest. But if this test is right—and it is right—Prophet Muhammad is a unique character, seeing that no other reformer, prophet, nor even any God-incarnate, could have and claim that love, devotion and obedience that came to Prophet Muhammad from his followers, who were not of low station or of inferior mental calibre, but men of position, rank, wealth and culture, and from his own kith and kin, those who knew the ins and outs of his life. For twelve years the early Muslims suffered frightful persecution at the hand of idolaters, and yet their number steadily increased. The community was scattered, many were driven into exile, yet it went on growing. Though its members were subjected to most cruel tortures, there were few apostates, and many converts to the faith of Allah. Did the personality of Prophet Muhammad—the most charming that the world have known—count for nothing in that steadfast and enduring growth.

In Prophet Muhammad we have the ideal personaility, who in his own lifetime moulds the character of his fellowmen, reforms them, puts new ideals before them, elevates them to a higher plane, and, in spirit of themselves, drives them onward upwards on the path of progress, to the fullness of a better and holier life.

Prophet Muhammad was surrounded by infidelity, drunkenness, immorality, oppression, irreligion and infanticide, true religion had vanished, and an admixture of idolatry, fetishism, nature, element and man-worship was prevailing everywhere, even among Christians and Jews. Above all, he had to face people who were immensely conservative, who would not stoop to any interference with their own ways, who were tenaciously attached to their old customs and habits, and would not tolerate any admonition from another. It was a hopeless task to reform them. But Prophet Muhammad came with a mission to do so, a mission that surpassed the mission of other prophets in its arduous nature. But did Prophet Muhammad hesitate or shirk it? Did he begin his work with words and deeds of compromise, as others did? Did he adopt half-measures, or try the gradual infusion of new thoughts? Were his actions ever influenced by expediency? No. He goes directly to the root of the evil. Sensitive, retiring and reticent as he was, he neither temporized nor kept silent. He felt the force of his convictions and had the courage to act up to them. He was never influenced by expediency, neither did he ever care for diplomacy. He was always direct, whether in reply, advice, or reproof. To the non-Muslim world, he would say, in the words of the Qur'an: Whoever desires a religion other than Islam—submission to God—it shall not be accepted from him, and in the hereafter he shall be one of the losers. To the Christian he would say: Jesus son of Mary, is only an apostle of God——believe therefore in Allah and His Apostle and say not, Three. Desist, it is better for you and they say the beneficent God has taken to Himself a son. Certainly you have made an abominable assertion. The heavens may almost threat, and the earth cleave asunder, and the mountains fall down in that they ascribe a son to God——say, God is one. He is independent, He is neither begotten nor begets. The Christians say: The Messiah is the son of Allah, these are the words of their mouths, they imitate the saying of those who were pagans before. Allah destroyed them, now they are turned away. To the Romish Church he would say: They have taken their Doctors of Law and their monks for Lords besides Allah. The Jews believed that they were the sons of God, and the Christians also thought themselves to be so, but Prophet Muhammad would admonish them and say: The Jews and Christians say we are sons of Allah and His beloved ones, say, why then does He chastise you. In addressing the Jews he said: Most of you are transgressors——Allah has cursed and brought His wrath upon (them) of whom He made apes and swine. To the hypocrites he would say: There is a disease in their hearts, so Allah added to their disease and they shall have a painful chastisement, because they lied. To those who would not listen to admonition nor care for warning he would declare—Allah has put a seal upon their hearts and upon their hearing, and there is a covering over their eyes and there is a great chastisement for them. Deaf, dumb, blind, so they will not turn back. Those were the days when salvation through vicarious atonemens, sacrificial rites, intermediaries and intercessions was a popular belief, and no one was prepared to bear or give countenance to any attempt that would expose the hollowness of that belief. And yet Prophet Muhammad falsified all these doctrines when he said : What shall I seek a Lord better than Allah. And He is the Lord of all things, and no soul earns (evil) but against itself, and no bearer of a burden shall bear the burden of another (v : 165). There does not reach Allah their flesh (of animals sacrificed) nor their blood, but to Him is acceptable rightenosness on your part (xxii : 37). So the intercessions of intercessors shall not avail others.

Arabia was a seat of different religions, each decrying the other while no religion, though it suffered in purity, was without some partial truth. The same state of things we find today. But Prophet Muhammad denounced sectarianism and the hostile attitude of the various religions towards each other, in the following words of the Qur'an : And the Jews say : The Christians do not follow anything (good) and the Christians say : The Jews do not follow anything (good) while they recite the (same) Book. Even thus say those who have no knowledge, like to what they say, so Allah shall judge between them on the Day of Resurrection in what they differ. Say : We believe in Allah and (in) that which has been revealed to us, and (in) that which was revealed to Abraham and Ishmael and Isaac and Jacob and the tribes, and (I) that which was given to in Moses and Jesus, and (in) that which was given to the Prophets from their Lord, we do not make any distinction between any of them, and to Him do we submit.

Those were the days when ritualism was the sum total of almost every religion. But Prophet Muhammad distinguished between a formal and ceremonial piety. He made faith in God, and benevolence towards man, the essence of religion. It is not righteousness that you turn your faces towards the East and the West, but righteousness is this, that one should believe in Allah and the Last Day and the angels, and the Book and the prophets, and give away wealth out of love for Him to the near kin and the orphans and the needy and the wayfarer and the beggars and for (the emancipation of) the captives, and keep up prayer and pay the poor-rate, and the performance of their promise when they make a promise, and the patient in distress and affliction and in time of conflict these are they who are true (to themselves) and these are they who guard (against evil).

The Arabs were extremely addicted to "drink" and gambling, but he would not allow even moderation, he would go directly to the root of it and would preach total prohibition thus : "O' you who believe intoxicants and games of chance and (sacrificing to) stones set up and (divining by) arrow are only an uncleanness, the devil's work, shun it, therefore, that you may be successful. His countrymen used to kill their female babies or bury them alive. It was a custom honoured by usage, but Prophet Muhammad uprooted it, saying when one is buried alive—for what sin was she killed. In short, no false belief or wrong doctrine remained of which the error or hollowness was not exposed. No evil custom or bad habit was left unrebuked. And yet Prophet Muhammad had any identity with the Deity. No extraordinary pretensions, no indulgence in hyperbolical language, no endeavour to cast a glamour round his character and personality. I am only a preacher of God's words, the bringer of God's Message to mankind, repeats he always.

Miracles he performed, but not to propagate his faith. He would plainly say he was but a man like others, he had no treasures, nor did he claim to know the secrets of the future. Say : I am only a man like unto you. Say : I do not control any benefit or harm for my own soul except as Allah pleases, and had I known the unseen I would have had much of good, and no evil would have touched me. I am nothing but a warner and giver of good news to people who believe. Say : I do not say to you I have with me the treasures of Allah, nor do I know the unseen, nor do I say to you that I am an angel. The Arabs were superstitious people. Had the Prophet so wished, he could have claimed any supernatural powers for himself. Many incidents occurred in his lifetime when people would have ascribed divine powers to him, but he destroyed all such vain suggestions by a plain denial. It is stated that on the day of the death of his son, the sun became totally eclipsed. Some of the pagans thought that the sun was in mourning for the sad event. They went to him with repentance, ready to accept his mission. But he would not take advantage of such subterfuges. He said surely the Sun and the Moon are two signs of Allah, they do not suffer eclipse in consequence of the death of anybody nor on account of any one's life.

Here is a man, a Reformer, a Prophet, a Messenger from God, who tripped himself of all the paraphernalia reported to have been possessed by those who came before him with a similar mission. He disowned all that might invite following, help, co-operation or sympathy. Thus he made no friends, but enemies of them all. He would not yield to solicitations nor accept a position of wealth, to prejudice the mission—a mission in no way contributing to his personal aggrandizement—but the mission of God, the mission of humanity and the mission of everything that is noblest and best, the mission to establish the Unity of God and, through it, the unity of the human race, the mission of raising degraded humanity to its destined elevation. In short, he deprived himself of all that could have smoothed his way to success, had he done otherwise, he would have been untrue to himself and insincere to his mission for which he had the call. He did not work miracles to achieve his object, but he worked what was more than a miracle, he worked against odds and achieved a success—such a success as has never come to any person before or since in religious or secular history, and that in the adverse circumstances to which he had been subjected. But to achieve this unique success he did not resort to things beyond human reach, in which case he could not have acted as an exemplar. He used all the honest and honourable means that are open to others, and so his life is an object-lesson to those who have to work for success against heavy odds and under adverse circumstances.

A Prophet comes to act as a guide and a model, Prophet Muhammad has a special claim to those qualifications. He is the Prophet in human colours, and consequently a true specimen for our imitation. He faces difficulties, and surmounts them as the report goes, had recourse to miracles to meet the difficulties in their way. One could understand the need of a miracle in order to strengthen the conviction of, or drive home, certain truths to a man in the street—it is a necessity and there is a genuine report of any number of miracles performed by the Holy Prophet for that purpose—but we, in our day, have to face similar difficulties in our life, and we cannot do miracles in order to surmount them. Moses saved his people from the Egyptian tyranny through a miracle, but Prophet Muhammad defended the city of Medina with his little band against ten thousand odds through his heroic and soldier-like measures which a commander of an army will be proud to follow with advantage. But Moses with all his miracles could not infuse that spirit of manliness into his followers which we observe in the ranks of Prophet Muhammad. Jesus had to complain always of the lack of faith in his disciples, though they saw many a miracle from the master, but Prophet Muhammad had a band of the faithful unique in their devotion to the master.

Few persons remember of their days of adversity when they come to power. High-mindedness and great strength of character alone can stand against the vicissitudes of life. To him who possesses these qualities change means newness of occasions that call forth such other noble qualities as could not be exhibited in his former state. In fact, every quality has its own occasion and demands special circumstances for its revelation. If trial gives man a character, success brings out his nobility of mind, if he possesses it. Humanity is not only softness of heart, it consists of various morals, tender and stern, and needs a variety of conditions for their development. If some find manifestation in penury, others demand affluence, if they are to appear in perfection. Very few of the Guides of Humanity were granted occasion to taste both. But Prophet Muhammad, to act as a perfect model for humanity, had to pass every phase of life. If prosperity brought out his generosity, his forgiveness, his hight-mindedness and his adversity gave him occasion to exhibit his patience, his fortitude and his trust in God.

There is one thing in him that shows that he had achieved that zenith of character and morality that must be the final goal of human endeavour, where man reflects Divine morals. Like all the ways and laws of God, Prophet Muhammad is unchangeable. In victory or in defeat, in power or in adversity, in affluence or in indigence, he is the same. He discloses the same character. Humility was, for example, his special characteristic throughout his career. His military triumphs, says Washington-Irving, awakened no pride or vainglory, as they would have done had they been effected for selfish purposes. In the time of his greatest power he maintained the same simplicity of manners and appearance as in the day of his adversity. So far from affecting regal state, he was displeased if, on entering a room, any unusual testimonial of respect were shown him. If he aimed at universal dominion, it was the dominion of the faith, as to the temporal rule which grew up in his hands, as he used it without ostentation so he took no step to perpetuate in his family.

After he became the sovereign of Arabia he still remained on terms of brotherhood with all believers. He had not to surround himself with guards and janitors, he moved in simple ways among the brethren, the guide, the peacemaker, and the trusted friend. Even at the zenith of his worldly power the good sense of Prophet Muhammad, says Gibbon, despised the pomp of royalty, the apostle of God submitted to the menial offices of the family, he kindled the fire, swept the floor, milked the cows, mended with his own hand his shoes and his woollen garments. Disdaining the penance and merit of an hermit, he observed, without effect and vanity, the abstemious diet of an Arab and a soldier. On solemn occasions he feasted his companions with hospitable plenty, but, in his domestic life, many weeks would elapse without a fire being kindled in the hearth of the Prophet, I would add a statement on record left by the Lady Ayesha to these quotations which I have purposely made in pursuance of an Arabic proverb that says that the best of testimony is that that comes from the other camp. For a whole month together we did not light a fire to dress victuals, our food was nothing but dates and water unless anyone sent us meat. The people of the Prophet's household never got wheat bread on two successive days.

This was the life he led and such were his humble ways when the whole of Arabia was at his feet. The entire town of Medina grew wealthy in the latter days of his life. Everywhere there was gold and silver, and yet the house of his own daughter showed no sign of riches, no trace of wealth or comfort. On the very day of his death his only assets were a few shillings, a part of which went to satisfy a debt and the rest was given to a needy person who came to his house for charity. The clothes in which he breathed his last had patches. The whole property being thus spent, the Prophet has been reported to have remarked : We of the class of Prophets neither inherit from others nor do we leave anything for others to inherit from us.

Character of the Prophet :

Prophet Muhammad was the embodiment of all virtues. He is not only the best of men but also the greatest of the Prophets. His morals are the Qur'an said Ayesha, the Prophet's wife. In other words, his daily life was a true picture of the Qur'anic teachings. He was an embodiment of all that is enjoined in the Holy Qur'an. Just as the Book of God is a code of high morals for the development of the manifold faculties of man, similarly the Prophet's life is a practical demonstration of all those morals.

Simplicity was the key-note of Prophet's character. He loved virtues for its own sake. High morals which formed an attractive feature of his character, were not an acquisition with him, but were ingrained in his very nature.

He was an affectionate father of the orphans and the distressed. He was very affectionate towards his family. He would assist his wives in their household duties. He would milk his own goats, patch his own clothes, and mend his own shoes. No work was too low for him. He worked like a labourer in the construction of the mosque. His habit of living was also marked by simplicity. Whatever was offered to him, he would cheerfully partake to it. The little food he had was always shared with those who came to see him. His ordinary food was dates and water or barley bread. Milk and honey were luxuries of which he was fond of, but which he rarely allowed himself. His dress was also simple. He did not like the males to wear silk. He was very particular about the neatness of his dress. His dwelling consisted of small rooms made of mud bricks. He would also make use of perfume.

The Prophet had a deep love for his friends. He met everybody with a smiling face. Sometimes he would enjoy innocent jokes with his friends. He would talk freely, never putting an artificial reserve to give himself an air of superiority.

His conduct towards the bitterest of his enemies says Amir Ali, was marked by moved clemency and forbearance. The Prophet's generosity towards his enemies stands unique in the annals of the world. Abdullah-ibn-Ubbayy was a sworn enemy of Islam, yet at his death the Prophet prayed to the Lord to forgive him. Punishment was never given where there was the least chance for the success of forgiveness. Generosity was extended to the followers of all creeds—Jews, Christians, idolaters, all alike. He did not confine his charity to his own-fold. In the administration of justice, the Prophet was scrupulously even-handed. Muslim and non-Muslim, friend and foe, were all alike in his eyes. In his dealing with others he never placed himself on a higher pedestal. He would conduct himself just as a man like others. He never rebuked his servants for their mistake. He never kept anybody in slavery. As soon as he got a slave, he set him free.

The Prophet never disappointed a poor or needy. He would feed the hungry, himself going without food. Never in his life, old abusive language escape the Prophet's lips. He never uttered even a harsh word. His integrity, his righteousness and his sincerity were of universal fame throughout Arabia, so much so that he was known as *Al-Amin*. Forgiveness was another most radiant gem in the Prophet's character.

Prophet Muhammad inspite of the fact that he became the sovereign of Arabia lead the life in simplicity. There was no pomp and show. He did not require any guards. He used to live amongst his peoples as their brother.

Prophet as a Social Reformer :

The Prophet was not only the founder of a new faith, the maker of a new nation but also a reformer of a great social order. Ever since the dawn of history, the world has seen many reformers in different ages and at different places but none could equal the Prophet of Islam in bringing a revolutionary change into a hitherto moribund and ignorant society.

At the time of the Prophet's advent, the Arabs were passing through a period of ignorance. The whole Arab social life was steeped in vices and immoralities. Idolatry and polytheism were the orders of the day. Drinking, gambling and adultery were the common practices of the people. Infanticide was in vogue among the Arabs and the women were the most degraded section of the society. They had no social or legal rights.

But the Prophet of God rose to the occasion and carried out his humanizing mission in the very teeth of the prevailing customs and ideas.

The Prophet understood well that the Arab society must get rid of social inequalities and there shall no longer be any privileged classes in the society. He could not find any reason why there would be difference between man and man on account of birth in a particular family or tribe or clan. Hence he upheld the doctrine of equality between man and man. He declared even himself as an ordinary member of mankind for he said, Surely I am a man like yourselves. Man and woman, master and slave, and king and subject all have equal right before the eye of God and of law. In other words, all have equal social rights. This is amply demonstrated in the daily prayers when high and low, rich and poor stand shoulder to shoulder before the Supreme Being—the greatest equalizing force on earth and heaven. Under his system a slave enjoyed the same civil right as a free man. Zayd, the liberated slave, was sometimes entrusted with authority over the proud Quraish.

Along with his venture to establish social equality and harmony he brought about a reconciliation between the conflicting religions of the world by pursuing a policy of religious toleration. He laid down that the Muslims should believe in all the Prophets of the world sent from time to time. None should speak ill of other faiths. He himself set up an example marrying the woman of the other faith. He once remarked : Do not abuse those whom they take up as gods besides Allah. Indeed, his aim was to establish a universal brotherhood of man so that the human race could live in peace and harmony with one another.

No longer the evil practices of the old days could prevail in Arab society. Drinking was prohibited and the practice of infanticide was severely dealt with. The people were asked to lead a pious and virtuous life. The Prophet said : The person who drinks liquor, who commits adultery and who steals, calls down upon himself severe punishment. Himself unlettered, he advised his countrymen to be seekers of knowledge. He once said : The worst man is a bad learned man, a good learned man is the best. Thus, by advocating the cause of learning and education, he fostered the development of an intellectual Arab society.

The Prophet brought about a thorough change in the condition of the females. The women were placed on a footing of perfect equality with men in the exercise of all legal rights and functions. For the first time, in the Muslim Law of Inheritance, rights of the females were recognised not only in the property of their parents but also in the property of their deceased husbands. Previously, girls had nothing to say about their marriage but now the Prophet gave them the right to choose their husbands. For, in Islam, marriage is regarded as a social contract entered into by the parties on a footing of equality and by free consent of the parties. Prior to the advent of the Prophet, the right to divorce their husbands by the wives was simply unthinkable, but now they were given the right to divorce their husbands under certain conditions. Of course they were cautioned to take recourse to this right, for he said, the thing which was lawful but most disliked by God was divorce. At the same time, the Prophet advised the women to be virtuous and dutiful to their husbands. He once said, "The worlds and all things in it are valuable but the most valuable thing in the world is a virtuous woman".

The Prophet made polygamy permissive, not binding. Besides, it was not invented by Islam but was a long standing custom in Arabia arising on account of the preponderance of females and dearth of males caused by frequent tribal wars. The Prophet regulated this evil system and put severe restrictions on it. The Holy Qur'an says, "Marry woman of your choice, two or three or four, but if you fear that you shall not be able to deal justly with them then only one".

The Holy Prophet sincerely believed in the principle of human equality. Hence, along with other reforms, he introduced measures for the emancipation of the slaves. Slavery was an ancient institution existing as a constant factor in the economic and social life of the Middle East and Europe. Prior to the advent of the Prophet none attempted to abolish this system. But he understood the evilness of the system and immediately provided measures for its speedy abolition. He made the emancipation of slaves a highly commendable act and enjoined kind and humane treatment of slaves, for as Muslims, slave and master stood on equal footing. Slaves were allowed to purchase their freedom by accumulating their wages, and fugitive slaves were set at liberty as soon as they reached to a Muslim country. The history of Islam is full of illustrations of the way in which slaves rose to the highest position in the state.

The Prophet was a socialist who aimed to bridge the gap of differences between the rich and the poor and the high and the low. He visualised a society where there should not be any exploitation by one section over the other. To help the needy and the distressed and to equalize the distribution of wealth he introduced *Zakat*, *Sadqah* and *Fitra* in the Muslim society. Besides he ruled that the social status of a person should not depend upon the economic position of that person but on how much he was devoted to God and His Prophet.

The Prophet did not come for a particular country or a particular people. He came for the saviour of entire humanity. His message was universal and cosmopolitan. The Holy Qur'an says, "Surely We have sent thee for the whole of mankind".

Indeed the Prophet dedicated his whole life to uplift the human race and cement the heterogeneous races into one universal brotherhood. We must agree with the view of Encyclopaedia Britannica which says, of all the religious personalities of the world Prophet Muhammad was the most successful.

Prophet as a Nation Builder :

Before the advent of the Prophet, the Arabs had no cohesion or unity among themselves. Politically, they were a disunited and discordant people. Bloodfeuds and tribal jealousies ran rampant. Trifle matter served as a match-stick to set ablaze the flames of war which continued for years together. The foreign influence reigned supreme in the different parts of peninsula. Hence, unity among the Arabs was the urgent need of the moment. The Prophet realised it and attempted to bring the whole of Arabia under one government by pursuing a policy of reconciliation among the various warring Arab tribes. He succeeded in his venture. The Prophet did not aim to build a nation conflicting to the Arabian peninsula alone but he visioned the establishment of one universal brotherhood. This brotherhood was based on religion instead of blood or family-based relations, and as such quite contrary to the established ideals of Arabia. So Hitti writes, "This was the first attempt in the history of Arabia at a social organisation with religion rather than blood as its basis".

The Prophet was not a mere founder of religion and of society, he was also a great statesman and nation-builder. The Prophet was "Caesar and Pope in one but he was Caesar without the legion of Caesar and Pope without the pretention of Pope". He was greatest of the Caesar, because he created one of the greatest nations". He founded the Republic in Medina, united the divergent elements into one homogeneous unit, and formed a code of law that governed all the tribes without any distinction of class and parentage.

The Prophet was a born democrat. The charter which he gave to the Medina granted security to life, property and religion to all peoples without any distinction of caste and creed. It also granted the people their birth rights—liberty, equality and fraternity. The noble spirit of fellow-feeling, brotherhood and amity which the Prophet infused in the minds of the people, who were so demoralised, brought them into a strong and compact nation.

The observation of Prof. Hitti is worth quoting, "Within a brief span of moral life Prophet Muhammad called forth out as unpromising materials, a nation, never united before in a country that was hitherto but a geographical expression. The state he established was a truly democratic one. The new Commonwealth included within its fold, Jews, Sabians and

Christians as citizens like the Muslims. It was based on the principles of equality of men. They were accorded religious freedom and political rights and other fundamental rights of citizens".

The more we reflect on the vastness of the achievement in the very brief span of ten years during which the achievement was accomplished, and the tough opposition that had to be faced more we wonder at the ability, tact, wisdom and greatness of the man who accomplished this revolution.

In the words of Edward Gibbon, "the revolution of Islam was one of the memorable revolution which have impressed a new and lasting character on the nations of the globe".

Main Events of the Life of the Holy Prophet

Quraish Opposed :

Never in the history of the world was the need so great, the time so ripe for the appearance of a Deliverer when the prospect of entire Arabia offered a most hoary and dreadful picture of disintegration nationality, socially and religiously in the 7th Century A.D. But Islam was not allowed to pass unopposed. In the beginning of his Prophetic career Prophet Muhammad had to sustain persecution and animosity from his own tribesmen—the powerful Quraish who formed an oligarchy and manned a lucrative system of priesthood.

Due to the spread of new religion—Islam, the Quraish found their power and influence swiftly passing away and their age-old religious institutions, heathen practices and lucrative priesthood all were at stake. Islam wanted to dismantle the existing structure of Arabia and to build a new society based on the doctrine of monotheism and the concept of universal brotherhood.

Ameer Ali rightly puts: "The new preacher's love was intensely democratic, in the sight of his Lord all human beings were equal. This levelling of old distinctions was contrary to all their traditions. Islam promised to abolish all sorts of inequality and strifes and to establish a society in which superiority was to be judged by character and ability and not by wealth and fortune, birth and status." Thus replacing of the old ideas and ideals by a society basically religious and intensely democrat, was highly unpleasant to them.

According to Joseph Hell "the main reason for the opposition of the Quraish, was not so much against the new teachings of Islam as against the social and political revolutions which they sought to introduce."

The denouncement of idolatry by the Prophet struck at the root of their pagan and heathen customs and oligarchy. The

Gospel of Brotherhood preached by Islam was distasteful to the arrogant and aristocratic Quraish, abandonment of manners and customs and habits of life to which they had been accustomed for generations and the adoption of payer, fasting and other rituals of Islam and strict rules of morality and good conduct prescribed by Islam were unpleasant and disagreeable to them. So they embarked upon organised persecution and torture.

Seeing his companions subjected to such ruthless tortures, Prophet Muhammad advised some of his companions to migrate to Abyssinia. Thus eleven of Meccan families followed by some eighty-three others went to Abyssinia (615 A.D). Hazrat Usman with his wife, Hazrat Ruqaya, the Prophet's daughter, were among those who migrated. The inhabitants of Abyssinia as well as their king, called the Negus were Christian by faith. The Quraish, as soon as they heard of their departure, despatched their men to King Negus. They demanded the extradition of the Muslim immigrants, who, they alleged, were guilty of an innovation in religion, in opposition to their ancestral faith as well as to Christianity. But King Negus refused to do so. The delegation returned unsuccessful.

The emigration to Abyssinia was of far-reaching consequence on the expansion of Islam. It convinced the Meccan unbelievers of the sincerity and resolution of the followers of Islam. A bright example of self-denial was exhibited by the believers to the effect that they were led to regard peril and exile in the cause of God as privilege and distinction. It also suggested the idea that the hostile attitude of the Meccan unbelievers, might secure for the followers of Prophet Muhammad a safe refuge within the limits of Arabia itself, as cordial as that offered by the Abyssinians. This gave birth to the idea of a greater *Hijrat,* the emigration to Medina.

The attempt of the Quraish to suppress the propagation of Islam ended in failure. Its adherents did not mind undergoing any amount of hardship, and they would rather suffer exile than give up Islam. Every effort was made to put an end of his life in an underhand manner, which failing, the Quraish made up their mind to make an open attempt on his life. But according to the social code of Arabia, every tribe was in honour bound to protect each of its individual members. The chief of the clan of Hashim at this time was Prophet Muhammad's uncle Abu Talib who, though he was not a Muslim, was ready to accord to Prophet Muhammad the full protection as Prophet Muhammad was a member of his clan. The leaders of Quraish, headed by Abu Jahl, appealed more than once to Abu Talib either to stop Prophet Muhammad from preaching the new religion or to withdraw his protection from him. Abu Talib, however, refused to do either of these things, and managed to secure the approval of the clans of Hashim and Muttalib.

Excepting Abu Lahb, the whole of the family of Banu Hashim had decided to stand by Prophet Muhammad, and fight for him till the last man. Eventually Prophet Muhammad's opponents, failed in their attempt to detach him from his clan, managed to bring together a grand alliance of nearly all the clans of Quraish against Banu Hashim, with the formation of the grand alliance a boycott of the clans of Hashim and Muttalib was instituted. Inter-marriage and commercial relations with them were strictly forbidden. This was a period of great hardship for the Banu Hashim, and of suspension of all propagating activities. But some of the gentle-hearted among the Quraish felt too much of the severity under which the Banu Hashim were subjected. On their strong pleadings the ban had been withdrawn.

Immediately after the withdrawal of the ban Prophet Muhammad lost his uncle Abu Talib, who has so far proved his mainstay. Shortly afterwards, his faithful wife Hazrat Khadijah, also died. Their death ushered in a new era of troubles. The Quraish redoubled their persecution. Hopeless now of success among the Meccans due to growing hostility of the Quraish the Prophet decided to go to Taif. But there also the Prophet did not receive any better treatment. Their people drove him from their city, pelting him with stones. In a mood of despair he returned from Taif to Mecca. He lived there for some time, retired from his people, preaching occasionally and confining his efforts mainly to the strangers who came to Mecca during the season of pilgrimage, hoping that some among them might listen to his words and give up their evil and inhuman ways.

"*Hijrat*" and its Causes :

Unable to bear brutal atrocities and animosities by his own clan and countrymen, the Prophet turned his mind to find out a new field for his activities. The persecution to which the Prophet was exposed at Mecca and the stubborn opposition to his mission there have a great historical importance, for it implied a change of front and a reversal of his scheme. When he was convinced that the turbulent and idolatrous Quraish would never bent their neck before the light of monotheism, the Prophet devoted his heart and soul to preach his doctrine to the half-pilgrims and half-traders who came from Yathrib to perform pilgrimage to Mecca. Among them he found the more earnest hearers. Struck by the earnestness and the truth of his words, six Yathribites embraced Islam in 621 A.D. they swore that they would not associate anything with God, nor commit adultery, nor steal, nor kill their children, and obey the Prophet in everything that was right. This pledge is known in history as the First Pledge of Aqaba. This happened in the 11th year of Islam. This first pledge of Aqaba marked an important epoch in the preaching of Islam because Islam now began to assume a universal role at Medina in combating other creeds. The peaceful penetration of Islam through the Prophet's diplomatic contact with the different tribes of Medina was so overwhelming that Islam brought within its fold at least a few members of all the tribes of Medina except the tribe of Banu Aus. Next year (in the year 622), the converted Yathribites came to Mecca to invite the Prophet to their city and took the oath that they would protect him and his faith from any danger whatsoever. This second pledge of Aqaba opened a new chapter in the history of Prophet's career.

When the Quraish got the inkling of the pledge, they planned to assassinate the Prophet. When a number of noble youths preyed round his quarters, the instinct of self-preservation swelled in him and he, accompanied by Hazrat Abu Bakr, went to hide in the mount Saur from where they started towards Yathrib and reached there on the 2nd July, 622 A.D. With his arrival the city was given a new name, Madinatunnabi—the city of the Prophet.

The chief causes which led to the migration of the Prophet may be summarised as follows:—

(1) Firstly, the diverse climatic conditions of the two places expedited it. Mild climate of Medina and sober temper of its people were very encouraging to the spread and development of Islam in Medina. On the contrary, Mecca had none of these facilities. This is why the Prophet met with the stiffest opposition in Mecca.

(2) Prophets were generally found not to be respected in their own countries. Prophet Muhammad was also not accepted by his own people. But he was recognised as the Prophet of Allah by the people of Medina and was earnestly requested to go to their city. The request was granted by the Prophet.

(3) The priest-class and the Quraishite aristocracy of Mecca vehemently opposed the new religion. They thought it quite against their interests. But in Medina there was no priest-class nor any religious aristocracy. So it was easier to preach Islam there with a better success than in Mecca.

The Medinites invited him in the expectation that through the personal influence and advice of the Prophet the long-drawn war between the two hostile tribes of Aus and Khazraj, which had almost paralysed the normal life of the people of

Medina, would end. On the religious side, *Hijrat* meant the acceptance of Muhammad as Prophet, and on the political side the acceptance of him as arbiter between the opposing factions in Medina.

The Prophet at Medina :

The condition of Medina before the arrival of the Prophet there, was like that of Mecca. Lawlessness was the order of the day. The tribes which inhabited it were at war with each other. There was no government to enforce law and order. The Prophet after his arrival there, abolished all tribal distinctions, and grouped the inhabitants under one general name, *Ansar*. He introduced law and order, established peace and thereby secured the goodwill of the Medinites.

Before the arrival of the Prophet, Medina was mainly inhabited by two tribes, namely, the Aus and Khazraj. For more than a century they had been at daggers drawn and lived in a state of incessant warfare. They were exhausted by this prolonged devastating war and, therefore, they badly needed peace and security without which their agriculture, trade and even normal life had almost come to a standstill. The Jews, on the other hand, were the most united, prosperous and cultured people in the peninsula. The Jews were almost on the point of capturing the ruling power of Medina, and one Abdullah-bin-Ubbay aspired to capture the power of Medina.

The *Hijrat* is a turning point in the career of Prophet Muhammad. A new and different element imbibed the religious programme of the Prophet. Here he began what may be called a politico-religious career. So long Islam was a pure religion, but after his migration to Medina Islam became a religio-political entity. The Prophet foundad a brotherhood—the brotherhood of Islam. He succeeded in establishing an alliance, embracing the rich and the poor alike on equal terms. Pride of family, of descent, of wealth, of power, in short, pride of everything had vanished and all the heterogeneous elements were fused into one nation.

Prop. Philip Hitti rightly remarks, this was the first attempt in the history of Arabia at a social organisation with religion rather than blood as its basis. And for the establishment of this social organisation, the importance or educative value of the disciplinary prayer can hardly be over-emphasized. The people wanting entirely in the sense of obedience and discipline were taught the values of uniformity, order and discipline through prayer.

Prophet Muhammad founded a state on the basis of the principles of equality, liberty and fraternity. The Arabs, the Jews and all the citizens of the new Islamic Commonwealth were placed on an equal footing, were allowed a free and equal patnership in the establishment of a new socio-political structure and in the advancement of mankind towards a fuller and richer moral ideal. There were no national or racial prejudices, no colour bars, no vested interests, no priesthood and no heredity nobility in the Islamic Commonwealth. No special benefits or privileges were reserved for anyone, not even the highest dignitary of the state. The intrinsic value of man was judged not by his rank or fortune but by his character and competence. Every man was given opportunities and scope to use his talents and abilities in the way he think fit, or he was given rank and position suitable to his qualities and attainments.

In order to weld together into harmonious political entity, Prophet Muhammad granted a character to the people with well-defined rights and obligations of the Muslims and the non-Muslims. This charter provided the provision for the foundation of a city state, a commonwealth, and a nation based on the bond of religious unity and faith, equality and democracy. Prophet Muhammad succeeded in rousing a sentiment of national unity among the everwarring tribes. This charter reveals the man in his real greatness—a mastermind, not only of his own age, but of all ages. The main provisions of the charter are reproduced as follows :

1. In the name of the Most Merciful and Compassionate God, given by Prophet Muhammad, the Prophet, to the believers, whether of the Quraish or of Yathrib, and all individuals of whatever origin who have made common cause with them, all these shall constitute one nation.
2. The state of peace and war shall be common to all Muslims, no one among them shall have the right of concluding peace with or declaring war against the enemies of his co-religionists.
3. The Jews who attach themselves to our commonwealth shall be protected from all insults and vexations, they shall have on equal rights with our own people to our assistance and good offices.
4. The Jews shall form with the Muslims one composite nation and they shall practice as freely as the Muslims.
5. The clients and allies of the Jews shall enjoy the same security and freedom.
6. The clients and allies of the Jews and Muslims shall be respected as patrons.
7. All true Muslims shall hold in contempt every man guilty of crime, injustice, or disorder, no one shall hold the culpable, though he were his next kin.

8. The guilty shall be pursued and punished.
9. The Jews shall join the Muslims in defending Medina against all enemies.
10. The interior of Medina shall be a sacred place for all who accept this charter.
11. The Jews, the allies of the Muslims, shall not declare war or enter into a treaty or agreement against the Muslims in alliance with their enemies.
12. All future disputes between those who accept this charter shall be referred, under God, to the Prophet.

The Prophet's constitutional charter at Medina is a standing monument of his political sagacity and statesmanship, a marvel of his insight and wisdom. This charter is the most significant from the historical point of view because it opened a new phase of the revolution of Islam by the addition of political constitution to the religious structure of Islam. It contained the germ of the Islamic state. It is the first written constitution in the world after the Greek age. During the ten years Prophet Muhammad presided over the Commonwealth of Islam a great change had come over the character of Arab people.

The Holy Prophet Muhammad was actuated by the following factors to issue this noble and novel charter of Medina. The chief motives behind the promulgation of the charter were to define the rights and obligations of the Muslims and the Jews, to make arrangement for the settlement and livelihood of the Meccan refugees, to establish a harmonious relation and understanding between the Muslims and non-Muslims, to secure a foot-hold for himself and a firm footing for his faith in the city of Medina, to strike out a political organisation and to ensure public security.

This new constitution of Medina brought with it a very important and revolutionary change to Arabia. It has two distinct parts, the first consisting of 23 sections effecting the refugees and helpers, and the second consisting of the remaining sections dealing with the rights and obligations of the Jewish tribes. By the promulgation of the charter, the Prophet welded heterogeneous tribes of Medina (*i.e.*, the Aus and the Khazraj and the *Ansars* and the *Muhajireens*) into one compact political entity. This charter delivered ruling powers to Prophet who assumed the role of the Magistrate and the head of the state. It recognised individual and public liberty, guaranteed the security of person and property of the people, and fostered the growth of civic virtues. This charter breathed a spirit of religious toleration of the Muslims, defined the rights and obligations of the Muslims towards each other and to the Jews. This document gave a death-blow to the archaic customs of the Arabs. The charter cast a lurid light on the Prophet's statesmanship and his religious toleration towards the minorities and non-Muslims.

The Battle of Badr (March, 624 A.D.) :

While the Muslims enjoyed perfect religious liberty within the walls of Medina, the fire of malice kept smouldering in the same proportion in the hearts of the Meccans. Hostility went on growing both in intensity and extent. Now that the Prophet and all the Muslims were safely settled at Medina, and were steadily gaining in power and influence, the Quraish could not remain inactive.

A war between Mecca and Medina was unavoidable, Abdullah-bin-Ubbay, an important personality of Medina possessed immense influence there. Before the immigration of the Prophet, the people of Medina were thinking of making him their overlord. Naturally enough when the Prophet arrived there, Abdullah's personality was eclipsed. He felt the sting of jealousy and maintained a hostile attitude towards the Muslims. The Quraish also instigated him to expel the Muslims from there, but a large number of his own tribesmen had already joined the fold of Islam. An attempt to offer an open resistance to the Prophet might lead to a civil war among his own people. Disappointed in Abdullah-bin-Ubbay, the Quraish began to incite the inhabitants of the strip of land lying between Mecca and Medina.

The success of the Quraishite propaganda among these people set the Muslims once more on their guard. On all sides they were hemmed in by enemies, and even within the walls of Medina. The Muslims, therefore, felt great concern with their safety. Attack was apprehended every moment from without and treachery from within. Thus came about what goes in the history of Islam by the name of the Battle of Badr.

By a strange coincidence, a Quraishite trading caravan under the leadership of Abu Sufyan was, about this very time, on its way back from Syria. Before departure, Abu Sufyan sent word to Mecca to arrange for the protection of the caravan. This has led to the unwarranted conclusion that the Muslims wanted to waylay the caravan, and hence followed the Battle of Badr. It is absolutely baseless to impute any such motives to the Muslims. In fact, the long-standing anxiety of the Quraish to crush the growing power of Islam, was the only cause that led to the battle. The Muslims were in fact dragged into it.

The fight took place in the valley of Badr, a few miles from Medina. The Muslim-strength counted only 313 including boys, all poorly armed, against a force of 1,000 strongfully equipped. Numerically the Muslim force was hardly one-third of the Quraish. Besides, the latter were composed of skilled veterans, while the Muslims had recruited even inexperienced youths. Therefore, neither in respect of number, nor in that of strength and skill, were the Muslims a match for the enmity. Abu Jahl was incharge of the Meccans. In the battle that followed, Prophet Muhammad won a signal victory over the Meccans. Abu Jahl died in action. In all, seventy of the hostile army fell in the field. Seeing their chief's fall, the rank and file were seized with confusion and took to flight. The Muslims pursued them, and took about seventy prisoners. On the Muslim side, the casualties were only fourteen.

The conflict of Badr is unique in the annals of warfare. It does often happen, that any army having smaller numerical strength but otherwise well-equipped, composed of valiant soldiers, well-disciplined and skilled in the use of arms, defeats larger hosts. But what makes the battle of Badr so strikingly unique is the fact that every form of weakness on one side is ranged against every form of strength on the other.

The importance of the battle can best be summed up in the words of Prof. Philip Hitti : However unimportant in itself as a military engagement, this *Ghazwat-e-Badr* laid the foundation of Prophet Muhammad's temporal power. Islam had own its first military victory. The spirit of discipline and contempt of death, manifested at this first armed encounter of Islam, proved characteristic of it in all its later and greater conquests. Hitherto Islam had been a religion within a State in Medina. After Badr, it passed into something more than a State-religion and itself become the State.

In the words of Joseph Hell, the victory of Badr resulted in the consolidation of the power of the Prophet in Yathrib. The most important result of the battle, however, was the defending of the faith of Prophet Muhammad himself and his closest companions in his prophetic vocation. After years of hardship and a measure of persecution.........there came this astounding success. It was a vindication of the faith which had sustained them through disappointment. Indeed, in the midst of the encircling darkness of despair the Muslims saw a ray of hope in this success.

The Battle of Uhud (March, 625 A.D.) :

The defeat at Badr was a blot on the honour of the Meccans. Revenge was therefore the watchword all over Mecca. Abu Sufyan was elected as leader and he solemnly pledged to avenge the disgrace of Badr. Abu Sufyan used all the means at his disposal to prepare a large force. The

Meccans at last set out under the leadership of Abu Sufyan with an army of 3,000 soldiers, of whom 700 men had coats of mail, and there were 3,000 camels and 200 horses. They encamped at the foot of the Uhud, a hill three miles north of Medina. In this neighbourhood there were fields of corn and they deliberately pastured their animals there in order to provoke the Medinites to come out to fight.

The Muslims could muster only 700 armed men. The Prophet was of opinion that they should not venture out to meet the enemy in open conflict, but rather stay within the four walls of Medina and repulse their onslaught. But the majority, consisting of the youths, inclined towards giving the enemy an open battle. The Prophet yielded to the decision of the majority. He laid the plan of attack and defence, ordering them to keep to their positions unless told to move. At the very beginning of the fight Abdullah-bin-Ubbay with his confederate of the Jewish tribe of Qaynuqa withdrew from the battle. In the excitement of battle the Muslims forgot all the instructions given to them by the Prophet. They began to fight without plan, and then fell on the Meccan camp without making sure that the enemy had really been defeated. The result was that the Meccan reserve, led by a notable general Khalid-bin-Walid, came upon them suddenly and scattered them. The Prophet himself was wounded and he fell. A cry rose. The Prophet is slain. This demoralized the Muslims further and many fled. The Battle of Uhud ended in a defeat for the Muslims. The causes of this Muslim discomfiture were unbounded confidence arising out of the victory at Badr and indiscipline and lack of steadfastness. If Uhud was not an out-and-out defeat for the Muslims, still less was it a Meccan victory. The Meccan strategic aim was the destruction of the Muslim community and nothing less, and they had fallen far short of this.........Prophet Muhammad was almost able to hold his own against Quraish, and Quraish were not capable of doing much more than holding their own against Prophet Muhammad.

After the Battle of Badr, the Jews of Medina, disregarding their agreement, entered into conspiracies with the Quraish to do injuries to the Muslims. The attitude of the hypocrites became more openly enimical. They made in a point to cause trouble to the faithful in every way. Insinuations against Muslim ladies in obscene verses were freely indulged in. They stooped even so low as to molest Muslim women in the street. One such incident resulted in the murder of a Jew and a Muslim and ultimately led to actual fighting between the two communities. The Jewish tribe of Qaynuqa, with whom the trouble arose were defeated and exiled from Medina. Another Jewish tribe, the Banu Nadir had friendly relations with the enemies of Islam. The Prophet apprehended some conspiracy against him by Banu Nadir and asked them to leave Medina. Some of them went to Khaybar and settled there.

The Battle of Trench (March, 627 A.D.) :

It was the supreme effort of the Meccans to break Prophet Muhammad's power. They organised a vast confederacy of friendly tribes. The Jews of Banu Nadir, now in exile at Khaybar and eager to regain their lands at Medina also helped a great deal in organising the confederacy. The Meccans had a large army of 10,000 men. To oppose this formidable host the Muslims could muster only 3,000 men. On the eve of this battle, the remaining Jewish clan Banu Qurayza who possessed several strong fortresses in the vicinity of Medina, was entrusted by the Prophet to guard the untrenched parts of the city. But the Jewish clan broke their faith with the Prophet and joined the Meccans.

The Meccan army besieged Medina on 31st March, 627, and this continued for 15 days. On advice of a Persian convert, Hazart Salman, Prophet Muhammad had adopted another form of defence, indeed, one hitherto unknown in Arabia. Whereever Medina lay open to cavalry attack he dug a trench, the *Khandaq*. The Meccans made several attempts to cross the trench but it was vigilantly guarded by the Muslims. The Muslims were sufficiently well-organised. After a fortnight spent in this way the Meccans gave up hope of success, and the great confederacy melted away in disgust. At last rain and storm utterly dissolved the Meccan army. On the military side the reason for the Meccan failure was the superior strategy of Prophet Muhammad, and probably also his superior information service and secret agents. Apart from these purely military considerations, the result was due to the relative unity of the Muslims and their discipline, in contrast to the lack of cohesion in the confederacy and the lack of confidence of the various groups in one another.

The Meccans thus tried their utmost to dislodge Prophet Muhammad from Medina, but he remained there more influential than ever. Their trade with Syria was gone, and much of their prestige lost.

It was considered unwise to allow the treacherous tribe of Qurayza to live near the city of Medina. So they were called that their punishment should be left to the judgment of the Auslite chief, Sa'd bin Mu'adh, whose clients they were. This man infuriated by their treacherous conduct, ordered for execution of all fighting men and enslavement of the women and children.

The Pact of Hudaibiya :

In the year 6 A.H. the Prophet with about 1,400 of his companions started on a pilgrimage to Mecca. By way of precaution, lest their motive should be misunderstood, it was strictly forbidden to carry arms. This would lay the Quraishite suspicions at rest, assuring them of the Muslims' peaceful intentions. On approaching the vicinity of the town, they found the Quraish ready to offer them armed resistance. Budail, the chief of the tribe of Khuza though not a Muslim, but well-disposed towards Islam, brought this intelligence to the Prophet, who sent him back to tell the Quraish that the Muslims had come to perform the pilgrimage and not to fight. The Quraish, it was also proposed, might conclude peace with them for a certain period. Having sent this word to the Quraish, the Muslims halted at Hudaibiya, a day's journey from Mecca.

Budail communicated the message to the Quraish. The wiser and experienced element was in favour of accepting the proposal of peace. They had good reasons to believe that they were unable to do any harm to Islam. Besides, with the conclusion of peace, they would be in a position to resume their trade with Syria, suspended so far in consequence of hostilities with the Muslims who commanded the route. Urwa was sent a plenipotentiary to discuss terms with the Muslims. The negotiations ended in a fiasco.

Another emissary was sent to the Quraish by the Prophet, but he was maltreated, and the camel on which he rode was killed. An armed Quraish detachment also came out to take the Muslims by surprise, but was itself taken prisoner. The Muslims, however, were not out for fighting, and hence let them all go. At last Hazrat Osman was commissioned to negotiate with the Quraish. The Quraish arrested him and kept him in custody. A rumour went forth that Hazrat Osman had been murdered. The Muslims had reasons to believe that the Quraish were bent upon fighting. It was a critical situation. The Muslims were practically unarmed and much smaller in number. The Quraish had every advantage on their side. The Prophet called upon his companions to pledge afresh, in view of the inordinately critical nature of the situation, that they would fight to the very last man, in the defence of their faith. Under a certain tree close by, the pledge was cheerfully taken. In the history of Islam this goes by the name of *Ba'tur-Ridzawan*.

The Muslims' resolve to shed the last drop of their blood in the defence of their faith, brought the Quraish to their senses. Their past experience stood them in good stead. They could now realise what such a resolve on the part of the Muslims meant. Thus chastened in spirits, they deputed one Suhail-ibn-Amr to resume peace negotiations. A truce was drawn up restoring a state of peace between the two parties for a period of ten years. The main clauses of the treaty were as follows :—

1. The Muslims shall this year return without performing the pilgrimage.
2. Next year they may come, but shall not stay at Mecca longer than three days.
3. They shall not take with them any of the Muslims already living in Mecca, and, on the other hand, they shall not stand in the way of any one from among themselves, should he wish to remain behind at Mecca.
4. Should any of the Meccans go over to Medina, the Muslims shall hand him over to the Meccans, but if any of the Medinite Muslims should rejoin the Meccans the later shall not restore him to the Muslims.
5. The Arab tribes shall be at liberty to enter into alliance with whichever party they choose.

The terms were extremely distasteful to the Muslims, but out of regard for the Prophet's peaceful attitude, they kept quiet. The leniency and magnanimity of the Prophet in concluding this treaty caused some discontent among his impulsive or stern followers. But the Prophet convinced them of his righteous stand and foretold about the ultimate good effects of the treaty.

The truce of Hadaibiya ultimately turned out to be triumph of Islam. It is borne out by the fact that on the occasion of his advance to Mecca about a year and-a-half later, the Prophet was accompanied by 10,000 comrades instead of 1,400, which was the number at the time of truce. How to account for this remarkable rise in the number of Muslims ? The fact is that the state of warfare which had so far prevailed between the Muslims and the non-Muslims, had created a wide gulf between them. General malice towards Islam would not permit the Arabs to mix with the Muslims. Hence they had so far no opportunity of coming into contact with the Muslims, and becoming acquainted with their Islamic virtues. It was for the first time since the inception of the Islamic movement that the gulf was bridged over. This afforded the non-Muslims an occasion to calmly ponder over the inherent virtues of Islam. The Arabs were bent upon destruction of Islam. They were therefore not well disposed to appreciate the teachings of Islam. Now that the barrier was removed and normal intercourse with the Muslims resumed, they were in a position to carefully study the moral and manners of the Muslims. Among large conversions to Islam after this treaty, the conversion of Hazrat

Khalid-bin-Walid and that of Hazrat Amr-bin-Aas proved to be greatly beneficial for Islam.

After the truce of Hudaibiya, the Prophet felt his position secure and despatched embassies to the neighbouring kingdoms. The envoy who was sent to Heracleus, the Byzantine Emperor, was well-received. The Emperor showed great respect to the Prophet. The Persian King Khosroe insulted the Muslim envoy, but the Persian Governor of Yemen named Bazan embraced Islam. Another Muslim envoy sent to the Christian prince of Banu Ghassan of Syria was treacherously murdered.

The Battle of Khaybar (628 A.D.) :

The Jewish malice against Islam, however, kept growing in bitterness. The exiled leaders of the Banu Nadir were preparing for an attack on Prophet Muhammad. They bribed a number of Arab tribes to joining them. The Jews fortified Khaybar with a number of strong fortresses such as Naim, Qamus, Sa'ad, Sal'am, etc. The Prophet on his return from Hudaibiya came to know of this and led an expedition against them. All these forts fell in quick succession except Sal'am and Qamus which were guarded by Marhab, a famous warrior of Arabia. Hazrat Abu Bakr who was commissioned to lead the attack failed to capture it. On the following day Hazrat Umar led the assault but with no better results. At last the Prophet assigned the command to Hazrat Ali on the third day. Marhab was killed and the fort was captured by Hazrat Ali. The Prophet, however, dealt with the Jews of Khaybar mercifully.

The Muta Expedition (629 A.D.) :

A Muslim envoy sent to the Christian prince, Shurahabil-ibn-Amr, of Banu Ghassan of Syria, was treacherously put to death in utter violation of inter-tribal usage. It would have been unwise to allow them any leisure to gather all their forces to fall upon the Muslims. The Prophet sent an army of 3,000 strongmen under the command of Hazrat Zayd. It should be noted that this was the only expedition ever sent outside Arabia during the life-time of the Prophet. The armies met at Muta and Hazrat Zayd was killed in the action. Hazrat Jafar took up the command but he also met with the same fate. He was succeeded by Hazrat Abdullah-ibn-Rawaha, who was also slain. At last Hazrat Khalid-bin-Walid took hold of the standard of Islam. Hazrat Khalid led back the army safely to Medina and saved the Muslim force from utter destruction.

Conquest of Mecca (630 A.D.) :

One of the clauses of the Peace of Hudaibiya ordained that the clans of Arabia were at liberty to side with the Quraish or the Muslims according to their discretion. Accordingly the tribe of Khuza'a had entered into an alliance with the Muslims while the clan of Banu Bakr with the Quraish. These two clans had long been antagonistically disposed to each other. It so happened that the Banu Bakr in alliance with the Quraish fell upon the Khuza'a and killed a large number of them. The injured people appealed to the Prophet for redress. The Prophet thereupon sent word to the Quraish telling them to accept either of these three conditions—That they should pay blood-money for those slain from among the Khuza'a or that they should dissociate themselves from the Banu Bakr, or that they should declare the truce of Hudaibiya as null and void. In reply, the Quraish preferred the last one. But Abu Sufyan realized his mistake and immediately hastened to Medina for the renewal of the truce. But the mission of Abu Sufyan was not successful due to his dupery.

The Prophet made preparations for the march on Mecca, and mobilized a force of ten thousand men from Medina. During the preparations for the expedition Prophet Muhammad took precautions to secure a large measure of secrecy. By now the tide had turned, the Meccans were not strong enough to fight such an army commanded by a general such as the Prophet, and they laid down their arms. Their leader, Abu Sufyan accepted Islam. Thus Prophet Muhammad entered the city which had so cruelly ill-treated him. It lay now completely at his mercy. But in the hour of triumph every evil suffered was forgotten, every injury inflicted was forgiven, and a general amnesty was extended to the population but the first thing he did in the *Kaa'ba* was to pray. The key was then returned to Hazrat Usman with the words that the charge of the sanctuary would ever remain with him and his descendants.

The conquest of Mecca practically decided the struggle for supremacy in Arabia. It elevated Prophet Muhammad to position in which it was natural for him to assert an authority paramount over the whole of Peninsula. Such a conquest without bloodshed is rare in the history of mankind, and through all the annals of the conquest, there has been no triumphant entry like unto this one. It was no small credit on the part of the Prophet of Islam to create circumstances in which his bitterest enemies surrendered to him without any fight. Foremost among the reasons for this success of Prophet Muhammad was the attractiveness of Islam and its relevance as a religious and social system to the religious and social needs of the Arabs. Again, Prophet Muhammad's own tact, diplomacy, and administrative skill contributed greatly. The conquest of Mecca also means the victory of Islam against idolatry. Truth has come and falsehood vanisheth.

The Battle of Hunayn (630 A.D.) :

With the conquest of Mecca the power and opposition of the Quraish had come to an end. But the hostile activities and preparations of other cities near that city demanded immediate attention. Malik bin Auf, the chief of the Hawazin tribe, collected his tribesmen and those of the Thaqif (Taif) who were in alliance with them and took from all a pledge that they would join in opposing the Holy Prophet. When the Prophet came to know about these developments he deputed Hazrat Abdullah Aslami to go there and report the true state of affairs. He brought the news that the Bani Hawazin and other tribes were bent upon war. The Prophet had therefore no alternative but to march against them at the head of 12,000 followers of whom ten thousand were from Medina and two thousand from Mecca. The enemy had a force of 20,000. The two armies met in the valley of Hunayn. The Muslims, who had been over confident, were somewhat dismayed at the huge mass of human beings and animals which they saw, for Hawazin had brought all their women, children and live-stocks, staking everything on the issue of the battle. The battle commenced with an attack by the tribesmen who were so firm in their determination that their army looked like an iron wall, and the ranks of the Muslims were soon dispersed. They fled away in all directions leaving the Prophet who had remained firm in his position with small band of followers. Of these Companions, the most distinguished were Hazrat Abu Bakr, Hazrat Umar, Hazrat Ali, Hazrat Abbas, Hazrat Fazl bin Abbas, Hazrat Usama bin Sayd, and Hazrat Aiman, the foster-brother of the Prophet. The Prophet countercharged the enemy. This turned the tide, and before long the enemy were in full flight. Some Thaqif fought bravely for a time, then fled to the safety of their walls. The fighting men were dispersed or taken prisoner or killed. Women, children, animals, and goods fell into the hands of the Muslims. The Holy Prophet divided the booty among the Muslim rank and file.

The Expedition of Tabuk (631 A.D.):

The brilliant success of Islam alarmed the neighbouring Christian Empire. She viewed with a jealous eye this rapid growth of Islam. A skirmish had once already taken place at Muta. About the year 631 a Byzantine attack on Arab was apprehended. Reports came to Medina that Heracleus was making arrangements for an invasion with the assistance of the Christians of Arabia. The Holy Prophet also started his preparations for defence. But there were a number of obstacles that stood in the way. The journey was long and the weather hot. The crops were ripe and ready for sickle and Medinites were reluctant to leave the city. The hypocrites took full advantages of these circumstances and did all they could to create dissensions among the Muslims and hamper their preparations. Nevertheless, the Prophet succeeded in persuading the wealthier among his followers to help the army. It was on the occasion of this expedition that Hazrat Abu Bakr gave away all that he possessed and Hazrat Usman also contributed generously. Women brought their ornaments and jewelleries to provide for the expenses of war. Eventually a large army of 30,000 was collected. Leaving Hazrat Ali incharge of the administration the Prophet marched with the army and halted at Tabuk midway between Medina and Damascus. To their surprise and also relief, the Muslims found that the apprehended attack did not materialise. John, the Governor of Jerusalem, begged for peace. The Prophet granted this and returned to Medina in perfect peace.

The Year of Deputation :

The ninth year of the *Hijri* is known in the Muslim annals as the "Year of Deputation". In that year deputations from the various clans and tribes kept pouring into Medina. Deputations also come to Medina from such distant places as Usman, Yaman and Hadramawt. Some of these tribes were converted to Islam. A written treaty, guaranteeing the privileges of the tribes, was often granted, and a teacher invariably accompanied the departing guests to instruct the newly-converted people in the duties of Islam, and to see that every evil practice was obliterated from their midst. Further the Prophet Muhammad instructed the teachers who were sent to the different provinces. "Deal gently with the peoples and be not harsh, cheer them, and condemn them not. And ye will meet with many people of the Book who will question thee, what is the key to heaven ? Reply to them, the key to heaven is to testify to the truth of God, and to do good work."

The Farewell Pilgrimage :

When the Holy Prophet Muhammad (peace be upon him) felt that his mission was accomplished, and under the impression of his approaching end, he determined to make a pilgrimage to Mecca. As this was his last pilgrimage, so it is known as *Hajjatul-Wida*. Hazrat Abu Bakr was authorised to lead the caravan of pilgrimage to Mecca. On his arrival at Mecca and before completing all the rites of the pilgrimage, he addressed the gathering emphasising on the points of his teachings. The sermon that the Prophet Muhammad delivered on this occasion was remarkable. It ran thus :

> "O people lend an attentive ear to my words, for I know not whether I shall ever hereafter have the opportunity to meet you here. Do you know what day is it today? This is the *Yaumun-Nahr* or the sacred Day of Sacrifice. Do you know which month is this ? This is the sacred town. So I apprise you that your lives, your properties and your honour must be as sacred to one another as this sacred day, in this sacred

> month, in this sacred town. Let those present take this message to those absent. You are about to meet your Lord Who will call you to account for your deeds......
>
> O my people you have certain rights over your wives, and so have your wives over you......They are the trust of God in your hands. So you must treat them with all kindness. And as regards your slaves, see that you give them to eat of what you yourself eat, and clothe them with what you clothe yourselves.
>
> O people listen to what I say and take it to heart. You must know that every Muslim is the brother of another Muslim. You are all equal. You are all members of one common brotherhood. It is forbidden for any of you to take from his brother save what the latter should willingly give. Do not tyrannize over your people.

Death of the Prophet :

Soon after his return to Medina the Prophet fell ill. One event of importance after the Prophet's return to Medina was sending out an expedition to Syria under the leadership of Hazrat Usman bin Zayd to avenge the death of Hazrat Zayd in the Muta expedition. The expedition, however, materialised after his death. According to a famous tradition the Prophet's illness lasted thirteen days. The illness was remittent. During his illness he stayed in Aisha's house close to the mosque and attended the public prayers as long as he could. Till his last breath Aisha kept to his bed-side and nursed him. His strength rapidly declined and the Prophet breathed his last on Monday, the *12th Rabi-ul-Awwal, 11th A.H.*/8th June, 632, at noon in the house of Aisha and was buried at noon on the following day. Thus died the great desert-bred Prophet of Islam who had given a new message of hope to man. He had achieved a great deal. To the pagan peoples of Western Arabia he had brought a new religion which, with its monotheism and its ethical doctrines, stood on an incomparably higher level than the paganism it replaced.

Conception of "Sunnah"

In a loose sense the term *Sunnah* and *Hadith* convey the same meaning, *i.e.,* the traditions of the Holy Prophet Muhammad. Primary meaning of *Sunnah* is pathway, "behaviour," "practice", manner of acting of "conduct of life". There are number of Quranic verses which indicate that the term *Sunnah* denote practice and behaviour. This term is not a new to the Muslims. In pre-Islamic Arabia this term was used for the past customs and exemplary conduct left by their ancestors. The *Sunnah* was used in the sense of peoples practice and individual behaviour which carries a normative element. Imam Abu Yusuf admonishes the Caliph to revive the *Sunnah* originated by righteous men, because revival of the *Sunnah* according to him, is a virtue which survives and never perishes.

When this term found a place in the Islamic Law it refers to the normative practice set up by the Prophet as a model. It may be noted that *Hadith* and *Sunnah* are two different things and not identical one. A *Hadith* is a narration of the behaviour of the Prophet Muhammad while the *Sunnah* is the law deduced from this narration. There are cases where a particular *Hadith* contains five *Sunnahs*, or three. Apart from this the *Sunnah* was used in the sense of established practice of the Muslims claiming to have come down from the time of the Prophet Muhammad. That is the reason that sometimes *Sunnah* contradicts *Hadith* and sometimes it is documented by *Hadith*. The difference between the early meanings of *Sunnah* and *Hadith* is that the former carried in its gamut the well-known traditions, the established practice and the agreed usages of the Muslims, while the latter was the narration of the fixed and definite laws enunciated by the Prophet Muhammad. But Imam Shafai insisted to take the *Sunnah* from the genuine tradition of Prophet Muhammad.

The Qur'an from time and again makes the Prophetic *Sunnah* as obligatory on the Muslims. The Qur'an speaks of the behaviour of the Prophet Muhammad as an ideal. Therefore the Muslims since the revelation believe and consider the conduct of the Prophet Muhammad as a model. Apart from this the actions of the community were governed by the Qur'an and it was Prophet Muhammad who gave its injunctions a practical shape and concrete form. Therefore the manner in which the Prophet Muhammad had acted upon the Qur'an has become the law of community. It can be noted that the Qur'an and *Sunnah* of the Prophet Muhammad are inter-related and interwoven. This may be called as an integral whole. Prof. Schacht rejects the concept of the Prophetic *Sunnah* as it was not used during the time of the Prophet Muhammad but Schacht perhaps did not take any recourse to the speech of the Prophet Muhammad made by him on the occasion of the Farewell *Hajj*. Moreover, Hazrat Umar, the Second Caliph sent emissaries to different towns in order to teach them the religions and the *Sunnah* of the Prophet Muhammad. Al-Hasan of Basra used the phrase "*Sunnah* of the Prophet" and his term has been frequently used by Imam Al-Shafai. There can hardly be any doubt that the Muslims considered the Prophet's behaviour and ideal pattern and example for them since the inception of the Revelation. This is quite sufficient proof for the existence of its concept from the early days of the Prophet Muhammad.

Prof. Schacht criticises that *Sunnah* in its Islamic context orginally had a political rather than a legal connotation. He is of the view that the concept of the *Sunnah* of the Prophet Muhammad appeared in connection with the assassination of Hazrat Uthman, the Third Caliph. He also links it with the *Sunnah* of Hazrat Abu Bakr and Hazrat Umar. He observes that the term *Sunnah* was introduced in the Islamic Law towards the end of the 1st century of the *Hijrah* by the Iraqis. He concludes that—

(1) The *Sunnah* was originally the practice of the Community and not the *Sunnah* of the Prophet which is a late development.

(2) The concept of *Hadith* came to be accepted later on but *Hadith* came to be forged on a large scale so much so that there is probably hardly any *Hadith* which may be genuinely from the Prophet Muhammad himself.

It may be noted that the Qur'an commands Muslims in general terms to follow the pattern of the Prophet's behaviour in all fields of life. The observations of Schacht are mere conjectures. He purposely ignores the testimony of the Qur'an to the necessity of this concept. As a matter of fact the Caliph, Hazrat Abu Bakr, has referred this term in legal context. If the second observation of Schacht is admitted it shall amount to the rejection of the whole corpus of *Hadith* which may be genuine from the Prophet Muhammad himself.

According to the early schools of law *Sunnah* was the practice of the community as supported by the well-known tradition from ths Prophet Muhammad, or the conduct of the Companions or the successors. Imam Al-Shafai regarded every well-founded authentic *Hadith* even though it may be an isolated one and whether accompanied by practice or not, as *Sunnah* of the Prophet Muhammad. During the lifetime of the Prophet Muhammad *Sunnah* implied the conformity of the acts of the Companions to the acts of the Prophet Muhammad, and therefore after his lifetime the Companions had with them the Qur'an, the conduct of the Prophet Muhammad and their own practice prevalent while he was alive. The Companions were not only the transmitters of the *Sunnah* but were also the interpreters and elaborators. They being the representatives of the life and conduct of the Prophet Muhammad the conduct and opinions of the Companions began to be regarded as exemplary by the succeeding generation. This widened the scope of the *Sunnah* to receive within its orbit new contents.

The practice that originated from the lifetime of the Prophet Muhammad continued in its pure form until the time of the first four Caliphs. At this time there were two channels before the people for knowing the real *Sunnah* of the Prophet Muhammad :

1. Practice.
2. *Hadith.*

For *Hadith* it was necessary that it must conform to the established practice. The Caliphs were very much particular about the *Hadith* and were habitual to put it to serve test if it does not conform to the practice. That test was very stringent in the case of solitary *Hadith.* Hazrat Abu Bakr was always tried to confirm the solitary *Hadith* by another Companion. Hazrat Umar, the 2nd Caliph was more cautious, he accepts the solitary tradition on the evidence of two witnesses. Hazrat Ali, the 4th Caliph recognized an individual *Hadith* when it is confirmed by oath. It is said for Hazrat Umar, the 2nd Caliph that he made generally official announcement of the solitary *Hadith* after being confirmed to the general public so that they may not be mistaken in future.

After the time of the Prophet and four Caliphs we find a derivation from the pure and continuous tradition. Different sects emerged and each endeavoured to prove its doctrines as part of the Islamic teaching and sought to endorse them by certain authority. There was free transmission of *Hadith.* The Ummayad Caliphs were not interested in protecting the purity and continuity of the ideal practice. The judicial authorities were under their control. Therefore, the established ideal practice could not survive in its practical form. The confidence vested in practice was gradually weakened and ultimately *Hadith* was regarded as the only channel for the ideal *Sunnah. Isnad* in *Hadith* gained significance and the community morally deteriorated.

Anyhow, the whole society was not swamped with forgers. The Companions were doing their job in the judicial and legal sphere. Their conduct was followed by the people as being an approximation to the ideal life of the Prophet. The practical aspect of their life had, therefore, a far-reaching effect on the conduct of the next generation of the successors. That is why when they exercised their own *Ijtehad* in certain matters, people accept as an authority and it become the *Ijma* of the community. These were in fact *Sunnah* of the Companions. The reason for such thinking was that people knew that the Companions of the Prophet could never deviate from the spirit of the *Sunnah* of the Prophet. Therefore, with the *Ijtehad* of the companions the element of the personal opinion entered into *Sunnah.*

During the second century of *Hijrah* a controversy arose amongst the jurists as to whether an isolated *Hadith* should be taken as *Sunnah* or conduct of the Companions.

During the Umayyad period ushered a new era of the development of *Sunnah*. During this period *Sunnah* came to include the rulings of the administrative authorities and the consensus of the jurists of each region. Due to the acceleration of individual independent thinking in law the personal opinions of the juris-consults also became the part of the authoritative source in law. Therefore, the *Sunnah* and local *Ijma* had come so close together that there was hardly any point of distinction.

Controversy in the view of Al-Awzai and Imam Abu Yusuf :

Al-Awzai regards *Sunnah* as the practice of the Muslims as came down to him from the time of the Prophet.

During the recourse with Imam Abu Hanifah he regards the following three as *Sunnah* :—

1. At the first instance he refers to the conduct of the Prophet as *Sunnah*.

2. The practice of the Companions and early Muslims.

3. The conduct of the political leaders.

If we examine the controversy of Imam Abu Yusuf and Al-Awzai the following facts will be evident :—

> That in a given situation the *Sunnah* may differ because one legist singles out certain incident from the life of the Prophet as relevant to the situation while the other argues it differently.

According to Imam Abu Hanifah, if a non-Muslim embraces Islam, leaves his home and property, his property will be included in the booty in case the non-Muslim territory falls to the Muslims. Al-Awzai disagrees with the view of Imam Abu Hanifah and in support of his contention refers the precedence of fall of Mecca did not take into possession the properties of the Muslims there and also did not make them captive. Here Al-Awzai stresses that the person most worthy to be followed and whose *Sunnah* would be adhered to is the Prophet. In reply to this contention Imam Abu Yusuf says that the example of Mecca is an exception and not a general rule. Imam Abu Yusuf cites another exception of the battle of Hawazan. In this battle the Prophet returned the captives to Banu Hawazin. It shows that he asserts that the Prophet's behaviour was right for him but others are not to take it as a precedent.

The following conclusions can be drawn from the above discussion :—

1. According to Al-Awzai others, too, can establish *Sunnah* but the *Sunnah* of the Prophet shall be supreme.

2. Where clear instructions are not available *Sunnah* can be determined by Ra'y applying a relevant incident of the Prophet's life to the situation.
3. There may be difference in determining the *Sunnah* on the basis of argument.
4. Even an exception from the general rule can be called as *Sunnah*.

Al-Awzai does not quote generally any tradition in the formal way of *Isnad*. He refers to a particular incident from the life without any support of *Isnad*. Whereas Imam Abu Yusuf generally quotes the tradition in a very formal way supported by the narrations, *i.e., Isnad*. Therefore, the emphasis on *Hadith* in Imam Abu Yusuf is greater than Al-Awzai. We find in some cases Al-Awzai bases himself only on practice without any reference to the Prophet but such thing is rare with Imam Abu Yusuf. Imam Abu Yusuf always bases himseif on the general practice but Al-Awzai sometimes bases himself on exceptions too. According to Al-Awzai every *Sunnah* of the Prophet whether general or exceptional should be followed.

Views of Imam Malik :

The practice with Imam Malik that he first relates the legal topic to the relevant *Hadith* from the Prophet then from some Companions, and lastly the practice and opinions of the lawyers of Medina. Afterwards he states the views of his own school. He gives great emphasis on the established practice of the people of Medina. Imam Malik sometimes rejects the tradition coming from the Prophet. In favour of the opinion of the Companion or the successor. This is due to the fact that the agreed and established practice of Medina was the ideal practice according to him. The established practice of the Muslims in Medina was the channel to judge the real *Sunnah*. The reason that the Companions had seen the Prophet behave in all sorts of condition and thus they themselves were taken by the next generation to be acting according to his model conduct. Therefore, by the time of third generation, the *Sunnah* of the Prophet was taken to have been established in the community. There were about thirty thousand Companions living at Medina. Their recognized, known and established practice was more reliable to them than an isolated tradition. A transition in its formal way would have been supported by ten to twelve persons. Therefore, the channel of practice was more reliable to them than the chain of transmission to know the real *Sunnah*.

Now the question arises whether for Imam Malik the *Sunnah* was the established practice of Medina without reference to the Prophet. The answer would be in the negative due to the following reasons :—

1. He discussed *Sunnah-al-Aitkaf* and specially mentioned to the Prophet's *Sunnah*.

2. He also made certain remarks while dealing with a particular problem:
   (*i*) "The practice since the time of the Prophet".
   (*ii*) "So has been the practice since the time of the Prophet".
3. In most cases he bases himself expressly on the conduct of the Prophet as narrated to him in the form of *Hadith*.
4. On one occasion while dealing with the position of *Wali*, he stipulates for the permission of *Wali* (guardian) for the validity of the marriage of woman. He based his arguments on a tradition from Hazrat Umar b. al-Khattab and the practice of the two legists of Medina.
5. Imam Malik follows the traditions those were practised generally, although he did not discredit the others too.
6. On one occasion he said that "*Hadith* is there, but we do not know what it really means."

Therefore, such a conclusion cannot be drawn that Imam Malik gave preference to the traditions of Medinese upon the traditions of the Prophet. There was the only difference in the mode of sorting out a real *Sunnah* from the Prophet.

View of Imam Abu Yusuf:

Imam Abu Yusuf defined the *Sunnah* as the conduct of the Prophet as practised by the Muslims after him. In his arguments the terms *Sunnah* and *Hadith* run together. He was very cautious in accepting the lonely *Sunnah* which is not in conformity with the well-known *Sunnah* and traditions. According to him *Sunnah* must be known to the men of learning and understanding in law.

The *Sunnah* was not the practice of the community alone. He takes the *Sunnah* primarily from the behaviour of the Prophet which became well-known for being acted upon and practised by the early Muslims. On one occasion Caliph Harun-al-Rashid inquired Imam Abu Yusuf about sending invitations to the infidels before waging war with them. In reply to this Imam Abu Yusuf referred various instructions of the Prophet which he used to send to his Companions on this matter and enlightened him on the practice of the Companions like Hazrat Abu Bakr and Hazrat Umar.

We find in his writings that the terms *Sunnah* and *Hadith* go concurrently. He mostly depends on the generally well-known traditions and the mere reference to the Prophet or the practice was not enough for him. He differs with Al-Awzai on the point of lonely *Hadith*. A lonely *Hadith* according to him is one which is foreign to the established practice and the abundant well-known traditions on the subject. As we know

Imam Abu Yusuf quotes, in his writings, *Hadith* very frequently at the same time he was very strict in sorting out a genuine *Hadith*. He had certain criteria to judge its authenticity. He does not recognize any *Hadith* which goes against the Qur'an and the well-known *Sunnah*. He made Qur'an and *Sunnah* as the touchstone for the test of the genuineness of *Hadith*. He warns against the solitary *Sunnah* and requires adherence to the *Hadith* followed by the community. A *Hadith* should be in conformity with the Qur'an and *Sunnah* and must be well-known to the lawyers.

He emphatically opposes the term *Madat-al-Sunnah* used by Al-Awazai, but he himself occasionally found using similar phrases in the course of his reasoning. According to him the source of *Sunnah* is of vital importance. He says "judgments should not be taken in the matters of lawful and unlawful merely on the basis of the statements, like the people have always been doing such and such, for people have been practising such what is unlawful and what should be practised. A decision should be based on the *Sunnah* of the Prophet and the practice of the early generations (*Salaf*)". But it may be noted that he in reliance upon the authorities was regional in approach. He had more reliance upon the local authorities and this tendency was resulted into the *Ijma* of the local scholars and differences in the *Sunnah*. This was the general trend amongst all the schools.

Views of Al-Shaybani :

In dealing with a particular problem he points *Sunnah*, then he supports it by quoting tradition from the Prophet and then the practice of the Companions. Afterwards he states the opinion of Imam Abu Hanifah and the scholars of Iraqis in general. He basis himself on well-known *Hadith* and on occasions uses the phrase "*al-Sunnat al-Morufah*". He criticizes Imam Malik and the Medinese for neglecting the traditions of the Prophet. But on many problems he differs from Imam Abu Hanifah and agrees with the Medinese on the basis of *Hadith*. He followed the view of Medinese on the point that Imam should lead the prayer standing and rejected the opposite view of Imam Abu Hanifah on the contention that Hazrat Abu Bakr, Hazrat Uthman, Hazrat Ali and others had ever led prayers in sitting condition.

It is evident from the above analysis that the *Sunnah* carried in its contents personal opinion of the jurists and the local colour of each region. The differences among the jurists of different regions were very acute. Even on crucial problems the *Sunnah* in its early stages was characterised by provincialism.

Chapter 2

The Period of Khulfa-i-Rashideen

HAZRAT ABU BAKR

(11-13 A.H./632-634 A.D.)

Prophet Muhammad (Peace be upon him) died in 632 A.D., with a great portion of Arabia converted to Islam. The death of Prophet Muhammad confronted the infant Muslim community with something in the nature of constitutional crisis. The Prophet had left no provision for the succession, nor had he even created a council on the lines of the tribal *Majlis* which might have exercised authority during the crucial transitional period. Immediately after the death of the Prophet three rival factions—The *Ansar*, the *Muhajirin* and the Banu Hashim, sprang up on the issue of Caliphate.

Contest in Election :

The *Ansar* claimed that they were the people who sheltered the Prophet in the hour of great crisis. A successor to the Prophet therefore be chosen from among their ranks. The *Muhajirin* were pushing the claim of Hazrat Abu Bakr as the best man for succeeding the Prophet. Basing upon the principle of legitimacy, the Banu Hashim reasoned that Allah and Prophet Muhammad could not have left the community of believers to the chance and whims of an electorate, and therefore must have made clear provision for its leadership by designating some particular person to succeed Prophet Muhammad. Hazrat Ali, the paternal cousin of the Prophet, was the one designed as the only legitimate successor. But the case of the Banu Hashim was very weak. The concept of legitimate succession was foreign to the Arabs at the time and it is probable that even if Prophet Muhammad had left a son the sequence of events would not have been different.

The situation was very grave. At the time of the Prophet's death Medina was full of sanctimonious hypocrites who were only waiting for the passing away of the Founder of Islam to deal a blow to the faith. In the meantime the *Ansar* gathered in the Saqifa Bani Sa'dah to discuss and settle the question of

Caliphate. When Hazrat Abu Bakr and Hazrat Umar were informed of this, they hastened to the scene. Hazrat Abu Ubaidah also accompanied them. On their arrival at Saqifa Bani Sa'dah they found that Sa'd bin Ubadah, on whom the choice of the *Ansar* fell, had just finished his speech. The *Ansar* were ready to accept him as successor of the Holy Prophet. One can imagine whether at such a critical juncture it was expedient to pass the time in lamentations or to take immediate steps for the nomination of a Caliph and the restoration of everything from chaos to settled order. The moment was critical.

It appeared that both the *Muhajirin* and the *Ansars* were on the point of falling out among themselves. Hazrat Abu Bakr stood up and recounted the services of the *Ansar* to the cause of Islam. But at the same time he impressed the fact that 'the Almighty God conferred upon the early *Muhajirin* a unique distinction', because they acknowledged him (Muhammad) as Prophet, accepted his faith, remained with him and shared his hardships in spite of the fact that all their people accused them of falsehood and had become their mortal enemies. And the determination of these people was shaken neither by the smallness of their numbers nor by the excess of their enemy. These are the people who have had precedence in worshipping God on earth and in having faith in Him and His Apostle. Consequently, they have the strongest claims on the Caliphate, and no one except the wrong-doer can have any contention against them in this matter. But the *Ansar* continued to press their claims. Altercations followed. Then the *Ansar* suggested that there should be two groups. But this meant the disruption of the unity of Islam. Hazrat Abu Bakr thought it prudent to stop this unhappy situation at any risk and stepping forward said, "I would agree to any one whom you select from these two"—pointing out to Hazrat Umar and Hazrat Abu Ubaidah and mentioning some of their virtues. But both of them said, "No, we cannot give preference to ourselves over you in this matter. You are undoubtedly the most excellent of the *Muhajirin*." Hazrat Umar, who was a very dynamic man and who had a strong personality, spoke for Hazrat Abu Bakr to the *Ansar*. It did not take him long to convince the *Ansar* and that Hazrat Abu Bakr was the most deserving man in Medina to be the first successor of the Prophet. When these two major groups agreed, the other two parties, which were in a minority, had to accept the decision. Hazrat Umar was the first to pay the homage of allegiance to Hazrat Abu Bakr. Hazrat Usman, Hazrat Abu Ubaidah and Hazrat Abdur Rahman bin Auf followed suit, and the populace then pressed forward with one accord to proclaim their allegiance to Hazrat Abu Bakr. So Hazrat Abu Bakr was elected. A rising storm was thus warded off and the people being satisfied took to the pursuits of normal life.

The Prophet was laid to rest in a grave dug in Aisha's chamber. On the following day the Muslims had assembled in the Prophet's Mosque to offer allegiance to Hazrat Abu Bakr. When it was completed, the newly elected Caliph rose and addressed the assembly. "O people ! I swear by Allah that I never coveted the Amirate either by day or by night, nor had I am inclination towards it. I never prayed to God openly or in secrecy to confer the same on me. In fact, a big task has been assigned to me which is beyond my power to fulfil except with the help of the Almighty Allah. I wished to see the strongest of men in my place this day. Now it is beyond doubt that I have been elected your *Amir*, although I am not better than you. Help me, if I am in the right, set me right if I am in the wrong, Truth is a trust ; falsehood, a treason. The weak among you shall be strong in my eyes until I secure his right if God will, and the strong among you shall be weak in my eyes until I wrest the right from him. No nation gave up *Jihad* in the path of Allah but Allah abased it ; and people who indulged in acts of shamelessness are bound to be subjected to Divine punishment. Obey me as long as I obey Allah and His Prophet, when I disobey Him and His Prophet, then obey me not. And now rise for prayers. May God have mercy on you."

His Accession :

On becoming Caliph the first care of Abu Bakr was to carry out the dying wishes of the Prophet namely the sending of an expedition under Hazrat Usman on the Syrian border to take 'the revenge of the murder of Hazrat Usama' father of Hazrat Zayd and the loss suffered by the Muslims in the Muta expedition. But situation within the Muslim state deteriorated. The news of the death of the Prophet was a signal for several of the Arab tribes to cast off their allegiance to the city-state of Medina. The members of the *Majlis-e-Shura* were therefore of strong opinion that the departure of Hazrat Usama would leave the city defenceless, and many were in favour of delaying the expedition. But Hazrat Abu Bakr, a man of strong attitude as he was, refused to comply with their proposal. The expedition had its effect. Hazrat Abu Bakr's boldness to send on expedition convinced the Bedouins of his position of strength at home.

The War of Apostasy :

The dynamic personality of the Holly Prophet held all Arab tribes together. Besides many Arab tribes considered their agreement with the Prophet as personal which ended with the death of the Prophet. As soon as the death of the Prophet was noised abroad, the unruly elements began to raise their heads. A number of tribes shook off the overlordship of Medina and refused to pay homage to the new

Caliph or accept his orders ; some of them even denied Islam. This was a serious situation. Islam never went deep in the minds of Bedouin tribes. So fast had been the rate of conversion to Islam after the conquest of Mecca that the Prophet was not able to do much towards educating the new converts the principles and teaching of Islam. He could only gather around him a nucleus of well-grounded men who had fully absorbed the principles of the revolution, but the distant parts of Arabia could not be educated as soon and the Prophet did not live long enough to make the necessary arrangements. It was physically impossible to arrange, in a few months that the Prophet lived after that, for the proper education or training of the masses scattered over a vast territory with very scanty means of intercourse and communication. Those who came in deputation to the Prophet from these distant tribes of the desert, took back a deep impress of Islam, but they were a drop in the ocean. So it is no wonder that after the death of the Prophet, they would break off from the authority of Islam.

Politically speaking, a centralised Government claiming and receiving the obedience of the individual had never been known in Arabia, where the tribes lived in complete independence. Moreover, the Arab tribes resented the ascendancy of Medina, the then Capital of the Muslim Empire. The hegemony of Medina became intolerable to the independent spirit of the Arab tribes.

The payment of *Zakat* was beyond the conception of the Arab mind. For the first time they were compelled to pay *Zakat* to the Central Treasury at Medina. Naturally, this meant subordination to authority and was disliked by the tribes. Their objection was not to Islam but to *Zakat*. The situation became very critical. Medina itself was threatened by the Bedouin hordes, at the Head of which stood the powerful tribe of Ghatafan. Many Companions including Hazrat Umar recommended with one voice that under the circumstances it would be advisable to follow a mild policy. To this Hazrat Abu Bakr replied indignantly : "You were so harsh in the days of ignorance ; but now after Islam you have become so low. Divine Revelations have ceased, and our Faith has reached perfection. Now should it be allowed to be mutilated during my life ? I swear by Allah that if even so much as a piece of string is withheld (from the *Zakat*) I shall order war against them".

The Arabs could not conform themselves to the strict rules of morality of Islam. The strong principles sanctioned by Islam and the observance of religious rites, such as five times prayers, observance of *Ramzan*, payment of *Zakat*, prohibition of drinking and gambling, marriage bindings, etc., were very much disturbing the free minded Arabs who were silent only at the fear of the Prophet.

There was a host of new aspirants to prophethood who, thinking the office of the prophethood a profitable concern, had declared themselves as prophets and began to attract people by liberalising the principles of morality and religious rites, such as drinking and gambling were declared lawful, *namaz* was reduced from five to three times, the *Ramzan* fast was completely abolished, marriage restrictions were put off and payment of *Zakat* was made voluntary.

False Prophets :

The first pretender to the prophetic role appeared in Yemen. He was Aswad Ansi. In the year 10 A.H. he subjugated Najran, took the capital of Yemen, Sanda, and conquered the entire province of Yemen. But he was killed by a relative of the slain Governor of Yemen, though the flames of rebellion kept blazing after his death. The next pretender who laid claims to prophethood was Musailama the liar, who, encouraged by the success of Aswad Ansi, proclaimed that the Prophet Muhammad had made him a partner in prophethood. He had gathered round him a number of Arabian tribes and proved to be the most formidable enemy of Islam.

The third pretender was Tulayha who was acclaimed as the Prophet of Banu Ghatafan. Sajah, a woman, was the fourth pretender who laid claims to prophethood. She came of the tribe of Banu Yarbu in Central Arabia.

The false prophets began to march upon the city of Medina, when Hazrat Abu Bakr was preparing to send Hazrat Usama on the Syrian border. Thus Hazrat Abu Bakr was amidst the internal and external dangers. He immediately called the meeting of *Majlis-e-Shura* and the question was put up there. The opinion of the members totally against the Caliph's view who all were of the view that either the Syrian expedition would be postponed or some compromising steps should be taken towards the false prophets, because the new-born Republic of Islam was not in a position to fight on both the fronts—external and internal. But the Caliph—a man of strong attitude as he was, refused to comply with either proposals of the members of the *Majlis-e-Shura* and expressed determination to send the Syrian expedition as well as to fight against the false prophets. His policy towards the successionists was unconditional surrender or war unto destruction.

The Caliph deputed Hazrat Ali, Hazrat Talha, Hazrat Zubair and Hazrat Abdullah bin Masud on strategic points to defend the city of Medina. The enemies who were encamped at a few miles distance at Dhi-Hassi, Dhul-Qissa, Daba and Abraque began to advance upon the city. The Caliph himself marched upon them (towards the direction of Dhi-Hassi) and repulsed their attack. Then he proceeded towards Dhul-Qissa. The Caliph attacked at night and succeeded in capturing Dhul-Qissa. After the fall of Dhul-Qissa, Daba was also occupied. The Caliph then concentrated his direction towards Abraque which after such prolonged fighting also fell into the hands of the Caliph. Meanwhile Hazrat Usama came back victorious from Syrian expedition. Now the Caliph made Hazrat Usama incharge of the defence of the city.

Hazrat Khalid bin Walid was sent against Tulayha, Hazrat Ikrima and Hazrat Shorabil bin Hasan were sent against Musailama, and Hazrat Zubair was sent against Aswad Ansi in Yemen. Hazrat Khalid bin Walid without much difficulty succeeded in defeating Tulayha who later on once again accepted Islam. Aswad Ansi died before Hazrat Zubair reached there. The death of Aswad facilitated the task of Hazrat Zubair and the whole area without much fighting was once again regained for Islam.

The greatest opposition was offered by Musailama who by marrying Sajah, a Christian prophetess, had arranged 40,000 soldiers. The two generals Hazrat Ikrima and Hazrat Shorobil were defeated by Musailama. The gravity of the situation prompted the Caliph to send Hazrat Khalid, 'the Sword of Allah' did not find the task easy one. On Hazrat Khalid's arrival at Yamama, Musailama moved forward and the two armies fought one of the stiffest battles. Tabari writes: "Never did the Muslims fight a more stiff battle." The Muslims unable to resist the pressure of the enemy's forces gave way and dispersed. But the Muslims soon recovered from the early reverses and attacked the enemy with fresh enthusiasm and vigour. They pushed back the enemy up to Hadiqa where Musailama had to take shelter within a high-walled garden city. The Muslims swarmed round the wall but found the gate closed. But Hazrat Bara bin Malik jumped from the wall, hazarding his life rushed to the gate and opened it. As soon as the gate was opened, the Muslims made repeated attacks on the enemy. Musailama was killed in the action and his soldiers began to flee in all directions without any order. The army of Islam thus obtained a brilliant victory. Tabari says that more than 10,000 infidels were killed on this occasion, and therefore it came to be known as the "Garden of Death." Other campaigns were conducted by various Muslim generals with the secessionists in al-Bahrain, Uman and Yemen. Thus the whole movement of Apostacy, also called *Ridda* War, came to an end.

Thus Hazrat Abu Bakr can be called the Saviour of Islam. He not only saved Islam from dissolution and disruption but also made it a world religion. The *Ridda* War reclaimed for Islam the allegiance of the whole of Arabian Peninsula. "But for him (Hazrat Abu Bakr) Islam would have melted away in compromise with the Bedouin tribes or likelier still, have perished in the throes of birth." (*Muir*).

The success of the *Ridda* War demonstrated to the world that truth shall prevail. Secondly, it was the victory of moral force over material force. Islam in its infant stage withstood the shock or evil forces which were actually mightier. Thirdly, the victory terrorised the enemies of Islam and proved that it had strength enough to resist them. Fourthly, the Muslims themselves were assured of the superiority of Islam and of its inherent moral strength.

The Byzantine and the Sassanian Empires :

At the beginning of the Seventh Century, the Middle East was divided between the two great rival Empires of Byzantine and Persia. The history of the previous three centuries was largely a record of their struggles. The Byzantine Empire with its great Capital of Constantinople was Greek and Christian in culture and religion. The Persian Empire of the Sassanids presents a certain general resemblance to Byzantine. Between 602 and 628 A.D. the last of the series of Perso-Byzantine was wars fought, which ended in the Byzantine victory.

After restoring order within Arabia, Hazrat Abu Bakr next addressed himself to the strengthening of the Persian and Syrian frontiers which led to a series of wars ending in the subjugation of the Byzantine and the Sassanian empires. "These were not started by the Muslims, nor was there the slightest attempt on the part of the Islamic leaders to impose their own way of life on the foreign peoples. True, Islam was a missionary religion and an expanding force. The Prophet himself had invited the ruling monarchs of the surrounding countries to accept Islam. But he had never, by word or deed, tried to trespass their domains. The blame rests with the foreign powers who tried to encourage the rebels and by sending them reinforcements attempted to shatter the nascent power of Islam."

Hira, a semi-Arab kingdom, paid its allegiance to the Persian monarch but it was strategically important to the Muslims for further expansion on the north and east. At the times of insurrection, the Arabs of Iraq and Chaldaea helped their neighbour rebel new Muslims and instigated them to revolt. Not only that they fell on Muslim territories but also plundered their properties. From the very beginning Hazrat Abu Bakr was anxious to take necessary steps to guard the Muslims against the tyranny of the Persians, but he could not get time to materialise his scheme on account of the Apostasy movement. However, Hazrat Abu Bakr sent an army under Hazrat Muthanna to protect the Muslims of the borderland from the depredations of the Persians. When the War of Apostasy was over, Hazrat Khalid bin Walid was sent with an army of ten thousand men to assist Hazrat Muthanna. Before opening the campaign Hazrat Khalid addressed a letter to Hurmuz, Governor of Chaldaea inviting him either to accept Islam or pay the tribute or be ready for the fight. The third alternative was chosen and in a combat to which Hurmuz invited Hazrat Khalid the former was killed. The battle now fought more furiously, and it was after considerable bloodshed that the Muslims succeeded in routing the Persians and winning the vicroty. This battle is called the 'Battle of Chains'. The battle of Hafir was followed by a more contested action at Madhar where the Muslims defeated a fresh army of the Persians that the Emperor had sent from Madain. In short, of the battles of Walaja, Ullis, Yaumul Maqar, Ain-ut-Tamar, Dumatul Jandal, Aubar, Zamil and Rirod that were now fought, each was more severe than the preceding one. As the Satrapy of Iraq was the main prop of the empire of the Persians and as their capital at Madain (near Baghdad), lay in it, they fought for it with the greatest courage and enthusiasm. But all their efforts proved fruitless and they had to bow their heads before the sword of Hazrat Khalid bin Walid. His attacks were so rapid and effective that the enemy found no time to breathe, and in the course of a few days the whole of the country was cleared of his armies.

The army of Hazrat Khalid besieged the city of Hira, inhabited mainly by Christians. The Satrap fled across the Euphrates and the city after resisting for sometimes capitulated on easy terms. They agreed to pay a yearly tribute in return for which the Muslims undertook to defend the city. The city of Hira was the first outside the Arabian peninsula to fall in Muslim hands and the treaty concluded with the inhabitants provided the model for such treaties of capitulations concluded subsequently. After the fall of Hira, Hazrat Khalid completed the conquest of Dumatul Jandal. Another important engagement took place at Firad, the meeting-place of the frontiers of Persia, Syria and Jazirah. This large gathering of the Muslims at Firad excited the jealousy of the Romans, and they decided to oppose them with the help of the Persian continents and the infidel Arabs. The two armies met near the banks of the Euphrates and the battle ended in the victory of the Muslims.

War with the Byzantine Empire :

Syria, a country on the north of Arabia, was dominated by the Byzantines. No natural barrier stands to separate Syria from Arabia. Moreover, it was peopled by the Arabs and its inhabitants spoke the Arabic dialect. So the Arab Muslims regarded it as an integral part of Arabia. So both for the security of Arabia and for the racial affinity with the people of Syria the annexation of Syria was essential for the Arabs. On the other hand, the Byzantines could not like and tolerate the emergence of a powerful Arab state in their borderland which differed from them in race and religion.

Moreover, by violating the principle of international morality, once the Ghassanid Christian Prince of Syria had murdered the Prophet's envoy at Muta. The consequent invasion of Syria by Muslims under Hazrat Zayd was humiliating to the Byzantines. To avenge these humiliations they conspired the Bedouin tribes and the Persians and gave them active support against the Muslims.

The Prophet had began preparation for a war against the Byzantines but for his sudden death the expedition was postponed. But the first action of the first Caliph was to send an expedition under the Command of Hazrat Usama whose father Hazrat Zayd was killed in the battle of Muta. He defeated the Byzantines at Obna, close to the Mediterranean, and returned with huge spoils of war.

After the return of Hazrat Usama, the Byzantines again rose against the Muslims. Hazrat Abu Bakr sent Hazrat Khalid bin Sayed against them (632 A.D.). But he was defeated by the enemies. Then the Caliph sent four generals against the Byzantines. Hazrat Amr was directed to command his division in Palestine (Southern Syria), Hazrat Shurahbil in Central Syria, Hazrat Yazid in Damascus, and Hazrat Abu Ubaidah, the Commander-in-Chief, in Northern Syria. The first battle fought in Syria took place in Wadi Araba, south of Dead Sea, in which Hazrat Yazid inflicted a defeat on Sergius, the Byzantine Patrician of Palestine. Ultimately Hazrat Khalid bin Walid the 'Sword of Islam', who was then in Hira, has turned to Syria to take up the command there. He left Hazrat Muthanna, incharge of the Iraq front. He on his way joined Hazrat Shurahbil and captured Basra. Then he proceeded to capture Damascus, the capital of the Eastern Roman (Byzantine) Empire. Hazrat Abu Ubaidah also came forward to help him.

When Heraclius heard of the movement of the Muslims he also made preparations for war on a large scale and encamped in Hims. He decided to despatch separate columns against the various armies of the Caliph in order to stop them from combining together. The Muslims were a little upset on seeing the large number of the Roman soldiers. It has been recorded by the historians that the Romans were two lacs while the number of the Muslim soldiers could not rise above 46,000 soldiers. Then the first significant victory on the Syrian front was won. The battle of Ajnadayn was the first serious Byzantine effort to dislodge the Arabs from Syria. The Byzantine army was headed by Theodore, brother of Heraclius. But the former was devoid of any cohesion and loyalty whereas the Muslims far excelled them in discipline and dash. The Roman horsemen, unable to bear the brunt of Muslim attacks turned back and fled away. Having thus discomfited the Roman cavalry, the Muslim force now fell upon their infantry and dispersed its ranks without much difficulty. The defeated Romans took shelter in the trenches. They were consequently slaughtered in large numbers. The number of Muslims who were slain in this action is stated to have been 3,000. "Before the break of the day the Romans had cleared off from the field, and the golden rays of the morning sun were greeted by the victorious banner of Islam which had been planted on the banks of Yarmuk. It was a splendid victory which, besides impressing upon the minds of the Romans the greatness of the Muslims, opened for them immense possibilities of further successes."

Death of Hazrat Abu Bakr :

Hazrat Abu Bakr fell ill in the summer of 634 A.D., and for fifteen days he was confined to bed. The Caliph was now anxious to settle the question of succession and to nominate a successor, lest it might involve his people into a civil war. Although from long experience Hazrat Abu Bakr was confirmed in the belief that none but Hazrat Umar could take the heavy responsibilities of the Caliphate still with a view to galvanizing public opinion, he consulted the elite of the Companions. Tabari writes that Hazrat Abu Bakr went up to the balcony of his house and addressed the people who had assembled below : "Would you accept the person," said the Caliph, "Whom I nominate as my successor ? I say it under oath that I have spared no pains in determining this and I have chosen Umar bin Khattab as my successor. Listen to me and comply with my wishes." All of them said with one voice, "We have heard you and we shall obey you."

Then he called Hazrat Usman and dictated the text of the ordinance appointing Hazrat Umar as his successor. He died on Monday, the 23rd August, 634 A.D. The funeral prayers were led by Hazrat Umar, and he was buried in the apartment of Aisha by the side of the Prophet. He was 63 years of age at the time of his death and his Caliphate lasted for two years three months and eleven days.

HAZRAT UMAR

(13-25 A.H./634-644 A.D.)

While Hazrat Abu Bakr consolidated Islam and saved it from extinction, Hazrat Umar secured its expansion. He was a great man ; a man of great powers, of iron will, of stern justice, of passionate loyalty, and one who had a remarkable gift for administration.

The Conquest of Syria :

The siege of Damascus, one of the most important centres of Syria, commenced in the time of Hazrat Abu Bakr but the city was reduced during the reign of Hazrat Umar. Hazrat Khalid bin Walid devoted more than usual care in laying siege to it. The rigour of the siege damped the hopes of the Christians. They had, however, this consolation that Heraclius was ready to back them up and a relieving force had alrealy started from Hims and was on its way to Damascus. But the relieving force despatched by Heraclius from Hims was stopped in the way and never reached its destination. Blank despair now stared the inhabitants of Damascus. In the meantime a son was born to the Governor of Damascus. The auspicious occasion was celebrated by all the citizens and before nightfall they were all overdrunked. Availing this opportunity Hazrat Khalid, accompanied by a few brave officers, scaled the wall and got down the other side and broke the locks and flung the gates wide open. The Muslim troops were standing ready outside. As soon as the gates flew open they rushed in like a tempestuous torrent and massacred the outlying picket. The city was easily conquered but no plundering was permitted. Hazrat Khalid had been very just in the terms he had given to the conquered, thereby setting a pattern which was followed later Muslim conquerors everywhere. The terms were approved by Hazrat Umar.

After the conquest of Damascus, the Muslims had turned in the direction of Jordan, where the Romans began to gather their forces sent by Heraclius to relieve Damascus. Thus an army of about 40,000 was brought up under the command of Siklar, a Roman general. A bloody battle was fought at Fihl, a town east of Jordan. The Romans gave way and fled in the wildest disorder. After this battle the rest of the town and strong-holds in the province of Jordan were easily reduced and in the terms of peace it was everywhere stipulated that the lives, goods and chattels, lands and houses, churches and temples of the conquered people would be under protection.

After the fall of Damascus and Jordan three important cities remained to be reduced which meant the subjugation of the whole of Syria. These were Jerusalem, Hims (Amasia) and Antioch. The Muslims made up their minds to reduce Hims first. The Romans attempted to oppose the advancing Muslims near Hims. At the very first onset of Hazrat Khalid, however, they were routed ; Hazrat Khalid and Hazrat Abu Ubaidah laid siege to the city. The inhabitants of Hims, disappointed on all sides, now begged for peace. Hazrat Abu Ubaidah left Hazrat Ubaida Bin Samat incharge of the place and himself marched on Himat. The citizens of Himat surrendered to Hazrat Abu Ubaidah. Hazrat Abu Ubaidah then proceeded towards Mirat-ul-Numan and the people of this place submitted without opposition.

The Romans on meeting with disaster at Damascus, Hims, and other places, fled to Antioch where Heraclius held his court. Heraclius in a desperate attempt to dislodge the Muslims from Syria mustered an army of some 50,000 under his brother Theodorus. Hazrat Khalid relinquished for the time being Hims, even Damascus and other strategic towns, and concentrated some 25,000 men at the valley of Yarmuk the eastern tributary of the Jordan. A fierce and decisive battle took place on the 20th August, 636 A.D. The heterogeneous host of the Byzantines crumbled down before the determined army of the Muslims like a house of cards. The chant of the priest and their prayers were of no avail. The battle was raged with fury and violence. The cavalry made good their escape. The infantry, roped together in companies, to prevent flight, were easily killed or hurled down in the steep bed of the river. Theodorus himself fell and the imperial army was converted into a fleeing, panic stricken mob. Opinion is divided as to the extent of the casualties on the side of the Romans. Tabari gives the number as over an hundred thousand while Baladhuri puts the figures at seventy thousand. On the side for the Muslims three thousand persons were killed. The fate of Syria was decided. One of the fairest provinces was for ever lost to the Eastern Empire. Herclius was in Antioch when the news of the terrible disaster reached him. Forthwith he prepared to repair to Constantinople. As he took his departure he turned about and exclaimed ! "Farewell, O Syria" !

Removal of Hazrat Khalid bin Walid :

It was at this stage that Hazrat Umar appointed Hazrat Abu Ubaidah Commander-in-Chief and recalled Hazrat Khalid bin Walid. The deposition of Hazrat Khalid constitutes an important incident in the course of events relating to the conquest of Syria. Certain excesses of Hazrat Khalid had displeased Hazrat Umar. He also felt highly dissatisfied at Hazrat Khalid's severities against some enemies. Once Hazrat Khalid made a grant of ten thousand dirhams to a poet. Hazrat Umar took a serious view of this. Hazrat Khalid, however, maintained that the contribution was from his own purse. Hazrat Umar was not satisfied with this explanation. Thus he wrote to all the provincial governors to inform them that he did not dismiss Hazrat Khalid because he was offended with him or because he deemed him guilty of breach of trust, but that he had seen that the people grew more and more attached to him and that he accordingly considered it adviseable to depose Hazrat Khalid so that his admirers might realize that everything is disposed of by God.

Capitulation of Jerusalem :

After the Yarmuk, Hazrat Abu Ubaidah, the new Commander-in-Chief, with his deputy the glorious Hazrat Khalid, went and besieged Jerusalem, the holy city of the Christians. Hazrat Abu Ubaidah led the attack on one side and Hazrat Khalid attacked from the other. Hazrat Khalid won his way through. Meanwhile the Christian High Priest surrendered to Hazrat Abu Ubaidah. The High Priest sued for peace on condition that Caliph Hazrat Umar should himself come to the Holy City and settle terms of surrender. Hazrat Umar decided to come and give his decision in person. The purpose of Hazrat Umar's coming to Jerusalem was not merely to receive the capitulation of the Holy City but also to set the whole government of the country upon a sound basis, to revise the treaties and to fix the taxes. The terms of settlement were equally wonderful. Hazrat Umar decided that the half conquered by Muslim armies would be Muslim territory and the half surrendered by the High Priest would remain under Christian authority though under the overlordship of the Muslim governor of the town. Everybody was satisfied with this agreement.

The whole of Syria from south to north was conquered between 633 and 640 A.D. "So swift and easy an acquisition of so strategic a territory from the first potentate of the age gave the newly rising power for Islam prestige in the eyes of the world and, that is more important, confidence in its own destiny. From Syria the hordes step into Egypt and thence made their triumphant way through the rest of northern Africa. With Syria as a base the onward push to Armenia northern Mesopotamia, Georgia and Adharbayjan became possible, as did the raids and attacks which for many years to come were to be carried on against Asia Minor. With the help of Syrian troops Spain in far-off Europe was in less than a hundred years from the death of the Prophet brought within the ever widening circle of Islam".

Towards the close of the year 17 A.H. a virulent plague broke out in Syria, Egypt and Iraq and raged with the greatest rigour for many months. Many a towering personality of Islam succumbed to it. These included such distinguished and august personages as Hazrat Abu Ubaidah, Hazrat Mu'adh bin Jabal,

Hazrat Yazid bin Abu Sufyan, Hazrat Harith bin Hisham, Hazrat Suhail bin Umar, Hazrat Utba bin Suhail. Some 25,000 Muslims died of it. This direful pestilence arrested the progress of Islamic arms all of a sudden. The army instead of attacking the enemy was involved in its own affliction.

Conquest of Iraq and Persia :

As a result of the first encounter between the Muslims and the Persians in the battle of Hafir during the Caliphate of Hazrat Abu Bakr, Hira and other neighbouring principalities had already fallen to the Muslims. Hazrat Khalid would have completed the conquest of Iraq but the affairs in Syria compelled Hazrat Abu Bakr to issue an order directing Hazrat Khalid to proceed at once to Syria. While marching to Syria, Hazrat Khalid left Muthanna, a Bedouin chief, incharge of the Iraq front. The absence of Hazrat Khalid was immediately availed by the Persians who with full preparation fell down upon Muthanna's force and almost annihilated them in the battle of Bridge on 26th November, 634 A.D. When the number of casualties was reckoned, it was found that out of an army of nine thousand only three thousand were left alive. This defeat exasperated Hazrat Umar and with all his energy he commenced preparation for a fresh attack on the enemy. The Muslim forces under the command of Muthanna encamped at Buwayb, a place near Kufa. The Persian army was under the command of Mehran. A pitched battle was fought here. The Christian fought heroically. Many Muslim officers were killed, but the iron will and perseverance of Muthanna turned the scale of war in favour of the Muslims. The Persian army was entirely annihilated. The conflict was brought to an abrupt close by the death of Mehran. The Persians fled in wild disorder. One of the marked effects of this victory was a decided improvement in the morale of the Arabs. After this battle the Muslims overran the whole of Iraq.

This defeat infuriated the new Persian Emperor called Yazdagird who came to the throne of Persia as a result of a palace resolution. The coronation of Yazdagird infused a new life into the empire. The Court and military officers took to their work with redoubled activity. All the forts and military outposts were fortified and strengthened. The conquered districts of Iraq on the prospects of receiving support from Persia, broke into revolt and passed away from the Muslim sphere of influence. Muthanna sent urgent message to Hazrat Umar who realising the gravity of the situation sent Hazrat Sa'd bin Abi Waqas as the Commander-in-Chief with large reinforcements of 20,000. Meanwhile Muthanna died. The Muslim army encamped at Qadisya, in the neighbourhood of Hira.

Before the battle started Hazrat Sa'd under the instruction of Hazrat Umar sent a deputation to Yazdagird, the Persian King, asking him to embrace Islam. Yazdagird made the following answer: "Do you not recollect that you were the most wretched and miserable people that the world ever saw? Whenever you showed signs of recalcitrance we had only to issue orders to the frontier land-owners who invariably succeeded in crushing your mutinous spirit and humbling you to dust". He called for a basketful of earth and asked one of the Muslim to carry it out of the city gates. The Muslims however accepted it as a happy augury and taking the load to the Commander-in-Chief, Hazrat Sa'd and said to him, "Accept our congratulations for the victory, the enemy has voluntarily surrendered his territory to us".

Battle of Qadisiya:

The battle of Qadisiya was a hardy contested battle which lasted for not more than three days. Rustam, in charge on the side of Persia, had an army of 60,000. While Hazrat Sa'd could muster only 30,000. Rustam displayed great skill in arraying the troops in battle order. Hazrat Sa'd was suffering from sciatica and being unable to move about could not personally take part in the action. He, therefore, entrusted the command to Hazrat Khalid bin Arafatah. On the first day the battle started amidst loud cries of *Allahu Akbar*. The Muslims displayed their valour and skill but an elephant corps began to do havoc in the ranks of the Muslims. Ultimately the tribsemen of Tamin, who were famous archers and lancers, rained such a blinding shower of arrows as to knock down all the elephant riders. On the second day also the fighting was severe but the issue remained undecided. On the third day also the elephants again began to create terror among Muslims. In order to make up the deficiency under which the Muslim army laboured from want of elephants. Qaqa had recourse to very ingenious device. He pierced the eyes for some camels which gave them a frightful appearance. On whichever side these artificial mammoths went the horses of the Persians shied and got out of control. On this day the number of casualties on the Muslim and Persian sides were two thousand and ten thousand respectively. On the fourth day the battle raged vigorously. The event, however, remained still undecided. Qaqa in one last and mighty effort resolved to force the result. He selected several renowned warriors from among the chiefs of the clans and made a rush in the direction of Rustam. A storm arose and the canopy of Rustam was blown into the river. While trying to flee he was detected and slain on the spot. Instantly there was complete confusion prevailed. Every Persian soldier fled for his life.

The Battle of Qadisiya sealed fate of the Persia as that of Yarmoke had sealed the fate of Syria. The Muslims gained immense booties. The booty, as usual, was distributed among the troops, a fifth portion being despatched to the Caliph's court. This victory paved the way for the Muslim advance into the plains of the Euphrates and the Tigris. As a result of it all the fertile lands lying to the Muslims. The victory of the Muslims was welcomed by the inhabitants of Iraq because the Muslims brought with them peace, security and better government.

Fall of Madain :

The Arabs followed up their victory by capturing Balal and Kutha. Kutha was a historical place where Nimrud is saidto have imprisoned Prophet Abraham. The Persian capital, Ctesiphon (Madain) on the eastern bank of river Tigris, was Hazrat Sa'd's next objective. With characteristic dash and energy he pushed ahead. When Hazrat Sa'd arrived at the bank of the Tigris he found neither bridge nor boat. The river was deep and boisterous but its turbulent elements could hardly effect the resolute and undaunted spirit of the Muslim army. They crossed the river Tigris without any severe loss. Yazdagird had already sent his family to Hulwan. He himself abandoned the city and fled. As Hazrat Sa'd entered Cteisphon he found silence reigning everywhere supreme. Hazrat Sa'd took possession of the royal palace. In the palace the pulpit was set up in place of the royal throne and the Friday prayers were said therein. This was the first Friday prayer that was performed in Iraq. The vast treasure of the palace greatly amazed the Arabs. Gold, silver, oranments, robes, spices, camphor and many other articles of luxury were acquired by the Arabs. The one-fifth of the booty was sent to the Caliph at Medina. The carpet and other ancient relics were sent in their entirety so that the Arabs might view the spectacle of the grandeur and magnificence of Persia as well as of the might and glory of Islam. The occupation of Ctesiphon brought the sons of barren Arabia into direct contact with the luxuries and comforts of the then modern high life.

After the fall of Madain (Ctesiphon) the Persians began to make preparations for war in Jalula and gathered a large army. Kharzad, brother of Rustam, who wis the Commander-in-Chief, displayed great skill in carrying out these preparations. With the consent of Hazrat Umar, Hazrat Sa'd placed the Muslim army under the command of Hashim and Qaqa. A fierce battle ensued and Persians being defeated fled further north. The Muslims put them to indiscriminate slaughter till, according to the historian Tabari, a hundred thousand men were slain. The spoils of war again were rich and plentiful. When Yazdagird got the news of the disaster of Jalula he left Hulwan for Rai. Hazrat Sa'd personally stopped at Jalula and despatched Qaqa at the head of some troops to Hulwan. A short and fierce struggle ensued in which the Persians were routed. Hulwan thus fell into the hands of the Muslims.

The proud Yazdagird refused to yield even after his defeat in Nehawand. Nothing could curb the restlessness of the Persians. They were constantly organising new levies to attack the Muslims and fomented insurrection in provinces which were in the possession of the Muslims. It should be noted that hitherto Hazrat Umar had not intended to undertake the general subjugation of Persia. The battles fought up to this time were defensive measures adopted by him with a view to maintain the integrity of his own country. But circumstances compelled him to undertake the general subjugation of Persia. Hamdan was thus subjugated in 642 A.D. and hoard of royal treasure amounting to 4,000,000 dirhams, was discovered from a fire temple. Adharbaijan fell in 643 A.D. Fars was conquered in 644 A.D. by Hazrat Abdullah ibn Amir. The province of Sistan was conquered by Hazrat Asim bin Umar. After this the great and distant province of Khurasan came under the possession of the Muslims. The subjugation of Makran, the coastal region of Baluchistan, shortly after 645 A.D. brought the Arabs to the very border's of Indo-Pakistan.

About this time two military cantonments were established at Basra and Kufa (638 A.D). The Arabs could not bear the climate of Obollo ; so they found out a better site at Basra on the coast of the Shatt-ul-Arab. It had a great strategical value to the Muslims, because it guarded the passage from the Persian Gulf to Mesopotemia. Kufa was established on the western bank of Euphrates. Both cities were laid out on regular lines. In course of time Kufa and Basra grew into important centres of culture. Moreover, from these centres, the Muslim advance was made to the east.

But not long the peace treaty was violated by Yazdagird. "Neither the prudence of the Caliph nor the moderation of his generals was of avail in preventing a fresh conflict with the Persians." Circumstances forced the Muslims to cross the limits set by Hazrat Umar. Khuzistan was occupied in 638 A.D. following raids on Arab territories by its rulers Hurmuzan. The Muslims pursued Hurmuzan further north and being defeated he surrendered. "It now became clear to Hazrat Umar that the ban against an advance towards the east must be withdrawn. In self-defence, nothing was left but to crush the Chosroes, and take entire possession of his realm." Thus Sir William Muir who is not well-disposed towards Islam repudiates all the charges of expansionism, imperialism and avarice laid at the door of Islam.

Yazdagird gathering the remnants of his army once again started hostilities against the Muslims. The news of the Persian preparations caused great excitement in Medina, and the Caliph at once hurried off reinforcements towards the frontier. Hazrat Umar nominated Nu'man bin Maqran as the Commander of the Muslim army. The great battle took place at Nehawand in 641 A.D. The Persians, who outnumbered the Muslims by six to one, were defeated with terrible loss. Nearly thirty thousand Persians were slain in this battle. The Persians never recovered themselves after this battle. The Arabs named this victory 'Victory of Victories.' Persia thus passed under Muslim domination.

Conquest of Egypt :

Hazrat Amr-bin-As was mainly responsible for the conquest of Egypt. Prior to his adoption of Islam Hazrat Amr had undertaken a number of trading expeditions to Egypt and he knew routes thoroughly. When Hazrat Umar undertook his journey to Jerusalem, Hazrat Amr waited upon him and spoke about Egypt. "Hazrat Umar felt reluctant at first from considerations of prudence, but Hazrat Amr's repeated representations prevailed upon him and gave his consent for the invasion of Egypt and four thousand troops were placed at Hazrat Amr's disposal." But it was a conditional permission : "Depart and may success attend you, but if you get a letter from me before reaching Egypt then mend your way back." On returning to Medina Hazrat Umar had consulted with Hazrat Usman and others who pointed out the risks and perils involved in it. Hazrat Umar, despatched a messenger to halt the advance of the column. Hazrat Amr, however, did not open the letter which he got just in time until he reached the Egyptian frontiers (December, 639 A.D). Hazrat Amr was victorious from the beginning. He first captured the town of al-Farama in eastern Egypt. He next conquered the important town of Bilbays. Soon he came before the walls of the famous fortress of Babylon, a very great Byzantine centre. He now felt that he needed more troops. Fortunately Hazrat Zubair bin al-Awwam, a leader of the *Muhajirin*, came up, with 6,000 more men. Leaving half his army to besiege Babylon, Hazrat Amr advanced and captured the town of Ayn Shams. Cyrus, the Commander of Babylon, was shut up in the fort. He asked, therefore, for terms. Hazrat Amr gave an answer which became famous in history. He said : "If you wish to accept Islam, you are welcome and your people are welcome. If you do so, you will become our brothers. But there is no compulsion in our religion. If, however, you do not wish to become Muslim, you can surrender and pay tribute. We shall treat you well. If you do not agree, then let us fight it out. God will decide." Cyrus surrendered and proceeded to Alexandria to forward the terms of agreement to Emperor Heraclius. Heraclius took the viceroy severely to task and exiled him. Meanwhile the siege went on for seven months. Annoyed at this stubborn resistance, Hazrat Zubair took the lead in deciding the issue. He got inside the fort by scaling the wall and flung the gate wide open and the entire army rushed in. The enemy, on seeing that the Muslims had the advantage, surrendered and the fortress was occupied (April, 641 A.D).

Muslims afterward marched upon Alexandria which was heavily garrisoned with 50,000 soldiers. Behind it lay the whole strength of the Byzantine navy, of which the city was the base. "The invaders, far inferior in number and in equipment, had not a single ship, no siege machines and no immediate source of supply for their man-power." Moreover, the Arabs suffered from the pounding of Catapults from the high walls. But the sudden death of Heraclius in February, 641 A.D. changed the whole situation. He was succeeded by his grandson Constants II who, restored Cyrus to power. Cyrus concluded the Treaty of Alexandria (November 8, 641 A.D.) by which the city was evacuated and a fixed tribute of two *dinars* per head was to be paid. The Emperor Constants, weak and young, ratified the treaty which meant the transference of one of the fairest provinces of the empire to the Arabian hands. With the fall of Alexandria the whole of country came under the possession of the Muslims. Afterwards the foundation of the new capital city of Faustat near Babylon was laid in 641 A.D. Since then Egypt became a part and parcel of the Commonwealth of Islam. Hazrat Amr was made the Governor of Egypt. It had been a great seat of culture for centuries.

Administration of Hazrat Umar :

The role of Hazrat Umar in the early history of Islam was most conspicuous for his territorial acquisition. After the conquest of Iraq, Iran, Syria, Palestine and Egypt within the short period of his ten years Caliphate transformed the infant state of Islam into a big empire and the biggest power of the then world.

But his Caliphate is not less conspicuous for his administrative reforms for which he is regarded as the practical founder of the administration of Islam. "During the 30 (thirty) years that the Republic lasted," says Ameer Ali, "the policy derived its character chiefly from Hazrat Umar, both during his lifetime and after his death."

Arab Nationalism :

Hazrat Umar's administration was guided by foresight, consideration and ultimate welfare of every section of the people in the state. The starting point in his policy was to consolidate Arabs and to fuse the Arab tribes into a nation. The Peninsula of Arabia must be preserved as the citadel of Islam free from all corrupt influences. This was to exclude all hostile and alien elements from Arabia, the birth-place of Islam, and to keep it exclusively for the Saracens. With this end the Jews had to leave Arabia. The experiences of the Prophet with the Jews, the rising of the apostates and the hostility of the Byzentines prompted Hazrat Umar to take this action. Moreover, it is a fact that Jews had never been really friendly towards the Muslims. The Jews of Khaiber had been told on the conquest of the city that they would be turned out whenever the state thought it necessary to do so. Their enmity towards the state became more open in the reign of Hazrat Umar. The Christians of Najran began secretly to prepare for war, for which they procured many horses and arms. Hazrat Umar, therefore, ordered them to quit Yemen and settle in Iraq. But it should be noted that they were duly indemnified for the loss of their lands. Historical evidence is, therefore, decisive that the expulsions were ordered in pursuance of political necessities, and no exception can be taken to them.

Military Communism :

The Muslim state of the first century was purely military state. Hazrat Umar's system, therefore, was one of military communism in which every Arab Muslim was a soldier.

In the language of Prof. Hitti, "Hazrat Umar's policy was to organise the Arabians, now all Muslims, into a complete religion—military commonwealth with its members keeping themselves pure and unmixed—a sort of martial aristocracy." With this end in view the Arabian Muslims were not to hold or cultivate landed property outside the Peninsula. In the Peninsula itself the native Muslims who owned land paid a kind of title (1/10 land revenue). Accordingly the Arab conquerors in Syria, first lived in camps at Jabyah, Hims, Amwas, Tabariyah, Ludh and Ramla in Palestine. In Egypt they were settled in Fustat and Alexandria. In Iraq, the newly built Kufa and Basra served as Headquarters. In making these rules which gave predominance to the Saracen he was not actuated by the motive to keep the Arabs distinct as a race from the rest of the Muslims, nor was difference of colour, race and nationality considered a bar to equality. Under Hazrat Umar the adoption of Islam or the introduction of clientage of a non-Arab into a Saracenic tribe raised him to the status of a born Arab. Of course, there were privileges attached to the dominant faith as had always been the practice in other countries and among other communities, which acted in inducing rapid abandonment of the older cults.

Domocracy :

Hazrat Umar established complete net work of civil administration. "Without having a pattern of example before him, Hazrat Umar yet laid the foundations of a democratic state, and though, owing to the peculiar conditions of the age, the principles could not be developed in all its aspects and implications, the pre-requisites essentials to a democratic form of Government were brought into being. During his reign there were two consultative bodies. The one was a general assembly which was convened by making a general announcement and in which only affairs of special importance were discussed. Matters pertaining to the appointment and dismissal of public servants, and ordinary matters of daily occurrence were discussed by this committee. Apart from the consultative assembly, every citizen had a voice in the state administration.

Provincial Governors and district officers were often appointed by election. Hazrat Umar's Government vouchsafed the right of every individual and the people exercised utmost freedom.

The Caliph enjoyed no special privileges. Nobody kept guards, no palace and no distinction in robes was maintained either by Hazrat Umar himself or by his subordinates so that there should not be any difference between the ruler and the ruled, and they were accessible to the public any time.

Death of Hazrat Umar :

The death of Hazrat Umar was very tragic. One day a Persian slave, Feroz by name, came to Hazrat Umar with a complaint that his master had imposed upon him a very heavy tax. Hazrat Umar promised to see into the matter. Next day when the people assembled in the mosque of Medina for prayer he mingled with the worshippers. No sooner had he commenced reciting the service then Feroz suddenly rushed from behind and struck Hazrat Umar. Hazrat Umar died three days after and was buried on Saturday the First Muharram, 23 A.H./644 A.D. The duration of his Caliphate was ten years six months and four days.

HAZRAT UTHMAN

(24-36 A.H./644-656 A.D.)

Hazrat Uthman bin Affan, the third Pious Caliph of Islam, was born in 573 A.D. in the Umayyad clan of the great Quraysh family. The Prophet had great admiration for him for his simplicity, piety and generosity and gave his two daughters in marriage to him, one after another. When the second daughter died, he said that if he had another he would have married her to Hazrat Uthman.

Hazrat Uthman did great services to the cause of Islam. He suffered persecution with the Prophet at the hands of the Quraysh and accompanied the emigrants to Abyssinia with his wife. Hazrat Uthman was a well-to-do man and he placed his wealth at the disposal of the Prophet for the services of Islam. In the construction of the mosque and well in Medina and meeting the cost of campaigns of Islam, Hazrat Uthman made very generous contributions of money next only that of Hazrat Abu Bakr. He took prominent part in all the activities of the Prophet and thus won for him a distinguished position in the Companions of his great teacher.

During the Caliphate of Hazrat Abu Bakr and Hazrat Umar, Hazrat Uthman was one of their principal counsellors and assistants in the affairs of the state.

Election of Hazrat Uthman :

In his sick-bed, Caliph Umar nominated a Council consisting of Hazrat Uthman, Hazrat Ali, Hazrat Talha, Hazrat Zubayr, Hazrat Abdur Rahman bin Auf and Hazrat Said bin Waqqas to elect a Caliph from among themselves, in the time of the death of Caliph Umar. Hazrat Talha was away from Medina. So the five nominees had to choose a successor of the deceased Caliph. The task was really a difficult one as the name of both Hazrat Ali and Hazrat Uthman were to be considered. In the time of the election, however, Hazrat Ali voted for Hazrat Uthman and Hazrat Uthman voted for Hazrat Ali, Hazrat Sa'd casted his vote for his kinsman Hazrat Uthman. As regards Hazrat Abdur Rahman and Hazrat Zubayr it is not known who voted for whom. However Hazrat Uthman secured the majority of votes and was elected as a Caliph. The Muslims took the Oath of Allegiance to him and thus approved the choice. The sixth person of the body of electors, Hazrat Talha, returned to Medina after the election was over. He also swore allegiance to Caliph Uthman.

Expansion of Empire :

Caliph Uthman ruled over the Muslim empire for about twelve years. During his Caliphate the Arab empire expanded in Asia and Africa. In the beginning of his reign, a rebellion was caused by the Persians instigated by Yazdjard. The Caliph suppressed the rebellion. This was followed by the advance of the Arab generals into Herat, Kabul, Ghazni and Central Asia. These territories were overran and the chiefs of Afghanistan, Balkh, Turkestan and Khorasan were forced to recognise the sovereignty of Caliphate and pay a tribute to the Caliph.

Establishment of Navy :

The Caliphate of Hazrat Uthman is particularly memorable for the establishment of the Arab navy. As a Governor of Syria, Hazrat Muawiya had to face the naval attacks of the Romans in the coastal regions of his province. To repel the invasions he felt the need of a navy. So, he built a navy and with its help fought successfully against the Roman invaders. Hazrat Muawiya even fitted out a naval expedition to the island of Cyprus. He defeated the Roman ruler of the place and forced the island to pay tribute to the Caliphate.

The Romans also raised Egypt from the Sea, and in 646 A.D. even occupied Alexandria. Hazrat Amr bin Aas however repulsed them and recovered the port. Again in 651 A.D. the Romans invaded Egypt with a large fleet. Hazrat Amr's successor in the Governorship of Egypt, Hazrat Abdullah, mustered a naval force and defeated the Romans in a naval engagement. The Arabs thus established their superiority in the sea.

Conquest of Tripoli :

In Africa, Hazrat Abdullah rivalled the glories of his predecessor, 'the victor of Egypt' by the conquest of the Roman colony of "Tripoli." With the object of putting an end to the Roman invasions and hostilities, Hazrat Abdullah advanced with an army to Tripoli. The Roman Governor Gregorius offered him battle with a force of 120,000 Romans. The Arabs defeated them with a terrible slaughter, and occupied the whole of the Roman province of Tripoli (652 A.D.).

Redaction of the Holy Qur'an :

A remarkable work of Caliph Uthman was the redaction of the Holy Qur'an. During his Caliphate it was found that there were different readings and versions of the Holy Qur'an in different parts of the empire, Hazrat Uthman resolved to remove the difference and collect the correct version of the Holy Qur'an. So he set up a board presided over by Hazrat Zayd bin Thabit. This board collected the authentic Holy Qur'an and the copy found with Hafsah, a wife of the Prophet was much helpful to his compilation. They made several copies of the redacted Holy Book. These copies were sent to different parts of the empire and the rest were burnt so that the authenticity of the Holy Qur'an could be maintained.

Caliph Uthman constructed a huge dam to protect Medina against floods and regulated the supply of water to the city. He built many roads, bridges, mosques, guest houses in different parts of the empire and extended the Prophet's mosques in Medina.

Charges Against Hazrat Uthman :

Caliph Uthman had a prosperous and successful reign in the early few years of his Caliphate. In the later part of his reign troubles broke out in the empire, particularly in Egypt and Iraq. The people brought charges of nepotism and favouritism against the Caliph. They said that he favoured his kinsmen, the Umayyads, with high posts, valuable properties. They charged the Umayyad governors with inefficiency, oppression and misappropriation of the property of the *Bait-al-Mal.* Discontent, disaffection and sedition ran apace in the empire.

Caliph Uthman appointed Marwan as his Principal Secretary, Muawiya, Walid bin Aqba and Abdullah bin Sa'd as Governors of Syria, Iraq and Egypt respectively. The appointment of his inefficient and selfish cousin Marwan to the high position was extremely unpopular. Caliph Uthman was not really responsible for appointing Hazrat Muawiya to the Governorship of Syria. In the Caliphate of Hazrat Umar Yezid bin Abu Sufyan was Governor of Syria and after his death Hazrat Muawiya eventually succeeded his brother to the Governorship. The appointment of Abdullah bin Sa'd, a foster-brother of Caliph Uthman, in place of Hazrat Amr bin Aas caused great disaffection and disturbances in Egypt.

It was also charged that the kinsmen of Caliph Uthman acquired private properties at the expense of the public property and crownlands. Hakam, father of Marwan, acquired the estate of Fadak and Hazrat Muawiya appropriated the crown-lands in Syria. The Caliph allowed Abdullah to keep for himself one-fifth of the spoils of the battle of Tripoli. Many other Umayyads in this way made private properties which were strictly forbidden in the Caliphate of Hazrat Umar. Talha also purchased the estate of Nashtasag in Kufa during the Caliphate of Hazrat Uthman.

The seditionists charged Caliph Uthman with extravagance and helping his relations with the money of the public treasury. In fact, the Caliph did not take even any allowance from the estate treasury. He had a big property and helped his kinsmen, the Umayyads, from his private property. This is known from his own statement recorded in Tabari's history. Hazrat Uthman said, "At the time of my accession to the Caliphate I was the biggest owner of goats and camels in Arabia. Today I possess neither a goat nor a camel, save the two used in pilgrimage...............It is alleged that I love my relations and give them riches. But my love others, I put upon them the obligations that are due from them. As regards favouring them, I give them whatever I can from my own property. As regards public property, I consider it lawful neither for myself nor for anyone else. Even during the times of the Prophet, Hazrat Abu Bakr and Hazrat Umar, I used to give large sums of my earnings. This I did when I was yet a youngman and as such stood in need of money. Now that I have reached a normal limit of my family age and my days are coming to a close and I have made over all my possessions to my family, the misguided people say such things of me. I take nothing out of it ; what I eat, I eat out of my own earnings."

On the complaints against the oppression and embezzlement of the Governors, Caliph Uthman called all the Governors and asked the complainants to come with their grievances. Nobody however came with any representation. The Governors advised the Caliph to inflict exemplary punishment on the mischief-mongers. But the tender-hearted Caliph Uthman did not like to have any bodyguard for his personal safety. Caliph Uthman thus showed leniency and this proved suicidal to him. The seditionists were encouraged in their activities.

Causes of Sedition and Assassination of Hazrat Uthman :

Many Muslims became jealous of the ascendancy of the Umayyads in the Caliphate of Hazrat Uthman. They found that the Umayyads were in high offices of state and they flourished in wealth and privileges. They did not have good opinion about the Umayyads. The Umayyads were the last to accept Islam and many of them accepted it in consideration of worldly gains, because they saw that they would lose by adhering to idolatry. Some of the Umayyads behaved in a very scandalous manner. Walid bin Uqbah, Governor of Kufa, appeared drunk in the mosque. So, many Muslims were disgusted with them and they did not have any sympathy for the Umayyad family.

Secondly in the Caliphate of Hazrat Uthman the *Ansars* of Medina found their position and influence was disappearing. They did not have their due share in the affairs of empire.

Thirdly, the ruling aristocracy of the Umayyads had completely eclipsed the Hashimites. The Hashimite chief Hazrat Ali and others lost their position and influence in the Caliphate of Hazrat Uthman. So the Hashimites were not favourably disposed towards Caliph Uthman and his Umayyad family.

Fourthly, the elevation of Marwan bin Hakam to the high position of the Chief Secretary of the State was extremely unpopular. A selfish and intriguing person, Marwan aimed at promoting and consolidating the position of the Umayyads in the Caliphate. His policy divided the Umayyads and Hashimites into two camps and denied the latter their rightful place in the Caliphate. This lost the Caliphate of Hazrat Uthman the services and support of that important branch of the Quraysh family.

Fifthly, Caliph Uthman's simplicity and leniency greatly accounted for his own disaster. Relying too much on Marwan, he left the reigns of Government in his hands and thus allowed the conditions to go from bad to worse. Being tender-hearted, Caliph Uthman also could not adopt a stern policy towards the seditionist. He could have dealt with the mischief-mongers with a strong hand and could averted the great calamity that befell him. But by character and temperament, Caliph Uthman lacked firmness, a quality which was so essential to govern an unruly people.

Sixthly, the banishment of Hazrat Abu Dharr Ghifari, one of the most pious Muslims of his time, irritated the feelings of the good Muslims. He had urged upon the Governor of Syria that the rich should be compelled to give a fraction of their wealth for the benefit of the poor. Hazrat Muawiya sent him to Caliph Uthman as a fomenter of discord and strife and the Caliph banished him to the village of Rabadah.

Lastly, some disgruntled and designing persons fomented sedition to promote their own interests. Abdullah bin Saba, a Yemenite Jew, who had become Muslim on a motive of self-interest, took the leading part in creating sedition against the Caliph. Being expelled from Busra, Kufa and Syria on account of his subversive activities, he went to Egypt and found there a more congenial field for his propaganda.

Rebellion :

Discontent against the Caliphate of Hazrat Uthman grew apace. In Kufa and Busra people rose against the Governors appointed by Caliph Uthman. Agitation became violent in Egypt where Abdullah bin Saba preached the right of legitimacy of Hazrat Ali to the Caliphate. He said that Caliph Uthman had wrongly usurped Caliphate. Abdullah even introduced the Jewish idea of Messiah asserting that Hazrat Ali would come as a Mahdi, a Redeemer to the earth after his death. Hazrat Ali had the largest followers in Egypt and Talha and Zubayr had great influence in Kufa and Busra.

The impetus to rebellion came from Egypt. The insurgents drove away the Governor. Then a body of 600 Egyptians, mostly volunteers started for Medina. On the way they were joined by the mutineers of Kufa and Busra. These deputationists placed their grievances before Caliph Uthman. The Caliph promised to redress their grievances and appointed Muhammad bin Abu Bakr, a man of their choice, as Governor of Egypt. Apparently the deputationist seemed satisfied and they left for their respective provinces. Shortly afterwards came back to Medina from their way and demanded the surrender of Marwan to them. When Hazrat Ali asked them the reason of their behaving in this way, they said that on the way they intercepted a letter from a special courtier of Caliph Uthman written by Marwan to the Provincial Governor instructing him to murder the deputationists as soon as they reached Egypt.

There is doubt about the authenticity of the letter. Hazrat Ali, however, interceded in favour of the Caliph and tried his best to dissuade them from violence. But the insurgents would listen to no reason. Caliph Uthman also did not agree to surrender his kinsman to them. So they besieged his house. In the hour of his peril, his friends and relations deserted him. On 17th June, 656 (35H) the rebels stormed the house and two Egyptians assassinated the aged Caliph when he was reciting the Holy Qur'an.

In the words of Wellhausen, "the death of Uthman is more epoch-making than almost any other event in the history of Islam." The assassination of Hazrat Uthman destroyed the idea of the sanctity of the person of Caliph. As the representative of the Prophet, the Caliph's person was considered sacred and inviolable for the Muslims. Of course, Caliph Umar was also assassinated ; but he was assassinated by a war prisoner and a non-Muslim. Caliph Uthman, on the other hand, was killed by the Muslims in an organised way. These Muslims felt that they had grievances against the Caliph and they were killing him for a cause. Their action established the notion that the Caliph was answerable to the Muslims for his actions and he could be removed if he failed to fulfil the obligations of his high office.

The right to remove the Caliph on reasonable grounds may be exercised by a people ; but the use of violence and murder of the Caliph is certainly not a right to be enjoyed by any section of the people.

Secondly, the assassination of Caliph Uthman revised the old tribal spirit of the Arabs which had disappeared as a result of the teachings of the Prophet.

Thirdly, this unhappy incident broke the unity of the Muslims. The Umayyads and Hashimites were sharply divided into two rival and hostile camps. It also introduced bitterness between the Medinite *Ansars* and the Meccan Umayyads.

Fourthly, the city of Medina lost its ascendancy in the Caliphate and the provincial cities like Kufa and Damascus came into prominence. The *Ansars* also lost their position in the Caliphate.

Fifthly, as a result of the troubles which broke out among the Muslims after the assassination of Caliph Uthman, the expansion of the Arab empire received a set-back.

Lastly, the assassination of Caliph Uthman introduced generations of civil war in Islam. The civil war first began between Caliph Ali and Talha-Zubayr, then Hazrat Ali and Muawiya. It resulted in the assassination of Hazrat Ali. The civil war renewed in the Caliphate of Muawiya and culminated in the tragedy of Karbala at the time of Yezid. It continued till Hazrat Abdullah bin Zubayr was killed by Hajjaj bin Yusuf in the reign of Caliph Abdul Malik. This assassination and the consequent civil war gave rise to Schism in Islam namely the Shias and Kharijis.

The murder of Caliph Uthman is the most unfortunate event in the history of Islam. Caliph Uthman was renowned for his piety and honesty. He was deeply religious and very simple in his life and habits. Modesty and generosity were the striking features of his character. But he lacked the firmness of mind and resolution which are very essential for a ruler. This accounted for his failure and tragic end.

HAZRAT ALI

(36-41 A.H./656-661 A.D.)

A boy of only nine years, but intelligent and brave, Hazrat Ali, son of Abu Talib, believed in the mission of the Prophet and was first among the young to accept Islam. From his infancy, he was brought up by his cousin Prophet Muhammad. The Prophet loved him as a son for his noble qualities and gave his affectionate daughter, Hazrat Fatimah in marriage to him a year after the *Hijrat* to Medina. Though a boy, Hazrat Ali had been the constant companion of the Prophet in the preaching of his mission and had been the foremost champion of Islam. He was a great warrior, and fought and distinguished himself in all the battles of the Muslims against the pagans and Jews.

Hazrat Ali excelled in both sword and pen. A scholar and orator, Hazrat Ali was the most accomplished man of the time. His sayings are proverbial in the profundity of thought and wisdom. He was known as the gate of knowledge. Because of his learning, wisdom and intelligence, his advice was very much valued by Caliph Abu Bakr and Hazrat Umar and he occupied the position of a prime counsellor in their Caliphate.

Hazrat Ali was a lion in bravery as well as in generosity and magnanimity. Simple, frank, sincere and large-hearted, Hazrat Ali was an embodiment of all humane virtues. But his simplicity, frankness and large-heartedness proved his great drawbacks as a ruler because he easily believed his men, so his shrewd enemies easily deceived him.

Election to Caliphate :

After the murder of Caliph Uthman confusion prevailed in Medina for about five days. Then Abdullah bin Saba, the leader of the Egyptian party, proposed that Hazrat Ali, as the rightful successor of the Prophet, should succeed to the Caliphate. All acclaimed it. Hazrat Ali at first refused to accept the Caliphate at such a time and circumstances. But considering the interests of Islam, he ultimately agreed to accept the responsibility of the Caliphate. So, on 23rd June, 656 A.D. everyone swore allegiance to him and he was declared the Caliph of Islam.

As a Caliph Hazrat Ali followed the ideal of Hazrat Abu Bakr and Hazrat Umar. He wanted to follow strictly the principles of *Bait-al-Mal*. He resolved to resume to the public treasure all the estates acquired by the Umayyads and others in the Caliphate of Hazrat Uthman. Caliph Hazrat Ali was also determined to replace all the Governors against whom the people had grievances. He appointed Uthman bin Hanif as Governor of Busra in place of Ibn Amir. Qays was sent to the Governorship of Egypt to replace Abdullah. The Governors of Kufa and Syria were asked to resign to make place for new Governors. The Governor of Kufa agreed to resign ; but Muawiya, the Governor of Syria, refused to obey him as a Caliph. So, Caliph Hazrat Ali had to face troubles with Muawiya.

Rebellion of Talha and Zubayr :

Shortly after his accession to the Caliphate, Hazrat Ali was called upon to deal with a rebellion of Talha and Zubayr.

Talha was one of the oldest and the most esteemed companions of the Prophet and a kinsman of Caliph Abu Bakr. Zubayr's mother was the aunt of the Prophet and his sister Hazrat Umme Habibah was married to the Prophet. He was a kinsman of Hazrat Uthman and a son-in-law of Hazrat Abu Bakr.

Talha and Zubayr at first accepted Hazrat Ali as Caliph. Afterwards they disowned him, because he did not agree to their demand that he would immediately punish the murderers of Caliph Uthman. Their demand was an impossible one. The immediate task of Caliph Ali was to restore order and consolidate his position in the empire where great confusion and troubles prevailed. Secondly to punish the murderers was not an easy task. Caliph Uthman was not murdered by a few individuals that they could be easily secured and punished. Large number of persons of Egypt, Iraq and Arabia were directly connected with this assassination. Hence, to punish the assassinators at this time of confusion and troubles would confound the Caliph and the Caliphate.

As Caliph Ali did not accept their demand, Talha and Zubayr withdrew their allegiance and started for Busra where they counted a large followers of their own. On the way they met Hazrat Aishah who was returning from the pilgrimage. Being informed of the assassination of Caliph Uthman, she was greatly shocked. When she heard that Caliph Hazrat Ali did not agree to punish the assassins, she joined Talha and Zubayr and returned to Mecca with them. They went from Mecca to Busra and made the Governor Ibn Hanif prisoner. Hazrat Ali's party was defeated and Busra passed into the hands of Talha and Zubayr.

Battle of Camel :

Caliph Ali desired to avoid war and settle the matters with Talha and Zubayr by peaceful means. As peaceful settlement seemed to recede in the distance, he advanced to subdue them and met their forces at Koraiba. Caliph Ali continued negotiations for a peaceful settlement. But many interested people did not like it. Their interests lay in the continuance of the trouble so that the Caliph might not give his attention to deal with the murderers of Hazrat Uthman. So the inevitable battle took place. It is known as the Jang-i-Jamal or the Battle of the Camel because Hazrat Aishah was present in the field on the back of a camel. The superior military talent of Hazrat Ali soon succeeded in vanquishing the rebels. Talha and Zubayr were killed while they were running away. 20,000 Muslims fell in this battle. Hazrat Aishah was taken prisoner. Caliph Ali sent her to Medina escorted by her brother Muhammad with due respect. After the battle Caliph established his authority in Busra. He then went to Kufa, which henceforth became his capital. From Kufa, he intended to deal with Muawiya.

Rebellion of Muawiya :

The Umayyad chief Muawiya bin Abu Sufyan, the Governor of Syria, aimed at the Caliphate and he exploited the situation created by the murder of Hazrat Uthman to his advantage. After the murder of Hazrat Uthman, many Umayyads left for Syria to Muawiya so that with the elevation of Hazrat Ali to the Caliphate, Muawiya stood at the head of the Association of the Umayyad families numbering many thousands. This greatly strengthened the hands of the Umayyad chief against Caliph Ali. Muawiya possessed vast estates in Syria, so also many of the members of his family. Even many Arab exiles in Syria acquired landed properties in that province. This greatly added to the strength of the Umayyad pretender.

Furthermore, Muawiya had at his disposal the entire resources of a vast and fertile province. He had also mustered the Syrian Arabs in his support. These people thought that by promoting the cause of Muawiya, they would further their own interests. So Muawiya had enough men and money to contest for the Caliphate with Hazrat Ali.

Lastly a shrewd man, Muawiya exploited the assassination of Caliph Uthman to discredit Caliph Ali in the eyes of the Muslims. He excited the feelings of the people by exhibiting in the mosque of Damascus the relics of murdered Hazrat Uthman and his wife Bibi Naila's amputated finger, which was cut off when she tried to save her husband. He demanded that Hazrat Ali should find out and punish the murderers or he should accept the position of murderer.

Battle of Siffin :

Thus strengthened Muawiya's refusal to recognise Hazrat Ali as Caliph and defied his order to dismissal. From Kufa Caliph Ali moved at the head of fifty thousand men to deal with the rebellion of Muawiya advanced with a large army to oppose the Caliph's army. The two armies faced each other in the field of Siffin. Caliph Ali wanted to avoid the bloodshed of the Muslims and settle the dispute by peaceful means. Muawiya demanded the immediate punishment of the murderers. It was impossible for Hazrat Ali to arrange for immediate punishment of the murderer at that time. Muawiya would not agree to make peace on any other condition. Hazrat Ali even suggested a personal combat to decide the issue of the Caliphate. But Muawiya would rather face a fierce tiger than meet Hazrat Ali, the Tiger of God, in a personal combat.

Proposal for peaceful settlement having failed, the battle began. On the second day of the Battle of Siffin, Hazrat Ali's gallantry and generalship was clearing the field off the vast forces of the enemy. 7,000 fell in the battle. Faced with a disastrous defeat, crafty Muawiya, on the advice of his cunning associate Amr bin Aas, fastened the copies of the Qur'an to the lances of the soldiers and thus demanded the reference of the dispute to the Qur'an. It was in fact a clever trick of Muawiya to escape disaster and deceive Hazrat Ali. Hazrat Ali saw into the ruse and desired to continue the battle. But his soldiers clamoured to stop fighting. So fighting stopped and Muawiya escaped destruction.

After fighting stopped, it was decided that the dispute should be referred to two arbitrators. Muawiya appointed his friend cunning Amr bin Aas to be an arbitrator from his side. Hazrat Ali's side was represented by Hazrat Abu Musa Ashari, who was no match for astute and shrewd Amr. The two arbitrators were assisted by 400 men of each side and in case the arbitrators could not come to a settlement, the issue would be decided by the majority of votes.

Curiously enough, the very soldiers of Caliph Ali who clamoured for the reference of the dispute to arbitration now denounced arbitration by men as sinful. They said that arbitration belongs to Allah only. In fact they did not like the settlement of the dispute and wanted the continuance of troubles for their own interests. Caliph Ali had given his word for arbitration and did not agree to renew fighting. So 12,000 of his soldiers left his camp and began to create troubles in the empire particularly in Iraq. These people are known as Kharijis. The Khariji trouble diverted the attention of Caliph Ali. This was a great relief to Muawiya. Hazrat Ali had to take up arms against them. He beat them severely at Naharawan. Many of the Kharijis fell fighting and the survivors escaped to Bahrein and other places.

It is difficult to ascertain what actually happened in the arbitration. There are confused versions about it. It is said that Amr explained to Hazrat Abu Musa that both Hazrat Ali and Muawiya should be deposed and fresh election should take place for the Caliphate. Accordingly when Hazrat Abu Musa first declared the deposition of Caliph Ali, Amr accepted it and proclaimed the installation of Muawiya to the vacant Caliphate. This treacherous proceedings of the arbitrators enraged Hazrat Ali's party men and the arbitration ended in a farce. Whatever might have been the truth of these proceedings, it is, however, certain that Hazrat Ali came out loser and Muawiya gainer from the arbitration. Hazrat Ali had the Caliphate to lose but Muawiya did not have the Caliphate to lose. Arbitration made Muawiya, who was a rebel Governor, an equal of Caliph Hazrat Ali.

Resolving to fight out the issue, Caliph Ali made preparations to advance to Syria. About this time Khariji troubles broke out and the Caliph had to proceed against them at Naharawan. While he was busy against the Kharijis in 658 A.D., Muawiya seized the opportunity to capture Egypt. He sent an army under Amr bin Aas, who defeated Hazrat Muhammad the Governor of Egypt and took possession of the province for the Umayyad chief. Muawiya thus immensely strengthened himself.

As Hazrat Ali had to face troubles at home created by the Kharijis and others, he found it impossible to deal with Muawiya. So he agreed to conclude a treaty with the Governor of Syria. As a result of this treaty, Muawiya was confijrmed in the possession of Syria and Egypt. This compromise settled the dispute between Caliph Ali and Muawiya.

Causes of Hazrat Ali's Failure :

The compromise settlement with Muawiya was, in fact a failure for Hazrat Ali. The various troubles which confronted Hazrat Ali from the very accession to the Caliphate mainly accounted for his failure to suppress the rebellion of Muawiya. The formidable rebellion of Talha and Zubayr weakened the position of Hazrat Ali and strengthened the hands of Muawiya. Rebellions were also afoot in Busra, Egypt and Perisa for independence. Caliph Ali had to deal with these rebellions and restore order in the empire. The Kharijis in particular greatly weakened his strength and kept him pre-occupied.

In men, money and resources, Muawiya was far stronger than Caliph Ali. Hazrat Ali possessed inadequate resources and commanded a people whose allegiance to him was fickle and doubtful. Muawiya on the other hand, had the vast resources of Syria and unflinching support of his family at his disposal. The Umayyads as well as the Syrians were solidly behind him and supplied with inexhaustible sources of strength.

Hazrat Ali was merely a general and a brave soldier. Muawiya was a shrewd diplomat and clever politician. He played fox where valour was of no avail. He cleverly exploited the murder of Hazrat Uthman to discredit and weaken Caliph Ali and to serve his design. Himself one of the shrewdest of the time, Muawiya made friends and alliance with Amr another craftiest man of the time. Failing in sword Muawiya and his associate deceived and defeated Caliph Ali by the game of cleverness and shrewdness in the battle of Siffin.

The compromise settlement of Hazrat Ali with Muawiya was not liked by the mischief-mongers, because it freed the Caliph to devote himself to the task of chastising them. The Kharijis planned to murder Hazrat Ali, Muawiya and Amr and choose a Caliph of their own ideas, freely elected from all Muslims. Accordingly Abdur Rahman, the Khariji zealot, struck a severe blow at Hazrat Ali as he was going to say his morning prayer in the mosque. The blow proved fatal and Caliph Ali died on 17 *Ramadan*, 40 A.H. corresponding 661 A.D.

"Thus died," says Col. Osborne, "in the prime of his youth, the best-hearted Muslim that ever lived". Caliph Ali reigned only four years and mine nonths.

As a Caliph Ali lived a very simple and ascetic life. He very scrupulously maintained the ideals of Islam and the principles of *Bait-al-Mal* and never spent, nor allowed others to spend a single farthing from the treasury. The death of Hazrat Ali was a great loss to Islam. With his death the Republic and the ideal days of Islam came to an end. The primitive simplicity and purity of the Caliphate disappeared. Muawiya transformed the Caliphate into a 'mulk' and established a dynastic rule in Islam. Medina, *Ansars* and Arabs of Arabia lost their influence in the Caliphate and the supremacy of Damascus and Syrian Arabs was introduced in the empire.

The four Caliphs who succeeded the Prophet in the leadership of the Muslims are known as the Khulfa-i-Rashideen or the Pious Caliphs. The period of the Pious Caliphs is the most glorious age in the history of Islam. In this period the ideals and teachings of the Prophet continued as a living force and the Caliphs followed the tradition of the great teacher in their ideals and policy. This period nourished the democratic ideas of Islam and worked out a Republican Government to which the Muslims look with pride and inspiration.

Though lasted only thirty years, the Republic of Islam is the most momentous period in history. It saved Islam, consolidated it and laid the basis of the greatness of the Muslims. The first Pious Caliph Hazrat Abu Bakr saved the Muslims from being divided on the issue of succession to the leadership after the death of the Prophet. He also saved Islam from the great danger of apostasy and false prophets and maintained the hold of the true faith in Arabia. The second Pious Caliph Hazrat Umar consolidated Islam in Arabia, converted the wild sons of the desert into a disciplined race of warriors and demolishing the Persian empire and Byzantine empire built a very powerful empire comprising Persia, Iraq, Chaldaea, Syria, Palestine and Egypt. The reign of the third Pious Caliph Hazrat Uthman witnessed farther expansion of the Arab empire in central Asia and Tripoli. It is also memorable for the establishment of the Arab navy. The reign of the fourth Pious Caliph Hazrat Ali was spent in meeting internal troubles. With his death in 661 A.D., the Republic of Islam came to an end.

Chapter 3

The Period of Umayyads

MU'AWIYA

(*A.H. 661/680 A.D.*)

Mu'awiya, the founder of the Umayyad dynasty, was the son of Abu Sufyan. Mu'awiya come into power, but except in Syria and Egypt, he ruled solely by the sword. He combined in his person ali the qualities of a ruler, politician and administrator. Mu'awiya was a keen student of human nature and acquired a keen insight into human mind. He secured the services of ablest leaders, administrators and politicians of the time. He was an orator of superb quality.

His Military Exploits :

After securing his position at home Mu'awiya embraced upon a vigorous foreign policy. Considerable extension of the Muslim dominion took place under him. He was a superb organiser of victories. In the words of Prof Hitti, "Mu'awiya's reign witnessed not only the consolidation but the extension of the territories of the Caliphate."

During the Caliphate of Mu'awiya, great progress was made in the East. The people of Herat rebelled and they were suppressed in 661 A.D. Two years later Kabul was also besieged. Similar operations were directed against Ghazna, Balkh, and Kandahar and other strongholds. In the year 676 A.D. Bokhara was captured and two years later Samarqand and Tirmid were occupied. In the Far East, another Muslim army under Mahalib, son of Abu Sufra, advanced as far as the banks of the Indus. Thus Mu'awiya brought the whole of Central Asian regions reaching up to the outskirts of Indo-Pak sub-continent under his sway. Rightly Hitti says, "Thus Mu'awiya became not only the father of a dynasty but the second founder of the Caliphate after Hazrat Umar."

The first invasion of North Africa has taken place in the reign of Hazrat Umar. Under Hazrat Usman the Arab forces had advanced as far as Barce. After the defeat of Gregorius the Byzantine Prefect, as the memorable battle fought not far from ancient Carthage, the Romans undertook to pay an annual tribute to the Arabs, who then withdrew from the country leaving small garrisons here and there. The Roman Governors re-occupied the abandoned territories, but their capacity and exactions were so intolerable that before long the natives themselves invited the Arabs to liberate them from the Byzantine yoke. Mu'awiya responded to their call, and an army under the celebrated Uqba, son of Nafe, marched into Ifrikia, beat down all opposition, and reduced the country to Arab dependency. In 670 A.D. Uqba built the famous military city of Kairowan to the south of Tunis to leap in check the fierce unruly Berbers, and also to guard against the Roman ravages from the sea. The brilliant march of Uqba and the crushing blows he inflicted on the Romans and the Berbers had the effect of keeping the country quiet for several years. With a slight intermission owing to his recall to Damascus, he ruled Ifrikia and its western dependency until his death in 683 A.D.

Siege of Constantinople :

The most striking incident in the Caliphate of Mu'awiya was the siege of Constantinople. An expeditionary force commanded by Yazid sailed through Dardanelles and landed in. For six years the Muslims beleaguered the Constantinople, capital city of Christendom, and for six years the valour of the Romans and the impregnable wall of the city held them at bay. Hard pressed from all sides Mu'awiya ordered for withdrawal of the siege.

Administration :

Caliph Mu'awiya built up a well-organised Government. "The situation when Mu'awiya came in power presented many difficulties. The administration of the Empire was decentralised and in disorder and the resurgence of nomad anarchism and indiscipline, no longer restrained by a religious or moral tie led to a general instability and lack of unity. The theocratic bond which had held together the early Caliphate had been irrevocably destroyed by the murder of Hazrat Uthman, the civil war that followed it, and the removal of the capital from Medina. The oligarchy in Mecca was defeated and discredited. Mu'awiya's problem was to find a new basis for the cohesion of the Empire." He thus transformed the religious sovereignty into a secular state. But it should be noted that the religious element in the Government and administration was not altogether absent. He observed the religious formalities and at times posed as the champion of Islam.

Mu'awiya brought about mighty and distinct changes in the administration of the country. The real basis for his Government is to be found in a strong and efficient army. He relied on his loyal and faithful Syrian army, who stood by him in the gravest hour of peril. Mu'awiya sought to build up with the help of loyal Syrians a stable Government on the lines of the Byzantine Government. He worked very hard for the smooth working of the system that he introduced.

Mu'awiya is credited to have been the first in Islam to establish a department of registry (*Diwanul-Kahatam*). Every ordinance issued by the Caliph was to be copied in a register and then the original one was to be sealed and despatched to its destination. Prior to this, open orders were sent out. Once so happened that to a man the Caliph had granted 1,000 dirhams from the Provincial Treasury. The letter in which the order was given was intercepted on the way and the amount was altered to higher figure.

Postal service (*Diwanul-Barid*) is said to have been introduced by Mu'awiya. The *Barid* (Post Master) informed the Central Government as to what was going on in the Provincial Administration. In this way, Mu'awiya enforced the authority of the Central Government. Mu'awiya established two Secretariates—one Imperial (Central) Secretariate whose medium was Arabic and the other Provincial Secretariate which used the Greek and Persian languages. Mu'awiya as a farsighted administrator, separated the finances from the political administration. He appointed a Governor in each province for political administration. But for the collection of revenue, he appointed in each province a special officer who bore the title of *Sahibul-Kharaj*. This officer was independent of the Governor and appointed by the Caliph. The Governor had to depend upon the *Sahibul-Kharaj* for money and this checked his power. Thus, out of chaos, he developed an orderly state.

Mu'awiya died in April, 680 A.D., after having ruled the Muslim Empire for about twenty years. On the whole Mu'awiya's rule was prosperous and peaceful at home and successful abroad. "No small measure of the success of the Caliph Mu'awiya should be attributed to the circle of collaboraters with whom he surrounded himself, particularly Amr-bin-al-Aas, the vicegerent over fertile Egypt al-Mughirah, the Governor of turbulent al-Kufa, and Ziyad bin Abih, the ruler of al-Basrah."

Nomination of Yazid :

In 679 A.D. Mua'wiya nominated his son Yazid as his successor. This was certainly a deviation from the principle followed by the Pious Caliphs. The system of leadership among the Arabs even before Islam was never hereditary. This was opposed to the old Arab conception and new Islamic ideals. Probably Mu'awiya thought that absence of any definite rule of succession to the Caliphate was likely to plunge the country into a confused civil war at the death of every Caliph. But this was not so strong a ground as his desire to maintain the Caliphate in his own line. He managed to secure an oath of allegiance for Yazid during his lifetime. He invited deputations in 676 A.D. from all provinces and important cities to take oath of allegiance for his son. Iraq and Syria submitted. Mu'awiya then proceeded to Medina and Mecca to secure the covenant of the people of Hijaz. In Medina the leading citizens including Imam Hussain, the son of Hazrat Ali, Hazrat Abdullah, the son of Caliph Umar, Hazrat Abdur Rahman the son of Abu Bakr, and Hazrat Abdullah, the son of Zubair refused to take an oath on any condition, Hazrat Abdullah bin Zubair was of opinion that Mu'awiya should follow one of the three precedents so far established. "It could be left to the free choice of the citizens as was in the case of Hazrat Abu Bakr. There could be nomination by the reigning Caliph provided the nominee was best by all criteria and was not related to the ruling sovereign. That was what Hazrat Abu Bakr did regarding Hazrat Umar. There could still be a third course, that is, the appointment of a board of electors for the selection of a Caliph. That was what Hazrat Umar did." But Mu'awiya was not convinced by these arguments.

Accession of Yazid :

Yazid had already been nominated by Mu'awiya during his lifetime. Yazid was both cruel and unscrupulous. He was tyrant who knew no piety or justice. His pleasures were as degrading as his companions were low and vicious. He was the most irreligious of the Umayyads. He infinitely preferred wine, music, and sport to the drudgery of public affairs. He was famous for his frivolity and dissipation.

Mu'awiya particularly warned Yazid against Hazrat Abdullah bin Zubair and advised him to deal gently with Imam Hussain after he had got victory over him in reverence to the blood of the Prophet that ran in his veins. Yazid soon after assuming the Caliphate sent orders to leading citizens in Medina calling for oath of allegiance to him. Both Imam Hussain and Hazrat Abdullah bin Zubair refused to acknowledge the Caliphate of Yazid.

The Tragedy of Kerbala :

The Kufans were groaning due to the cruelty and misrule of the Provincial Governor appointed by Yazid. So they decided to help Imam Hussain against Yazid and with that end in view summoned him to Kufa.

Although warned by many against the fickleminded Kufans, Imam Hussain left Medina for Kufa. He had received innumerable letters from the Kufans assuring him of their full support.

Moreover, he had sent Hazrat Muslim bin Aqueel (his cousin) to Kufa to ascertain the real position there. He sent favourable report from there. But later he was caught and killed by Ubaidullah bin Ziyad, Yazid's Governor of Iraq. But the news of his death did not reach Imam Hussain.

The report of Hazrat Muslim encouraged Imam Hussain and he set out with about two hundred of his kinsmen and friends towards Kufa. After crossing the desert of Iraq Imam Hussain received the news of Muslim's death. Advancing forward he met Yazid's cavalry forces under Al-Hurr of Banu Tamin tribe. Keeping Kufa on his right, Imam Hussain and his men proceeded along the western bank of the Euphrates. Meanwhile Obaidullah bin Ziyad sent an army of 4,000 men under Umar bin Sa'd to meet Imam Hussain and his supporters. On the first day of the month of Muharram Imam Hussain pitched his camp on the plains of Kerbala on the bank of the Euphrates at a distance of twenty-five miles to the north of Kufa. Obaidullah pressed upon Umar bin Sa'd not to yield to the request of Imam Hussain, but to push forward and demand unconditional surrender of Imam Hussain. Imam Hussain tried to postpone the battle for some time so that he might reinforce his strength. But finding the opposite side unyielding decided to fight, whatever might be the consequences. Most probably from a sense of honour he did not turn back and refuse to desist from fighting for truth.

On the 9th day of Muharram Imam Hussain suggested to his relatives to return to Medina, but none agreed to that proposal. The infant son of Imam Hussain was then down with fever. Not a drop of water would be given to his parched lips. The women-folk and children passed the night in alarm and suspense. On the 10th of Muharram in the morning Imam Hussain got ready with his small band of followers for the ensuing fight. Ubaidullah sent Shimar to bring Imam Hussain to Kufa dead or alive. In the midst of uproar and lamentation of women and children the battle commenced. The first victim of enemy's attack was Qasim, his nephew, the son of Imam Hasan. One after another fell martyrs. At length the thirsty Imam Hussain with his infant son Hazrat Ali Asghar in his lap proceeded towards the bank of the Euprates, but the arrows of the enemies did not allow him to proceed further. The infant son Hazrat Ali Asghar was hit and killed. At long last Imam Hussain was pierced by an arrow. The profuse bleeding and acute pain compelled him to lie down on the field. At once the enemies fell upon him and severed his head from his body. When the severed head of Imam Hussain, the beloved grandson of the Holy Prophet, be smeared with blood, was placed before Ubaidullah bin Ziyad, people shrank with fear and disgust. As the Governor was turning the head of Imam

Hussain an old man cried aloud, "Gently, it is the Prophet's grandson. By Lord I have seen the very lips kissed by the blessed mouth of the Prophet." The ladies of Hussain's family together with his son Hazrat Ali, later called Imam Zain-ul-Aabidin, were sent to Yazid, who deplored at their fate, treated them with every mark of respect, and sent them to Medina. The coldest heart even melted at his inhuman sight. In the words of Edward Gibbon : "In a distant age and climate the tragic scene of the death of Imam Hussain will awaken the sympathy of the coldest reader."

Thus ended a noble soul. The massacre of Imam Hussain and his family was an event of greatest momentous. The rift that existed between the Hashmies and the Umayyads was further strained and the dissension ultimately weakened the Umayyad power and continued to act as a potent factor for the disintegration of their empire. Whatever may be the historical consequence of the death of Imam Hussain at Kerbala, one thing is clear that it divided the Muslims into hostile camps for all time to come.

The horrors of Kerbala tragedy ran apace throughout the length and breadth of Islamic world. The account of the tragedy added fresh fuel to the hatred and indignation of the people of Medina. They rose in open rebellion against the authority of Yazid. Yazid sent in hasten special Governor to pacify the people. At his suggestion the notables sent a deputation to Yazid to seek redress for Imam Hussain's family. The deputation, however, returned disappointed. Enraged at this, the Medinites under Abdullah bin Hinzala, proclaimed Yazid's deposition and drove his Governor from the city. This made Yazid furious. He sen a large army under Muslim the son of Uqba. The Medinites met the army of Yazid at a place called Harrah, where a desperate battle took place. The Medinites were defeated with terrible loss. "The flower of the Medinite chivalry and the noblest Companions of the Prophet, both *Ansars* and *Muhajirin*, perished in the disastrous fight—disastrous to Islam in more ways than one. The city which had sheltered the Prophet, and which was sanctified by his life and ministry, was foully desecrated." The colleges and hospitals built under the early Caliphs were either closed or demolished, and Arabia relapsed into a wilderness. Medina never recovered her prosperity.

The army then proceeded to Mecca, where Abdullah bin Zubair had set up as a rival Caliph. He came to oppose the army of Yazid. For two months the Holy City was besieged and all cruelties were penetrated against it. In course of the fights that followed great damage was done to the *Kaaba* and other sacred edifices. But in the meantime Yazid died. "Thus ended the inglorious reign of an Umayyad, who is remembered in the Muslim history for his brutal attack on the

Prophet's family and the plunder of the Holy Cities of Mecca and Medina. Muslim tradition regards Imam Hussain as a martyr and Yazid as a murderer.

MU'AWIYA II

(64 A.H./583 A.D.)

Yazid was succeeded by his son Mu'awiya II. He was a man of mild disposition. A period of crisis and uncertainty followed, which witnessed the first ominous appearance of large-scale tribal strife among the Arab themselves. The death of Mu'awiya II after a rule of only six months was followed by and interregnum and the outbreak of the second civil war in Islam. Abdullah bin Zubair had been acknowledged as Caliph all over Hijaz, Iraq and Khorasan. Al-Kufa also went over to Ibn Zubair.

MARWAN I

(64-66 A.H./683-685 A.D.)

On the death of Mu'awiya II, he was succeeded by his brother Khalid. At that time Khalid was a mere boy so the Umayyads refused to acknowledge him as their ruler. The leading Umayyad courtiers elected Marwan, the old counsellor of Hazrat Uthman. He was a cousin of Mu'awiya I, and wielded considerable influence among the Umayyads. He won the support of Khalid's partisans by promising him the Caliphate when he would reach manhood. He also secured the adhesion of Amr, his own cousin, who had a considerable followers in the clan by a similar promise. Meanwhile Abdullah bin Zubair was acclamied Caliph in the Holy Cities. Egypt, Basra and Kufa also acknowledged his authority. The Umayyads in Syria were divided. A part of Syria and even a section of people in Damascus espoused the cause of Abdullah bin Zubair. The house of Umayyad was almost tottering. But age had not dimmed Marwan's genius for intrigue. He won the support of a section of Syrian by bribe and by lavish concessions to their chiefs. Marwan then marched against the partisans of Ibn Zubair. A battle took place at Marj Rahat, a few miles to the north-east of Damascus. It was fortunate for Marwan that Ibn Zubair did not move out of Mecca. Had he moved out of Mecca, Ibn Zubair would have been able to crush the Umayyad dynasity. However, Marwan obtained a victory and the partisans of Ibn Zubair were annihilated. The whole of Syria now passed under the rule of Marwan. Egypt was also regained. Marwan's trouble was not yet over. He had to deal with the Kufan penitents. They were so-called because they repented the desertion of the cause of Imam Hussain and his family. They rose in arms, vowing vengeance upon his murderers

Their leader was Sulaiman. They killed a large number of Umayyads. The Kufans were ultimately defeated by a overwhelming force sent against them by Marwan. Sulaiman and his followers were killed.

Finding his position sufficiently secured, Marwan withdrew his promise to Khalid. He also forced Amr, whom he had also nominated as his successor, to resign the right to the throne in favour of his own sons, Abdul Malik and Abdul Aziz. This arrangement offended the mother of Khalid whom Marwan had married with the object of reconciling the partisans of her son. One day he grossly insulted Khalid and on the same night the enraged mother put Marwan to death. In fact the story of the Umayyads is from now on the story of the Marwanids.

ABDUL MALIK

(66-86 A.H./685-705 A.D.)

Abdul Malik, son of Marwan, after the demise of his father, was inaugurated as Caliph in the year 685 A.D. Under the rule of Abdul Malik the Umayyad Kingdom reached its zenith in power and glory. He represented a new spirit and reflected a lustre on the dynasty.

At his accession and during his first decade as Caliph Abdul Malik was amidst many foes, and like his illustrious predecessor, Mu'awiya, whose counterpart he was, had to face enemies on various fronts. But his courage, resoluteness and wise policy destroyed the valour, vindictive zeal of his rivals. Mukhtar, the leader of the party of penitents, was his chief enemy whose battle cry was the vengeances for Imam Hussain. The revolt of the rival Caliph Abdullah bin Zubair vexed the peace and tranquillity of the Empire of Mesopotamia. Amr bin Sa'id, a cousin of Abdul Malik and Governor of Damascus, also raised the standard of revolt. There outbreak dangerous hostilities between the Mudarites (the Northern Arabs) and the Himyarites (the Southern Arabs) in Khurasan. The Kharijites also rose in revolt against the Umayyads. As a typical Umayyad, Abdul Malik, with his usual extraordinary ability, applied himself happily to the task of consolidating his position on the throne of the Caliphate of Islam in a brave and resolute manner. It would not be unfair to call him the second founder of the Umayyad dynasty.

Rise of Mukhtar :

During Abdul Malik's Caliphate, a scheming adventurer, named Mukhtar cast himself in the rule of avenger of the murder of Imam Hussain. He was the son of Abu Ubaidah, who was killed in the Battle of Bridge (October, 634) waged by Caliph Hazrat Umar for the conquest of Iraq. He professed allegiance to Hazrat Muhammad bin al-Hanfiya, the son of Hazrat Ali by a lady of the Hanifa tribe. Kufa, which was then under the authority of Abdullah bin Zubair, was their first target of attack. Mukhtar quite popular here as the 'Avenger' of Imam Hussain's murder. But the Governor of Kufa suspected Mukhtar of his sinister motives and so he was siezed and cast into prison. Shortly after, Mukhtar was released from the prison and gained possession of Kufa with the help of the Kufan 'Penitents'.

Muktar's main target was Ubaidullah bin Ziad, the man responsible for the tragedy of Kerbala. For this end, Mukhtar sent his army against Ibn Ziad under Malik al-Ashtar. But in the meantime the citizens of Kufa rose in rebellion against Mukhtar and Al-Ashtar was immediately recalled. A terrible conflict ensued and Mukhtar emerged victorious. Finding Mukhtar occupied in Kufa, Ibn Ziad had taken Mosul and was advancing Iraq. Mukhtar hurried off the army under al-Ashtar to meet his enemy. The armies met on the bank of Zab, a tributary of the Tigris, in August, 686 A.D. Al-Ashtar inflicted a crushing defeat on Ubaidullah and Ubaidullah fell among the dead. Thus the tragedy of Kerbala was avenged. This victory made Mukhtar for the moment undisputed master of Mesopotemia.

This resounding victory of Mukhtar roused the jealousy of Abdullah bin Zubair, but the latter had no faith in this ruthless fanatic. Meanwhile the people of Kufa, being oppressed, by the oppressive rule of Mukhtar, approached Mus'ab, brother of Abdullah bin Zubair who was the Governor of Basra. This offered an opportunity to Mus'ab to try arms with Mukhtar. Mus'ab set out for Kufa with a splendidly equipped army. On the approach of Mus'ab to Kufa Mukhtar took refuge in the fort. For several months the siege continued and at last Mukhtar gave a battle in which he was slain. The entire army of Mukhtar, some 8,000 men, were all killed. The movement of the non-Arab Muslims of which Mukhtar was the leader, failed for the present. Fortunately for Abdul Malik this dangerous adventurer was eliminated by Mus'ab. Again Kufa came under the control of Abdullah bin Zubair.

Abdul Malik was so long quiet. He had been watching the bitter strife between Mukhtar and Abdullah bin Zubair in which the former lost his life. He now decided to strike his enemies one after another. He applied himself with extraordinary ability and exemplary courage to strengthen his position. Meanwhile, a rebellion broke out in Syria. Amr bin Sa'id, the cousin of the Caliph declared himself Caliph in Damascus. Abdul Malik sent an army against Amr and after some engagements, he offered an amnesty on which the fighting ceased. A few days later he invited Amr and treacherously murdered him with his own hands.

Having strengthened his position Abdul Malik turned against Mus'ab, brother of Ibn Zubair, who had been ruling Kufa on behalf of his brother. He mobilized force against Mus'ab put to death the leading persons who were connected with him and routed Mus'ab, his son Yahya and his lieutenant Ibrahim bin al-Ashtar. Even he did not spare Anas bin Malik the respected Companion of the Prophet. He had to wear around his neck a collar bearing the viceroy's seal. Human lives to the number of 120,000 were lost in his hands. He is represented by the Arab historians as a blood-thirsty tyrant, a veritable Nero.

We know that during the Caliphate of Mu'awiya, Africa was conquered by Uqba. But the Muslims suffered a terrible reverse in Africa when in 683 A.D. the Berbers, under the leardership of Koseila, rose in rebellion and overwhelmed Uqba, who with his entire army perished in the fight. Abdul Malik sent an army under Zubair for the reconquest of Africa. Zubair was eminently successful in destroying Koseila and the united forces of the Berbers. The whole province was cleared of the enemy. Being encouraged by this success Zubair sent out expeditions for the subjugation of the outlying parts. This proved a fatal mistake. The Greeks and Bebers taking advantage of the absence of his army took Zubair by surprise and cut him to pieces. Africa again slipped out of the hands of the Muslims. Abdul Malik sent another force under Abdul Mailk Hassan bin Nu'man to restore the lost prestige of Islam. He after a hard fight, recaptured Kairwan. The city of Carthage was stormed and the Romans and Berbers were defeated in the open field. About this time the Berbers acknowledged the authority of a woman, who is called by the Arab historians the Kahina. For five years she remained the queen of Africa. She wanted to throw off the Muslim yoke. Abdul Malik despatched another army to the assistance of Hassan. The Kahina then swore allegiance to Abdul Malik. Africa passed once more under the Umayyads.

The death of Mus'ab inflamed the fury of Abdullah bin Zubair who vehemently opposed the authority of Abdul Malik. Abdul Malik ordered Hajjaj bin Yusuf to march against Abdullah who held himself as the Caliph in the Holy City of Mecca. He restored and repaired the House of *Kaaba* that had been subjected to destruction by the army of Yazid. Hajjaj reached Mecca in January, 692 A.D. with a letter of pardon from Abdul Malik to Ibn Zubair, if the latter would submit. Ibn Zubair turned down the offer. Hajjaj then besieged the city and subjected the inhabitants to all violence. The siege of Mecca lasted for seven months. Ibn Zubair lost all hopes and in despair consulted his mother Hazrat Asma, the daughter of Caliph Abu Bakr, whether he should submit to the yoke of the Umayyad or die fighting. "The aged lady, in the heroic spirit of the Arab matron, answered that if he believed in the justness of his cause, it was his duty to fight to the last, but if he thought he was in the wrong, he should submit......Bidding her farewell, he kissed her renderly on the forehead, and then issued sword in hand, determined to conquer or to die. Ibn Zubair died fighting in October, 692 A.D. His head was sent to Damascus. The body of Ibn Zubair was handed cover to his mother Hazrat Asma. Thus ended the life of Abdullah bin Zubair, a man of noble character. He was extremely pious and had won the support and symapathy of al-Hijaz for his claim to the Caliphate. "There was much to admire in Abdullah's character", remarks Ameer Ali, "crafty and ambitious, he was yet cast in a heroic mould, and a strong sense of justice distinguished him from most of his compeers." On the death of Ibn Zubair Abdul Malik was now the undisputed master of the Islamic Empire.

The Kharijites had stolen an opportunity in the contest between Abdullah and Abdul Malik to stir up a spirit of defection. Goaded into fury by the insensate persecution of the tyrannous Umayyad Governors, they fought wildly and reckless of their lives, and after a sanguinary battle they sustained a crushing and ignominous defeat at the hand of Muhallab, a lieutenant of Abdul Malik. The east Iraq thus was cleared of the revolt but he had to lay down his arms before the irresistible onslaught of Hajjaj. After the Khariji menace in Iraq was suppressed, Abdul Malik brought all the eastern parts of the Muslim Empire under his subjection.

Throughout the reign of Abdul Malik the leading figure was undoubtedly Hajjaj bin Yusuf who stands in the annals of Islam as the incarnation of cruelty. For sometime after the sack of Mecca, he remained as the Governor of Arabia but repeated rebellions in Iraq necessitated his appointment as Governor of that province. When he became the Governor he crushed the power of the Kharijites. He also quelled the internal troubles and restored order in Iraq. Peace was granted to those who survived the great killing on condition that they would supply him 25,000 cavalry.

WALID BIN ABDUL MALIK

(86-96 A.H./705-715 A.D.)

After the death of his father Abdul Malik, Walid ascended the throne of Damascus in 705 A.D. His reign inaugurated an era of comparative peace and prosperity. He was fortunate that no internal fued or, dissension disturbed his reign. The Kharijites menace ceased to the best of his reign, for the Kharijites were put down with an iron hand in the time of his father. Walid was fortunate in having under him some generals who possessed uncommon ability and indomitable courage like the heroes of the first generation under Hazrat Abu Bakr and Hazrat Umar. This peace and tranquility naturally led to the expansion of the Empire and its all-round development.

Walid very wisely followed the policy of his father in administrative affairs. He retained the services of Hajjaj as the viceroy of Iraq. To appease the family of Abdul Aziz, who held the title of the Caliphate after Abdul Malik, the former' sson Umar was appointed Governor of Arabia. Umar bin Abdul Aziz distinguished himself as a pious and prudent ruler. Umar bin Abdul Aziz brought considerable developments in the Holy Cities of Mecca and Medina. He beautified and enlarged the mosque of Medina. Walid generously helped him with men and materials. Under Walid's instruction, Umar made all the roads and passes leading towards Mecca easy to the pilgrims. The people of Iraq, repressed and harassed at the hands of Hajjaj, flocked to Arabia to be saved from his tortures. Thus Arabia proved to be an asylum for the oppressed and the down-trodden. Hajjaj complained to the Caliph against Umar bin Abdul Aziz for giving shelter to his notorious subjects and as a result Walid had to yield to the pressure of Hajjaj and removed Umar bin Abdul Aziz from his Governorship.

After the death of Muhallab, his son Yazid was appointed Governor of Khurasan but Hajjaj had certain misgivings against Yazid. Yazid along with his brothers was thrown into prison on the charge of embezzlement, and subjected to the cruelest torture. Yazid, however, succeeded in effecting his escape from the prison house, and took refuge with Sulaiman, the Caliph's brother at Palestine. Through the intercession of Walid the life of Yazid was saved.

Invasions of Qutayba bin Muslim :

Qutayba bin Muslim replaced Yazid as a Governor of Khurasan. Qutayba was a great warrior. He advanced into the central Asian provinces every summer and gained permanent holdings beyond the river Oxus. Qutayba's first advance was directed against Balkh, Tukharistan and Ferghana. In 705 A.D. he recovered Tukharistan with its capital Balkh. The surrounding provinces around Bukhara were subdued (706-709 A.D.). Samarqand threw off the Muslim yoke. Qutayba then proceeded with a large army to meet the situation. The king of Samarqand sued for peace and agreed to pay a heavy tribute (710-713 A.D.). Khwarizam was also conquered. Qutayba then crossed the Jaxartes for the first time and brought the Muslims in touch with the Mongols and the Buddhists. Taking Khojanda, Shash and other cities of Farghana, Qutayba reached Kashghar and the confines of China.

Conquest in Indo-Pakistan :

From a very remote antiquity, the Arabs were renown international traders. They carried on trade also with India. They served as intermediaries in trade between Europe and India. After the advent of Islam, fired with enthusiasm of this new faith of international outlook, the Arabs entered a remarkable carrier of expansion. Their conquest of Persia, however, opened the way for systematic expeditions to Indo-Pakistan. It is reported that as early as 637 A.D., an Arab expedition was sent to plunder the western coasts of Indo-Pakistan. But Caliph Hazrat Umar disapproved this and prohibited further expedition. But after Hazrat Umar's death in 643 A.D., the Arabs conquered Makran (in Baluchistan).

Invasion of Muhammad bin Qasim :

It was during the time of the Umayyads that the Arabs took up the Indian expeditions seriously. The immediate cause for this was that during the period of Caliph Walid some Indian pirates plundered eight vessels full of valuable presents sent by the ruler of Ceylon to the Caliph Walid and his Governor Hajjaj bin Yusuf, near the coast of Debal in Sind. An army was sent by Hajjaj to chastise the pirates and to demand indemnity from Dahir, the then Hindu Raja of Sind. But the punitive expedition failed and Arab general was killed. Hajjaj then vowed vengeance upon the Hindus and set out a fresh expedition under Muhammad bin Qasim. He attacked the Kingdom of Raja Dahir. Raja Dahir tried his best to save his country from the hands of Muslims but was ultimately defeated and killed. The Sind, Multan and a part of the Punjab were annexed to the Muslim Empire.

Muhammad bin Qasim's work of conquest was left incomplete. After his death the Hindus expelled the Muslim Viceroy. But the chief causes of the failure of the Arab power in Sind were : (*a*) the sudden death of Muhammad bin Qasim ; (*b*) the stubborn resistance of the Rajput princes ; (*c*) Sind being a barren and desert land was not attractive for the Arabs, so the

Caliph withdrew his support. Unsupported by the Home-Government the Arabs in Sind continued a very precarious existence. Sind remained a province under the Caliph for a century and half. But when in 871 A.D., the Caliph abandoned his support, Sind became a prey to disorder. The Arab settlers then established small dynasties. These lasted for about three centuries and were eventually conquered by Muhammad Ghori.

Pacification of Africa :

During the Caliphate of Abdul Malik, Hasan bin Nu'man pacified and reconquered Africa. He was succeeded by Musa bin Nusayr to the Governorship of Africa in 708 A.D. The removal of Hasan encouraged the Berbers of North Africa to throw off the Muslim yoke. They had miscalculated the energy and vigour of the new viceroy. He led an army against them and succeeded in suppressing their formidable revolt. By adopting a conciliatory policy, Musa reconciled the Berbers to the rule of Islam. But the Byzantine from the islands of the Mediterranean harassed the Muslims of North Africa. Musa sent out an expedition against them and succeeded in capturing Majorca, Minorca and Ivica. "Under the Muslim rule these islands soon became extremely flourishing. As in other places, the Saracens erected beautiful buildings, introduced various kinds of handicrafts and otherwise materially improved the country."

Conquest of Spain :

The most notable event of Walid's reign was the conquest of Spain. On the eve of the Muslim conquest, the social, political and economic conditions of Spain were in a deplorable state. Spain was a province of the Roman Empire under the Imperial rule. When the Roman Empire was overrun by the Teutonic races, such as Vandals and Visigoths. The Visigoths established their domain over Spain. They became Christian and set up a very inefficient and corrupt government. Whilst Africa was enjoying the blessings of toleration and justice, and was advancing with rapid strides in the path of material prosperity under the Muslim rule, the neighbouring Peninsula of Spain groaned under the iron heel of the Goth. Never was the condition of the country or of the people so bad or so miserable as under the grinding yoke of the Gothic kings."

About this time Musa bin Nusayr ruled over Africa. With his position consolidated in Africa, Musa cast his longing eyes to south-western part of Europe. The kingdom of Spain was then ruled by Roderick. Roderick usurped the throne of Spain by disposing and murdering its former ruler Witiza. Count Julian, the Governor of Ceuta, was highly displeased with Roderick and entered into negotiations with Musa over the suitability of the conquest of Spain. Julian was the son-in-law of Zitiza.

Musa sought for the sanction of Caliph Walid for leading an expedition into Spain. Permission was granted. In 710 A.D. Musa sent Tariq bin Ziyad with few hundred men to the other side of the channel on fact-finding mission. The report was favourable. In 711 A.D. Musa sent Tariq bin Ziyad, whom Musa had appointed Governor of Tangier, with 12,000 men to fight Roderick. When Roderick received the news of Muslim invasion, he hastened to repel the invader with 100,000 men. The two armies unequally matched in numbers met in the valley of the Wadi Lakho. A furious battle was followed for seven days. Tariq offered intense opposition to Roderick on the bank of the Guadalete. "The sons of Qitiza and also his brother Bishop Oppas, who had joined Roderick at his request and led the two wings of the Spanish army, broke away from the main force after the first onslaught, not because they wanted the Muslims to succeed but because they hated the usurper and desired his downfall." Tariq was irresistible and the Gothic army was completely routed. Roderick was drowned in his flight.

The victory was followed by the capture of Malaga and Granada. Cordova fell without much difficulty after two months' siege. Tariq, guided by Count Julian, marched towards Toledo, the then Gothic capital. Toledo fell almost without any resistance into the hands of the Muslims. Bishop Oppas was appointed Governor of Toledo. In recognition of his services Count Julian was given the province of Ceuta. Treaties were made with various cities. In many causes the terms granted were more favourite than had been the case under the Gothic rule. Christians and Jews were left completely undisturbed, but they had to pay a fixed tribute. The conquered subjects were mostly Christians, but gradually a number of them embraced Islam.

These exploits of Tariq attracted the attention of Musa who now set out with a large army of 18,000 men and landed in Spain in 712 A.D. Musa chalked out new line of victory and stormed Sidonia and Carmona. The city of Merida fell after a prolonged siege. Musa met Tariq near Toledo, received him angrily, struck him on his head with his whip and demanded an account of the booty. Friendly relations were, however, restored. The two generals then separated—Tariq for Saragossa and Musa for Astorga and Salamanca. By the joint effort of Musa and Tariq, Saragossa was stormed. Musa, then occupying Taragona and Barcelona, reached as far even as to Gerona on the French border. In the mean time the news of Musa's ill-behaviour with Tariq reached Damsacus and the Caliph recalled Musa from Spain in 713 A.D.

Before leaving Spain Musa made all necessary arrangements for the administration of the newly conquered country. He appointed his son, Abdul Aziz, the Viceroy of the new province,

Abdullah, another son and a great warrior, was left in charge of Africa ; whilst Abdul Malik, the youngest ruled over Morocco, and Abdus Saleh held the command of the coast and of the fleet, with Tangiers for his headquarters.

The Muslim conquest of Spain opened a new and glorious chapter in the history of the country. "The conquest of Spain, which is told by Muslim historians with many romantic circumstances, marks the nearest approach that the Arabs ever made to world-Empire." The peninsula of Spain was saved from the tyranny, corruption and misrule of the Goths, and a new regime of justic and equity was established. The principle of universal brotherhood was extended to all. Individual liberty and civic rights were given to the people. It swept away the cruel rights and powers of the privileged classes. The people were freed from grinding taxation, and an equitable system of taxation was introduced in the country. The earning members of non-Muslim families had to pay *jizya*, but it was extremely light in its incidence, for it varied according to the means of the payer. But people leading a monastic life, and women and children in general, were exempt from this tax. The slaves and the serfs were freed. Trade and commerce were fostered. Agriculture was promoted by irrigation. The cultivators peacefully carried on their agricultural works without any interference from the landlord.

Religious toleration was granted to the Jews and Christians. No one was troubled about his faith ; every man, woman, or child was free to worship as he liked. They were allowed to be governed in accordance with their own laws and by their own judges. "The Christians themselves preferred the mild, generous and beneficent rule of the Saracen to the grinding tyranny of the Goth or Frank, and flocked back into the cities and villages which they had at first abandoned through terror. Never was Andalusia so mildly, justly, and wisely governed as by her Arab conquerors."

Hajjaj bin Yusuf :

Al-Hajjaj, the young school master of Taif in Hijaz, who had laid down the pen and taken up the sword in support of the tottering Umayyad throne, was appointed Governor of Arabia by Caliph Abdu Malik. In two years Hajjaj, pacified Hijaz and with it Yaman and even Yamamah to the east. He was summoned by Abdul Malik to perform a similar task in turbulent and dissatisfied Iraq, whose people were men of Schism and hypocrisy. Here the Alids and the Kharijites had continuously made trouble for the Umayyads. In disguise accompanied by twelve cameleers he suddenly appeared in Kufa. The proclamation of his policy in unequivocal terms showed the Iraqis from the very start that his would be no kid-glove methods of dealing with a disloyal populace.

He perpetrated almost reign of terror in Kufa and the same scene was enacted in Basra. In fact no head proved too mighty for the relentless Umayyad viceroy to crush, no neck too high for him to reach. Even Anas bin Malik, the respected companion of the Prophet, accused of sympathy with the opposition, had to suffer in the hands of this tyrant. Human lives to the number of 120,000 are said to have been sacrificed by this Governor of Iraq, who is resented by the Arab historians, as a blood-thirsty tyrant, a veritable Nero.

Hajjaj continued to govern the Eastern provinces even after the death of Abdul Malik. He appointed Qutayba bin Muslim as the Governor of Khurasan. This great warrior advanced into the central Asian provinces every summer and gained permanent holdings beyond the river Oxus. Another important event in 712 A.D. in the eastern theatre of war was the conquest of Sind by Muhammad bin Qasim, a cousin and also son-in-law of Hajjaj bin Yusuf.

SULAIMAN

(96-99 A.H./715-717 A.D.)

Walid bin Abdul Malik was succeeded by his brother Sulaiman who proved himself an unworthy son and an unworthy brother. In his short reign of two and-a-half years, he did many foolish things. He was disposed favourably towards the Yemen Arabs and hated the Hijaz Arabs. He was fond of pleasure and good cheer. Immediately upon his accession Sulaiman opened the prison-doors and freed the people who were imprisoned by Hajjaj bin Yusuf. He removed the revenue-collectors appointed by Hajjaj, and abolished most of the oppressive taxes. "Had he rested content with removing the burdens that had been laid upon the people by Hajjaj there would have been nothing unworthy to record of him." But Sulaiman had a grudge against Hajjaj who supported Walid when he wanted to set aside the right of succession of him (Sulaiman) in favour of his (Walid's) son. Hajjaj was fortunate to die before Walid and thereby escaped the wrath of Sulaiman but it fell with terrible severity on his family and adherents.

It has already been discussed that Walid recalled Musa from Spain on account of the quarrel that had taken place between the latter and Tariq. When Musa reached the capital Walid had died. Sulaiman deposed him from all commands and cast him into prison. He laid such heavy demands upon him that he was reduced to poverty and when released from the prison, he was forced to beg from door to door in order to earn his livelihood. Sulaiman is even suspected of having connived at the murder of Abdul Aziz, the son of Musa, whose administration of Spain had been so successful and prosperous.

Tariq also retired from active life and he died in obsecurity. In Khurasan, the great general Qutayba also rose in revolt against the new Caliph and was killed in the civil war that broke out afresh between the Yemen Arabs and Hijaz Arabs. Yazid bin Muhallab, who fell from favour during the Caliphate of Walid returned to power again as Governor of Khurasan. To please the Caliph he undertook expeditions to Jurjan and Tabaristan and sent eneormous booties to him.

Sulaiman was persuaded to send a costly expedition against Constantinople at the instance of Leo, a Byzantine general. To ensure success this double-faced traitor offered himself to act as a guide to the invaders. Dazzled by the prospect of success, Sulaiman sent an army under Maslamah. He crossed the Hellespont without any opposition and laid siege to the city. The Romans offered Maslamah a large subsidy to raise the siege. This was refused, and the Romans were reduced to submission. The Roman king Theodorius II who ruled Constantinople, was either killed or deposed, and Leo was raised to the throne. The Muslim troops were defeated and after one year of siege they withdrew. The Muslim army also suffered from hunger, pestilence and frost. But such was the prestige of Muslim army, that the Christian world, instead of being triumphant at the repulse of the Muslims heaved a sigh of relief that their advance in this area was checked for a time. On the Western front, however, al-Hurr bin Abdul Rahman the Muslim Governor of Spain who succeeded Musa bin Nusayr, crossed the Pyrenees and invaded France.

Sulaiman died at Dabik on the Byzantine frontier after a short and not very glorious reign. On his death-bed he nominated Umar bin Abdul Aziz as his successor. Sulaiman's character was made up of contradictions. Generous towards his partisans, he was as cruel, as his father, towards the enemies.

UMAR BIN ABDUL AZIZ

(99-101 A.H./717-720 A.D.)

Sulaiman was succeeded by Umar bin Abdul Aziz, a ruler who stands out in singular contrast with his predecessors, and whose brief reign is regarded by many Muslims as the sole bright spot in a century of godless and bloodstained tyranny. There had been nothing like it since the days of his illustrious namesake and kinsman, Hazrat Umar bin al-Khattab. His mother, Umme Asim, was a grand-daughter of Hazrat Umar-I. His reign opened a happy augury for the people as well for the empire. He was exemplarily religious and devotedly pious, whose business in life was to promote the well-being of the subjects. He is regarded by the Muslims as the fifth pious Caliph. He was the symbol of simplicity. So great was his piety that even the fanatical Kharijites recognised him as one of the lawful Caliphs of Islam. Pious and upright, simple and austere he inaugurated an interlude of peace and justice.

The rule of Umar was a marked departure from all pompous display of the Umayyads. When he assumed the office of the Caliphate the royal grooms brought before him the finest steeds to choose from. But he preferred his own humble equipage. He had the horses of the royal stables sold by public auction and the proceeds deposited in the *Baital-mal.* He also asked his wife to return to the treasury all the jewellery and valuable presents she had received from her father and brothers and she ungrudgingly complied. He then called upon his Umayyad kinsmen to surrender their properties for the state. The garden of Fedak which belonged to the family of the Holy Prophet and which had been appropriated by Marwan, was given back to the heirs of the Prophet. He ordered for the discontinuance of the practice of cursing from the pulpit the sacred memory of the Caliph Hazrat Ali and his descendants. Certain properties in Mecca was restored to the family of Talha. "Laxity of morals was reprehended ; the smallest oppressionment with condign punishment ; and the burdens imposed by Hajjaj and his myrmidons on the converts of Iraq, Khurasan and Sind were removed." Poets and orators found no favour at his court, which was thronged by divines and men of ascetic life. He warned his Governors that they must either deal justly or go. He would not allow political consideration to interfere with his ideal of righteousness, but, as Wellhausen points out, "he had practical ends in view of his piety made him anxious for the common meal no less than for his own salvation."

Umar was above party bias. He was in the habit of appointing the pious, the honest and the efficient. His sense of justice was very keen and he gave more importance to the Qazi than to the Governor. He was a veritable father of his people, but at the same time he was very prompt in punishing the dishonest. Thus Yazid bin Muhallab was thrown into prison on the charge of embezzlement. To his Governors, Caliph Umar gave the following instructions : "Do not think lightly of any sin ; do not try to depopulate what is populous ; do not try to exact from the subjects anything beyond their capacity ; take from them what they can give ; do everything to improve population and prosperity ; govern mildly and without harshness ; do not accord presents on festive occasions ; do not take the price of sacred books (distributed among the people) ; impose no tax on travellers, or on marriages, or on the milk of camels ; and do not insist on the poll-tax from any one who has become a convert to Islam."

Though a zealous Muslim he was tolerant to the Christians and Jews. The Christians of Damascus appealed to him to give them back the Cathedral of St. John, which Walid had seized from them and converted it into a mosque. It was difficult for Umar to concede to this demand but he allowed them to have the Church of St. Thomas which was not theirs by right. The Jews of Najran has to pay nearly 2,000 pieces of cloth as tribute in spite of great decrease in their number. During the Caliphate of Umar II, their number had decreased from 40,000 to 4,000. Umar, therefore, reduced their tribute from 2,000 pieces of cloth to 200. Umar was, however, not in favour of the employment of the Jews and Christians to the Government services. He issued an order to his Governors to this effect that none but the Muslims would be appointed to office of trust. But he restored to the Christians and the Jews the churches and synagogues to which they were entitled under the ancient capitulations, and which had been wrongfully taken away from them.

The new-converts of Mawali so long occupied an intermediary position between the Arab-Muslims and the non-Muslims. Umar announced that these Mawali must be placed on a footing of equality with the Arabs. Under his rule, the Mawali were exempted from taxes of *kharaj* and *jizya* and provisions were made so that they might receive pensions from the state. This provided the great incentive for conversion and multitudes began to flock to the Faith.

The short, Caliphate of Umar II, though devoid of stirring events, is highly attractive due to certain new and noble features in the fabric of the Government. The striking feature in his revenue administration was the revival of the old system introduced by Hazrat Umar I. He prohibited landownership by the Muslims in foreign land. The customary *jizya* was abandoned and *kharaj* was excused to the landholders. He made it a principle that a Muslim whether of first rank or second, whether of pure blooded Arab or Mawali, need pay no tribute and forbade the Muslims to devote themselves to agricultural pursuits in foreign countries. But Umar II did not succeed in this financial policy since the royal treasury was highly depleted due to the exemption of taxes and ever-increasing conversion to Islam. The children of the fighting Arabs used to receive pensions during the pious Caliphs, but this system had been curtailed by Mu'awiya, and withheld by Abdul Malik. Umar II restored pensions to the children of the fighting Arabs. His policy ruined the machinery of the Government because his attachment to the old and patriarchal system of taxation was no longer suitable to the demand of the time. Though inspired by the best of intentions, Umar's policy was not successful. Umar died at the age of 39 and was buried at Dair Simon near Hims.

YAZID II

(101-105 A.H./720-724 A.D.)

Umar II was succeeded by Yazid II, the third son of Abdul Malik. His reign marked the revival of conflict between the Mudarites and the Yamanites. Yazid was married to a niece of Hajjaj, and all his predilections and sympathies were on the side of the Mudarites. Umar II had carefully maintained the balance between the two rival tribes. Under Yazid the Yamanites were to feel full-weight of Mudarite revenge. This was in part the result of the harsh, not to say cruel policy which had been pursued under Sulaiman by Yazid bin Muhallib against the family of Hajjaj to make them disgorge their ill-gotten gains. Even the niece of Hajjaj, the wife of Yazid II was not spared. During the reign of Umar II, Yazid bin Muhallib was cast into prison. When Yazid bin Muhallib heard in his prison at Aleppo that Umar II was ill, he bribed the guards and escaped to Iraq where he raised the standard of revolt against the succeeding Caliph Yazid II whom he considered as his great enemy.

When Yazid II came to power, he, being influenced by his wite, determined to the vengeance on Yazid bin Muhallib. The Caliph mobilised a huge army under Muslama against Yazid bin Muhallib. The two contending armies met on the battlefield of Akra, on the right bank of the river Euphrates. The result was that Yazid bin Muhallib was defeated and slain. The effect of the rising of Muhallib and his ultimate death was very great. The rivalry between these two camps convulsed the whole Arab empire into a series of bloody strifes which weakened the Arabs.

Yazid proved a worthless king. The Kharijites who, during the last reign, had refrained from acts of aggression, now issued against the man whom they considered an unjust and ungodly tyrant. Yazid had a great passion for *Harem* life. Durıng his reign a slave-girl Habbaba and a songstress Sallama were great favourites of the Caliph and their influence was supreme at the Court. The death of Habbaba so overwhelmed him with grief that he died a few days later. The annalist records one meritorious act to the credit of this monarch which is worthy of note. His Governor at Medina had proposed to marry Fatima, the daughter of Imam Husain, the martyr. The lady refused his proposal. The tyrant threatened her with ill treatment. Fatima appealed to Yazid. Yazid deposed the Governor and severely punished him.

Yazid's short and inglorious reign only has tened the process of disintegration of the Umayyad empire. It was in this reign that the propaganda in favour of the descendants of Abbas began to be actively prosecuted.

HISHAM

(105-125 A.H./724-743 A.D.)

On the death of Yazid II, his brother Hisham ascended the throne. He had to confront serious difficulties on his accession. The peace and tranquillity of the Empire was disturbed by conflicts between the Umayyads and the Hashimites. The Abbasid propaganda has already cast slurred light on the fortunes of the dynasty. His mild and upright administration did a lot to restore peace and prosperity but all his virtues could not make amends for the misdeeds of his predecessors and the dynasty was on its downward move towards the unhappy fall. In this gravest hour of peril there were a number of other troubles, the incursion of Turkomans and Khazars from north, the rivalry between the Mudarites and Yamanites (Himyarites) and the rise of the fanatical Kharijites.

What was perhaps more dangerous, as far the Umayyads were concerned, was the rising of the Abbasid movement against their house. The Abbasid movement mobilised all the discontented elements and with their help and co-operation dealt a death-blow to the tottering empire. The leader of this movement was Muhammad, the great grandson of Abbas, the Prophet's own uncle. Muhammad cleverly advanced the claim of Hashimites to the throne as against the discredited Umayyads whose indifference to the cause of Islam was constantly emphasized. The Shiaites and Kharijites, and the religious Muslims as well the public firmly supported the Abbasid movement, hoping to be relieved from Umayyad tortures and misrule. Thus the Hashimites were united in a common cause against the Umayyads.

Khalid-al-Qasri :

The conflict between the Yamanites (Himyarites) and Mudarites created an acute problem in the Caliphate. The Caliph appointed Khalid-al-Qasri Governor in the eastern regions. A man of enlightened views, and himself a Yamanite, Khalid held the balance between the two rival stocks with tact and judgment, and during the whole of his administration there was hardly any trouble. His treatment of the Christians and Jews was considerate, just and liberal ; he repaired their churches, and threw open to them offices of emolument and trust. His wise and statesmanlike tolerance exposed him to the attacks of fanatics. He effectively kept in check the Kharijites of Iraq and fought fiercely with them. But unfortunately for the Umayyads Khalid after long years of faithful service incurred the displeasure of his master, who dismissed him in 737 A.D. His successor Yusuf reversed his policy to the Jews and the Christians, and earned the hatred of the Shiah by persecuting the family of Hazrat Ali. Zaid bin Ali, a grandson of Imam Husain was accepted by a section of people in Kufa and its surroundings, as Caliph. News of this reached Yusuf, who kept himself in readiness when a party of Zaid's followers rose in revolt in Kufa. In the battle that followed Zaid was defeated and killed (740 A.D).

Throughout the twenty years of Hisham's reign there were serious troubles in Khurasan. There was a violent conflict between the Mudar and the Himayar. The newly converted Muslims in Sughdiana rose in revolt against the Deputy Governor who after promising the remission of the taxes to such people as would embrace Islam, tried to re-impose the taxes. The insurgents were joined by some of the colonists under an Arab chief named Haris. They also received support from the head of the Turkoman hordes who roamed towards the west of Transoxiana. Serious efforts were made to quell the insurrection, but without success. At last Khalid, the Viceroy of Iraq, deputed his brother Asad to restore order in the disturbed province. Asad proved an utter failure and was succeeded by Nasr bin Sayyar. Nasr was a man of moderate views. He succeeded in settling the difference between the Mudar and the Himayar. The Sughdiana were also brought back to allegiance by promise of good treatment. Nasr conducted the administration of the province with reputation.

Whilst these events were taking place in Central Asia, the Muslims in Armenia were hard pressed by the formidable Turkish hordes of the Khazars and the Alans. The Muslim Army under Al-Jarrah was destroyed and the general himself was slain in 730 A.D. A fresh levy was sent to the Muslim army. The calamity as thus retrieved, and after repeated engagements the Khazars were driven back and the family of Jarrah was recovered. Then the Caliph's brother Muslama was sent to take command of the country. Muslama ravaged the whole country when he was too overtaken by the Turkomans and lost his life in a fight. It was now Marwan (grandson of Marwan I) who was sent as Governor of Armenia and the Caspian border. He beat back the Khazars and recovered the country as far as the Caspian Sea.

Hisham also revived the war with the Byzantines The expeditions were led by the two sons of the Caliph. The Muslims were successful and the hero of these campaigns was al-Battal. He, however, lost his life in a battle in 740 A.D.

It was no fault of his that the empire had already declined. His virtues alone failed to prevent this downward move. Moreover, the Abbasid propaganda had carefully undermined the foundation of the dynasty and the empire.

Hisham was a keen patron of arts and letters. Von Kremer writes that "Hisham bin Abdul Malik unquestionably one of the ablest of the Umayyad sovereigns, was as much a warrior as a scholar." Hisham's Chief Secretary Salim was a renowned man of letters. He had translated some works of Aristotle in Arabic.

Campaigns in Africa :

There were great reverses in Africa where the Muslims suffered greatly. The whole of North Africa was convulsed by the revolt of the Berbers and the Kharijites. A new sect of fanatics called Saffarides had about this time appeared in Mauritania. The oppressive rule of the viceroy's son, who was active on behalf of his father at Tangiers, roused them to fury marched towards Kairowan. The Muslim army which opposed the enemy, was destroyed in the battle known as "the Fight of the Nobles." This defeat threw into disorder the whole of Northern Africa. Hearing this disaster, Hisham then appointed Kulsum to the command of the Muslim army in 937 A.D. But Kulsum also proved failure. Hisham then appointed Hanzala to the Governorship of Africa. "He combined the religious enthusiasm of the days of Omar with gentleness of heart unusual in that age. Standing in the great square in front of the Cathedral Mosque, he addressed the people that the struggle between the pent-up Muslims and the rebels outside was one of life and death, that a Berber victory would mean the promiscuous slaughter of the inhabitants, in which neither age nor sex would be spared. Hanzala succeeded in restoring peace and prosperity in North Africa by defeating the Berbers and the Kharijites in the battle known as "the Field of Idols." One hundred and eighty thousand Berbers, with their principal leaders, are said to have been killed in the fight, whilst the Sarcenic loss, though severe, was not so great. So long Hanzala held the reins of office the country was free from disturbance. Under his mild and just government North Africa soon recovered its prosperity.

Affairs in Spain and France :

In Spain also disorder and revolt reigned supreme. After the death of As-Samh in the battle of Toulouse, Abdur Rahman was elected by the army in his place, but he held the office only fór a few months. Anbasah was appointed to the Governorship of Spain in 721 A.D. He succeeded in restoring order to some extent. Shortly after Hisham's accession Anbasah crossed the Pyrenees with a view to restore the shattered prestige of the Muslim arms in France. Carcassone was stormed ; Nimes fell into the hands of the Muslims and the whole of Southern France was overrun. "The conquests of Anbasah," writes a Christian historian, "were due more to tact and management than to force ; and his efforts to conciliate the good-will of the inhabitants strengthened the Saracenic positions in Southern France." Anbasah was killed in 725 A.D. Abdur Rahman again resumed command after six years in 731 A.D. His appointment was hailed by all in Spain. Abdur Rahman proved himself as the ablest and the most patriotic ruler that country ever had under the Umayyad domination. "Animated by a natural desire to avenge the check sustained by the Saracens before Toulouse, and envious to emulate the glorious achievements of Tariq and Musa, he persistently endeavoured to create an army which would prove irresistible in its advance towards the north." He marched with a vast army and subjected the whole county up to Poitiers. He also defeated Usman bin Abu Nessa, the Muslim Governor of the province beyond the Pyrenees who in concert with the Duke of Aquitaine raised the standard of revolt. It was then the Duke of Aquitaine, realising the danger, appealed to the Frankish king Charles Martel to come to his help. Charles, readily responded and with a vast army marched to the south. Abdur Rahman met the combined army of the enemy at Tours, on the southern bank of the Loire river in northern France. The Muslims, though outnumbered by the vast multitude of the fighting forces of Christendom, fought with reckless bravery as usual and pierced the steel-clad wall of the Franks again and again. The battle lasted three days. On the third day Abdur Rahman was struck down by an arrow. The fall of general threw the whole army into disorder and the Christians, committed great havoc. When night fell, the Muslim Amirs assembled in a council ; they debated long on whether they should continue or retreat. They saw that the Franks were very strong and victory over them was now out of the question. They therefore decided to retreat. "On the plains of Tours" says Ameer Ali, "the Arabs lost the empire of the world when almost in their grasp. In subordination and intertribal jealousies which have been the curse of Moslem communities, led to the disastrous issue." "To the Christians it meant the turning point in the military fortunes of their eternal foe. Gibbon and after him other historians, would see in Paris and London mosques, where Cathedrals now stand, and would hear the Qur'an instead of the Bible expounded in Oxford and other seats of learning, had the Arabs won the day."

WALID II

(125-126 A.H./743-744 A.D.)

Hisham was succeeded by Walid II, son of Yazid II. He is described by the Arabian writers as "a libertine, a wine-drinker, and a breaker of the divine commands". He did not observe the ordinary rules of morality and led a corrupt and wicked life. At the outset he showed kindness to the poor, the lame, and decrepit and thereby won popularity. But this popularity was neutralised and made abortive by a fickle temperament and debased nature, which often ended in cruel deeds. He proved extremely cruel to his cousins, the sons of Walid. Khalid-al-Qasri was made over to his cruel enemy Yusuf, who put him to death. It was during his reign that Yahya, son of Zaid, the Alid, was most cruelly put to death. Profane and dissolute Walid soon alienated the sympathy of the people. Yazid, the son of Walid raised the standard of revolt against him. The Yamanites who suffered terribly at the hands of Walid whole-heartedly supported Yazid. The people attacked his palace and put him to death.

YAZID III

(126 A.H./744 A.D.)

Upon the death of Walid II, Yazid was raised to the throne. He was a just and religious ruler. He reduced certain taxes and removed the dishonest officers of the state. "Had he lived long enough it is probable that he would have proved a capable sovereign, but his reign too short and too disturbed to admit of reform or improvement." He died after a reign of six months. He was followed by his brother Ibrahim, who ruled barely for two months and ten days. He is not included in the category of the Caliph.

MARWAN II

(127-132 A.H./744-750 A.D.)

The Last of the Ummayyads :

Marwan II ascended to the throne when the Umayyads were passing through a period of great turmoil and strife. The conflicting forces were at work to undermine his authority. The Yamanites who had failed to secure his favour remained hostile to him. They revolted against his authority wherever it was possible. The Kharijites attempted to create distrubances in different parts of the country. The Abbasid propaganda was also spread over with greater intensity in the eastern part of the empire. As a result of these troubles Hims and Palestine first rose to rebellion which was suppressed with great difficulty. The Kharijites revolted in Iraq which was followed by revolts and rebellions in other parts of the empire.

The main centre of trouble was Khurasan where the Abbasids concentrated their activities. The quarrel between the Himyarites and the Mudarites were going on in full swing. The Abbasids fully utilised this anarchical condition in the East. Abu Muslim, the leader of the Abbasids, was planting successfully the banner of the Abbasids in different cities of the east. Abu Muslim issued a manifesto inviting the followers of Hashimites to rise. On the 25th of Ramazan, 129 A.H. (May, 747), the people were summoned, and vast multitudes, all clothed in black, in sign of mourning for the chiefs that had fallen or been murdered, flocked to the hill-top lighted by large bonfires. The black banner of the Abbasids was unfurled. The Umayyad garrisons were expelled from Herat and other places in the Far East. At the head of a Yamani tribe Abu Muslim entered Merv, the capital of Khurasan. Nasr, the Governor of Khurasan, was defeated by Kahtaba, General of Abu Muslim. Nasr appealed to Marwan for help. Marwan was so busy with the Kharijites that he could not respond to the appeal of Nasr immediately. However, Marwan directed the viceroy of Iraq to despatch reinforcements for the assistance of Nasr. But it came too late. Khurasan and Farghana had fallen entirely into the hands of Abu Muslim. Kahtaba pursued Nasr and inflicted on him a defeat which completely demoralised the Syrian forces. Nasr then fled towards Fars, but died on the way.

Meanwhile, the political condition of the eastern provinces started deteriorating. Marwan appointed spies to find out the man who was the originator of the risings. It was discovered that the descendant of Abbas, Ibrahim was the man for whom Abu Muslim was working. Marwan had him arrested. But this had no effect on the fortunes of the Abbasid movement. Kahtaba, the famous General of Abu Muslim, then advanced westward. He was accompanied by Khalid bin Barmak who became the founder of the Barmakid family. They crossed the Euphrates and came to the field of Kerbala where Imam Husain fell fighting. A fierce and sanguinary battle took place in which Yazid, the Umayyad Governor of Iraq was defeated. Kahtaba was either drowned in the river or fell on the field. His son Hasan took command and forced Yazid to retire to Wasit. Thus Kufa was captured.

Soon after Ibrahim died through a house falling over him. Before his death Ibrahim nominated his brother Abdullah Abdul Abbas as his successor. Thus in the mosque of Kufa Abdul Abbas was proclaimed the Caliph of the Muslim Empire in Oct., 749 A.D. Abu Salama, who had been one of the busy agents of the Hashimites in Khurasan was designated as "the Wazir of the House of Muhammad." Abdul Abbas assumed the title of "As Saffah" or blood-thirsty.

Meanwhile, events were progressing rapidly in the East. In 749 A.D. Marwan's son was defeated by Abu Ayun. Marwan resolved to fight the last desperate battle with the Abbasids. He collected a strong army of 120,000 and crossed the Tigris and advanced upon the Greater Zab. The Abbasid forces was headed by Abdullah bin Ali, an uncle of the Caliph. Here the Syrian army was defeated and Marwan took to flight. At Damascus, the Umayyads offered some resistance ; but the city was stormed, and the Governor was slain, and the capital of Syria and practically of the whole empire, passed into the hands of the Abbasids. Marwan was followed from place to place, at last he was found in Egypt and slain. Thus came an end to the career of one of the vigorous rulers of the time and with him perished the Umayyad dynasty.

Causes of the Fall of the Umayyads

There are many causes which contributed to the downfall of the Umayyads.

According to Ibn Khaldun, the decline of a dynasty is a natural phenomenon of history. The effective life of a dynastic empire could not be more than the span of the life of a human being. And a period of hundred years is generally the largest term that a man can expect to live. "This natural form can only be avoided by a thorough reform. The Umayyad dynasty had existed about ninety years and family had already degenerated beyond all recovery."

Mu'awiya set aside the principle of election and declared Yazid as his heir-apparent. Republicanism was replaced by hereditary monarchy. The principle of Islam that the head of the state must be elected by the people was ceased to be operated. Thus the Umayyads lacked the full support and co-operation of the people.

The weakness of the ruling family was the first and foremost cause of the fall of the Umayyad dynasty. Among the Caliphs with the exception of Mu'awiya, Abdul Malik, Walid I, and Umar II, all others were weak and incompetent. Hisham was the fifth and last true statesman of the Banu Umayyah. His four successors proved incapable if not dissolute and degenerate. Even before the time of Hisham, it became the fashion for the Caliph, as exemplified by Yazid II, to pass time in chase and over wine-cup and to be absorbed more in music and poetry than in the Qur'an and state-affairs. Due to increased wealth and a super abundance of slaves, was rampart. Even the reigning family could no longer boast of pure Arabian blood. Yazid III was the first Caliph in Islam born of a slave mother. His two successors were also sons of such freed women. The characteristic vices of civilization, especially those involving wine, women and song, had seized upon the sons of desert and were beginning to sap the vitality of the youthful Arab society. In the words of Von Kremer, "The rule of the Umayyads was regarded by their contemporaries in no way as a continuation of the rule of the Prophet and his Companions, inasmuch as it rested not upon Islam which was the mainstay and strength of the first Caliphs, but upon conquering force. This fact, indeed, formed the greatest source of weakness to the Umayyads and explained the constant opposition to their rule raised in the name of Allah and His Prophet, which the Umayyads had ever and alone to face and overcome.

Non-Arabian Muslims in general and Persian Muslims in particular had good reasons for dissatisfaction. The Umayyad

Caliphs displayed throughout a hostile attitude towards them. Far from being granted the expected economic and social equality with Arabian Muslims, they were instead generally reduced to the position of clients. These Mawali Muslims had genuine grievances against the Umayyads. Von Kremer rightly states: "The utterly unsympathetic policy of the Umayyads towards their subject races endangered more than anything else existence of this dynasty. It inaugurated that tremendous social movement which was directed against not them alone but against the entire Arab rule."

Mu'awiya had initiated the wise and farsighted policy, though undemocratic, of nominating his son as successor, but the antiquated Arabian tribal principle of seniority in succession stood in constant conflict with the natural ambition of the ruling father to pass the sovereignty to his son. Of the fourteen Umayyad Caliphs only four, Mu'awiya I, Yazid I, Marwan I, and Abdul Malik had their sons as immediate successors. The already complicated problem was rendered more complicated by the precedent established by Marwan who designed his son Abdul Malik as his successor, to be followed by his second son Abdul Aziz. Abdul Malik also tried to divert the succession from his brother Abdul Aziz to his son Walid, in the meantime designating his other son Sulaiman as the second nominee. Walid in his turn made an unsuccessful effort to deprive his brother Sulaiman of his right in favour of his own son. All these manoeuvres were, of course, far from being conducive to the stability and continuity of the regime.

Negligence in administrative affairs and lack of interest in public works on the part of many Umayyad Caliphs made the Umayyad rule very unpopular. The officials were corrupt and selfish. The Caliphs entrusted the administrative works mostly to the selfish corrupt officials and nobles, who looked more to their own interests, and the interests of the people and country suffered at large. As a result the administration became slack and inefficient.

The age-long tribal rivalry weakened the Umayyad dynasty. Islam temporarily united the warring Arab tribes but the old tribal feud began to reassert itself. The tribes of Rabia were sharply divided into the northern Arabs, also called Mudarites, who generally inhabited Iraq and the southern Arabs, the Yamanites (Himyarites) who were mainly inhabiting Syria. The Umayyad Caliphs supported one section of the Arabs against the other according to their suitability. This policy convulsed the whole Arab empire into a series of bloody strife between the two sections. The polarisation of the Muslim world by this dualism of two groups, precipitated the downfall of the Umayyad dynasty.

The opposition of the Shias too was a factor of no less importance. They never forgot the tragedy of Kerbala and the subsequent indifference and ill-treatment to the Prophet's family. The cursing on Hazrat Ali in the Khutba and propaganda against the Alids strengthened the anti-Umayyad movement. The Shias secured the sympathy of the people by their whole-hearted devotion to the descendants of the Prophet.

Lastly, the Abbasid movement dealt a death-blow to the tottering empire. This movement cleverly put the claim of the Abbasids to the Caliphate as the descendants of the Prophet. The Shias and the supporters of Alids also supported this movement. The Kharijites and non-Arab Muslims (Mawali) were also cleverly brought in this movement.

Abu Muslim, the leader of the revolt, was peculiarly fitted for the task entrusted to him by the Abbasid Imam. An impassive exterior, which no adversity or success could affect, however slightly, concealed a pitiless and cruel heat. "The gravest events could hardly disturb the serenity of his countenance" says an old author. "He received the news of the most important victories without expressing the least symptom of joy; under the greatest reverses of fortune he never betrayed the slightest uneasiness; and when angered, he never lost his self-command." A Machiavellian dexterity in playing upon the vanity of Mudhar and Himyar and the bitterness which animated both, enabled him to carry out his design with sufficient immunity from either side.

Abu Muslim championed the cause of the House of Al-Abbas. Khurasan became the centre of Abu Muslim's activity. The condition of the country was very favourable. The high handedness of Hajjaj bin Yusuf alienated the sympathy of the people of the eastern provinces from the Umayyad dynasty. The Arab Muslims always looked down upon the non-Arab Muslims who were regarded by them as inferior race. This created a gulf of difference between the Arab-Muslims and the non-Arab Muslims. Abu Muslim very tactfully secured the support of the non-Arab Muslims whose cause was championed by him. The power of the Syrians, who were loyal to the cause of the Umayyads, was also weakened due to the age-long rivalry between the Hijaz-Arabs (Mudharites) and Yemen Arabs (Himyarites). In these elements of discontent and disaffection, Abu Muslim found his materials for the revolt.

With the fall of the Umayyads, the glory of Syria passed away, its hegemony ended. The Syrians awoke too late to the realization that the centre of gravity in Islam had left their land and shifted eastward, and though they made several armed attempts to regain their former importance, all proved futile.

Treatment of Ummayyads Towards the Alids

Yazid I was though the first yet not the only exception in giving bad treatment to the descendants of Hazrat Ali. The tragedy of Kerbala had of course stigmatised him as the enemy of Alids and the destroyer of Imam Hussain and his family members ; but to a great extent it has been exaggerated. In the unmatched battle of Kerbala Imam Hussain and his family members and his supporters were murdered not according to the direct order of Yazid but because of the whims of the subordinate officers like Obaidullah, the Governor of Kufa, Umar bin Saad, the commander of the Umayyad forces in the battlefield and Shimar, the heartless soldier who cut off the head of Imam Hussain along with those of the dead relations accompanied by the ladies of his family, was sent to Yazid in Damascus, he was horrified to see that and cried out, "Oh Heaven excuse me, I never ordered to put off the heads of the fallen persons" and hurriedly sent back the ladies to Medina and there they were provided with pensions which of course were not accepted. Besides this, there was no other act on the part of Yazid to show his cruelty against the descendants of Hazrat Ali. Nevertheless, the tragedy of Kerbala was enough to defame him for ever.

After Yazid, during the reign of Marwan I, his son Abdul Malik and grandson Hisham, Alids were given worst treatment than that of Yazid. The supporters of Imam Hussain, by that time grouped themselves into a separate sect called the "*Shias*". About this time, there arose a group of penitents (*Tawwaban*) in Kufa, who visited the tomb of Imam Hussain at Kerbala and passed a whole night in a bitter cry and self-reproach for having deserted Imam Hussain and his family on the battlefield of Kerbala. Their leader was Sulaiman. He carried first every thing before them but they were ultimately defeated by an overwhelming force sent against them by Marwan. Sulaiman and his lieutenants were killed, and they shattered remnants of "the Penitents" retreated upon Kufa. It was about that time that Mukhtar a scheming adventurer, cast himself in the role of avenger of the murder of Imam Hussain. He professed allegiance to Muhammad bin Hanifa, the son of Hazrat Ali by a lady of the Hanifa tribe, and was joined by a number of elements, the Persian Mawali for instance and all other supporters of Hazrat Ali's family. Kufa, which was then under the authority of Abdullah bin Zubair, was their first target of attack and the city fell to Mukhtar. He then sent his army against Obaidullah, the man responsible for the tragedy of Kerbala, and Malik al-Ashtar, the Commander of Mukhtar, inflicted a crushing defeat on Obaidullah at the Battle of Zeb (686 A.D.) where Obaidullah himself fell dead. Thus the tragedy of Kerbala was avenged.

The resounding victory of Mukhtar against the Umayyads roused the jealousy of Ibn Zubair who sent his brother Musab to try arms with the adventurer. On the approach of Musab to Kufa Mukhtar took refuge. For several months the siege continued and at last driven by hunger and thirst Mukhtar gave a battle in which he was killed with nineteen of his trusted followers. The entire army of Mukhtar, some 8,000 men, were all mercilessly butchered. Hajjaj bin Yusuf proved no less cruel to the Alids.

During the reign of Hisham, Khalid bin Abdullah al-Qasri, the Viceroy of Eastern provinces and the Chief Councillor of Hisham, when showed sympathy to the Shias was put into prison, and also the Shiite Imam and all the prominent Shia leaders were thrown into prison and their properties were confiscated.

The only exception from among the Umayyad Caliphs was pious Umar bin Abdul Aziz who took steps to mitigate enmity between the Umayyads and the Alids. The garden of Fedak, which belonged to the Prophet, he gave it back to the family of Prophet. Hitherto it had been customary under the Umayyads to rebuke Caliph Ali and his decendants. Umar ordered the discontinuance of the practice, and directed that instead of that a prayer should be offered to turn the hearts of the people towards charity, forbearance and benevolence. He also added the word "*Karam Allah Wajha*" with the name of Hazrat Ali.

Thus the cruel treatment meted out to the House of Hazrat Ali, apparently seemed a political matter but in fact it took a religious colour and not only divided Islam but also brought about Schism in the political system of Islam—one group believing democracy, the other in the hereditary system of Government.

Chapter 4

The Period of Abbasids

The Abbasids inherited from the Umayyads a great empire. They were in a position to achieve more because the ground had been prepared for them by the great Umayyads and the early Abbasids took advantage of this. "This replacement of the Umayyads by the Abbasids in headship of the Islamic community was more than a mere change of dynasty. It was a revolution in the history of Islam, as important a turning point as the French and Russian revolution in the history of the West. It came about not as the result of a palace conspiracy or Coup d'etat, but by the action of an extensive and revolutionary propaganda and organisation, representing and expressing the dissatisfaction of the important elements of the population with the previous regimes and built up over a long period of time. Like most revolutionary movements it was a coalition of different interest, held together by a common desire to overthrow the existing order, but doomed to break up into conflicting groups once victory was obtained."

With the establishment of the Abbasid rule, the seat of government was removed from Syria to Iraq (*i.e.*, from Damascus to Baghdad). The Syrians lost their predominance in managing the affairs of the state. The Iraqite, who freed themselves from the Syrian tutelage, became all and all in the administration of the Muslim empire.

"With the change of dynasty, the internal mode of government also changed. Whether Persian influence had a particular effect upon it may or may not be the case, but it certainly became quite non-Arab. By the conquests the Arabs had become a ruling nobility as distinguished from the vanquished. The geneological net of their tribal system extended superficially over the provinces of their kingdom. Under the Umayyads this primitive system still persisted in its fundamentals, though it soon showed itself to be no longer tenable, but under the Abbasides it disappeared along with the difference of the condition which it presupposed. The Abbasides were not elevated, like the Umayyads, over a wide-spread aristocracy, to which they themselves belonged ; the Khurasanites, by whom they were supported, were not their blood, but only their instrument. The whole body of the Muslims stood in the same relation to them, without natural gradation of political rights, they alone had the divine right to rule as heirs of the Prophet. From a technical point of view, no obstacles stood in the way of fashioning the government as seemed in conformity with the interest of the cause and their own interest. They brought greater order into the government especially into the taxation system and the administration of justice, as they showed themselves zealous in opposing and redressing the grievances of those who applied to them as the supreme court of appeal. But they suppressed the general living interest in politics which in earlier times was part of the religion to a far greater extent than the Umayyads had contrived to do. The Muslims, Arabs and non-Arabs, were simply subjects and were no longer allowed to take part in public affairs. They were relegated to the realm of trade or agriculture, and at the most might conspire in the secret."

Added to this, the Abbasids lost their own Arab race, because, we know, that the Abbasids came to power with the help of the Mawali (new-converts). Thus we see that the Umayyad Caliphate, unlike the Abbasid Caliphate, was international in character in which the Arabs formed one of the may Component races.

Explaining the cause which led to the loss of power of the Arabs, Sir William Muir writes, "To their hard life and martial fire were mainly due the first spread of Islam and material prosperity of the Caliphate. But the race had by this time lost much of its early hardihood and vigour. Enriched with the spoils of the conquered peoples, the temptations to pride and luxury had gradually sapped their warlike virtue, and so they either settled down with well-filled harems, living sumptuously at their ease, or, if they still preferred the field, yielded there to petulance, rivalries and insubordination, preferring too often the interests of person, family, and tribe to the interest of Islam." The national glory was replaced by self-aggrandisement.

Under the Abbasids, the old Arabian aristocracy was replaced by a class of Government Officials. The Abbasid Caliphate had been greatly influenced by the Persian influences. Khurasanians formed the Caliphate bodyguard, and the Persians occupied the important posts in the Government of the Abbasid Caliphate. "Gradually Persian titles, Persian wines and wives, Persian mistresses, Persian songs, as well as Persian ideas and thoughts won the day. Al-Mansur, we are told, was the first to adopt the characteristic Persian head-gear in which he was naturally followed by his subjects.

Persian influence, should be noted, softened the rough edges of the primitive Arabian life and paved the way for a new [illegible] distinguished by the cultivation of science and scholarly pursuits. In two fields only did the Arabian hold his own. Islam remained the religion of the state and Arabic continued to be the official language of the state registers." Another marked feature of the Abbasid revolution was that there came into existence a Muslim State as opposed to the Arab State, in which all elements of the population had their share of power. "It gave practical effect to the democratic enunciation of the equality and brotherhood of man. The acceptance of this fundamental principle of racial equality among all the subjects helped the early sovereigns of the house of Abbas to build up a fabric which endured without a rival for over five centuries."

ABUL-ABBAS AS-SAFFAH

(*133-37 A.H./750-754 A.D.*)

Abul Abbas was declared the first Caliph of the Abbasids in the mosque of Kufa in 750 A.D. He referred to himself as as-Saffah (the blood-shedder) in his inaugural *Khutba* from the mosque of Kufa. This was ominous, since the incoming dynasty, much more than the outgoing, depended upon force in the execution of its policy.

As-Saffah was a blood-thirsty man. He justified himself by saying that the Umayyads deserved all that could be done to them. No doubt he had to take strong measures to make his position secure, as there were a great many risings early in his reign, and these risings continued in the reigns of his successors. Kufa was especially troublesome. The Kufans would not take as-Saffah seriously. They had started so many conspiracies and new movements. As-Saffah therefore, used an upper hand in suppressing the reactionaries. In order to impress the people he posed as a holy man.

As-Saffah then adopted a policy of exterminating the members of the Umayyad family. His uncle Abdullah used every cruel method to sweep away from the surface of the earth all the members of the fallen house. Once he invited ninety of them to a function and then slaughtered them treacherously; Abbasid agents and spies travelled the length and breadth of the Empire to hunt down fugitive persons of the fallen family. One of the few fortunates who managed to escape this universal massacre was Abdul Rahman, a grandson of Hisham. He succeeded in founding a glorious rule of the Umayyads in Spain. "Nor was this Abbasid persecution merely confined to the living Umayyads; the dead among them were not to be spared. The Abbasids desecrated the tombs of the Umayyads, took out the mortal remains from their eternal slumber and burnt them to ashes. There were two escapes, the tomb of Mu'awiya by mere accident and that of Umar bin Abul Aziz, whose piety was indisputable." This ill-treatment brought its natural consequences. A revulsion of feeling took place in their favour in various parts of the country, and the partisans of the fallen house rose against as-Saffah in Damascus, Hims, Kismisrin, Palestine, and Mesopotamia. These risings were of course quelled down. The insurgents laid down their arms on favourable terms.

As-Saffah was now the undisputed master of Asia and Egypt, and West Africa also acknowledged his authority. In the distribution of the Governorships, he was careful to entrust them either to members of his own family or to men who had distinguished themselves by services in his cause. In spite of the arrangements made by the new ruler, the empire was still unsettled, and the Byzantines seized the opportunity of ravaging the Muslim territories on the north. The peaceful inhabitants were either massacred or carried into captivity, and the country was laid waste.

Feeling insecured in the fickle and pro-Ali Kufa, Saffah built a courtly residence, 'Hashimiya', in al-Anbar. Kufa's sister city Basra was also avoided for the same reason. Hashimiya thenceforward became the official headquarter of the Abbasids. Saffah died of small-pox in June 754, A.D. Before his death he nominated Abu Jafar, his brother as his successor to the throne.

ABU JAFAR AL-MANSUR

(*137-59 A.H./754-775 A.D.*)

As-Saffah was succeeded by his brother Abu Jafar who assumed the title of al-Mansur (victorious). He proved to be, Hitti remarks, "one of the most successful though most unscrupulous of the Abbasids." Although Saffah is the first sovereign of the Banu Abbas, Abu Jafar must be regarded as the real founder of the dynasty. The power the family wielded, and the influence they exercised, were due to his foresight. He laid the foundation of the church which maintained and enhanced the prestige of the pontifical throne, and in later years he became the chief source of its strength. "With a remarkable knowledge of human nature, he conceived and carried out, in course of his long reign, the gradual formulation of those doctrines which, whilst they added to the hold of the sovereign on the imagination of the people, by enlisting other interests on the side of the trade, helped to create a powerful hierarchy bond and devoted to the new dynasty."

He firmly consolidated the dynasty and never shrank any act of cruelty when the interests of the dynasty were involved. "Saffah's cruelty" Amir Ali writes, "was due to vindictive frenzy, his successors' bloodshed sprang from calculation. Cold blooded, calculating and unscrupulous, he spared none whom he thought in the least dangerous to himself or his dynasty."

Rebeliation of Abdullah :

Hardly had he been seated on the throne than Abdullah bin Ali, his uncle, who was Governor of Syria under Saffah, rose in revolt. The late Caliph Saffah had promised him the Caliphate as a reward for his campaign against Marwan II who was defeated and slain in the battle of Zab. So Abdullah contested the Caliphate with Mansur who directed Abu Muslim to crush the rebellion. In a well-fought battle near Nasibin, Abu Muslim inflicted a heavy defeat on Abdullah bin Ali. He fled away with his family to his brother Sulaiman bin Ali at Basra, and there remained in concealment until Sulaiman was removed from his Government. He was ultimately put to death by utmost trickery when after seven years of imprisonment he was ceremoniously removed to a house built on salt surrounded by water which forthwith collapsed and killed the boarders.

Fall and Death of Abu Muslim :

The next target was Abu Muslim. After the battle of Nasibin, Abu Muslim desired to return to Khurasan of which he was the Governor. He had been the most leading figure in the Abbasid movement. He was extremely popular in Khurasan and he could, by raising his finger, destroy the House of Abbas. His attitude also now became overbearing. The removal of such a dangerous subject now became the first consideration of Mansur. Abu Muslim was invited to the court. He was received with consideration, and for a time the honours shown to him were almost legal. One day while he was having a talk with the Caliph, the agents of the Caliph fell upon him all of a sudden and killed him outright. Abu Muslim had raised the dynasty from the dust but his immense power and influence at Khurasan aroused the suspicion of Mansur who had him murdered.

The murder of Abu Muslim caused an insurrection among his followers in Khurasan under one Sanfad, the Magian, who cast himself in the role of avenger of Abu Muslim. The rebellion for a time kept the whole country from Ray to Nisapur in constant turmoil. But they were defeated and dispersed.

Rising of Rewandiyah :

In 758 A.D. a curious new sect of Persian extremists the Rawandiyah looked upon Mansur as the "Providence who supplied them with food and drink". They considered the commandant of his body-guard as the incarnation of the Angel Gabriel. "They believed in doctrines such as the immanence of Divinity and transmigration of souls. They announced the Caliph as the adumbration of the Deity." Their unwelcome and blasphemous enthusiasm, which provoked the religious section of the people, caused Mansur to imprison several of the Rawandiyah. Mansur asked them to desist from such preaching, but thereupon they revolted. The revolt was ruthlessly suppressed.

Rebellion of Muhammad and Ibrahim :

Mansur's treatment of the decendants of Caliph Ali forms the darkest page in Abbasid history. Suyuti says that "Mansur was the first who occasioned dissensions between Abbasids and Alids." Mansur regarded the descendants of Hazrat Ali as the possible rivals of the dynasty and he was bent on crushing them. Throughout the Umayyad period, they led a retired life, and devoted their time and energy in religious and literary pursuits. They were held in high esteem by the people of Medina. But it was during the reign of Mansur that the Alids and their supporters became disillusioned with the Abbasid rule and openly flouted their authority. Mansur put into prison Abdullah, the great grandson of Hazrat Ali together with his sons Muhammad and Ibrahim who managed to escape from prison. In the meantime there was a rebellion in favour of Muhammad. Mansur sent his nephew Isa with a huge army to crush Muhammad. The heroic fight ended in the death of the later in 762 A.D. After the death of Muhammad his brother Ibrahim continued the rebellion at Basra. Fars, Ahwaz and Wast were occupied by the rebels. For a time Kufa was threatened and the Caliph passed his days in great anxiety. At last the Caliph's army from Ray under his son Al-Mahdi and from Medina under Isa closed upon the rebels. In the battle that followed Ibrahim was defeated and slain. Many famous men of Basra, who had joined Ibrahim were either executed or put to torture. In Medina, the properties of Hazrat Hasan and Hazrat Hussain were confiscated. All the privileges Medina enjoyed were withdrawn. He even threatened with death the venerable Imam Jafar Sadiq for asking for a release of his properties. He threw into prison Imam Abu Hanifa, and had Imam Malik cruelly flogged.

Baghdad Founded :

Mansur laid the foundation of the city of Baghdad in 762 A.D. Hashimiya was very near to Kufa. In his search for a safer site he found one on the right bank of the Tigris ; there he founded the city of Baghdad. The construction was completed in four years ; a sum of 4,883,000 dirhams was spent and about a hundred thousand architects and artisans were employed. The city was circular in shape, and surrounded by double walls. The palace stood in the centre, with the cathedral mosque closeby. The streets were laid out regularly, and were of forty cubits wide. There were several gates to the city, each surmounted by a lofty tower, which was guarded night and day by relays of soldiers. During Mansur's reign a family came to power which played a prominent role in the reign of four Abbasid Caliphs. This was the family of the Barmakis, whose head was Khalid bin Barmak. Khalid was appointed *Vizier* and his descendants held the position with the later Caliphs. The Barmakis were all able men and gradually became very rich and powerful.

In Jazira (Mesopotamia) the Khazars revolted and the revolt was suppressed. When the Kurds showed signs of disaffection in Mesopotamia Khalid bin Barmak who was the Chancellor of exchequer, was sent to Mesopotamia as its Governor. Khalid, by a mixture of firmness and justice, soon put down the rebellion there.

In Africa the Kharijites were very turbulent. The Kharijites did not recognise the Abbasid rule and became an incessant source of trouble to Mansur. Mansur sent his Generals over and again to fight against them but with no better result. At last in 765 A.D., Mansur appointed Aghlab as the Governor of Africa. He ruled successfully for nearly two years, but he fell in an action with the Kharijites near Tunis. He was succeeded by Umar bin Hafs, who proved himself a successful ruler and held his post for nearly three years. The Kharijites again rebelled and besieged Kairowan. Umar was killed in action and the capital fell into the hands, of the rebels. Being enraged Mansur sent a force under Yazid bin Muhallib a man of indomitable energy and great administrative power. Yazid curbed the Kharijites, killed their leaders and within a few months established peace in Africa. He held the Government of Africa for fifteen years, until his death in 787 A.D.

With Mansur began an unending border strife between the Abbasids and Byzantines in Asia Minor. Unconsciously, the Byzantines and Abbasids were following old traditions. Asia Minor had been the battle ground of East Europeans and West Asiatics for centuries. The Greeks and Persians had fought over this land. The Byzantines and the Sassanids had fought there for two centuries. Now the later Byzantines and the Abbasids were continuing the struggle of East and West. With the Abbasids, it began as a defensive war. Seeing that the Muslims were at each others' throats, the Byzantine had been harassing the border for some time. Mansur could not tolerate such a thing for long, and sent an army against the Byzantines.

The Christians had captured the fortresses of Malatyh in Armenia and Messisah in Galicia, but the Muslim army soon recovered them.

The Muslim army now directed against Tabaristan, to the South-West of Caspian. The inhabitants still followed the ancient cult, and threw off the Muslim yoke. Suddenly they rose in revolt and massacred a large number of the Saracens. Mansur led an expedition which resulted in the annexation of Tabaristan to the Muslim Empire. This took place in the year 759 A.D. Hardly had this conquest been achieved the people of Deilien created troubles for the Muslims. They adhered to the Magian religion, and were only nominally subject to the Muslim rule, raided into the Muslim territories. They were driven back after some hard fighting.

Mansur made an attempt to recover Spain where Abdur Rehman had established an independent Umayyad Caliphate in 765 A.D. The invading force was defeated by Abdur Rehman.

Mansur died in October, 775 A.D. on his way to pilgrimage to Mecca and was buried in the holy city. Before his death he had his son Mahdi nominated as his successor.

MUHAMMAD AL-MAHDI

(159-69 A.H./775-785 A.D.)

Al-Mansur was followed by his son al-Mahdi. His rule, remarks Sir William Muir, "is mainly noticeable as a mean between the rough and vigorous rule of the first Abbasids and the palmy days which followed".

He was a mild and generous ruler. Immediately on his accession to the throne he endeavoured to remedy the harshness and rigour of his father's rule. He was particularly kind and compassionate to the poor and distressed. The treasure left by his father enabled him to make profuse charities. He started his reign by setting at liberty all persons, except those who were undergoing imprisonment for dangerous crimes. He released from prison Hasan, the son of Ibrahim, and conferred on him a substantial allowance. He restored to the Holy cities their ancient privileges that had been withdrawn by his father and allowed them again to receive their supplies from Egypt. He also gave back to the descendants of the Prophet the properties confiscated by his father. Once in his pilgrimage to Mecca, he distributed nearly three crore dirhams in charity among the people of Hejaz. The mosque of the Prophet was rebuilt and beautified under his orders. The existing schools and mosques were enlarged in all principal cities. He fixed pensions for lepers and poor people. He built the inns and wells on the pilgrims' route and guards were provided for the protection of pilgrims and travellers.

Mahdi did not resort to violent methods to curb his enemy. Once a son of Marwan attempted a rising in Syria but was defeated and taken prisoner. Mahdi detained him for a while then set him at liberty with substantial pension. Marwan's widow was also treated with consideration and kindness.

The Caliphate of Mahdi saw the rise of an impostor named Hisham bin Hakim who posed as "the veiled prophet of Khorasan". Hisham was small, repulsive looking man, and in order to hide his ugliness always wore a golden mask. He thus acquired the name of Mokanna, over the veiled. He obtained a large following, and for a time successfully defied the imperial forces, but was finally over-powered and killed.

Al-Mahdi was a tolerant ruler, though he did not encourage heresy. A certain Shaikh, called Ibn Abdul Quddus was preaching doctrines which were a disguised form of Zoroastrianism. The followers of this sect were called Zindiqis. "They undermined social conventions and religious beliefs. Mahdi showed no mercy to these persons, they were hunted without pity, and placed under a ban as the enemies of morality." This stopped all wayward thinking.

Byzantine Raids :

The Romans or the Byzantines made a treaty with Mansur. In contravention of the previous treaty the Byzantine raided into Muslim territories and ravaged the frontier province far and wide. They took Maraash and reduced it to ashes. Mahdi sent Hassan bin Kahtaba to stem the hostile tide of the Byzantines. Ibn Kahtaba succeeded in defeating the Byzantines. Leaving his son Musa as regent at Baghdad, Mahdi himself marched by Mosul towards the seat of war. Harun was sent forward with Generals like Isa bin Musa, Abdul Malik bin Saleh and Hassan bin Kahtaba against the Romans. Harun defeated the Byzantines and restored peace in the frontier. Harun so distinguished himself that his father gave him the title of al-Rashid (Follower of the right path) and proclaimed him second in succession after his brother Musa al-Hadi. Harun was appointed viceroy of the west including Armenia and Azerbaijan. The Byzantines could not forget their humiliating defeat at the hands of the Muslims. Again the Byzantines attacked the Muslims. Harun hurried to repel the invaders. The Romans were routed with slaughter, and the Saracenic army marched towards Constantinople. The Byzantine Queen Irene, the widow of Leo VI, who held the Government in the name of her minor son Constantin, sued for peace and agreed to pay a heavy annual tribute to the Muslims.

During the time of Mahdi Baghdad became the centre of intellectual activities. Music, poetry, literature and philosophy began to flourish. He was very generous in his patronage of artists, writers, thinkers and philosophers. Not only was encouragement given to Muslim thinkers and scholars, but even Zoroastrian studies were stimulated. Mahdi improved roads, and commerce increased in his time. Travelling became easy and more visitors came to Baghdad. In every way Mahdi's reign, though short, was important, because it was a period of vital preparation.

Mahdi was so much pleased with Harun that he called upon Hadi to give precedence to Harun. He summoned Hadi from Gurgan to Baghdad for this purpose. But Hadi refused to comply. Thereupon Mahdi accompanied by Harun set out for Gurgan with an army. But he died on the way, at a place called Masandan. Mahdi was forty-three years of age when he died.

MUSA AL-HADI

(*169-70 A.H./785-786 A.D.*)

Mahdi was succeeded by his elder son Musa al-Hadi. "He is described as headstrong, obstinate, and hard-hearted, but brave, energetic, and generous, and devoted to literature."

Immediately on his accession to the throne Hadi found a strong rival in Harun, his younger brother. The mothers of the two were bitterly opposed to each other, each working against her rival. Hadi even strove hard to set aside the right of succession of his brother Harun in favour of his (Hadi's) son Jafar. He threw into prison Yahya bin Khalid, Harun's Principal Adviser, and several others of his brother's servants whom he considered opposed to his design. Being disgusted with the intrigues of the Caliph, Harun left the capital for his own personal safety. The short reign of Hadi witnessed a formidable Alids rising. One of the scions of the Alids named Idris, a brother of Ibrahim and Muhammad made good his escape from Medina and went to Maghrib al-Aksa where he founded the celebrated Idriside dynasty. In 786 A.D. Hadi fell victim to a fatal disease and succumbed to it.

HARUN AR-RASHID

(*170-94 A.H./786-809 A.D.*)

Upon the death of his brother, Hadi, Harun ascended the throne in accordance with the bequest of Mahdi. With his accession, the Abbasid Empire entered into an era of brilliant epoch. He was one of the ablest and noblest rulers of the Abbasid dynasty. He ruled for twenty-three years, his reign was crowded with events and with glory for Islam. He travelled greatly himself, and though he went on Hajj nine times he lived life fully and denied himself no pleasure. "His name appealed to romance-writers and he figures largely in 'The Arabian Nights', the book, fantastic though it gives some idea of the might and majesty of Harun al-Rashid and the glory of Arab civilization." Even stripped of all the glamour of romance, history would place him as indisputably one of the greatest rulers of the world.

"The Ninth Century opened with two imperial names standing supreme in world affairs : Charlemagne in the West and Harun ar-Rashid in the East." Of the two, Harun was undoubtedly the most powerful and represented the higher culture." The two great monarchs had also entered into friendly relations with each other and in this they were prompted by mutual self-interest. Charlemagne cultivated Harun as a possible ally against the Byzantines, who were also hostile to Harun. Harun desired the friendship of Charlemagne against his rival and deadly foes, the Umayyad rulers of Spain who were also no friends of Charles. This friendship resulted in exchange of a number of embassies and presents. This unique international prestige that Harun enjoyed resulted in his being diplomatically approached by some Chinese Kings. The Muslim historians are absolutely silent on these diplomatic relations, and all these informations could be procured from the Christian sources.

The early part of Harun's reign was greatly troubled by the Kharijites. They revolted several times in his reign, but their risings were suppressed without difficulty. One of these insurrections is remarkable for the appearance of a young girl named Laila who defied the imperial authority on many occasions. The revolt was begun by her brother Walid, son of Tarif. When he fell, she assumed the command. She repeatedly gave battle to Harun's troops. Damascus was harassed by Mudharite and Himyarite strifes. Harun allowed the two factions to weaken themselves by internal dissensions. In the end he intervened, and with a firm hand put a stop to their disorders. Similar trouble broken out in Mosul.

After the death of Yazid-bin-Haithem Muhallib (appointed Governor by Mansur in 772 A.D.) in 787 A.D., trouble broke out in Africa. Yazid's brother Ruh was appointed Governor of Africa by Harun in 787 A.D. Ruh succeeded in suppressing the revolt and ruled over Africa successfully for several years. But again trouble started there and Harun sent his most trusted General Harsama as Governor. But he also could not tackle the situation very successfully, so he resigned. Thereafter, Ibrahim bin Aghlab put a proposal to Harun that he would not only restore peace and prosperity in Africa but also remit 40,000 dinars annually to the capital. Harun accepted Ibrahim's offer and granted him the hereditary Governorship of Africa. Since then new dynasty came into being called the Aghlabides.

In Armenia the turbulent people of the Khazars, instigated by the Greeks, rose in revolt. "The atrocities and the devastation they caused are described as unheard of and unparalleled. Harun sent two of his best Generals to crush them. The revolt was put down and peace was restored. In Asia, the rule was conducted with vigour and energy. In 787 A.D., the whole of Kabul and Sanjar was annexed to the empire, and the Muslim domination was extended as far as Hindukush.

Nomination of Successors :

In 791 A.D., Harun al-Rashid under the pleasure, of his Empress Zubaida and her brother, Isa-bin-Jafar, nominated his three sons, Al-Amin, Al-Mamun and Qasim, as his successors one after another, after his death. Harun took special care for the education of his children. Mamun was confided to the tuition of Jafar bin Yahya, whilst Qasim was entrusted to the care of Abdul Malik bin Saleh, a cousin of the Caliph. In order to give political training to his sons, Harun made the empire in three parts. Amin get the charge of the western regions, Mamun the charge of the eastern regions and Qasim the charge of Mesopotamia. Harun had a great admiration for the intelligence and political wisdom of Mamun.

In 802 A.D. Empress Zubaida went to Mecca for pilgrimage with her sons. Finding that the people of Mecca suffered greatly from scarcity of drinking water, she constructed at her own expense the famous canal which is called Nehr-i-Zubaida. This canal proved an inestimable blessing to the Meccans.

War with the Byzantines :

Mention has been made of the treaty between Irene and al-Mahdi, the father of Harun. In 791 A.D., they broke the treaty and invaded the Muslim territories; their Army was repulsed with great slaughter. The Muslims attacked the Islands of Cyprus and Crete and forced the Byzantines to come to terms with them. Meanwhile Irene blinded her young son, Constantine VI, and seized the throne. She held the reins of Government for five years. In 802 A.D. a Romam officer named Nicerphorus murdered Queen Irene and usurped the throne. He was arrogant and had nothing but contempt for the infidels. He was determined as Ibn Khaldun tells us "to break the peace that had been established between the Muslims and Irene". So he wrote a very rude letter to Harun : "From Nicephorus, King of Greeks, to Harun, the King of the Arabs. Irene had paid the money the double of which then shouldst have paid to her. It was but a woman's weakness. Therefore return what thou hast taken or the sword shall decide." Harun wrote a reply which has been preserved in the pages of Ṭabari famous Arabian historian :

"In the name of God the Compassionate and the Merciful. From Harun, the Commander of the Faithful to Nicephorus, the dog of the Romans.

Indeed I have read the letter, O son of an infidel mother. As for the answer it is for thine eyes to see and for thine ears to hear."

Without any loss of time Harun at once started towards the frontier and inflicted a crushing defeat to Nicephorus. The boast of Nicephorus was levelled to dust and after this defeat he agreeed to pay an increased tribute. Hardly had Harun returned to the capital, Nicephorus, thinking it impossible the Caliph would take the field again in that bad season, violated the treaty. But he mistook his courage and determination. Harun immediately huried of with his army to the scene. "Nicephorus was astonished on the bold and rapid march of the Commander of the Faithful who repassed, in the depth of the winter, the snows of mount Taurus ; his stratagems of policy and war were exhausted ; and the perfidious Greek escaped with three wounds from a field of battle everspread with forty thousand of his subjects." Nicephorus again implored for peace, and his prayer was granted. This time beside the tribute, Nicephorus agreed to pay a personal impost on himself and on his family. But "over and again when Harun was engaged elsewhere, Nicephorus broke his treaty, and as often was beaten." This process went on unabated and culminated in the capture by the Caliph of Heraclea and Tyana in 806 A.D. He begged for peace and signed a treaty by which he agreed to pay a much large tribute. But the following year taking the advantage of Harun's preoccupation in some tributes the Greeks again advanced and raided into the Muslim territories. This time Harun al-Rashid could not retrieve the defeat as his hands were engaged in an insurrection in Khurasan.

The policy of Harun al-Rashid towards the Greeks was not beyond criticism. It was short-sighted policy of the Caliph to accede to their prayer when they over and again did not observe the treaty obligations. "For better would it have been for the peace of the world and for civilisation, had a term been then put on the Byzantine rule, and Constantinople been taken by the Saracens. The bitter end of all these treacherous breaches of agreement was to inflame religious hate.

Rise and Fall of the Barmekis :

In managing the administrative affairs the first three Abbasid Caliphs received powerful assistance from a noble and ancient Persian family, the celebrated Barmekids. In Harun's time their prestige was second only to that of the Caliph.

According to Masudi, Barmak was originally a title borne by the High Priest on the great Magian fire-temple at Balkh. Khalid, the son of one of the dignitaries—whence he and his descendants were called Barmekids; when Central Asia was overrun and subdued under the command of Qutaiba bin Muslim he embraced Islam.

Khalid took very significant part in the Abbasid movement under the leadership of Abu Muslim. His rise in the Abbasid court may be traced from the time of Al-Saffah who raised him later to the post of Chief Minister. Khalid thus became the founder of the illustrious family of Wazirs. Khalid was again appointed Governor of Mesopotamia. In 765 A.D., when the Alids revolted at Musul, he was appointed Governor there.

Caliph Mahdi appointed Yahya, son of Khalid, as the tutor of Harun. When Harun had been nominated successor to the Caliphate, Yahya was made his Counsellor and Wazir. Harun called him "father" as a mark of affection, and always deferred to his counsel and advice. The moment he came to the throne, Harun appointed Yahya as the Wazir of the empire, and vested him with absolute power. Yahya's administration was wise, firm and benevolent, no detail was neglected, and the well-being of the people was made a primary duty. His sons, Fazal, Jafar, Musa, and Muhammad, were also men of great ability, and possessed of administrative capacity of highest order. Fazal had successively held the Governorships of Khurasan and Egypt. Jafar likewise had been Governor of various important provinces. Later on when, owing to his old age, Yahya resigned, Jafar was entrusted with the office, the duties of which he discharged with signal success. For seventeen years this remarkable and gifted family governed he empire of Harun with fidelity.

These Barmekids had their palaces in eastern Baghdad, where they lived in grand style. Here Jafar's palace, al-Jafarin became "the nucleus of a large group of magnificent residences later occupied by al-Mamun and transformed into the Caliphate palace." The buildings stood by the Tigris with spacious gardens. Fabulous fortunes were amassed by the members of the Barmekid family. They vied with even the Caliph in bestowing rich presents on poets and panegyrists. Their generosity was proverbial. A number of canals, mosques and other public works owe their existence to the initiative of the Barmekids. Al-Fazal is credited with being the first in Islam to introduce the use of lamps in the mosques during the month of Ramzan. Jafar acquired great fame for eloquence, literary ability and penmanship. He was also a leader of fashion.

The fall of the Barmekids was as sudden as their rise. For seventeen years the family of Barmak had served the monarch with unswerving fidelity and extraordinary ability. The people were prosperous and happy, the empire had grown rich and strong, national wealth had increased, and the arts of civilised life were, cultivated everywhere. But their grandeur and magnificence, their benefactions and lavish charity, which made them the idols of the masses raise, a host of enemies who were determined, to bring about their ruin. Many causes have been assigned for the fate which eventually overtook them.

The true cause of the fall of the Barmekids, according to Ibn Khaldun is to be found "in the manner in which they seized upon all authority, and assumed the absolute disposition of the public revenue, so much so that Harun was often forced to the necessity of asking for and not obtaining from the Chancellor, small sums of money. Their influence was unlimited, and their renown has spread in every direction. All the high offices of the state, civil as well as military, were filled by functionaries chosen from their family, or from among their partisans. All faces were turned towards them ; all heads inclined in their presence ; on them alone rested the hopes of applicants and candidates ; they showered their bounties on all sides, in every province of the empire, in the cities as well as the villages.

The Barmekids were Persian in origin. The Arabs—the ruling aristocracy could not tolerate such supremacy of the foreigners. Moreover, they were accused of excessive sympathy with the Persians. According to Jurji Zaydan, the Bermekids were Shias and their forefather Khalid had shown allegiance to Alids. The Arabs generally belonged to the Sunnite sect and they could not bear the supremacy of the Shiite Barmekids in the court of Harun 'al-Rashid. The leader of the Arab group, Fazl bin Rabi, the Chamberlain, secretly gave a false report to Caliph that the Barmekids were intriguing for the overthrow of the Abbasids.

Whatever might have been the real reasons, Harun acted thoughtlessly and inhumanly. The faithful services of generation were forgotten in the blind fury of suspicion and despotic anger. Jaffar was put into death in 803 A.D. and his body was split up into pieces. Old Yahya and his three sons—Fazl, Musa and Muhammad were thrown into prison. Their property was confiscated. The old and faithful Yahya died in prison in 806 A.D. Fazl followed him to the grave three years later. Musa and Muhammad appeared to have been released after the death of their father. All the property of the family, said to have amounted to 30,676,000 denar in cash exclusive of farms, palaces and furniture, was confiscated. Thus the celebrated house founded by Khalid fell, never to rise again.

In 809 A.D. a rebellion broke out in Khurasan. Leaving Qasim at Raqqa and Amin at Baghdad Harun proceeded to the eastern part of his dominions. Mamun accompanied his father.

While Harun reached the neighourhood of Tus, the illness from which he had been suffering took a serious turn. He immediately sent for all the members of his family and addressed them as, "All who are young will get old, all who have come into the world will die. I give you three directions : observe faithfully your engagements, be faithful to your Imams, and united among yourselves ; and take care of Muhammad and Abdullah. (Amin and Mamun) ; if one revolts against the other, suppress his rebellion and brand his disloyalty with infamy." Harun died in March, 809 A.D. in the prime of his life at the age of forty-seven.

AL-AMIN

(*194-198 A.H./809-813 A.D.*)

After the death of Harun al-Rashid, according to his behest, Amin, the elder son, ascended the throne. Amin was educated under the guardianship of his mother Zubaida and maternal uncle Isa. But soon a struggle for the throne began with his brother Mamun.

Temperamentally the two brothers differed with each other, though both had received the same education ; and in oratory, a necessary accomplishment for an Arab prince, both stood on an equal footing. Amin was the son of Zubaida, the Arab queen of Harun. The Arab faction at court favoured Amin. Mamun was the son of a Persian lady. He was the idol of the people of Khorasan, who called Mamun "the son of our sister". Amin inherited the culture of Baghdad. He was pleasure-loving, frivolous, addicted to sensual pleasures and loved to remain surrounded by jugglers, buffoons, astrologers. He gave himself up to pleasures of life and left the affairs of the state in the hands of Fazl-bin-Rabi. In character and competency Mamun was far superior to Amin.

Civil War between Amin and Mamun :

There existed a sharp rivalry and jealousy between the Arab Amirs and the Persian Amirs of the court for securing supremacy in the administration of the country. The nobles and dignitaries of the court were split up into two camps—the Arabs supporting the cause of Amin and the Persians advocating the cause of Mamun.

Whilst Mamun was engaged in organising the principality that had been left to him, Amin was fast driving to ruin the country subjected to his rule. Instead of employing his energy or resources for the defence of the empire, he involved himself in a war with his brother. Mamun was summoned to Baghdad ; he excused himself saying that he could not safely leave the province. Amin thereupon deposed him from the Government and nominated his infant son Musa as his successor to the throne. Mamun replied to this breach of faith by drawing a cordon on his western frontier. No person was allowed to enter the province without undergoing an examination in order that the emissaries from Baghdad might not temper with his subjects.

The breach between the two brothers was now complete. All the Persian Generals stood by Mamun. Amin sent a huge army of 50,000 soldiers under Ali bin Isa bin Mahan against Mamun. Mamun sent Tahir bin Husain with 40,000 soldiers to face Ali. Tahir defeated and killed Ali bin Isa in a battle near Rai in 811 A.D. Then Amin sent another army under Abdur Rahman bin Jabala. Tahir defeated this army also and occupied Hamadan. Mamun also sent his two other Generals, Harsama and Zubair who after defeating Amin's Generals occupied the whole of Persia. Mamun now assumed the title of Ameer-ul-Mumineen. Fazl bin Sahl was invested with supreme command.

Then Mamun's Generals, Tahir and Harsama set out against Amin. They had reduced Ahwaz, Yemana, Bahrain, and Oman, and then captured Wasit. The rapidity of his movement, and the submission of the East Arabian seaboard, had its effect upon other places. Abbas bin Hado, who was Amin's Governor at Kufa, acknowleged Mamun's authority. He was followed by Mansur bin Mahdi, Governor of Basra, and Daud bin Isa, Governor of Holy cities. They were all treated with marked consideration, and confirmed in their appointments. Then the Generals of Mamun advanced towards Baghdad from different directions. They laid siege to the city which lasted for several months. Great damage was done to Baghdad in the course of the siege. The notables and leaders began deserting Amin. At last, Amin was driven to take refuge with his mother and family in the citadel built by Mansur on the western bank of the river. Here also his position soon became untenable, and he was advised by the few counsellors that still remained by his side to make a dash for Syria, but he proposed surrender on condition of being taken to Mamun, for he trusted his brother's fidelity.

Accordingly an agreement was made that Harsama would take him to Mamun at Merv. Accordingly Amin left the place and boarded the boat with Harsama to cross the Tigris. As the boat proceeded to the east bank, some Persian soldiers captured and killed him. Thus died Amin at the age of 28, after a reign of four years and eight months. When Mamun received the news of his brother's unhappy end, he was overwhelmed with grief. He punished the murderers of Amin and in order to make up for the loss of his brother he adopted Amin's children as his own children.

The conflict between Amin and Mamun was regarded as Mamun marked the triumph of the Persians over the Arabs. William Muir says : "The victory of Mamun over his brother, was once more like the overthrow of the Umayyads by the Abbasids, the victory of the Persians over the Arabs."

MAMUN THE GREAT

(198-218 A.H./813-833 A.D.)

The civil war being over, and Mamun being victorious, ascended the throne of Baghdad. The twenty years of Mamun's Caliphate may be divided into two parts, *viz.*, (*a*) Mamun's thirst for learning urged him to engage himself in cultural pursuits and philosophical discussions at Merv, leaving the charge of the Administration to Fazl bin Sahl. (*b*) During the later fourteen years, Mamun assumed the reins of Government in his own hands.

Administration of Fazal Bin Sahl :

Mamun's thirst for knowledge urged him to engage himself in cultural pursuits and philosophical discussion at Merv, leaving the charge of admission to Fazl bin Sahl. Fazl bin Sahl began to misuse the power which was entrusted to him by Mamun. Fazl was anxious to keep the sovereign at Merv. No news regarding the real state of affairs in the West was allowed to reach the Caliph, and he was kept in complete ignorance of the events that were taking place in Iraq and Syria. Fazl did not have an easy time in the beginning. He had to spend years in putting down one rebellion after another. Nasr bin Sabbah, an Arab chief faithful to the memory of the late Caliph rose in Mesopotamia, and defied the Imperial troops for over five years. In Iraq, the Bedouins rose against Hassan bin Sahl, who had been appointed by his brother as Governor of Iraq. The Shiites believed in Divine Right, which meant the right of the House of Hazrat Ali to rule. To them there was no difference between an Ummayad and an Abbasid Caliph. Hence they rose whenever and wherever they could. An Alid commonly known as Ibn Tabataba fomented troubles in Kufa. He invited the people to take the oath of allegiance to the family of the Prophet. He was supported by one Abu Saraya. Combining their forces they defeated Hasan bin Sahl, and made themselves masters of whole of Southern Iraq. In Hijaz a son of Imam Jafar al-Sadiq was elected Caliph. The whole country from the borders of Persia to Yemen was thus involved in strife. But none of this news was allowed to reach Mamun.

Influence of Imam Ali ar-Raza :

While at Merv, Mamun, fell under the influence of the Shia and had long cherished the desire of making over the Caliphate to its rightful owner, who according to him, was Imam Ali ar-Raza the eighth Imam of the Shia. He gave one of his daughters in marriage to him and declared him his heir apparent. He also changed the colour of the Abbasid flag from black to green, green being the colour of the House of Hazrat Ali. The news threw the Abbasid faction in Baghdad in open rebellion. They at once raised Ibrahim, a son of Mahdi and uncle of Mamun, to the Caliphate. There was confusion in Iraq and Hijaz. In this crisis, Imam Ali ar-Raza informed the Caliph the true state of affairs and requested him to proceed towards Baghdad. Other men also advised Mamun to go to Baghdad and assume the reins of government in his hands. Thereupon, Mamun decided to proceed to Baghdad. He had not passed Tus, however, when his son-in-law, Imam ar-Raza fell ill. All that was possible was done for him by way of treatment, but Imam ar-Raza died and was buried at Tus, which was called Meshhed, after this event, the Shias were not satisfied with the cause of his death and believed that he had been poisoned. Before the arrival of the Caliph at Baghdad Fazl fell victim at the hands of an assassin.

In 819 A.D. Mamun took over the charge of the empire. With his coming to power, all disorders ceased. Mamun applied himself vigorously to the work of reorganising the administration. The Government of the Holy City was entrusted to an Alid, Kufa and Basra were given to the two brothers of the Caliph. Tahir bin Hussain was made the Governor of Khurasan. Son of Tahir, named Abdullah, was entrusted with the Government of Syria and Egypt, together with the task of reducing Nasr Okaili. After some hard fighting the rebel was put down. After restoring order Abdullah proceeded to Egypt, where an insurrection was in progress. He crushed the rebels in a single battle. Abdullah's benign and tolerant rule satisfied the Christian subjects. About this time, a large number of Spanish Muslims were expelled by Hakam I, the Umayyad sovereign of Spain. They took refuge in Egypt and their unruly conduct caused distrubances in Alexandria. Abdullah called upon them either to deliver up their arms or to leave the province. They asked for permission to go to Crete, which was at once accorded. On their departure, they were supplied with such assistance as they needed for the conquest of the island. They conquered Crete and settled there. In the meantime a Kharijite rebellion broke out in Khurasan. It was put down by Tahir. Tahir became semi-independent and on Mamun's death founded the dynasty of Tahirids in Khurasan.

In 826 A.D., the Caliph married Khadija Buran, the daughter of Hassan bin Sahl. The marriage was celebrated with unprecedented pomp and pageantry. Buran exercised considerable influence upon the Caliph. Her charity was profuse, and she founded several hospitals in Baghdad.

During his reign, Mamun had a short encounter with the Byzantines. The throne of Byzantine was then occupied by Theophilus, the son of Michael. They massacred a large number of Muslims. To repel the enemy Mamun took the field in person, and in three successive campaigns completely crushed the enemy. The Romans were obliged to sue for peace. In order to prevent the ever-recurring attacks of the Romans, Mamun erected a military stronghold, at Tayanna in Asia Minor. But before its completion, Mamun died in 833 A.D.

Rise of Mutazilites :

The Mutazila movement started at the end of the first century A.H. The origin of this movement takes us back at the famous divine and ascetic, Hassan of Basra. One day he was asked to give his opinion on a point regarding which the Murijites and the Kharijites held opposite views, namely, whether a Muslim who had committed a great sin should be deemed a believer or unbeliever. While Hasan was considering the question, one of his pupils, Wasil bin Ata replied that such persons were neither believers nor non-believers, but should be ranked in an intermediate state. Hasan disagreed with Wasil and thereupon Wasil seceded from his school and founded a new school of his own. On this account the followers of Wasil were named Mutazilites, *i.e.*, Schismatics. "Although the story may not be literally true, it is probably safe to assume that the new sect originated in Basra among the pupils of Hasan, who was the life and soul of the religious movement in the first century A.H." The Mutazilites were the upholders of free will and rationalism and rejected predestination.

Its emergence was noteworthy as it was an ethical reaction against the doctrinal and practical excesses of the fanatical Kharijites. It also launched a vehement attack on the ethical laxity of the political confirmists, namely, the Murijites. While the Murijites were predestinarians, the Mutazilites were free-thinkers. Their difference with the Kharijites lies in the fact that while the Mutazilites put less emphasis on work to be the only measurement of true belief. During the second century the Rationalists were brought into contacts with Greek logic and philosophy. So in the early stage of the movement, there was hardly any foreign influence and they were more rigid puritans than rationalists.

The Mutazilites maintained that Allah alone is eternal. Allah's essence and attributes are identical and can never be separated ; to assert any separation between the two, they said, amounted to heresy. Secondly, the Mutazilites reject the orthodox view, that the Qur'an is eternal. They maintain that the Qur'an is created and expressed in letters and revealed to the Prophet in time, in place, and in the local language. The miracle of the Qur'an is in its teaching and not in its language. If the eternity of the Qur'an is accepted, then there would be two eternal things, one Allah and the other the Qur'an. But this is against the laws of Islam. The acceptance of the eternity of the Qur'an is fundamentally opposed to the Qur'anic principle of Divine Unity, which is the cardinal principle of faith. Thirdly according to the Mutazilites, knowledge is attained through reason which gives man the ability to distinguish between good and bad, between the real and not real. If reason judges an action to be good, it is good, and if evil, it is evil. Distinction between good and bad is within the power of human reasoning. Revelation only confirms what reason dictates. It is reason that the worth of Revelation is understood and the sanctity of the religion is believed. One must not obey the law of religion without reflecting and knowing its truth. Theology should be subject to investigation and based upon rationalistic foundations and logical conclusions. Fourthly, the Mutazilites strongly oppose anthropomorphic view of Allah and maintain that Allah has no form and as such no vision of Him is possible. The Qur'anic promise that virtuous will be rewarded with the vision of Allah, should be interpreted in an allegorical sense. Fifthly, regarding the theory of Divine Justice the Mutazilites held that man has freedom of will and they reject the idea of intercession of the Prophet on behalf of the guilty Muslims on the Day of Resurrection and considered that man does not stand in need of a mediator to reconcile him with Allah. Each man will be judged according to his deeds. In short, they were extreme free-thinkers.

The Mutazilites received royal patronage from the Abbasid Mamun, who was a free-thinker, stimulated the influence of the Mutazilite doctrine and proclaimed a decree manifesting the doctrine of the creation of the Qur'an as the only truth, binding upon all Muslims. Hence Mutazilism became a "state church" under Mamun. "His two immediate successors followed in his foot-steps and tried to continue his work, but without his ability or the breadth of his comprehension. Under them Rationalism acquired a predominance such as it has perhaps not gained even in modern times in European countries. The Rationalists preached in the mosques and lectured in the colleges ; they had the moulding of the character of the nation's youth in their hands : they were the chief counsellors of the Caliphs, and it cannot be gainsaid that they used their influence wisely."

This philosophy was vehemently opposed by Imam Ahmad bin Hanbal, a great jurist of his age and the founder of the Hanbali school of jurisprudence. He has been regarded as the embodiment of traditionalism and his system was truly a bulwark of orthodoxy against the Mutazilites. He abandoned the Mutazilites' conception of the created Qur'an and maintained the doctrine of the eternity of the Qur'an for which he was persecuted by Mamun.

AL-MUTASIM

(A.H. 833/842 A.D.)

Mutasim became the Caliph of the Abbasid empire after the death of his brother Mamun. Mutasim's accession was viewed with objection by a section of the army who wanted Abbas, son of Mamun, as their ruler. However, the trouble was averted. It is difficult to understand at this distance of of time the reasons which led Mamun to supersede his son Abbas, who was popular with the army certainly with the Arabian section. Possibly he may have thought him impressionably and not likely to pursue the policy he had laid down for the guidance of the state. Perhaps he considered the stronger and maturer character of Mutasim as more certain of maintaining a continuity of action.

Mutasim was also a champion of Mutazilism. At his court freedom of discussion was allowed on all matters except the dogmas of the new faith. Persecution of the non-Mutazilites was strictly enforced like in the reign of Mamun. The famous Imam Ahmad bin Hanbal was again cast into prison.

One most important event of his reign is the formation of a standing army composed of the Turks. These Turkish soldiers were recruited to counterbalance of the power of the Khurasanian bodyguards, whose pretentions the Caliphs were unable to tolerate. But the influx of Turkish body-guards and soldiers who were originally slaves proved to be much more formidable than the Khurasanians. The highest position in the army came to be occupied by them and Arab elements were furthermore relegated to the background. This army gradually became very powerful and ultimately proved ruinous to the Caliphate. They were commanded by their own officers who were directly under the Caliph. In course of time, they assumed the role of deposing and setting up sovereigns at their will and pleasure. These Turkish soldiers became a source of terror tc the people. The capital city grew tired of the activities of these haughty creatures.

Change of Capital :

The Caliph removed with his favourite corps to a place called Samarra, some sixty miles up the Tigris. He built there a palace for himself, with barracks for two hundred and fifty thousand soldiers. A part of the city was allotted to the Turkish chiefs. Mosques and schools were also built. It was not long before Samarra began to rival Baghdad in splendour, except that it never took the place of Baghdad as a great intellectual centre.

Revolt of Zatts:

His reign is remarkable for the revolt of the Zatts in the lower regions of Iraq. These Zatts were a strange people who had migrated to Persia a few centuries before from India when the Sassanids were the emperors of Persia. They were then called Jats and had been settled near the Tigris and the Euphrates. They had always been a troublesome people. They could not settle down and were rough and violent in their ways and would not keep to anything for long. The Jats had rebelled under al-Mamun, but the rising had not been a very big affair. Under Mutasim they organised a revolt on a large scale and began to loot caravans and raid settled areas and towns in Iraq. They levied tolls on the boats passing that way and finally supplies to Baghdad were cut off. Mutasim had to take strong measures and at last defeated them. They were forced to migrate to the border province of Cilicia in Asia Minor. Many Jats settled in Cilicia, but a few bands passed into Europe and took to a wandering life.

During the reign of Mamun the rebel Babak perpetrated havoc in the northern provinces. Mutasim sent Afshin, one of his best Turkish Generals, against them. After a series of carefully conducted operations, Afshin captured Babak's stronghold. His son and other relatives submitted, and were sent to Baghdad. He and his brother escaped to Armenia where they were seized by an Armenian chief and delivered to Afshin. They were brought to Baghdad, their crimes against humanity were too great for pardon. They were first paraded in the streets on an elephant, and then put to death.

Byzantine Emperor Theopilus having entered into agreement with Babak invaded the Muslim territories sacked and burned their cities, put the men to the sword, and carried away the women and children into slavery. Mutasim's birth place was reduced to ashes. The men were either killed or blinded with red-hot irons, others were subjected to mutilation. The news of these barbarities threw Mutasim into a furious rage, and he swore dire vengeance. Rapidly collecting his army, he marched against the treacherous and brutal Greeks and inflicted on them terrible defeat. The Caliph then marched on the birth place of Theopilus and after a siege of fifty days, it was carried by storm, and razed to the ground. Mutasim now directed his march towards Bosphorus with object of striking a final blow at the Greek power. But the discovery of a dangerous plot within his own camp withheld him. Some of the Arab Generals, jealous of the influence possessed by the Turks, and disgusted with the way in which they were treated by the Caliph, entered into a conspiracy with the young and misguided Abbas to assassinate Mutasim. The plot was discovered by chance, and appeared to be so extensive that it upset the Caliph's plans. Abbas and his fellow conspirators were executed.

In 839 A.D., Maziar, the Magian prince of Tabaristan, revolted against the Caliph. Under the impression that Abdullah bin Tahir would not be able to suppress Maziar's revolt and that Mutasim would be compelled to appoint him as Viceroy of the East in place of Abdullah, Afshin secretly instigated the Magian chief to fight to bitter end. But Maziar was captured by Abdullah and sent to Baghdad. In the Caliph's presence, he exposed Afshin's treachery, and showed the letters he had received. Maziar was executed, and Afshin was imprisoned and put to death.

Mutasim was a man of firm views and quick action. He was not inimical to intellectual or philosophic pursuits and the quickening of the Arab mind that had come to flower under al-Mamun continued under him. He upheld the dignity of his office. He is said to have promoted agriculture, and taken a great interest in the development of the natural resources of the empire.

AL-WATHIQ

(223-228 A.H./842-849 A.D.)

Mutasim was succeeded by his son al-Wathiq. Wathiq's character has been grossly misrepresented by the ortho dox Muslim writers. In reality, he was a very capable ruler, a nerous in his ways and liberal in his ideas. His Government was firm and enlightened. A great patron of liberal thought, he gave much money to charity and encouraged learning to the full. With a literary turn of mind he leaned great proficiency in music, and is said to have composed a hundred airs and melodies. The state was prosperous during this time and industry flourished, the trade between East and West, which was made easy by the Abbasids and had greatly increased, rose to new heights.

Religious controversies raged high in his time. "He tried hard to diffuse the Rationalistic doctrines among the people, but his endeavours were counteracted by the reactionary jurists." There was a serious uprising in Baghdad under the leadership of one saint Ahmad bin Nasr against the policy of persecution of the non-Mutazila. Ibn Nasr was captured, tried for heresy and executed. Wathiq continued the fatal mistake made by his father, by favouring the Turks at the expense of the Arabs and the Persians. He appointed a Turkish officer, Ashans by name, with whose ability he was impressed, as the Lord Lieutenant or Naib of the Caliphate.

AL-MUTAWAKKIL

(847-861 A.D.)

Al-Wathiq died young and was succeeded by al-Mutawakkil. He ruled for fifteen years and under him commenced the decline of the empire. He was a very orthodox Caliph indeed and was keen for the restoration of orthodoxy. The *Ulema*, who had not played a very prominent role in the reigns of the earlier Caliphs, came into their own. Rationalism was banned. He liberated Imam Ahmad bin Hanbal. He then started controlling and later suppressing the Mutazilite scholars. Kazi Abu Duwad and his son, prominent Mutazilites, were thrown into prison, and their property was confiscated. A large number of them died at his hands.

Al-Mutwakkil was equally intolerant to the Alids. The Garden of Fadaq, belonging to the Prophet's family, once again confiscated by Marwan, then released by Umar II, was again confiscated.

Taking advantage of this inner disturbances at the Abbasid centre, the Byzantines took heart. They overran the Muslim province of Cilicia in South Asia Minor and attacked and captured Dmietta in Egypt. People became very dissatisfied and this gave an opportunity to the Turkish Guard to become turbulent. Mutawakkil tried to shift his capital to Damascus to escape the guard, but he could no longer do. He was ultimately put to death.

LATER ABBASIDS

(861 A.D. to 1262 A.D.)

The glory had begun to fade during al-Wathiq. Mutawakkil was followed by twenty-seven Caliphs in succession, none of them being competent. The Caliphs became less and less powerful as the years went by, until they held but a shadowy existence at the Centre. They became tools in the hands of their ambitious and corrupt Ministers. Their weakness and incompetence were exploited by the Provincial Governors and officers, who carved out many independent kingdoms in the course of time.

Mutawakkil was succeeded by Muntassie. "He is described as a pious and just sovereign, forbearing and generous in character, possessed of a keen intellect and honestly desirous for the welfare of his subjects." He died after a short reign of six months.

The next Caliph was Mustain, a grandson of Mustasim. He was raised to the throne by the powerful Turkoman Chiefs. They allowed him no power of authority. Unable to stand the tyranny of his Turkish guards, Mustain escaped to Baghdad. Turks now raised Mutazz, a son of Mutawakkil, as Caliph. Mutazz occupied the throne for three years. He was forced to abdicate in favour of al-Muhtadi. Al-Muhtadi was a man of sound character, noble, virtuous and just. He tried to assert his power and rule the state according to law. This soon brought him into collision with the Turks. He was seized by the insurgents, and after considerable ill-treatment was forced to abdicate. He died in the prison. Mutamid, the eldest surviving son of Mutawakkil, was then proclaimed Caliph. He was weak and pleasure-loving man. He was a mere show-boy and in reality the empire was governed by his brother Muwaffik, a man of ability and of great military talents. Mutamid was succeeded by his nephew Mutazid, the son of Muwaffik. He was a "bold and active man, a vigorous and wise administrator, and a capable soldier." His greatest achievement was the restoration of Egypt to Caliphate. He was successful in his wars with the Romans, and several cities were either recovered or taken from them. Mutazid's rule was undoubtedly beneficent.

Mutazid died in 902 A.D. and was succeeded by his son al-Muktafi. Al-Muktafi proved a wise and just ruler. He won the love of the people by restoring to the rightful owners the lands and gardens that had been acquired by Mutazid for building his palace. Muktafi died after a short reign of five years, and was succeeded by his brother al-Muktadir. He occupied the throne for nearly twenty-five years. He was fortunate in having the services of the virtuous and able Ministers such as Ibn Furat and others, who maintained the dignity of the empire in the beginning of his reign, but towards the end it declined rapidly, owing to the sovereign's recklessness. Towards the end of his reign the real power of the Government was in the hands of his mother, a woman of noble character and wonderful ability. After the death of Muktadir another son of Mutazid, named Abu Mansur, was raised to the throne with the title of al-Kahir. He was cruel. He was soon deposed and blinded. The Turks then placed ar-Razi, a son of Mukadir, on the throne. Soon after his accession, Mohammad bin Raikm, Governor of Wasit and Basra, seized the supreme power. But he was overthrown by Turkish General Bajkam.

Ar-Razi was succeeded by al-Muttaki, another son of Muktadir. He was a mere puppet in the hands of a Turkish General named Tuzun. In his reign the Greeks raided as far as Edessa, slaughtering the Muslims on all sides. After his death, Tuzun placed al-Mustafi, a brother of Muttaki on the throne. But he was deposed and blinded. Al-Muti, another son of Muktadir, was then installed as a Caliph. Al-Muti struck with paralysis, abdicated in favour of his brother, who was placed on the throne under the title of at-Taii. At-Taii was also deposed and forced to abdicate in favour of his brother, who was placed on the throne under the title of al-Kadir. Kadir is described as a virtuous man, distinguished for his piety and noble character. He gave large portion of his income in charity. Kadir was followed by his son Abu Jaffar Abdullah, who took the title of al-Kaim. Like his father, he was also virtuous, pious, devout and learned. "He was assiduous in the cultivation of learning", says the annalist, "skilled in writing, and prompt to do justice and benevolence." He remained in power for nearly twenty-four years.

Kaim was followed by his grandson Abu Kasim Abdullah who ascended the throne under the title of Muktadi. Muktadi was pious and virtuous and administered his private domains with care. He was succeeded by his son Abdul Abbas Ahmad, under the title of al-Mustazhir. Ibn ul-Athir describes him as humane, virtuous, and liberal, of generous disposition and gentle manners, and a patron of the learned. Had he lived in a more favourable times, he would probably have made some figure in history." The Christians had enjoyed the utmost toleration under his rule. He had occupied the pontifical throne for twenty-five years. He was succeeded by his son Abu Mansur, under the title of al-Mustarshid. Mustarshid was put to death by Masud, brother of Sultan Mahmud. Mustarshid was succeeded by his son Rashid who, however, did not occupy the throne beyond a few months. Upon Rashid's deposition, Abu Abdullah, son of Mustazhir, became Caliph under the title of al-Muktafi. He succeeded in recovering his temporal authority in the home provinces.

The Caliph Muktafi was succeeded by his son Abul Muzaffar Yusuf, under the title of al-Mustanjid. He was a capable ruler, generous in his ways and liberal in his ideas. He abolished all oppressive and illegal imports within his territories, and maintained order and peace with firmness. He was a man of firm views and quick action. He was succeeded by his son, Abu Mohammad Hassan, under the title of Mustazil. Mustazil had succeeded in regaining his temporal power over Iraq, lower Mesopotamia, Fars, Shewaz, and the Deltaic provinces. He was succeeded by his son Nasir who was an able and successful ruler. He created a powerful army, seems to have been respected and feared by all the neighbouring princes. His long reign of forty-seven years was glorious and blessed with splendour, peace and prosperity reigned everywhere. Upon his death his son, Zahir, ascended the throne. Ibn ul-Athir describes him as a just, mild, and benevolent sovereign, recalling the days of Umar bin Abdul Aziz. His reign lasted only for a year. His son Abu Jaffar Mansur ascended the throne under the title of al-Mustansir. He maintained the power and grandeur of the Caliphate. He was brave and chivalrous man, and a just, wise, and pious ruler. He was succeeded by his son Abu Ahmad Abdullah, who received the title of al-Mustassim. "Weak, vacillating, and fond of pleasure, his reign was one continuous record of disturbance, and disorder at home and disaster at abroad, culminating in his destruction and that of his family."

The Fall of the Abbasids :

The death-knell of the Abbasid Caliphate was sounded with the invasion of Halaqu Khan and sack of Baghdad in 1258 A.D. Baghdad the seat of culture, the eye and centre of the Saracenic world was ruined for ever. The population before the sack was over two millions ; according to Ibn Khaldun, "one million six hundred thousand people perished in the slaughter of six weeks". "The invasion of the Tartars", says Ibn ul-Athir, "was one of the greatest of calamities and the most terrible of visitations which fell upon the world in general and the Muslims in particular. With the destruction of Baghdad, the Abbasid Caliphate collapsed. The Abbasid Caliphate though produced many illustrious Caliphs could not be built on permanent basis.

Chapter 5

Muslims in Spain & North Africa

SPAIN

The conquest of Spain by the Arabs is a brilliant chapter of their history. It speaks a volume of the military skill of the Arabs. Following are the causes that led to the conquest of the Peninsula :

Causes of Conquest :

The Muslims were expanding the dominion far and wide. They conquered North Africa which was separated from Spain by a strait only. So it was natural that they could conquer the Peninsula. Moreover, on the eve of the Muslim conquest, the social, political and economic conditions of Spain were in a deplorable state, and the evil was long standing. Spain was the province of the Roman Empire. When the Roman Empire was overrun by the Teutonic races the hope of better condition disappeared, rather it deteriorated. The country was split into a number of petty states.

The religious intolerance of the Gothic rulers paved the way for Muslim conquest of Spain. They could not tolerate any religion except Christianity. There were many Jewish inhabitants in Spain. They were terribly suppressed by the Gothic kings, chiefs, nobles, and priests. They tried to rise in arms which, however, made slaves to the Christians. The Saracenic province on the otherwise of the Strait of Gibraltar was regarded as a heaven of safety and many Spaniards had found refuge in Muslim Africa, so it was natural that at the first shock the Gothic Government would fall and these people would naturally join with the Muslims who had already gained reputation for better Government and universal brotherhood. When the Muslims invaded Spain these people supported them.

The social condition of Spain was a prelude to the Muslim conquest. The social fabric was in deplorable condition. The people were divided into three classes. The nobility formed the privileged class and were exempted from the payment of taxes. The lower class people who formed the vast majority of the population were reduced to utter ruin and misery. Never was the condition of the country or the people so bad or misruled as under the grinding yoke of the Gothic king. Thus the society was filled with poverty, distress and inequality. Under this condition they were looking for a deliverer, and they found it in the Muslims.

ABDUR REHMAN

(756-788 A.D.)

Spain became a part of the Muslim empire during the reign of Walid bin Abdul Malik. Since then it continued to be a part of the Muslim dominion. The people of Spain were happy and prosperous under the Muslim rule. It remained a part of the Umayyad Caliphate till the outbreak of the Abbasid revolution. The. Abbasid succeeded in establishing their authority in different parts of the empire except Spain where a son of the Umayyad house inaugurated an independent rule.

The founder of this independent Umayyad dynasty was Abdur Rehman I, the grandson of the 10th Umayyad Caliph Hisham. He was one of the very few Umayyads who escaped from the terrible vengeance of the first Abbasid Caliph, As-Saffah, "The story of his narrow escape and his five years' wandering through Palestine, Egypt and North Africa in disguise is one of the most dramatic episodes of the Arabic annals". After a sojourn of five years in Palestine, Egypt and Africa, he at last reached Geuta. He was given shelter there by a Berber who were the family of his maternal uncle. Thence he sent his servant Badr to negotiate with the Syrians in Spain. The Syrians were the foremost supporters of the Umayyad House and they readily welcomed the adventurous youth of their favourite dynasty. Being assured of their help Abdur Rehman went to Spain where he was accorded a warm reception in 755 A.D. The charming personality of this young adventurer and great name of his family won for him the popular support. The weak Abbasid Governor Yusuf gave him battle at Masarah. The battle of Masarah was a decisive battle in the history of Islam. Yusuf, the Abbasid Governor of Spain was defeated as Caliph Mansur could not send him help in time. Abdur Rehman became the master of Spain and installed himself on the throne of Spain as an independent Amir (756 A.D.). Thus within the sixth years of the fall of Umayyad rule a new Umayyad dynasty was established in Spain.

For some years he saw his authority disputed sometimes by the Berbers, sometimes by Yamanites, sometimes Tahirites. After finally establishing his authority in and around Cordova. Abdur Rehman took steps to punish the rebel Chiefs. The

Yamanite chief Abu Sabbah, Governor of Seville, who had plotted against Abdur Rehman after the battle of Masarah, was deposed and killed. The Yamanites of the south were also defeated, 20,000 of them were killed and their power was crushed. Matari, rebel Yamanite chief of Niebla, was also defeated and killed. Hisham bin Urwah, the former Governor of Toledo, raised a standard of revolt. Toledo was reduced to submission and the rebel leaders were put to death. The Berbers also created serious troubles. Their leader was Shaqna, a school master claimed himself a Fatimid and descendant of the Prophet. But ultimately he was killed by his own men.

Abdur Rehman had not yet finished with his enemies, he had to face a formidable coalition formed by the Arab chiefs of eastern Spain. They wanted to drive Abdur Rehman out of Spain. They now sought help from Charlemagne the Great of France. Charles was known as the champion of Christianity. So he welcomed the idea of doing as much damage as he could to a Muslim power, and came with a large army. Charles crossed the Pyrenees and fought a number of engagements with the Muslim forces, but he met with stiff resistance. Things were in this state when word reached him that the Saxons of Germany, who had been recently conquered, had revolted. Charlemagne had to return to France without achieving any thing. He left the army under the command of Roland, the greatest Christian knight of the times in Europe. He was attacked by the mountaineers and suffered terrible loss in man and materials. In the battle of Roncesvaltes that followed Roland was defeated and killed. Thus the object of the coalition, *viz.*, to overthrow Abdur Rehman was foiled. The fortress of Saragossa was captured by the royal force in 780 A.D. Abdur Rehman then crushed the Arab leaders. The authority of the Umayyad was now firmly established, and although his reign continued to be disturbed by risings and conspiracies, even in his own family it was uniformly successful. He died at the age of 59 years in the year 788 A.D. and was buried in the Palace of Cordova.

Achievements and Character :

Abdur Rehman, the founder of the Umayyad rule in Spain, was a young hero. He was adventurous, ambitious and energetic. He was a kind-hearted and well-meaning ruler. He was a very talented man and had progressive ideas. Though slow in determination, he was preserving in fulfilling his objects. Although in resisting the attempt against his authority he often employed harsh and cruel measures, he was naturally of a mild disposition. Abdur Rehman made no claim to the Caliphate. He was content with the simple title of Ameer.

Abdur Rehman, a prince of untiring energy, boundless ambition and indomitable will thus well-founded an independent state on the soil of Europe, pacified the country from anarchy and civil war and freed it. Abdur Rehman saw the society of Abdualsia composed of heterogeneous elements such as the Arab noble, non-Muslims, Spanish Muslims, Tahirites, Y amanites and Mudharites. He broke their power and position andestablished peace and created a highly organised and well-trained army of 40,000 mercenary Berbers and also constructed a powerful navy. Mansur acknowledged that he (Abdur Rehman) found a mighty Empire although he had nothing to rely on except his statesmanship and perseverance.

Having consolidated himself on the throne, Abdur Rehman turned to the art of peace. He proved equally successful in the art of peace as he had proved in the art of war. He beautified the cities of his domain. Two years before his death in 788 A.D. Abdur Rehman founded the great Mosque of Cordova which was completed and enlarged by his successors. With its forest of stately columns and its spacious outer court of this monumental structure, transformed into a Christian Cathedral at the reconquest by Ferdinand III in 1236 has survived to the present-day under the popular name "La Mezquita" (the mosque). He also built a bridge over the Guadalquiver. Abdur Rehman was greatly interested in gardening, and outside Cordova he constructed for himself the pleasure-garden called "Munyal al-Rusafa."

He made Cordova the most attracting centre of learning and culture in Europe. His patronage of letters attracted men of learning to his court. "Among the literary figures of his court mention may be made of Aby al-Mutahshsha, the poet, Shaykh Abu Musa Hawari, Isa bin Dinar, Yahya bin Yahya and Said bin Hasan". The Arabs of Spain were the teachers of Europe, and the Universities of Cordova, Toledo, and Seville served as the fountainheads of culture for Arab and non-Arab, Muslim and Christian, Jew and Gentile for centuries to come.

Abdur Rehman proved a wise administrator. He divided empire into six provinces under Provincial Governors. He divided the Government into three organs,—judiciary, revenue and civil. He was an enlightened and benevolent ruler. He ruled until his death in 788 A.D., with the tempered severity and justice which made his dominion the best organised in Europe, and his capital the most splendid.

HISHAM

(*788-796 A.D.*)

Abdur Rehman was succeeded by his son Hisham. He was a good man, given to study and pious works. He was considered to be a model of virtue. His reign was marked by a number of rebellions and of which he successfully crushed. He had to deal with a rebellion of his own brothers, Sulaiman and Abdullah. They declared their independence and mobilised their forces at Toledo. Hisham tried to pacify them but in vain. Ultimately he had to march at the head of an army of 20,000 strong against Sulaiman. A battle that followed near Boulk in 790 A.D., the army of Sulaiman was completely routed. After reducing Sulaiman, Hisham marched to take Toledo which was defended by Abdullah. Being unable to cope with the strong imperial army Abdullah surrendered. Hisham was good enough to grant him a fief near Toledo. He then marched to Ebro to quell the insurrection of Matrup, the son of Sulaiman, who had invited Charlemagne into Spain. The rebel was killed and Saragossa and Barcelona again acknowledged the authority of the Umayyad sovereign. Sulaiman again made the necessary preparations for a final engagement with his brother, but Muawiya, the son of Hisham, defeated his uncle in a pitched battle at Lorca in 790 A.D.

Taking advantage of Hisham's engagement in dealing with his rebel brothers, the Yamanites, under the leadership of Saiyd bin Husain, raised rebellion at Tortosa in 788 A.D. But Saiyd was defeated and killed by Musa bin Fortunio. In recognition of his services, Musa was appointed Governor of Saragossa.

After restoring peace in his own dominions, Hisham turned his attention towards the north. The repression of the Christian frontier tribes had become a matter of vital necessity, for their raids were incessant and disastrous. They burnt, they massacred, they devastated wherever they went. It was then, as now, a conflict between civilisation and barbarism. Hisham considered it necessary to teach a lesson to the Franks, whose rulers had pursued a most treacherous policy towards the Saracenic Spain, and had for some time past fomented all the disorders within the Peninsula. With this object he sent forward two armies—one marching through Catalonia, entered France, overran Cerdagne, recaptured Narbonne and several other places, and inflicted a terrible defeat on the count of Toulouse.

Hisham was a pious man. He entertained a profound respect for Imam Malik, the founder of one of the four principal Sunni Schools of law. He did his utmost to introduce the Maliki system into the Peninsula. He encouraged the students of theology to make journeys to Medina in order to learn Maliki doctrines. The Maliki theologians were given high posts in the state. The Kitab "al-Muwatta" written by Imam Malik was copied and circulated throughout the empire.

Hisham was a just, mild and generous ruler. He reigned for only eight years but during this short period he did immense good to the poor and invalid. His charity was unbounded to his subjects. "Dressed in simple garb he was found in streets of Cordova, mix with the people and acquaint himself with their complaints and grievances, he frequently watched by the bedside of the sick and lowly and listened to the tale of their cares and burdens". His administration was firm and vigorous, disorders were repressed with a strong hand and no misdeed was allowed to pass unpunished. Corrupt officers were dismissed and never appointed. He stopped the collection of unlawful taxes. He restored the great bridge of as-Smah, completed the Cathedral mosque begun by his father, and embellished the cities of his father.

Hisham was equally interested in the cultivation of literature. He encouraged learning to the full. He established schools for the study of Arabic. He was fond of Arabic poetry and was himself a poet. The famous poet Amr bin Ali Ghaffar adorned his court.

Hisham was very regular in his religious duties. He rewarded those Muslim subjects who attended the congregational prayer and also observed fasting. Hisham died at the age of forty in 796 A.D. His rule lasted for about eight years. Before his death he had nominated his son al-Hakam as his successor.

HAKAM I

(796-822 A.D.)

Hakam I succeeded his father Hisham I to the throne of Spain. He was not kind and noble man. He loved to surround himself with pomp and pageantry. Hakam was by nature pleasure-loving and he enjoyed life as it came to him. He was addicted to wine.

Revolt of Faqihs :

Soon after his succession, Hakam was faced with a formidable rebellion of the renegades, led by a Faqih. The Faqihs obtain considerable influence over the renegades who lived in the southern suburbs of the city of Cordova, the then Capital of Muslim Spain. Owing to the generous though perhaps mistaken, policy of Hisham, the Faqihs had become a power in the land. He excluded them from all interference in affairs of state. "Frustrated thus in their hopes of power, and full of clerical pride, they became demagogues." So the Faqihs united themselves and denounced Hakam as irreligious. The Faqihs tried to inflame the bigotry of the Muslim Spaniards, among them their influence was unbounded. The bulk of population throughout the peninsula consisted of converts of Islam or Muwallad, these Muwallad were looked down upon by Arabs of pure blood They were Yahya bin Yahya, the leader of the Faqihs, entered into a plot with a section of the nobility to raise an uncle of Hakam to the throne of Cordova. But the plot was detected and the leading Faqihs and nobles, about seventy-two in number, were killed. Yahya secured safety by flight.

Revolt of Sulaiman and Abdullah :

Sulaiman and Abdullah, Hakam's uncles, were still alive. They once again tried to seize the throne, Sulaiman mustered a large army at Tangiers and then crossed over to Valencia. Abdullah won over some men to his side and seized Toledo. He proceeded to the Frankish Emperor Charlemagne at Aix-la-Chapella to solicit his assistance. While Hakam was making preparations to lead an expedition against his uncles news reached him that Louis and Charles invaded the Muslim territories and Alfonso, the Gallician chief, invaded Aragon. Hakam proved himself equal to the task and displayed the greatest energy. He marched at the head of a large army to the frontier in 796 A.D. This campaign met with unexpected success and both the Franks and the Gallicians were defeated and exterminated from his domain. Then Hakam marched upon Toledo. In the battle that followed Sulaiman lost his life and Abdullah was pardoned on submission. While Hakam was thus occupied, the Franks seized Barcelona. The loss of this valuable and important town was due to the treachery of its Governor. Charlemagne thus obtained a stronghold in Spain.

In 805 A.D., Cordova was convulsed by a formidable revolt. Hakam trusted no one and increased the number of his body-guards, composed mainly of the negroes. They were haughty and many of them were not Muslims. There was constant trouble between them and the people. "One day when Hakam was going as usual to the mosque to say his prayers, a citizen insulted him to his face much to the gratification of the people. Hakam was infuriated at this insult and had ten men executed in punishment. This enraged the Cordovans all the more. The Faqihs continued to inflame the passions of the Cordovans. Yahya fomented a movement for rebellion. Hakam put it down with an iron hand. Their principal leaders were either killed or executed, and the rest of them expelled. Many of them took ship and sailed East. They came to Crete, the island to the South of Greece and conquered it. Crete remained under Arab rule for a hundred and fifty years.

Revolt of Toledans :

Toledo was still an important city in Muslim Spain. The Toledans had never forgotten that their city was once the capital of Spain, and the memory of its former glory rankled in their hearts and increased their animosity against the Arabs. The inhabitants of Toledo were mainly neo-Muslims with an important Christian minority. They refused to obey the orders of the sovereign or to receive as their Governor any one who was not acceptable to them. The first rebellion took place in 797 A.D., under Ubaidah bin Hamid. Amrus bin Yusuf, a Muwallad from Huesca, who held command at Talavera, was deputed to restore order. A tactful man and a good administrator, he won over some of the principal citizens, and with their help induced the people to acknowledge the authority of Hakam. Ten years they revolted ; later they revolted under the leadership of Gharbib, a neo-Muslim poet. Amrus bin Yusuf was again deputed to restore peace and order. His appointment was accepted by the people of Toledo, as they believed that Amrus was inimical to the king. When the Crown Prince Abdur Rehman visited the city in 813 A.D. Amrus one day invited the principal citizens into the Castle and put them to death. Their dead bodies were flung into a ditch. This event is known in the history as "the Day of the Ditch."

ABDUR RAHMAN II

(822-852 A.D.)

Hakam was succeeded by his own son Abdur Rahman, surnamed Ausat. His succession was not uncontested since Abdullah son of Abdur Rahman I made an attempt to occupy the throne. This, however, failed and Abdullah had to submit.

Soon after his accession to the throne Alfonso II the Chief of Leon, made an incursion into the districts of Medina—Salim and Aragon. His example was followed by the other chiefs of the North. Count Borel of the Gothic March attacked Muslim territory. A strong force was despatched under Abdul Karim bin Mughith and Obaidullah bin Abdullah for their punishment. The Christians were thoroughly beaten and their towers and fortresses were raised to the ground, and Leon itself was destroyed. On their submission they were required to pay a heavy tribute and give hostages for their future good behaviour. The Franks also took advantage of this occasion and entered Catalonia which was under the Arab control. They suffered a disastrous defeat and were driven across the frontier. In 838 A.D., the Christians took possession of Pamplona, but they were defeated and the city was reoccupied by the Muslims. Barcelona and Galicia also fell into the Muslim hands. The Christians were expelled from the north-east of Spain. In 839 A.D. Louis attacked Medinaceli but was defeated with heavy loss by Musa, the frontier Governor.

Invasion of Normans :

It was in this reign that the Normans invaded the Spanish coastal towns of Lisbon and Cadiz. They sacked the island in the Guadalquivir and the city of Seville and killed a large number of people. An army sent by the king of Cordova inflicted a crushing defeat on the Normans. They fled but reappeared when they sacked Al-Geciras and raided the coastal towns. Again they were defeated by the Muslims.

The reign of Abdur Rahman was not free from internal troubles. "The Christians of Merida rose in rebellion under the leadership of Mahmud bin al-Jabbar a former tax collector and Sulaiman bin Martin. The cause of this rebellion is said to have been the imposition of taxes on articles of daily use and the tyranny of the Ministers and tax collectors." Abdur Rahman put it down with an iron hand. The miscreants were brought to submission and 7,000 rebels were killed. A fresh revolt broke out in Toledo, in which the neo-Muslims and the Jews took part. It was headed by a neo-Muslim named Hashim. But Hashim was defeated and killed and the rebles were dispersed.

Revolt of Christians in Cordova :

During the close of his reign the fanatical section of the Christian population in Cordova rose in revolt. This rebellion assumed the most menacing attitude. They despised the Muslims and vilified their Prophet. The Christians had no cause of complaint against the Arab rule. They enjoyed complete religious, social and economic freedom and were given important posts in the administration of the state. The Christians were greatly influenced by the Arab literature and language. They also adopted the Arab manners and customs even without embracing Islam. The Arabicised Christians or Mozarabs were hated by their fanatical brethren who denounced them as irreligious. The leaders of this section of community were a priest, Enlogius and his friend Alvaro. They fomented the discontent and in this way increased the bitterness of the bigoted sections. "The vilification of the Prophet Muhammad and of Islam by the Christians had great significance in the history of the Muslims in Spain. It demonstrated the uncompromising attitude of the Christians who were averse to Muslim rule and deprecated every thing Muslim". Abdur Rahman had to take effective action in the matter and it resulted in tbe voluntary martyrdom of many men and women.

Achievements and Character :

Abdur Rahman's reign was one of peace and splendour, the people were prosperous and the revenues ample. The administrative machinery was re-organised and the viziers were given special powers.

Abdur Rahman was devoted to arts and letters, and loved the society of men of talent and learning. Dozy remarks,

"Never had the court of the Sultans of Spain been so brilliant as it became under the rule of Abdur Rahman." Learned men and famous musicians flocked to his court. The renowned musician Ziryab was attached to his court. "The love of music, which became afterwards a national characteristic of the Spanish Arabs, began at this time to develop itself, among all classes of the people." Abdur Rahman made generous gifts to his poets, musicians and artists. Abdur Rahman was no mean as scholar himself and used to take part in the discussions which were a regular feature of his Court. The grace and elegance of his Court permeated the whole Arab society.

Abdur Rahman II made Cordova a second Baghdad. He was a keen builder. He beautified the city with edifices, mosques, fountains and gardens. He made arrangements for the supply of water to the city of Cordova. New roads were built. Mosques were constructed in the principal cities of the dominion.

His reign constitutes a glorious epoch of Umayyad rule in Spain. Thus Sedillot remarks "the splendid culture, the polished chivalry, the delicacy, grace and elegance of Arab manners which European chivalry afterwards attempted to imitate, date from this epoch." After a long and prosperous reign of thirty years Abdur Rahman died in 852 A.D.

MUHAMMAD I

(852-886 A.D.)

Abdur Rahman II was succeeded by his son Muhammad. I His reign was marked by a series of domestic troubles.

Immediately after his accession, the people of Toledo being assisted by the chief of Leon again revolted in 854 A.D. Muhammad I hurried off with a large force and compelled the rebels to submit. About 8,000 Christians were killed. A younger son of Muhammad I remained at Toledo to restore peace. The Christian zealots of Cordova also revolted. They had been punished but not crushed by the mild Abdur Rahman II. These Christians carried on reasonable correspondence with the French king, Charles the Beld, and invited him to attack Spain. Muhammad I took drastic actions against them. Repressive measures were adopted to stamp out mutiny in the Capital. Their monastery of Tabanos, the hot-bed of fanaticism, was demolished. Their leaders were hanged.

Reappearance of Normans :

Taking advantage of the internal troubles the Normans appeared for the second time in 859 A.D. on the coasts of Spain. They devastated Malage and other coastal towns. They were pursued by the Spanish fleet, and after a hotly-contested fight driven off with the loss of several ships. In the meantime the

Franks took advantage of the internal disturbances and invaded Spain. The Galicians and the Navarrese followed suit. Punitive expeditions were sent at regular intervals against the Christian princes of Galicial Leon and Navarre. In 861 A.D. Navarre was overrun and its capital captured. In 865 A.D. the prince of Leon sued for peace, which was granted on an unconditional surrender.

Towards the end of his reign, Muhammad I had to face rebellions of a few Muslim chiefs. In Aragon a Muslim Spaniard, Musa by name, made himself master of Tudela, Huesca and Toledo submitted to Musa. He resisted the royal authority as long as he lived and established himself firmly in Saragossa. His independence was recognised by Muhammad I. Musa assumed the kingly title After Musa's death in 862 A.D., Muhammad I recovered Saragossa but ten years later Musa's sons once again expelled the royal troops and declared their independence. In 868 A.D., the Meridans rebelled under the leadership of a neo-Muslim, Ibn Marwan. With the help of the chief of Leon he defeated the royal force and laid waste the districts of Seville and Niebla. Royal forces were sent against him again and again but could not suppress him. Besides, a mountainous chieftain Umar bin Hafsun too raised a formidable revolt. The revolt was fomented by the Franks and the Christians of the Frontiers. "It is surprising," says Ameer Ali, "That the Arab kingdom did not break to pieces under the weight of these troubles. The success with which it passed through the ordeal at this period shows considerable vitality in the dominant race, and no little ability on the part of the rulers." The king sent his son Munzir, the hair apparent to put down the revolt. Munzir captured Saragossa and launched expeditions against Ibn Marwan, who was given a crushing defeat. Saragossa had again been conquered by the Aragonese rebels, who were led by Muhammad, a grandson of Musa, who joined hands with Ibn Hafsun. But Munzir gave them a crushing defeat and expelled them to the hilly regions.

Achievements and Character:

Muhammad I was a wise, just and brave ruler. Ibn al-Athir tells us that he was first to organise the Government of Andalusia (on a regular basis) and to frame rules and regulations for the administration of the state. He improved the condition of the people by his generosity. He was an incessant worker. He looked into the minutest details of the administration. "Once a treasurer made a mistake of fifteen dirhams in keeping the account of a sum of one hundred thousand dinars and fifteen dirhams. The king detected this and returned the account book for correction but the secretaries and treasurers would not trace the mistake and so the king had to point it out at last." He carried on wars relentlessly against the rebels and thereby saved the Empire from grave crisis and almost sure annihilation.

Muhammad I was patron of learning and a lover of science. He was himself a poet, writer and an orator. He like his father was a lover of beauty and embellished the capital by building, edifices and monuments. After a reign of thirty-four years Muhammad I died on the 4th August, 886 A.D. at the age of 65 years.

MUNZIR

(886-888 A.D.)

Munzir succeeded his father and ascended the throne of Cordova. He gave enough proof of his abilities by suppressing many revolts in his father's reign. His reign was not peaceful one. The Spanish people were disloyal and always ready to rebel against him. Some independent principalities had also been carved out. Ibn Hafsun, the most stubborn enemy of the Umayyads, was still ruling independently over vast territory. The Franks had established themselves and the greater part of Leon, Aragon and Catalonia was under the possession of the Christians. Munzir marched in person against Ibn Hafsun and besieged his fort. But before his attempts could bear any fruit he died only after a reign of two years. Dozy says, "he was poisoned by his physician at the instigation of his brother." Munzir was a gifted man with energy, prudence and bravery. "Had a longer life been vouchsafed him, there can be no doubt he would have succeeded in restoring complete order in his kingdom."

ABDULLAH

(888-912 A.D.)

Munzir was succeeded by his brother Abdullah to the throne of Spain. He came to power at a very critical time. Ibn ul-Athir writes "Andalusia became filled with disturbances and rebels rose on every side, and thus it remained throughout his reign. He found himself opposed not only by the native Spaniards but also by the Arab nobles. In Seville and Elvira too there were unrest and disorders. Revolts broke out in every part of the Kingdom. The Yamanites and Mudarites were at daggers drawn with each other. A strong king was the need of the hour but Abdullah being weak failed miserably to control the situation.

At the beginning of Abdullah's reign, serious riots broke out between the Arabs and the Spaniards in the districts of Elvira and Seville. The Arab chiefs established themselves in some of the strongest castles and defied the royal authority.

Sawwar was the leader of the Arabs in Elvira. Sawwar concluded treaties with the Arabs of Regio, Jean and Calatrava. An independent state was established in Seville in the person of Ibrahim bin Hajjah.

Taking advantage of the chaotic conditions of the country Umar bin Hafsun made an attempt to extend his authority in every direction. He even cast his covetous years to the throne of Cor supported by the Christians of Cordova. Umar extended his influence northwards. He had occupied all the chief fortresses to the south of the Guadalquivir and became the undisputed leader of the Spaniards. The position of Abdullah became very precarious. He sent a large force against Umar under the Command of Obaidullah. Obaidullah was successful in beating Umar. This was the turning point in the fortunes of the king, and the victory of Obaidullah saved the monarchy. Umar concluded a treaty with Abdullah. But when Abdullah demanded one of his sons as a hostage he refused and fighting began again. Abdullah took it wise to conclude a Peace Treaty with Umar in 901 A.D

After a troubled reign of twenty-five years, Abdullah died in 912 A.D.

ABDUR RAHMAN III

(912-961 A.D.)

Abdur Rahman III was the ablest and the greatest of the Umayyads of Spain. He succeeded the throne of Spain in 912 A.D. at the age of 23. He had a strong and charming personality, unerring judgment, resoluteness and courage. His reign opened a happy augury for the peninsula as it marked the dawn of an era of peace, prosperity and splendour. He has justly been called the saviour of the Muslim empire of Spain. During his predecessor Abdullah the condition of the Spanish empire became very deplorable for his weak, mean and selfish policy. It was in decaying stage and threatened with danger. Many Provincial Governors declared independence. He, on his accession, found the Umayyad the most weak and shrunk but he left it the most strong and extended. In fact, during his reign the Umayyad rule in Spain reached its climax. He came to the throne when Spain was passing through peace and order throughout the country.

After his accession to the Spanish throne Abdur Rahman III demanded in a proclamation of unconditional surrender of his subjects irrespective of caste and creed. Throwing away the policy in winning back the criminals, seditionists within the fold of his suzerainty. Far from being rash his policy was dictated by the intellectual and political tendencies of the day. His grandise scheme, besides the wholesale destruction of forces of anomaly and disruption, was to found a kind of political equilibrium and to restore the peace and stability of the distracted empire of Umayyads. He was endowed with every talent and quality necessary to strike fear and to win their sympathy and confidence.

Abdur Rahman proved himself the man of honour. His were those qualities of resoluteness, daring which characterize leaders of men in all ages. His hold and wise policy quelled all the rebellions, established his authority from the river Ebro to the Atlantic and from the foot of the Pyrenees to the Gibraltar. In April, 913 A.D. he himself led the troops against the rebels of the south. His evident desire to share with them not only the glory but also their fatigues and perils, evoked an extraordinary enthusiasm on their morale. In the first campaign the fortress of Ecija was captured. In a compaign of less than three months he captured the province of Elvira and Jean. Their strong castles were captured and dismantled and the entire tract was purged of brigands and pacified. Muhammad, the Governor of Seville, submitted to Abdur Rahman in 913 A.D., and offered him his services. After a long period of thirty-one years' continued struggle at length Ibn Hafsun, the most stubborn enemy of the Umayyads was smashed and his fort Babastro was occupied. Similarly the rebels in the west were brought to subjugation. Merida and Beja submitted. The neo-Muslim chief of Oksonobn was reduced to submission. After a siege lasting two years the Toledons capitulated unconditionally.

Wars with the Christian Kings :

The Christians were the most inveterate enemies of the Muslims. The Christians of the north, who were beginning to organize themselves, has a few tiny kingdoms of their own and were determined to fight Islam. Nobody can blame them for they were fighting for their homeland and their religion. It took them nearly five hundred years to win, though they fought the Muslims whenever they could. In 914 A.D., Ordono II, the Leonese Chief, invaded Muslim dominions, Abdur Rahman was then heavily engaged with the conflicts with Fatimid Caliph Muiz of Egypt. Yet an army was sent against the Leonese under the command of Ahmad bin Abi Abdah. The Muslim Commander was killed and the army routed. Ordono by joining hands with his ally Sancho, the chief of Novarre, again took a bold stand against the authority of Abdur Rahman III and was determined to crush the Muslims. In June, 920 A.D. Abdur Rahman took over the command of the army in person. No opposition was met by the Muslims till it crossed the Ebro. Ordono was defeated. Abdur Rahman captured Osma, San, Estevan, Clunia and several other places of importance. Then he turned his attention towards Sancho, the

Naverrese chief. The Naverrese destroyed the vanguard of Abdur Rahman's army and then waited in the defiles to cut his main force into pieces. "The Christians now committed a serious mistake, instead of remaining on the mountains they descended into the plains and audaciously accepted the battle the Muslims offered." After this brilliant victory Abdur Rahman returned, to his capital in September, 920 A.D. Ordono and Sancho again raided the Muslim frontier province, captured Nayera and Viguera in 923 A.D., killed many men and took away women and children as prisoners. Abdur Rahman repulsed their attacks, penetrated as far as Pamplona, the capital of Naverre, and destroyed many of its fortresses. Sancho tried several times to oppose but was as often beaten. In 925 A.D., Ordono's death was followed by a war of succession among his sons in which Ramiro II emerged victorious. He allied himself with the rebel Governor of Saragossa plundered the frontiers of the Muslim Empire. The Leonese were joined by the Navarrese. After the death of Sancho, his son Garcia, under the regency of his mother Tota, held the chieftaincy of Naverre. Abdur Rahman at once marched against them. He swept through Castile and Alva, raising to the ground the fortresses and towers of the Gablicians. But soon a formidable league was formed against Abdur Rahman. In 934 A.D., Muhammad bin Hashim, the rebel Governor of Saragossa, offered his services to Ramiro. The whole of north was thus arrayed against Abdur Rahman, the danger was one of extreme magnitude, but he met it with his usual energy. Saragossa was capitulated with great promptitude and its Governor was pardoned and re-appointed to his post. Tota, sustaining defeat after defeat, sued for peace and acknowledged Abdur Rahman as the lord of Navarre. Thus with the exception of Leon Abdur Rahman became the undisputed master of Spain.

Soon after this event, the Christian rulers of Leon and Navarre again revolted. Abdur Rahman led an expedition against them and reduced them to subjection. He established peace in the North where he had advanced the Muslim frontier line running from Lerida on the Atlantic to the source of the Ebro. After the death of Ramiro II his son Ordono III, sued for peace in 955 A.D. A treaty was concluded on terms favourable to the Christians.

Abdur Rahman assumed the title of Caliph :

Hitherto, the Umayyad rulers of Spain had been content with the designation of Amir or Sultan. In 929 A.D., Abdur Rahman took the title of al-Nasir and resumed the Caliphate of his Umayyad ancestors. Thus there were two Caliphs at this time in the world of Islam : the Abbasid Caliph in Baghdad and the Umayyad Caliph in Spain. The weakness of the Abbasid Caliphate might have prompted Abdur Rahman to assume the title of Caliph. The later Abbasid Caliphs were puppets in the hands of the Buwayhids, the Umayyad rulers of Spain so long abstained from assuming these titles thinking that the titles of Caliph and Ameer ul-Muminin appertained to the custodian of the Holy Cities of Mecca and Medina. But now the Holy Cities were held by al-Muiz, the Fatimid. "The sovereign of Cordova naturally considered that the defence the Omayyads of Spain had hitherto shown to the Caliph of Baghdad was now misplaced, and felt himself justified in assuming the titles of Caliph and Ameer ul-Muminin."

Fight with the Fatimids :

After the overthrow of Aghlabid rulers, the Fatimids, an extreme sect of the Shiite, now became dominant in North Africa. They sent their agents into Spain to work against the Umayyad rulers. Al-Mahdi negotiated with Ibn Hafsun to secure a footing in Spain. They had underestimated Abdur Rahman, who was a dangerous person to annoy. Abdur Rahman led an expedition into Africa in 917 A.D., and obtained possession of Morocco and Ceuta in the year 918 A.D. and 931 A.D. respectively. He also sent a fleet to the Barbary coast (modern Algeria and Tunisia) to attack and harass Fatimid shipping. These attacks and counterattacks continued for many years.

Character and achievements :

Abdur Rahman III was unquestionably the able and most gifted of all the Umayyad sovereigns of Spain. He had found the kingdom in a chaos, torn by factions, and parcelled among a number of feudal chieftains, a prey to anarchy and civil war, and exposed to continual raids on the part of the Christian tribes of the north. In spite of these innumerable obstacles he had saved Andalusia and made it greater and stronger than it was before. Order and prosperity reigned throughout his empire. The police organisation was so perfect that the stranger or the trader could travel in the most inaccessible tracts without the least fear of molestation or danger. To transmit news rapidly relays of horses were posted at various points. Vast sums of money were spent in the construction of roads and repair of public buildings. Castles, bridges, schools, colleges and libraries were to be found everywhere in the country. Hospitals for the sick, rest houses for the destitutes and orphanages were constructed. The splendid hydraulic works and the scientific system of irrigation which made the most sterile lands fruitful, evoked the admiration of the traveller. Commerce and industry, arts and sciences were also encouraged and developed. Cordova, Seville and other cities and numerous industries of wool, cotton, silk, leather and metal which improved the economic condition of the people and added to the wealth of Spain. By this time a new middle class of Muslims had grown up which took to industry and commerce very eagerly. The commerce of the country had increased to such an extent that the customs alone supplied the most considerable portion of the state-revenue. The low price of commodities and disappearance of beggary testify to the general prosperity of the people.

Abdur Rehman's court was one of the most glamorous in Europe. Envoys from the monarchs of Germany, Italy had flocked in his court. "The Emperors of England, France, Germany and Italy were but pygmies compared with the brilliant Abdur Rahman III." He established the absolute power over all classes of his subjects. He held the African despots at a distance and curbed the growing power of the Christians in the north. The power of the Arab nobles was crushed and a just and firm administration was set up in the cities and provinces. Abdur Rahman maintained a well-disciplined standing army. The Christians and Jews had settled down and became part of the Spanish Arab nation. He was tolerant to the non-Muslims. Churches were allowed to be built. He established a kind of political equilibrium and invited men of every religion to his church. Abdur Rahman III fused all the races of the country into a veritable nation. The Christians were employed freely in the service of the state.

It was during his reign that the arts and sciences were encouraged and developed. Dozy tells us that one-third of the state revenue annually was spent on the advancement of learning and culture. Historians like Ibn al-Ahmar, astronomers like Ahmad bin Nasr, philosophers like Ibn Masarrah and physicians like Said and Yahya bin Ishaq flourished during the time of Abdur Rahman III. Greek learning had been patronized in Muslim Spain. Many Greek works were translated into Arabic. The universities of Cordova and other Muslim towns rose to great height of achievement. Spain had seventy-five libraries in his time.

Abdur Rahman was a great builder. "Cordova," Hitti remarks, "with half a million inhabitants, seven hundred mosques and three hundred public baths, yielded in magnificence only to Baghdad and Constantinople." He built near Cordova a beautiful palace called al-Zahra which was considered a marvel of Muslim art. This royal palace with its four hundred rooms accommodated hundreds and thousands of slaves and guards. It was made of white marble imported from Nurmidia and Carthage. To construct this palace 10,000 workmen with 1,500 beasts of burden laboured foı a score of years. He illuminated a road of Cordova extending up to ten miles with strong lights when there was dearth of good roads in England and Paris.

Summing up his achievements, it may be said that his was the golden age of Spain. Appreciating his achievements, Dozy opines that, what excites the admiration and wonder of the students of this glorious reign is not so much the work achieved as the workman himself. Hitti says, "never was Cordova so prosperous, Andalusia so rich and the state so triumphant as it was in the reign of Abdur Rahman III. He was, indeed, the most enlightened sovereign that had ever a country produced. His meekness, his generosity, and his love of justice became proverbial." His ideas were typical of a modern monarch rather than of a medieval Caliph. He raised the ruined country to a condition such as wildest imagination can hardly conjure up.

Abdur Rahman III breathed his last on October, 961, A.D., after a long reign of forty-nine years.

HAKAM II

(961-976 A.D.)

Abdur Rahman III was succeeded by his son Hakam II under the title of al-Mustansir Billah. He retained the Ministers of his father and appointed Jafar al-Asqalabi, as his Prime Minister. Hakam had, for some years before his father's death, taken an active part in the administration of the state. Masudi speaks of Hakam as the most distinguished man of his time for his justice and excellent qualities. He was a wise and just, praise and the fame of his justice and wisdom had already spread into distant lands.

War with the Christians :

Soon after Hakam's accession the Christians of the North rose against him. Sancho and Garcia, the chiefs of Leon and Navarre respectively had made treaties with the late Sultan towards the close of his reign. But after the accession of Hakam II, these Christian chiefs threw off the Saracenic yokes under the impression that Hakam, who was known to be of a pacific and scholarly disposition would not insist on the terms of the treaties and even if he did declare war he would not have equalled his father's military achievements. But Hakam proved himself equal to the task. Hakam II personally led an expedition. Gonzalez suffered a heavy defeat at his hands and fled across the frontiers. Hakam then sent his General Ghalib against the king of Leon. With the help of the Muslim Governor of Saragossa, Ghalib had beaten Garcia and occupied the main cities. The border towns of Catalonia were attacked and destroyed. The principal cities were taken by storm. Sancho then submitted Gonzalez of Castile and Garcia of Navarre also submitted in 966 A.D. Their example was followed by their confederates, the counts Borrel and Miron. "This successful campaign," writes Dozy, "ended in the subjugation of all the Christian princes of the North."

The rival Fatimid Caliphs wanted to unite the whole Muslim-world under their rule. They had engaged agents in the cities of Spain and created troubles. The danger was however very skillfully averted.

In 972 A.D., Hakam sent an expedition under his General Ghalib into the western part of North Africa with a view to check the advance of al-Muizz, the Fatimid Caliph in Cairo. Hakam extended his supremacy over Morocco by defeating the Idrisids in 975 A.D.

Hakam II was a just and enlightened ruler. He observed the religious rites strictly and enforced the precepts of Sunna throughout his dominion. He attended public worship every Friday and distributed alms to the poor. The use of wine was strictly forbidden by him. He established peace within the country. He was tolerant to other religions and the people enjoyed complete religious freedom. Agriculture was improved. The natural resources of the country were properly exploited. Trade and commerce was encouraged and the country became rich and prosperous. The Caliph took interests in public works as well. The highways were repaired. Wells and fountains for the travellers were provided along the road. Hostels for the poor and hospitals for the sick were built.

Hakam II was, however, more known for the development of learning and culture. "Hakam," says Ibn Khaldun, "loved literature and the sciences, and showered his munificence on men of learning." "Hakam completed the civilization of Spain, and made Cordova shine like a lighthouse upon the darkness of Europe" says Joseph McCabe. The University of Cordova flourished under him. The Christian, Jews and Muslim students came here for higher studies not only from Spain but also from other parts of Europe, Africa and Asia. In the capital alone there were twenty-seven free schools. No town, however small, was without its school. Each principal city possessed a separate institution for higher study. He invited Professors from the East to the University of Cordova. His liberality towards the Spanish as well as the foreign scholars, scientists, and philosophers was unbounded. Abu Faraj, the author of the "Kitabul-Aghani" and the historian Hamadia received his munificence.

During his reign, the state of culture reached to such a high level that Dozy remarks, "In Spain almost everybody knew how to read and write, whilst in Christian Europe, save and except the clergy, even persons belonging to the highest ranks were wholly ignorant." This good and virtuous Caliph died on October 1, 967 A.D. and with him ended the glory of the Umayyads in Spain.

HISHAM II

(*976 A.D.*)

Hakam II was succeeded by his son Hisham II. He was only eleven years of age at that time. Due to his minority his mother Sultana Subh and the Secretary of State, Muhammad bin Abi Amir, took up the work of administration at their hands. Muhammad bin Amir, ambitious as he was, seized all powers and assuming the title of Hajib al-Mansur became the virtual master of the state. The Sultana became a mere puppet in his hands.

HAJIB AL-MANSUR

(*976-1002 A.D.*)

The original name of Hajib al-Mansur was Muhammad bin Abi Amir. His forefathers were men of letters and highly respected in the court. His great grandfather Abdul Malik al-Ma'afiri came to Spain and settled at Torrox in the province of Algeciras. His father Abu Hafs Abdullah was a jurist who died at the close of the reign of Abdur Rahman III.

Muhammad started his career as an ordinary man. From his earliest days he had been cherishing great political ambitions. While still a student he was confident of his intelligence, sagacity and diplomacy and predicted that one day he would be the most powerful man in Spain. After passing the Law Examination from the University of Cordova, he began to earn his livelihood as a court writer of petitions to the Qazi of Cordova. Hakam II appointed him as the steward of his young son Hisham II. His charming personality and pleasing manners soon made him a favourite of the ladies of the royal harem and especially the Queen of Hakam II, Sultana Subh. The Queen later on appointed him the steward of her personal property. Next he was appointed superintendent of the mint at Cordova. By his liberal gifts, Mansur built up a party of his own devoted to his interests. Mansur's first aim was to satisfy every caprice of the Sultana and to load her with gifts. In 972 A.D., he was appointed Sahib al-Shurtah of Cordova. As a prefect of Cordova he worked with zeal and impartiality. By dint of merits he rose to a high position and at the age of thirty-one he held five to six key posts. He was next appointed Controller-General of Finance.

Such was his position when Hakam II died. Sultana Subh exercised a great influence in the affairs of the state. Mansur in alliance with the young Caliph's mother made his influence felt in all the affairs of the state. Mansur first of all suppressed the "slaves" with the help of the then Prime Minister Mashafi. With the help of his father-in-law, Ghalib, Mansur overthrew

Mashafi and the other nobles who were opposed to his ascendancy. By now Sultana Subh had turned against Mansur. She even sought the help of the ruler of Morocco to overthrow Mansur. However, Mansur succeeded in persuading Hisham to issue a decree entrusting him with all affairs of the state. Thus Muhammad bin Abi Amir became the unrivalled master of Spain and assumed the title of al-Mansur Billah.

Mansur's first step was to get control over the army. With that in view he made up his mind to reorganise the army. His aim was to rank Spain among the leading states of Europe. The army organisation was defective. Too much power was laid in the hands of the chiefs of the army and there were few soldiers at the disposal of the crown. In order to gain for himself the devotion of the army, Mansur drew his recruits from the Berbers of North Africa and from the Christian, of the north of Spain. Though these soldiers were paid from the public treasury, yet they regarded themselves not the servants of the state but of Mansur himself. Strict discipline was then enforced in the army and his favourite officers of ability were appointed. To eliminate tribal jealousies Mansur distributed the Arabs among the divisions of the Berber and Christian mercenaries. Amir Ali writes that "Mansur's wonderful talent for army organisation had made him the ideal of the soldiers. His solicitude for the well-being and discipline of the soldiers was constant and unceasing." Dozy remarks that with the splendid army, Mansur gave to Spain a power "which it had not enjoyed even in the times of Abdur Rahman III."

Al-Mansur proved himself equally successful in military affairs as in civil. According to Ibn Khaldun, Mansur undertook fifty-two campaigns against the Christians of the North. He defeated the Christian chiefs of Leon, Castile, Aragon and Navarre in a series of battle. The generalship of al-Mansur impressed the Christians of the North of Spain in such a way that they shuddered at his name.

Al-Mansur was the most remarkable man of his age. After Abdul Rahman III, he was the greatest warrior and statesman in Europe in the Tenth Century. He was undoubtedly a man of genius and the predominant figure of his age. His authority was so much dreaded that scarcely any revolt disturbed the peace of the country during his time. Arab-Spain was raised to a high level of prosperity. He won for Spain a position which she never enjoyed after that. He was equally interested in the material prosperity of the country. Many new roads and bridges were constructed, trade and commerce was fostered. Agriculture was improved. He enlarged the mosque of Cordova. Considering all these achievements Dozy remarks that "not only his country but civilization itself was under obligation to him". Dozy again writes that al-Mansur was in many respects a great man and yet even without judging him too strictly by the immutable canons of morality, we find it impossible to love and difficult even to admire him.

Al-Mansur was a liberal patron of art and culture. He fostered Arab culture and civilisation in Spain and gave encouragement to every branch of science. According to Joseph McCabe, he was only second to Hakam II in the encouragement of men of letters and the patronage of scholars. Mansur's court was thronged by men of letters and scholars. He was a poet who had composed a distinguished work on Arabic literature which contained philalogical comments, anecdotes, verses and proverbs. Poets and historians received stipends from the royal treasury.

Decline of the Muslim Power in Spain

(*1002-1008 A.D.*)

After the death of Hajib al-Mansur, he was succeeded by his son Abdul Malik, surnamed al-Muzzaffar. He followed in the footsteps of his father in the management of the state. During his rule Muslim Spain continued to be prosperous at home. He remodelled the army with new contingents recruited mainly in North Africa. Commerce, industry and agriculture flourished. He won several victories over the Christian tribes. He was successful in putting down the risings and continued to govern with a strong hand as long as he lived. Abdul Malik was poisoned in September, 1008 A.D.

Abdul Malik was succeeded by his brother Abdur Rahman, nick-named Sanchol to the Hajibate. He was very unpopular with the people for his flagrant immorality. He was addicted to wine and ridiculed the sacred ceremonies of Islam. He lacked the ability of his father and brother but succeeded in obtaining from Hisham II his nomination as heir apparent to the Umayyad Caliphate. This caused discontent among the Qurayshites and the Umayyads who had unflinching devotion for the Caliphs. He aggravated the prevailing discontent by compelling the soldiers to use the turban of the theologians instead of the helmet. When Abdur Rahman had hardly left the Capital on an expedition to the north, the Cordovans forced Hisham to abdicate in favour of Muhammad bin Hisham bin Abdul Jabbar bin Abdur Rahman III.

Muhammad was proclaimed Caliph under the title of al-Mahdi in 1008 A.D. The new king plundered the palace of as-Zahira and reduced it to ashes. Abdur Rahman deserted by his followers, was taken prisoner and put to death. Thus was the Amirid despotism overthrown for ever. But the new Caliph did not reign long ; he soon alienated both the slaves and the Berbers by dismissing a large number of them from the military diwan. By his debauchery and licentious habit he also alienated the theologians who now lamented their bad choice. The ferocious Berbers fell off, and put forward another candidate of their own. They supported Sulaiman bin Abdur Rahman III. Cordova now became the theatre of fightful riots. Mahdi appealed for help to the Catalans and his rival Sulaiman invoked the assistance of the Christians of Castile and Leon. Thus the Muslims, instead of dictating terms to the Christians, supplicated their aid for the destruction of their Muslim rivals. Mahdi was at last defeated and killed. Sulaiman then seized the person of the helpless Hisham who was either killed or allowed to escape. Sulaiman was installed as a Caliph under the title of al-Mustain billah. He, however, did not live long to enjoy the fruits of his ill-gotten victory. Another revolted to his fall and death.

After the fall of Al-Mansur's family, the Umayyad Caliphs in Spain became puppets in the hands of the Berbers. During this period of confusion, they raised Abdur Rahman V, a grandson of Abdur Rahman III to the Caliphate. He was killed soon after his accession by the royal guards. Muhammad was the next person to occupy the throne. The people became ferocious when he appointed a weaver as his Prime Minister. The mob killed his Prime Minister and Muhammad escaped in the guise of a woman. The last Umayyad Caliph of Spain Hisham III was overthrown by the Berbers in 1035 A.D.

NORTH AFRICA

Conquest of Mu'awiya :

The conquest of North Africa was an important event of Mu'awiya's reign. Before proceeding with the conquests in Africa, we should know the Arabic terminology applied by the Arabs to different parts of North Africa : (*a*) The Arabs called the lower Nile valley as Misr, the modern Egypt. (*b*) To the west of Egypt, lay the Italian territory Lybia. The eastern side of it was known to the Arabs as Cyrenacia and that of western part as Tripolitania. Further west of Lybia, we have the French territory Tunis. This whole region was known to the Arabs as Africa. To the west of Africa, lay the territories of Algeria and Morocco. This whole region from Algeria to Morocco was known to the Arabs as 'Al-Maghrib'.

The first invasion of this province had taken place in the reign of Hazrat Umar. Under Hazrat Usman the Arab forces had advanced as far as Barea. After the defeat of Gregorius the Byzantine Prefect, at the memorable battle fought not far from ancient Carthage, the Romans undertook to pay an annual tribute to the Arabs, who then withdrew from the country leaving small garrison here and there. The Roman Governors re-occupied the abandoned territories, but their capacity and exactions were so intolerable that before long the natives themselves invited the Arabs to liberate them from the Byzantine yoke. Mu'awiya responded to their call, and an army under the celebrated Uqba, son of Nafe, marched into Africa, beat down all opposition, and reduced the country to Arab dependency. In 670 A.D. Uqba built the famous military city of Kairowan to the South of Tunis to keep in check the fierce unruly Berbers, and also to guard against the Roman ravages from the sea. The brilliant march of Uqba and the crushing blows he inflicted on the Romans and the Berbers had the effect of keeping the country quiet for several years. With a slight intermission owing to his recall to Damascus, he ruled Africa and the Western dependency until his death in 683 A.D.

The most striking incident in the Caliphate of Mu'awiya was the siege of Constantinople. An expeditionary force commanded by Yazid sailed through Dardanelles and landed in. For six years the Muslims beleaguered the Constantinople, capital city of Christendom, and for six years the valour of the Romans and the impregnable wall of the city held them at bay. Hard pressed from all sides Mu'awiya ordered for withdrawal of the siege.

Reconquest of Africa :

During the Caliphate of Mu'awiya, Africa was conquered by Uqba. But the Muslims suffered a terrible reverse in Africa when in 683 A.D. the Berbers, under the leadership of Koseila, rose in rebellion and overwhelmed Uqba, who with his entire army perished in the fight. Abdul Malik sent an army under Zubair for the reconquest of Africa. Zubair was eminently successful in destroying Koseila and the united forces of the Berbers. The whole province was cleared of the enemy. Being encouraged by this success Zubair sent out expeditions for the subjugation of the outlying parts. This proved a fatal mistake. The Greeks and Berbers, taking advantage of the absence of his army, took Zubair by surprise and cut him to pieces. Africa again slipped out of the hands of the Muslims. Abdul Malik sent another force under Abdul Malik Hasan bin Numan to restore the lost prestige of Islam. He, after a hard fight, recaptured Kairowan. The city of Carthage was stormed, and the Romans and Berbers were defeated in the open field. About this time the Berbers acknowledged the authority of a woman, who is called by the Arab historians the Kahina. For five years she remained the queen of Africa. She wanted to throw off the Muslim yoke. Abdul Malik despatched another army to the assistance of Hasan. The Kahina then swore allegiance to Abdul Malik. Africa passed once more under the Umayyads.

Pacification of Africa :

During the Caliphate of Abdul Malik, Hasan bin Numan pacified and reconquered Africa. He was succeeded by Musa bin Nusayr to the Governorship of Africa in 708 A.D. The removal of Hasan encouraged the Berbers of North Africa to throw off the Muslim yoke. They had miscalculated the energy and vigour of the new viceroy. He led an army against them and succeeded in suppressing their formidable revolt. By adopting a conciliatory policy, Musa reconciled the Berbers to the rule of Islam. But the Byzantine from the islands of the Mediterranean harassed the Muslims of North Africa. Musa sent out an expedition against them and succeeded in capturing Majorca, Minorca and Iviea. "Under the Muslim rule these islands soon became extremely flourishing. As in other places, the Saracens erected beautiful buildings, introduced various kinds of handicrafts, and otherwise materially improved the country."

Campaigns in Africa :

There were great reverses in Africa where the Muslims sufferred greatly. The whole of North Africa was convulsed by the revolt of the Berbers and the Kharijites. A new sect of fanatics called Saffarides had about this time appeared in Mauritania. The oppressive rule of the viceroy's son, who was active on behalf of his father at Tangiers, roused them to fury, and, joined by the Berbers, they rose *en masse*. They killed the Governor and seized the city. Taking Tangiers, they marched towards Kairowan. The Muslim army which opposed the enemy, was destroyed in the battle known as "the Fight of the Nobles". This defeat threw into disorder the whole of Northern Africa. Hearing this disaster, Hisham then appointed Kulsum to the command of the Muslim army in 937 A.D. But Kulsum also proved failure. Hisham then appointed Hanzala to the Governorship of Africa. "He combined the religious enthusiasm of the day of Omar with gentleness of heart unusual in that age. Standing in the great square in front of the Cathedral Mosque, he harangued the people that the struggle between the pent-up Muslims and the rebels outside was one of life and death, that a Berber victory would mean the promiscuous slaughter of the inhabitants, in which neither age nor sex would be spared. Hanzala succeeded in restoring peace and prosperity in North Africa by defeating the Berbers and the Kharijites in the battle known as "the Field of Idols". "One hundred eighty thousand Berbers, with their principal leaders, are said to have been killed in the fight, whilst the Saracenic loss, though severe, was not so great. So long Hanzala held the reins of office the country was free from disturbance. Under his mild and just Government North Africa soon recovered its prosperity.

The Abbasids :

In Africa the Kharijites were very turbulent. The Kharijites did not recognise the Abbasid rule and became an incessant source of trouble to Mansur sent his Generals over and again to fight against them, but with no better result. At last in 765 A.D., Mansur appointed Aghlab as the Governor of Africa. He ruled successfully for nearly two years, but he fell in an action with the Kharijites near Tunis. He was succeeded by Umar bin Hafs, who proved himself successful ruler and held his post for nearly three years. The Kharijites again rebelled and besieged Kairowan. Umar was killed in action and the capital fell into the hands of the rebels. Being enraged Mansur sent a force under Yazid bin Muhallib, a man of energy and great administrative power. Yazid curbed the Kharijites, killed their leaders and within a few months established peace in Africa. He held the Government of Africa for fifteen years, until his death in 787 A.D.

Harun Al-Rashid :

The early part of Harun's reign was greatly troubled by the Kharijites. They revolted several times in this reign, but their risings were suppressed without difficulty. One of these insurrections is remarkable for the appearance of a young girl named Laila who defied the imperial authority on many occasions. The revolt was begun by her brother Walid, son of Tarif. When he fell, she assumed the command. She repeatedly gave battle to Harun's troops. Damascus was harassed by Mudharite and Himyarite strifes. Harun allowed the two factions to weaken themselves by internal dissension. In the end he intervened, and with a firm hand put a stop to their disorders. Similar trouble broke out in Mosul.

After the death of Yazid bin Haithem Muhallib (appointed Governor by Mansur in 772 A.D.) in 787 A.D., troubles broke out in Africa. Yazid's brother Ruh was appointed as Goveror of Africa by Harun in 787 A.D. Ruh succeeded in suppressing the revolt and ruled over Africa successfully for several years. But again trouble started there and Harun sent his most trusted General Harsama as Governor. But he also could not tackle the situation very successfully, so he resigned. Therafter, Ibrahim bin Aghlab put a proposal to Harun that he would not only restore peace and prosperity in Africa but also remit 40,000 dinars annually to the capital. Harun accepted Ibrahim's offer and granted him the hereditary Governorship of Africa. Since then a new dynasty came into being called the Aghlabids.

Professor Mahmood Brelvi in his book entitled "Islam in Africa" described about the conquest of Muslims after 761 C.E. as follows :

The destruction of Abul-Khattab's army by Syrian troops gave Ifriqiyyah back to the Arabs in 761 C.E. Forty years of bloody fighting and numberless battles (300 according to Ibn Khaldun) were required before they could again assert their sway in the Eastern Maghrib. The remaining lands were quite lost to them. States, with a Berber population under leaders of Arab descent, were, set up in various places, quite independent of the Abbasid Caliph : for example, the kingdom of Tahrat or Tagdemt (founded by Imam Ibn Rustam of the Ibadis in the Central Maghrib), that of Sijilmasa (under Banu Midrar) ; that of Tlemsen (founded by Abu Qarra, the leader of Banu Ifrin) ; that of Nukur ; that of the Perghawata (on the shores of the Atlantic Ocean) ; and, lastly, the kingdom of Fas (founded in the beginning of the Ninth Century C.E. by the 'Alid Idris II with the help of the Berber tribes, the Miknasa, Sedrata and Zwagha). Only the semi-independent dynasty of the Aghlabids (802-908 C.E.) recognised the suzerainty of the Abbasids. They raised, from the Berbers, their troops for the conquest of Sicily.

Thereafter, the support of the Berbers assured the supremacy of the Shiite doctrines in the Maghrib. The Ketama tribe furnished Da'i Abu Abdullah with the troop, who fought the Aghlabids and laid the basis of the Fatimid power for Mahdi 'Ubayd Allah. Although the Fatimids succeeded in suppressing the Berber Imamate of Taharat, they could not, however, prevent the Idrisids from retaining their power in the Western Maghrib. The Fatimids were also unable to make vassals of the Maghrawa and Zenata, who, out of hatred for the Fatimids placed themselves under the Umayyads of Spain. And, lastly, the Fatimids had to put down the revolt of the Kharijis, led by Abu Yazid (942-44 C.E.), from which they only emerged victorious with the help of the Sanhaja of the Central Maghrib.

The Fatimids :

The Fatimids soon turned their attention to the east and, as soon as Caliph al-Mu'izz was firmly established in Egypt, they lost interest in the Maghrib. In the east of North Africa, the Sanhaja displayed the Ketama and supported the Zirids, who were Governors of Ifriqiyyah (*i.e.*, Tunisia) and Tripolitania. In the west of North Africa, since the Idrisids had fallen, the power passed into the hands of the Zenata, who become independent. In the beginning of the Eleventh Century C.E., the Zirid kingdom broke up; the Hammadid kingdom was formed in the centre of the Maghrib, the rulers of which recognised the authority of the Caliph of Baghdad. In the middle of the Eleventh Century, as has been seen, the invasion of the Arab Hilali tribes from Egypt devastated Ifriqiyyah and part of the Maghrib and modified radically the ethnography of North Africa.

Almoravids and Almohads dynasties :

At this time, two Berber dynasties, the Almoravids and the Almohads, each proclaiming different reformed religious doctrines, succeeded in establishing their preponderance, for a time, in North Africa. The triumph of the Almoravids was that of the Lemtuna (nomadic Berbers from Sahara, between Southern Morocco and the banks of the Senegal and the Niger). They were converted to Islam in the Third Century A.H., and were taught the true doctrines of Islam by the 'marabout' Ibn Yasin in order to propagate the faith among the people of the Sudan, the Sahara and Southern Morocco. Their chief, Yusuf bin Tashifin, founded Marrakesh in 1062 C.E., subdued all Morocco and Central Maghrib, drove back the advancing Christians in the Iberian peninsula by the victory of Zallaqa in 1086 C.E. deposed the Andalusian Amirs, and became the sole master of Muslim Spain.

The Masmuda of Deren, converted the Unitarianism (Tawhid, whence the name Almohads) by the preaching of Ibn Tumart, rose against them. Led by a Kumiya Berber of great ability, named 'Abd al-Mu'min, they soon put an end to the Almoravid rule. The empire, founded by the Almohads, was even larger than that of their predecessors. Although 'Abd al-Mu'min was not actually able to conquer all Spain, he destroyed the Hammadid kingdom of Bejaya and the Zirid kingdom of Ifriqiyyah, drove the Christians out of the ports (they had seized), and made himself the lord of all the country between the Gulf of Sidra and the Atlantic. A great Berber empire, thus, extended over the whole of North Africa. Like the Almoravids, the Almohads, too, could not keep the orthodoxy in religion. One of them, Ibn Mamun, cursed the memory of Ibn Tumart and raged against true believers. A century after the death of 'Abd al-Mu'min, the last of his descendants, Abu Dabbus, came to an inglorious end as the leader of a robber band in 1279 C.E.

By this time, the Maghrib was partitioned among new powers—the Marinids in Fas, the 'Abdal-Wadis at Tlemsen and the Hafside in Tunis. In Morocco, the tribes of the mountain regions were in a constant state of revolt against the Marinids ; in Central Maghrib, the Banu Wemannu of Warsenis, the Zwawa of the Jurjura, the Kabyle of Constantine, the peoples of the Zab and the Jerid, threw off the yoke of the princes of Constantine, Bejaya and Tunis. Since the Fourteenth Century, the Berbers form a cordon on the frontier of the land of the Negroes parallel to that formed by the Arabs on the borders of the two Maghribs (Morocco and Algeria) and Ifriqiyyah or Tunisia. In the Fifteenth and Sixteenth Centuries, the 'marabouts' came to them from the legendary Sakiyat al-Hamra, believed to be a regular nursery of Muslim missionaries and saints.

At the present-day, the Berbers are scattered over an immense area, bounded on the east by the oases of Siwah, the desert of Libya, and the mountains of Tibesti ; on the west by the Atlantic, and on the south by the Hausa countries, the middle course of the Niger and the Senegal. Of all the parts of North Africa, Morocco is the one in which the Berber element is the most important. It predominates in the Rif, in the various ranges of the Atlas, in the Sus, in the valleys of the Wed Nun and of the Dra'a, and in the oases.

There are some Berber tribes in the mountains of the lands of Barca, in the Ghuryan, the Jebel Ifrin and in the Jebel Nefusa—the religious stronghold of the Ibadis. They are also met with in the oases of Siwah, Awjila, Saqna, Timissa and in the Fezzan:

Berber dialects are spoken among the Jerbi (island of Jerbia), who, like the Nefusi, belong to the Ibadi sect, among the Troglodytes of the Matmata and in the Jebel (Secon). The Khumir have been Arabicised.

Kabylia in the north and the Awras in the south-east have been the great centres of resistance of the Berbers. In the Algerian Sahara, the oases of Wed Righ and Wargla, the oases of the Mazb, peopled by the Ibadi Berbers and the Qsurs of Moghar, mark the road between south Constantine and South East Morocco.

Long subjected to Turkish domination, the peoples of North Africa fell, one after the other, under the control of the great colonial powers: Britain, France and Italy. The Mediterranean became a sort of a European lake and North Africa a prolongation of that Western Europe of which the ambitions and rivalries had the results we are all familiar with.

Chapter 6

Post-Mongol Muslim Period

MUSLIMS IN INDO-PAKISTAN

On Qutbuddin Aibak's sudden death the Amirs and Maliks of Lahore placed Aram Shah on the throne of Delhi with the title of Sultan Aram Shah. Aram proved himself quite incompetent to rule and was soon set aside in favour of Iltutmish, the then Governor of Badaun.

ILTUTMISH

(1211-1236 A.D.)

Iltutmish began his career as a slave of Qutbuddin. He rose to eminence by sheer dint of merit, and it was solely by virtue of his fitness that he superseded the hereditary claimants to the throne.

The Mongol Invasion :

It was during the reign of Iltutmish in the year 1221 A.D., that the Mongols appeared for the first time on the bank of the Indus, under their dreaded leader Chengiz Khan. Chengiz Khan made the Mongols the greatest political and military power in Asia. He overran the countries of Central and Western Asia with rapidity, and when he attacked Jalaluddin, the last Shah of Khwarizm the latter fled to the Punjab and sought asylum in the dominion of Iltutmish. Iltutmish wisely refused to give shelter to Jalaluddin. Jalaluddin entered into an alliance with the Khokars, and after defeating Nasir-ud-din Qabacha of Multan, plundered Sind and Northern Gujrat and went away to Persia. The Mongols plundered Sind and Western Punjab, but repulsed due to the terrible heat of the Punjab, they did not advance into the heart of India. India was thus saved from a terrible calamity.

Conquest of Iltutmish :

As soon as the Mongol threat was over, Iltutmish started a series of conquests. He first turned his attention to Bengal. Bengal was then ruled by Ghiyasuddin Khalji, who had declared independence and assumed royal title. He issued the coins and read Khutba in his own name. He is said to have subjugated Jannagar, Kamrup, Tirhut and 'Bang'. He transferred his capital from Devkot to Gaur-Lakhnauti. In 1225 A.D., Iltutmish marched against him, but Ghiyasuddin avoided war and concluded a treaty with him. But as soon as he returned to Delhi, Ghiyasuddin reasserted his independence and occupied Bihar. In 1127 A.D. the Sultan sent his eldest son Nasiruddin Mahmud towards Bengal. He captured Lakhnauti and killed Ghiyasuddin. Then he was appointed as the Governor of the province, but his promising career was cut short by early death in 1229 A.D. Thereafter, Alauddin Daulat Shah Khalji became the Governor of Bengal. But he was driven out by Ikhtiyaruddin Balka, a partisan of Ghiyasuddin. In 1230-31 A.D. Iltutmish defeated and killed Balka and Bengal was brought under the control of Delhi. Malik Alauddin Jani was installed as the Governor of Bengal.

Iltutmish then turned his arms against the Hindu chiefs. Ranthambor and Gwalior which had asserted independence were recaptured. The Sultan next invaded Malwa, took the fort of Bhilsa and captured and sacked Ujjain. He thus completed the conquest of the Northern India.

RUKNUDDIN FIRUZ

(1236 A.D.)

Iltutmish had nominated, on his death-bed, his daughter Raziyya as his heiress. But the nobles of his court took it as insult to bow their heads before a woman and disregarding the deceased Sultan's wishes, raised to the throne his eldest son Ruknuddin Firuz. This was an unfortunate choice. Ruknuddin was unfit to rule. He indulged in low activities, neglected the affairs of state, and squandered away its wealth. The management of public business slipped into the hands of his unscrupulous mother, Shah Turkan, who was originally a handmaid in the *Harem*. The whole kingdom was plunged into disorder. The Central Government lost its authority over the provinces. The Maliks rebelled against the royal authority, and the Governors of Oudh, Multan and Badaun joined them. The queen-mother and Firuz were made captives and were thrown into the prison. Firuz died in November, 1236 A.D.

RAZIYYA SULTANA

(1236-1240 A.D.)

After the death of Ruknuddin, Raziyya was proclaimed as Sultan. She did not find the throne of Delhi a bed of roses. Nizamul-Mulk Muhammad Junaidi, Ruknuddin's Wazir, and some otner nobles, did not recognize her accession and organised an opposition against her. But by her astuteness and superior diplomacy, the queen soon overpowered her enemies and restored order throughout the kingdom. In the words of Minhaj-us-Siraj, "from Lakhnauti to Debal and Damrilah all Maliks and Amirs tendered obedience and submission".

Raziyya was not, however, destined to enjoy a peaceful reign. She seemed to give offence to orthodox Muslim opinion by casting off female garments and by abandoning the prevalent seclusion or *purdah*. She marched in person against her enemies and conducted the affairs of her Government with considerable ability in open *Darbar*. But the main charge brought against her was that she showed undue favour to the Abyssinian slave Jalaluddin Yaqut, who was elevated to the post of master of the stables. This offended the Turkish nobles. The first man who revolted openly was Ikhtiyaruddin Altuniya, the Governor of Sarhind. The queen marched with a large army to suppress the revolt but was defeated and put in the custody of Altuniya. Yaqut was put to death and the nobles raised her brother Muizuddin Bahram to the throne. Meanwhile Altuniya, whose exclusion from the rewards of successful rebellion was, naturally a bitter disappointment to him, had released Raziyya from prison, married her and then marched towards Delhi. In October, 1240 A.D., Altuniya was defeated along with the queen by Muizuddin Bahram. She was put to death with her husband.

MUIZUDDIN AND ALAUDDIN

The removal of Raziyya was followed by a period of disorder and confusions. The new Sultan, Muizuddin Bahram Shah was a worthless and incompetent ruler. His reign saw the growing influence of the nobles who were known as the 'Forty'. During his rule the country knew no peace and tranquillity. The only important event of his reign was the invasion of the Mongols. In 1241 A.D., the Mongols invaded the Punjab, sacked Lahore, and laid the city waste. The king was too feeble to take any steps against them. The 'forty' besieged him in the White Fort at Delhi and put him to death (1242 A.D.)

The nobles now raised Alauddin Masud Shah, a grandson of Iltutmish, to the throne. His brief inglorious reign presents little noteworthy events except a rebellion in Bengal, a Hindu rebellion in Bihar, and an invasion of Punjab by the Mongols. In June, 1246 A.D., Masud was deposed and thrown into prison, where he died shortly after.

NASIRDUDIN MAHMUD

(1246-55 A.D.)

Nasiruddin Mahmud was an amiable and unassuming prince, possessing the virtues of continence, frugality, and practical piety, and a taste for calligraphy, which led him to employ his leisure in making copies of the Qur'an. For the greater part of his reign he was under the influence of Ghiyasud-din Balban, a Turkish slave whom Iltutmish had purchased and married to one of his daughters. Balban proved a capable Minister and for twenty years served his master. In fact, the record of Nasiruddin's reign is the list of Balban's achievements.

The pressing external danger of the reign was menace of Mongol invasions. The Mongols had not only sacked Lahore and levelled its buildings with the ground, but had so devastated the country west of the Jhelum that no cultivation remained. The turbulent Hindus of the Doab and also the Meos of Mewat were in rebellion. On the advice of Balban, Nasiruddin first set out to recover the Punjab. The Khokars were subdued, and a marauding force of Mongols fled when it found itself confronted with Balban's army. The Doab was reduced to obedience and the Meos were severely chastised. Balban's reward for these services was promotion to the post of lieutenant of the kingdom. This made Kutlugh Khan, Imaduddin Raihan, and some of the 'forty' jealous of him. They made a conspiracy against him and persuaded the king against him. The leader of the conspiracy was Raihan. Consequently Balban was dismissed from his post. Raihan's arrogance soon displease the Turkish nobles and Balban was again brought back to his previous post and position. Henceforward he was supreme in the kingdom. Balban now tried to crush the power of his opponents. Kutlugh Khan who rose in revolt in Oudh was suppressed. Balban next dealt effectively with all other rebels. Towards the close of this reign an envoy of Halaku Khan, the grandson of Chengiz Khan, came to the court of Delhi. The mission assured Nasiruddin that no Mongol raids would in future be permitted.

Nasiruddin died without an heir, on February 18, 1266 A.D. He was a pious, God-fearing and kind-hearted ruler who patronised the learned and sympathised with the poor and the distressed. It was during his reign that Minhajus-Siraj, his Chief Qazi, wrote the valuable history 'Tabakat-i-Nasiri' named after the Sultan.

GHIYASUDDIN BALBAN

(1266-87 A.D.)

In his early life, Ghiyasuddin Balban was a slave of Iltutmish. But soon he began to rise high by dint of his merit and ability. His political career may be divided into two parts : as a Minister of Nasiruddin (1246-66 A.D.) and as a Sultan of Delhi. As a Minister of Nasiruddin, Balban served the Delhi Sultanate for 20 years during which he repelled the menace of Mongol inroads and suppressed the rebellious Hindu chiefs. In fact, the history of Nasiruddin's reign is the history of Balban's achievements. Sultan Nasiruddin had no male child, so he had nominated Balban (his Minister and father-in-law) as his successor. On his accession Balban was confronted with a formidable and difficult task. The Turkish nobles became turbulent and took recourse to plots and intrigues. The prestige of the Sultan had sunk very low. Robber-bands infested the neighbourhood of Delhi. Above all there was the danger of recurring Mongol raids. The condition of the country at his accession has been aptly described by Ziauddin Barni in the following words : "Fear of the governing power, which is the basis of all good government, and the source of the glory and splendour of all states, had departed from the hearts of all men, and the country had fallen into a wretched condition. Thus, a strong ruler was the need of the time."

With the help of the army he suppressed with merciless severity all rebellions and disorders within the empire. The peace of the empire around Delhi was seriously disturbed by the Rajputs of Mewat. They not only plundered travellers on the roads but even carried their depredations into the heart of Delhi. They used to come prowling into the city, giving all kind of trouble, depriving the people of their rest. So great was their audacity that the western gate of the capital had to be closed at the time of afternoon prayer and even the garb of a mendicant was no protection against their high handedness. He suppressed the Mewatis with an iron hand, ordered all the jungles and forests to be cleared of the robbers. He next turned to the turbulent Hindus of Doab, captured their strongholds and ruthlessly chastised them. To keep them in check he established military posts at several places and garrisoned them with Afghan soldiers. The rebel Hindus of Ketehr (Rohilkhand) were also dealt terribly. By these drastic measures the roads were freed from robbers and the vicinity of Doab was made safe. In 1268-69 A.D., Balban led an expedition into the Salt Range, punished the recalcitrant Hindus. In a nutshell, by his stern attitude towards the ambitious nobles and unruly chiefs. Balban did much to restore order and to secure the stability of the Sultan.

Rebellion in Bengal :

Balban's principal military operation was directed against Tughril Khan, the Governor of Bengal. Tughril Khan was appointed Governor of Bengal by Balban in 1268 A.D. Being influenced by unwise counsellors, Tughril declared independence in 1279 A.D. He assumed the title of Sultan, struck coins and caused the Khutba to be read in his own name. He attacked Jajnagar, carried off a large booty consisting of valuable goods. The booty was lavishly distributed among the nobles, soldiers and subjects. Sedition became so common that the soldiers as well as citizens ceased to fear the sovereign power, and gave their adhesion to the rebellious Governor.

Balban was grealy perturbed by the news of this revolt. He at once sent a large army to Bengal under Amir Khan but he was defeated by the rebel Governor. Balban became so much enraged at the defeat that he ordered Amir Khan to be hanged. Another army was sent to Bengal under Malik Targhi, but this expedition, too met with a like fate. Hethen decided to march in person to Lakhnauti with a large army, accompanied by his son, Bughra Khan. He found Lakhnauti almost deserted, for Tughril had already fled from his capital with his troops and adherents. Balban continued his march and advanced into Eastern Bengal in pursuit of Tughril and his men. Tughril was captured and beheaded in 1281 A.D. On returning to Lakhnauti the Sultan inflicted exemplary punishments on the relatives and adherents of Tughril. "On either side of the principal bazar, a street more than two miles in length, a row of stakes was set up and the family and the adherents of Tughril were impaled upon them. None of the beholders had ever seen a spectacle so terrible and many swooned with terror and disgust." Before leaving Bengal he appointed his second son, Bughra Khan, Governor of Bengal, and instructed him to be dutiful in the work of administration. "Understand me and forget not that if the Governors of Hind or Sind, of Malwa or Gujrat, of Lakhnauti or Sonargaon, shall draw the sword and become rebels to the throne of Delhi, then such punishment as has fallen upon Tughril and his dependents will fall upon them, their wives, their children, and all their adherents."

Mongol Invasions and his Frontier Policy :

Balban's chief anxiety was the fear of the Mongol invasions. The Mongols had by this time established themselves at Ghazni and from that vantage ground began to raid Sind and the Punjab. Fear of Mongol invasions was a vital factor in determining his policy. He thus abstained from following the policy of expansion, reorganised the army and re-constructed forts and strengthened the defence line of the frontier. To check their depredations Balban appointed his eldest son, Prince Muhammad, Governor of Multan, while his second son, Bughra Khan, was placed in charge of the frontier district of Samana. Their combined operations warded off the Mongol attack for a time. But in 1279 A.D., the Mongols renewed their invasion under Tamar Khan and ravaged the upper Punjab and even crossed the Sutlej. Prince Muhammad lost his life in repelling the attack. The death of this excellent prince gave a rude shock to the old Sultan. It cast him into a state of deep depression and he died in 1287 A.D.

KAIKOBAD

(1287-90 A.D.)

When Balban died in 1287 A.D., his nobles raised Kaikobad, son of Bughra Khan to the throne. Bughra Khan did not oppose his son's accession, but assumed in Bengal the royal title of Nasiruddin Mahmud Bughra Shah. Kaikobad's reign was worthless. He was a dissolute young man, quite incompetent to bear the burden which had exhausted even his stern grand-father. Kaikobad became a puppet in the hands of an officer named Nizamuddin who encouraged him in all sorts of vices in order to retain his hold upon the young king. The affairs of the Government fell into disorder. All these things reached the ears of Bughra Khan who came to Delhi to meet his son. He advised his son to refrain from such vices.

Intrigues soon became rampant and the nobles began to quarrel for power. After the death of Nizamuddin, Malik Firuz became the Ariz-i-Mamaluk. His elevation offended the powerful Turkish nobles who looked down upon the Khalji tribe. Soon after this Kaikobad was struck down with paralysis. The Turkish nobles put on the throne Kaikobad's infant son Kayumars. This alarmed Malik Firuz who occupied Delhi, caused Kaikobad to be murdered, and ascended the throne on March, 1290 A.D. Tus ended the dynasty of the Turkish Slave Sultans of Delhi.

THE KHALJI DYNASTY

There is a difference of opinion among the historians as regards the origin of the Khaljis. Major Revaerty sought to prove that Khaljis could not be classed as Afghans or Pathans, and he assigned to them a Turkish origin. But the contemporary author Ziauddin Barni describes the Khaljis as different from the Turks and remarks that with the death of Kaikobad, the rule of the Turks in Indo-Pakistan came to an end. Modern view is that the Khaljis were a Turkish tribe, but, having been long domiciled in Afghanistan, had adopted some Afghan habits and customs.

JALALUDDIN FIRUZ KHALJI

(*1290-96 A.D.*)

Jalaluddin was the most powerful of the Khalji chiefs. He was seventy years old when he became Sultan. At first he was not much liked by the nobles and the populace of Delhi. He had to make Kilokri the seat of Government, and for some time he could not even enter Delhi. Gradually he established his authority, and as Barni writes, "the excellence of his character, his justice, generosity and devotion, gradually removed the aversion of the people and hopes of grants of land assisted his conciliating, though grudgingly, and unwillingly the affection of his people."

The one noteworthy military enterprise of the Sultan was an expedition against Ranthambhor. The hostile Rajputs shook off the authority of the Delhi Sultanate and declared their independence under Rana Hamir Mal. The Sultan marched against the Rana, but ultimately he changed his mind from capturing the fort as he was not willing to shed blood.

In 1292 A.D., he successfully defended his kingdom against a strong Mongol invasion and repulsed the invaders from Lahore. About 3,000 Mongols, who had surrendered, embraced Islam and they came to be known "New Musalmans." They were allowed to settle near a suburb of Delhi. "This was an ill-advised concession", remarks R.C. Majumdar, "which produced trouble in the future. The "New Musalmans" proved to be turbulent neighbours of the Delhi Government and caused it much anxiety."

The most noteworthy event of Jalaluddin's reign was a daring raid into the Deccan, undertaken by Alauddin, his nephew and son-in-law. The Sultan was very affectionate to his nephew and appointed him Governor of Kara in the district of Allahabad. In 1292 A.D. Alauddin invaded Malwa with the Sultan's permission, plundered Bhilsa, and carried an immense booty to Delhi. But Alauddin exceeded his authority and plunged into the heart of the Deccan, a country as yet free from penetration by the Muslims. He moved southward and marched through Berar and Khandesh and surprised Raja Ramchandra of Devagri, plundered his capital and compelled him to surrender Ellichpur. He then returned to Kara with an enormous quantity of gold and many precious jewels. "This daring raid of the Khalji invader", remarks the authors of "An Advanced History of India," "not only entailed a heavy economic drain on the Deccan, but it also opened the way for the ultimate Muslim domination over the lands beyond the Vindhyas."

ALAUDDIN KHALJI

(*1296-1316 A.D.*)

On the death of Jalaluddin Firuz, the adherents of Alauddin Khalji proclaimed him Sultan in 1296 A.D. With the reign of Alauddin began what may be called imperial period of the Sultanate, during which the kings of Delhi extended their authority, directly or indirectly, over the whole of the Indian peninsula.

His early difficulties, on his accession to the throne Alauddin had to face a critical situation of plots and revolts. The Jalali nobles had not yet forgotten the murder of the old Sultan and were secretly trying to avenge it. The Queen-dowager, Malika Jahan, who in the language of Barni was "one of the silliest of the silly", had in the meanwhile placed her younger son on the throne under the title of Ruknuddin Ibrahim. Her elder son, Arkali Khan dissatisfied with some of her acts, had remained at Multan. On hearing this Alauddin hurriedly marched for Delhi. Ruknuddin gave him no resistance and fled to Multan with his mother and her faithful Ahmad Chap.

Without any opposition, Alauddin occupied the vacant throne in the words of Barni, stands : "The throne was now secure, and the revenue officers and the keepers of elephants with their elephants, and the magistrates and the chief men of the city came out to Alauddin, and a new order of things was established. His wealth and power were great ; so whether individuals paid their allegiance or whether they did not, mattered little, for the Khutba was read and coins were struck in his name."

Mongol Invasions :

The ever-recurring Mongol raids formed a source of constant anxiety and alarm to Alauddin. The contemporary chroniclers tell us that between the years 1297 and 1307 A.D. Alauddin had to face as many as five or six formidable Mongol raids, besides many minor incursions. Within a few months of Alauddin's accession, a large horde of the Mongols invaded India, but Zafar Khan repulsed them near Jullunder.

In 1297 A.D., the Mongols under their leader Amir Daud, the ruler of Transoxiana made an attempt to conquer Multan, the Punjab and Sind but Ulugh Khan inflicted a crushing defeat upon them. The Mongols appeared again under their leader Saldi. This time also Zafar Khan vanquished them, and sent their leader with about 2,000 followers as prisoners to Delhi. But the most dangerous crisis occurred in 1299 A.D. when an army of 200,000 Mongols under Qutlugh Khaja suddenly appeared in the vicinity of Delhi. This time their object seemed not plunder but conquest. Zafar Khan charged them furiously but was killed in action. But Mongols for some unknown reasons soon withdrew. Next invasion took place in 1303 A.D. when the Mongols came to India and encamped near Delhi. "But the danger was averted through the good offices of Nizamuddin Aulia." In 1304 A.D. there was another Mongol raid under Ali Begand Khaja Tash. They penetrated as far as Amroha. Malik Kafur and Ghazi Malik were sent against them. The Mongols were completely beaten back with heavey losses and about 8,000 Mongols were captured and sent to Delhi. The last Mongol invasion during his reign took place in 1307-1308 A.D., when a chieftain named Iqbal-mand led an army across the Indus. But he was defeated and slain. The Mongols, disappointed by repeated failures in all their invasions and terrified by the harsh measures of Alauddin, did not venture to trouble him again.

Alauddin took effective measures to guard the North-Western Frontier against further invasion. He followed the policy of Balban. He added to the forts of Delhi, reconstructed the old forts of the frontier. He raised the number and efficiency of the army. The outposts of Samana and Dipalpur were garrisoned and kept in a state of defence. He also dealt severely with the Mongol converts, known as the "New Mussalmans", who had settled in the suburbs of Delhi, as they were looked upon as a source of danger and conspiracy.

His Conquests :

Alauddin's reign is memorable for the expansion of Muslim dominion in India. "With it began", as Sir Wolseley remarks, "the Imperial period of the Sultanate," which lasted for nearly half a century. He first effected a thorough conquest of Northern India and then turned his arms against the South. He was the first ruler of Indo-Pakistan who brought the whole of this sub-continent under his sway.

Alauddin's first military operation was directed against Gujarat in 1297 A.D., which was then ruled by Baghela (Chaulukya) King Rai Karnadeva II. Ulugh Khan and Nusrat Khan, Alauddin's principal lieutenants, were sent to Gujarat at the head of a large army. The capital was besieged and captured. Karnadeva and his daughter, Devala Devi, fled away and took refuge with King Ramchandradeva of Devagiri. Karnadeva's beautiful wife Kamala Devi was taken to Alauddin, who later on became his favourite wife. Nusrat Khan plundered the rich forts of Gujarat and brought away enormous booty. Gujarat was placed under the charge of a Muslim Governor.

Alauddin next turned his arms against the strong fortress of Ranthambhor which was then ruled by a Chauhan Prince named Hamir Deva. He had given shelter to some of the "New Mussalmans", and this offended Alauddin. Moreover, strategically, the great fort of Ranthambhor was a danger to the Delhi empire. So in 1299 A.D. Alauddin sent Ulugh Khan and Nusrat Khan to capture Ranthambhor. Hamir Deva stoutly defended his country and Alauddin's Generals were facing this that Alauddin marched in person towards Ranthambhor. Ranthambhor was occupied after one year's siege. Hamir was put to death and Ulugh Khan was appointed to govern Ranthambhor.

Alauddin's next victim was Mewar, the land of the brave Rajputs. According to Tod, the famous chronicler of the Rajputs, Alauddin organised an expedition against Mewar to gain Padmini, the beautiful queen of Rana Ratan Singh. But this has now been proved as a fiction. The real cause was Alauddin's natural desire to subdue a strong principality lying so near Delhi. Alauddin personally invaded Mewar and besieged Chitor. The poet Amir Khusru, who accompanied the Sultan, has left for us a valuable account of the campaign. He said that Chitor was gallantly defended by two Rajput leaders, Gora and Badal, but all resistance proved failure. Chitor fell to Alauddin on August 26, 1303 A.D. The fort was entrusted to Khizr Khan, Alauddin's son, and the town was renamed Khizrabad. The conquest of Chitor was followed by the reduction of Malwa, and the cities of Ujjain, Mandu and Chanderi fell into the hands of the Muslims. Thus by the year 1305 A.D. Alauddin became the master of practically the whole of Northern India.

Emboldened by these successes, Alauddin turned his attention to the conquest of the Deccan. He was the first Muslim conqueror of the Deccan. It was but natural for an ambitious ruler like him to extend his influence over the South after the North had been brought under control. The profuse gold of the Deccan also might have attracted his attention. Moreover the political condition of the South provided an incentive to Alauddin for launching upon a new career of conquest. The Deccan and the Peninsula were then divided between great Hindu kingdoms ; Devagiri on the west, Telingana in the east, and the Hoysala kingdom to the south of the Krishna and Tungabhadra, and the Pandya kingdom under Kulas Khara. Besides these principal kingdoms, there were other petty states. Internal dissensions among these States offered an opportunity to the ambitious designs of Alauddin.

In 1307 A.D., Alauddin sent an army against Ramchandradeva of Devagiri. Ramchandradeva had given refuge to his enemy, Karnadeva of Gujarat, and had withheld the promised tribute. Malik Kafur mercilessly ravaged his territory and forced him to come to terms. Ramchandradeva was allowed to rule as a vassal king.

Next Kafur was sent against the Kakatiya kingdom of Warangal. An expediton sent by Alauddin against Kakatiya Prataparudradeva in 1303 A.D., had failed. But this time the Kakatiya king found it difficult to cope with Malik Kafur. The king shut himself up in his impregnable fortress, but after a prolonged seige, was compelled to surrender in 1310 A.D. Kafur returned to Delhi with an immense amount of booty carried, as Amir Khusru writes, "on a thousand camels groaning under the weight of treasure."

After the subjugation of Devagiri and Warangal, Alauddin soon determined to bring under his authority the kingdoms in the farther south. So, in November, 1310 A.D. Alauddin sent a large army under Malik Kafur and Khaja Haji against Vira Ballala III, the Hoysala King of Dorasamudra. The Raja was taken by surprise and submitted without resistance. The Hoysala King paid an enormous booty and accepted the authority of the Delhi Sultan.

Kafur next turned against the Pandys kingdom in the far south. A fratricidal struggle in the royal court furthered his design as one of the parties implored his help. Kafur reached Madura, the capital of the Pandya in 1311 A.D. and captured an immense booty. Amir Khusru tells us that Kafur advanced as far as Remeswaram, leaving a Muslim Governor at Madura, Kafur returned to Delhi.

In 1312 A.D. Sankaradeva, son of Ramchandradeva, being encouraged by the absence of Kafur from the Deccan withheld the tribute promised by his father to the Delhi Sultan, and tried to assert independence. So, Kafur again marched from Delhi, and defeated and killed Sankaradeva. Thus the whole of Southern India came under the sway of the Delhi Sultan.

Deccan Policy :

Alauddin's Deccan policy was quite different from the policy he adopted in Northern India. In the North he adopted the policy of annexation. But in the Deccan he was not an annexationist. He did not replace the ruling Hindu Kings. He allowed them to retain their kingdoms on the condition of acknowledging his supremacy and paying an annual tribute. Alauddin realised that it was difficult to maintain effective control over the distant provinces of the South. The policy of ruling the Deccan through tributary princes speaks of his wisdom and statesmanship.

Shahabuddin :

After the death of Alauddin, there ensued a bloody struggle for power. Kafur tried to establish his influence as the supreme authority in the State. He set up on the throne Shahabuddin Umar, an infant son of the deceased Sultan, and made himself the regent and the virtual dictator of the State. Goaded on by the ambition of seizing the throne, Kafur perpetrated the most horrible crimes. He blinded Khizr Khan, the eldest son of Alauddin, and killed or imprisoned most of the other members of the royal family. He plotted further crimes but his murderous career was cut short, after a "criminal rule" of thirty-five days, by the slave guards of the palace.

QUTBUDDIN MUBARAK SHAH

After the death of Kafur, Mubarak the third son of Alauddin, ascended the throne under the title of Qutbuddin Mubarak Shah. He began his reign vigorously. He marched into the Deccan and defeated Raja Harapala of Devagiri who had revolted. But soon he gave himself up to the foulest vices. He left the conduct of the State affairs in the hands of a low-born Hindu convert, styled Khusru Khan seized the throne in 1320 A.D. by killing Mubarak.

KHUSRU KHAN

Khusru ascended the throne of Delhi under the title of Nasiruddin Khusru Shah. He abused his ill-gotten power in the most shameless manner. He gathered round him the lowest rabble of Delhi and for five months the city was a veritable pandemonium. These low-born adventurers offended the Muslim aristocracy. Ghazi Malik, Governor of the Punjab, with the support of all defeated nobles of Delhi in September, 1320 A.D., killed Khusru. The nobles persuaded him to accept the throne under the title of Ghiyasuddin Tughluq Shah.

GHIYASUDDIN TUGHLAQ

(1320-25 A.D.)

The opening scene of the Tughlaq dynasty was staged in the reign of Ghazi Malik who ascended the throne of Delhi under the title of Sultan Ghiyasuddin Tughlaq. Firishta tells us that his father was a Turki slave of Balban and his mother was a Jat woman of the Punjab. He had risen to high position by dint of his personal merit, and at the time of Alauddin Khalji had distinguished himself as a guardian of the frontier province against the Mongols. The choice of Ghazi Malik as the ruler of Delhi by the nobles was amply justified. "When he assumed the reins of office," remarks Dr. Ishwari Prasad, "the empire of Delhi was in a state of confusion, and it was with great tact, prudence and firmness that Ghiyasuddin restored order and recovered the moral prestige of the monarchy."

MUHAMMAD BIN TUGHLAQ

(1325-1351 A.D.)

On the death of Ghiyasuddin Tughlaq, his son Juna Khan, under of the title of Muhammad bin Tughlaq ascended the throne in 1325 A.D. On the second year of his accession he had to face the rebellion of his cousin Bahauddin, and the revolt of the Governor of Multan. Both were defeated and killed. To add to his troubles a Mongol army under Tarmashrim invaded India and reached the outskirts of Delhi. The danger was averted by the device of buying off the enemy. The empire which Muhammad inherited from his father was one of the largest to which any king of India has over succeeded. His reign constitutes the most momentous period in the history of medieval India. It falls broadly under two parts : (*a*) 1325-1335 A.D., and (*b*) 1335-1351 A.D. The first part was comparatively prosperous and peaceful ; the second witnessed increasing troubles culminating in rebellion and disintegration.

The last fifteen years of Muhammad bin Tughlaq was not peaceful. The year 1335 A.D. was a year of rebellions and disorders. Revolts broke out in Bengal, Oudh, Gujarat, and the Deccan. Some of these revolts were put down in the most ruthless manner.

The first important rebellion was that of Jalaluddin Ahsan Shah in Mabar and it occurred in 1335 A.D. The Sultan personally marched to chastise the rebel. But a sudden outbreak of cholera in the royal camp compelled him to abandon the expedition. Jalal proclaimed his independence and founded the independent Muslim kingdom of Madura. During Sultan's absence from Delhi Amir Halajun revolted in the Punjab, killed the Governor of Lahore and declared his independence. But Halajun was defeated and Lahore was occupied.

In Bengal Fakhruddin proclaimed himself independent and struck coins in his own name. The Sultan of Delhi, then preoccupied with other troubles, could do nothing to subdue him, and Bengal thus became an independent province.

Rebellions followed in quick succession also in other parts of the Empire, the most formidable one being that of Ainul-Mulk, the Governor of Oudh and Zafarabad in 1340-41 A.D. In 1340-41 A.D. when Ainul-Mulk was transferred from Oudh to Devagiri he was persuaded by some miscreants to believe that this transfer was a preliminary step towards his fall. So he revolted, but was defeated and captured.

When troubled on all sides by rebellions, Muhammad bin Tughlaq invoked the shade of the Abbasid Caliph of Cairo and received from him the diploma of investiture. But the Caliph's blessing neither restored his waning popularity nor relieved his embarrassments. He was faced with serious difficulties in almost all parts of his kingdoms. In the Deccan Hari Hara and his brother founded the kingdom of Vijayanagar in 1336 A.D. The Deccanese organised a national movement against the Muslim rule and freed Warangal. The foreign Amirs revolted in Devagiri and the foundation of the Bahmani Kingdom was laid by Abul Muzaffar Alauddin Bahman Shah. While Sultan was busy in suppressing the revolt at Thatta (Sind), he was attacked with fever and died on 20th March, 1351 A.D. Such was the end of this unlucky monarch. "And so", says Badauni, "the King was freed from his people and they from their King."

FIRUZ SHAH TUGHLAQ

(1351-88 A.D.)

The death of Muhammad bin Tughlaq occurred in peculiarly unfortunate circumstances, and, while anarchy at Delh was probable, anarchy in the army, leaderless and beset by dangers, was immediate. A contemporary historian, Barni, writes that the late Sultan has nominated Firuz as his heir-apparent. His statement is corroborated by another contemporary historian, Shams-i-Siraj Afif. Accordingly the nobles urged Firuz to ascend the throne and save the dispirited army from destruction. Firuz accepted the throne with great reluctance. But in the meanwhile Khwaja Jehan proclaimed a child to be the son of Muhammad, but Khwaja Jehan soon submitted to Firuz.

Firuz was a contrast to his cousin. He was a man of peace and lacked soldierly qualities. He lacked ambition, courage and the ruthless zeal for war which was unnecessary qualification for success in his age.

Firuz led two expeditions against Bengal to bring it back to the allegiance of Delhi but his attempts failed. Haji Ilyas who had styled himself Shamsuddin Ilyas Shah was an independent ruler of North Bengal. He had established his authority over both Eastern and Western Bengal and invaded Tirhut. Thereupon Firuz marched from Delhi, at the head of 70,000 horsemen (November, 1353 A.D.) to repel them. Ilyas retired to Ikdala, a village situated on islands in the Brahmaputra, and protected by the dense jungle along the rivers banks. Firuz was unable to reduce this stronghold and was obliged to retreat. In the language of Thomas, "the invasion only resulted in the confession of weakness."

Three years later Firuz again invaded Bengal at the request of Zafar Khan, son-in-law of Fakhruddin Mubarak Shah who had established his independence in Eastern Bengal. Ilyas conquered Eastern Bengal in 1352 A.D. and thus shattered Zafar Khan's hopes of succeeding his father-in-law. Mubarak took refuge at the court of Firuz where he had been favourably received. On the flimsy pretext of vindicating Zafar's rights Firuz marched from Delhi in the spiring of 1359 A.D. On his way to Bengal Firuz founded the city of Jaunpur, in memory of his cousin, Fakhruddin Juna (Muhammad bin Tughlaq). When he arrived in Bengal, Sikandar, son and successor of Ilyas Shah, like his father retired to Ikdala. Thus the second siege was no more successful than the first, and Sikandar obtained peace on very favourable terms.

Firuz retired to Jaunpur, and in the autumn of 1360 A.D., led an expedition into Orissa. The Raja of this place submitted and promised to send an annual tribute. His next military exploit was the reduction of the fortress of Nagarkot. After a long siege Firuz compelled the Hindu chief of Nagarkot to submit.

In 1361-62 A.D., Firuz turned his arms against the Jam (ruler) of Sind with a view to punish the people of Thatta for their disloyalty to Muhammad bin Tughlaq. He marched towards Thatta at the head of an army of 90,000 horses, 480 elephants, and 5,000 boats. The ruler of Thatta Jam Babaniya strongly defended his city. Moreover sudden outbreak of pestilence swept away one-fourth of the imperial army and the Sultan was compelled to retreat to Gujarat. Afterwards, when fresh reinforcement came, he resumed the attack and forced the Jam to submit. The Jam was granted a liberal pension and his brother Tamachi was allowed to govern.

Fall of the Tughlaq Dynasty :

After the death of Firuz Tughlaq a number of weak princes sat on the throne of Delhi, and the story of their reigns is a record of intrigues and revolts. The last of the Tughlaqs, Mahmud became King in 1394 A.D. His was a tragic reign. Four provinces namely Malwa, Gujarat, Khandesh and Jaunpur became independent. A famine, which lasted for twelve years wasted the Deccan and last but not the least was that in his reign the terrible Timur invaded India.

Invasion of Timur :

When the Sultanate of Delhi was on the brink of disintegration, Amir Timur, one of the most terrible military leaders known to history, invaded India. Timur, son of Amir Turghay, was born in Transoxiana in 1336 A.D. He ascended the throne of Samarqand at the age of 33 and then embarked upon the career of aggressive conquests. He conquered Persia, Afghanistan and Mesopotamia had announced his intention of invading India, and Pir Muhammad his forerunner, had already occupied a frontier province. The wealth of India naturally excited his temptation to invade this land and the greater stimulus was the disintergration of the Empire.

Early in 1398 A.D. Timur joined his grandson, Pir Muhammad at Multan and marched on Delhi. He massacred the people of Talamba, defeated Jasrat the Khokar on the Sutlej, captured Bhatnair and massacred its inhabitants, and then marched on towards the capital, plundering, massacring and enslaving people. On December 10, 1398 A.D., having crossed the Jumna, he occupied Loni, and made its headquarter. Sultan Nasiruddin Mahmud and Mulla Iqbal endeavoured to oppose him. But Timur, crossing the river, fell upon and defeated Mulla and Mahmud. Timur occupied Delhi, on December 18 and agreed on the mediation of the Muslim divines, to spare the citizens. He ordered the people of Delhi to pay a vast sum of money, but when his soldiers went from house to house to collect it there were fights in the streets in which some of Timur's men were killed. Enraged at this, he ordered the people of Delhi to be massacred. His orders were carried out, and for days human blood flowed freely and heaps of dead bodies made the roads impassable. Timur had no desire to stay in India. On January 1, 1399 A.D., Timur retired, marched back through Meerut which he took by storm and whose inhabitants he massacred with accustomed barbarity. He then captured Kangra and sacked Jumna. Having appointed Khizr Khan Sayyid to Government of Multan and Lahore, Timur recrossed the Indus with an immense booty and a large train of captives, many of whom were sent to Samarkand to teach the people there the famous handicrafts of India.

THE SAYYIDS

(1414-1451 A.D.)

With the death of Sultan Mahmud in 1413 A.D., Khizr Khan Sayyid who claimed to be a descendant of the Prophet, became practically the master of Delhi and founded the Sayyid dynasty which lasted for thirty-nine years. Their territory consisted of Delhi and the country round its wall. Khizr did not assume royal style but professed to rule as a viceroy of Timur's son and successor, Shah Rukh. But his allegiance to Timur was nothing more than a political fiction, for the coins struck by the Sayyids bore the names of the regular Sultans of Delhi of the last dynasty and not that of Timur. The history of Khizr Khan is mainly a tale of perpetual struggle to retain some control over Delhi and its immediate neighbourhood. Khizr Khan's authority was confined to Delhi, the Doab and the Punjab. But the turbulent Hindu chiefs of Etawah, Kamila, Katehr, gave him no rest. He died in 1421 A.D. He lived like a true Sayyid and never indulged in unnecessary bloodshed. Firishta extols Khizr Khan as "a great and wise king, kind and true to his word, his subjects loved him with a grateful affection and raised his son Mubarak Shah to the throne".

Khizr Khan was succeeded by his son Mubarak Shah. His reign lasted for thirteen years, which is as uneventful and dreary as that of his father. A few expeditions against the Khokar Chief, and the Hindus of the Doab exhaust the history of his reign. Mubarak was a kind and generous king. The contemporary chronicler praises him as 'A clement and generous sovereign, full of excellent qualities'. He was murdered in 1434 A.D.

Mubarak left no son, and the nobles at Delhi enthroned Muhammad Shah, the son of his deceased brother, Farid. Muhammad found it difficult to cope with the forces, of disorder and rebellion. The Hindu chief ceased to pay tribute and Ibrahim Shah of Jaunpur seized several parganas belonging to Delhi. He ruled for about 12 years. He died in 1445 A.D. and was succeeded by his son Alauddin Alam Shah. Alam

Shah, the last of the Sayyids, abdicated in favour of Bahlul Lodi, an Afghan noble, and retired to Badaun where he passed the rest of his life in the contemplation of God.

THE LODIES
(*1451-1526 A.D.*)

On the abdication of Alam Shah Bahlul Khan, belonging to the Lodi tribe of Afghans, ascended the throne in 1451 A.D. This new dynasty came to be known as the Lodi dynasty. Bahlul was active and war-like, and was resolved to restore the kingdom to its former pre-eminence. He would be puppet in the hands of none, and one of his earliest acts was to imprison Hamid Khan, an old Minister at whose invitation he had ascended the throne. He also frustrated an attempt on the part of Mahmud Shah Sharqu of Jaunpur to get possession of Delhi. He then reduced the turbulent chiefs of provinces to submission and infused some vigour into the Government. Thus Ahmed Khan of Mewat, Dariya Khan of Sambhal, Isa Khan of Koil, Mubarak Khan of Suket, Raja Pratap Singh of Mainpuri and Bhougoan, Qutb Khan of Rewari and the chief of many districts of Doab, which had caused so much trouble were made to acknowledge the authority of Delhi. But the most important event of his reign was the conquest of Jaunpur to effect this he had to wage a long war lasting for twenty-six years against Husain Shah, the last Sharqi King of Jaunpur. Bahlul appointed his son Barbak Shah, as the Viceroy of Jaunpur. The conquest of this kingdom restored the old frontier of the Delhi empire as far as Benares.

After Bahlul's death, his second son Nizam Khan was proclaimed King under the title of Sultan Sikandar Shah (1418-1577 A.D.). The early days of his reign were not peaceful : those who had opposed him he was obliged to have recourse to arms against them. Among them was his brother, Barbak, whom he defeated, and generously re-appointed to Jaunpur. But Barbak failed to deal effectively with a serious rebellion of the Hindu Zamindars of the province. Sikandar suppressed the rebellion and removed his brother from the Government of the province. The Zamindars sought help of Husain Shah, the Sharqi Sultan, who came at the head of large force but was defeated and compelled to take rescue in Bengal, where he passed the remaining years of his life in obscurity. Sikandar thus strengthened his position. He also annexed Bihar and Tirhut, reduced Gwalior to subjection and concluded a treaty with Alauddin Shah of Bengal. He did not spare even the haughty Afghans. His dominion included the country between Sutlej and Bundelkhand, thus recalling the earlier supremacy of the Delhi empire.

Sikandar was the ablest ruler of the Lodi dynasty. He has been highly praised by contemporary as well as by some later writers for his excellent qualities of his head and heart. A firm, vigilant and upright ruler, he entertained kind feelings for the poor and the needy. He listened to the complaints of the poor himself and tried to redress them. Sikandar was a strong ruler. He kept the Afghan barons in check and strictly enforced his orders. An efficient system of espionage kept the Sultan informed of every thing that happened in his empire. He abolished corn duties and patronised trade and commerce. He encouraged learning and took a special interest in the study of medicine. During his reign the country was prosperous and living was exceptionally cheap.

IBRAHIM LODI

(1517-26 A.D.)

After the death of Sikandar Lodi nobles at Agra raised to the throne his eldest son Ibrahim, but a faction advocated the partition of the kingdom and enthroned Jalal Khan, Ibrahim's younger brother in Jaunpur. Ibrahim marched against Jalal Khan, defeated him and thus baffled the attempt of dividing the empire. Ibrahim possessed military skill but was devoid of administrative capacity. He sought to enhance the dignity of his position by crushing the pretensions of the powerful Afghan nobles. Firishta says that contrary to the custom of his father and grandfather, he made no distinction among his officers, whether of his own tribe or otherwise, and said publicly that all around should be considered as subjects and servants of the state, and the Afghan chiefs who had hitherto been allowed to sit in the presence, were constrained to stand in front of the throne with their hands crossed before them. This assumption of superior airs gave mortal offence to the proud Afghans. Ibrahim was confronted with a difficult situation. The territory of the empire had increased in extent ; the feudal aristocracy who looked upon their Jagirs as their own right, and purchased by their swords rather than as due to any bounty or liberality on the part of the sovereign had become ungovernable. His drastic measures provoked the resentment of their half-loyal nobility and paved the way for the disruption of the Afghan empire.

Ibrahim was not wholly to blame. The break up of the empire was bound to come sooner or latter. The discontent of the nobles reached its climax and Daulat Khan Lodi, a semi-independent Governor of the Punjab, invited Babur, King of Kabul, to invade India. Babur responded to the call of Daulat Khan, invaded India and defeated Ibrahim on the field of Panipat in 1526 A.D. Ibrahim was killed in action and with him the Delhi Sultanate came to an end.

BABUR

(1526-30 A.D.)

Zahiruddin Muhammad Babur was born on Friday, the 24th February in 1483 A.D. His father, Umar Sheikh Mirza, the fifth in descent from the great Timur, was the ruler of Ferghana or Khokand, a small but beautiful country on the upper course of the Jaxartes. He was connected on his mother's side with Chengiz Khan. He was not a Mughal. In his Memoirs 'he calls himself a Turk.' But curiously enough the dynasty he established came to be known as the Mughal dynasty. "Mughal had, in fact, become a generic term for warlike adventures from Persia on Central Asia, and although Timur and all his line oathed the name, as that of their bitterest foes, it has been their fate to be branded with it, and it now seems to be too late to correct the error."

When only eleven years old, Babur lost his father. Babur showed remarkable courage. Babur had an early training, well-fitted to make him a great warrior and ruler. On succeeding to the throne, he at once made plans to recover the empire, in Central Asia of his great ancestor, Timur. Twice he took possession of Samarkand, but on each occasion he was driven out, and for a time, even lost the capital of Farghana.

These defeats made Babur a wanderer, as he writes in his Memoir, "Moving from square to square like a king on a chess-board." But he never lost courage. At last after many changes of fortune, Babur decided to leave Farghana to seek his fortune elsewhere. With the help from the king of Khurasan, he boldly crossed the Hindukush and took possession of Kabul and Ghazni in 1504 A.D. But Babur once more desired to re-establish his position in Central Asia, as a successor of Timur. Being able to secure the help of Shah Ismail Safavi of Persia against Shaibani Khan, the Uzbag chief, Babur tried once again to occupy Samrqand, but failed.

Being frustrated in his attempt to retain Samarqand Babur returned Kabul. He now decided to try his fortune in the east. The wealth of India had already tempted his adventurous spirit and fired his imagination. He started brisk military preparation for his Indian campaign. His first Indian invasion was directed against the Yusufzais in 1519 A.D. An expedition was also sent against Bajaur in 1520 A.D. In 1524 A.D., Babur advanced up to Dipalpur which he stormed. But he had to fall back on Lahore and return to Kabul. He depended on the co-operation of Daulat Khan Lodi and Alam Khan, on whose invitation Babur invaded India, but they turned against him when they found that he had no intention to give up Indian conquests. The whole situation was now different. Babur was now fully determined to crush the tottering Afghan kingdom of Delhi. "I placed my foot in the stirrup of resolution," writes Babur, "and my hands on the reins of confidence of God. I marched against Sultan Ibrahim in whose possession the city of Delhi and kingdom of Hindustan at that time were."

First Battle of Panipat (1526 A.D.) :

Babur marched from Kabul in November, 1525 A.D. and the Punjab easily came into his hands. Daulat Khan Lodi was compelled to submit. But the more formidable task was to conquer Delhi which was his main ambition. So he marched directly on Delhi, and at Panipat, that "historic site" where the fate of India has been thrice decided, he came in contact with Ibrahim's great army of 100,000 on the 21st April, 1526 A.D. Babur's resources were inadequate for this enterprise but he had the strength of character and experience of a veteran General. When, on the morning of the 21st April, 1526 A.D., the Delhi army advanced to attack, they found the front of the opposing army protected by ditches and hurdles, and havoc was made in their ranks by Babur's guns and match-locks. By noon, hemmed in and attacked on all sides, Delhi army was completely broken, and many thousands including Sultan Ibrahim were slain.

Babar and the Rajputs—Battle of Khauna :

Babur next had to face a most formidable chieftain Rana Sangram Singh, better known as Rana Sanga of Mewar. The Rana, disappointed by Babur's complete success was determined to fight Babur. To Babur, Rana Sanga was certainly a more formidable adversary than Ibrahim. Rana Sanga marched with an army, composed of 120 chiefs, 80,000 horses and 500 war elephants, and the rulers of Marwar, Amber, Gwalior, Ajmer and Chanderi. Sultan Mahmud Lodi also joined them. So it was a huge army and Babur found that his solidiers were showing signs of panic. He had a dramatic personality and decided to make a gesture. He publicly renounced his drinking of wine, and made another heart touching speech. The speech produced the desired effect and the officers and as well as the men swore by the Holy Book to stand by him. In the battle that followed at Khauna on 16th March, 1527 A.D., the Mughals fought with a fearless bravery that broke the ranks of the valiant Rajputs. Rana Sanaga died fighting and the Rajputs were defeated. This was a decisive victory. It made Babur king of Central India, as he had already conquered Doab.

Babur and the Afghans—Battle of Gogra :

The power of the Rajputs was now crushed. Babur next turned against the Afghans in the east. Mahmud Lodi, brother of Ibrahim, had seized Bihar and a large part of the eastern country had declared for him. Babur first sent his son Askari with a large force against the rebellious leader and himself followed a little later by way of Allahabad, Benaras and Ghazipur. Jalaluddin Babar Khan Lohari submitted to him. Mahmud raised the seige and retired, while the great Afghan army dissolved. Babur occupied Bihar. Mahmud fled and took refuge with Nasrat Shah of Bengal. He warmly supported Mahmud, less from love of the Lodi Dynasty than from fear of Babur, having conquered Bihar, should invade Bengal. In fact, Babur marched towards Bengal, and defeated the Afghans in the famous battle of the Gogra on 6th May, 1529 A.D. A treaty of peace was concluded with Nasrat Shah of Bengal.

Thus as a result of three battles, Babur had reduced northern India to submission. He left an empire which included Badakhshan, Afghanistan, the Punjab, Delhi, the open plain of Bihar and territories stretching southwards to a perimeter marked by the forts of Biyana, Ranthambhor, Gwalior and Chanderi.

Babur did not live long to enjoy the fruits of his victories. He died on December 26, 1530 A.D.

HUMAYUN AND SHER SHAH

(*1530-56 A.D.*)

Babur was succeeded by his eldest son Humayun who ruled for ten years. He was courteous, brave, accomplished, and capable, on occasion of displaying great energy, but not of sustained effort. He lacked political wisdom and diplomatic skill, as well as strong determination and preservation of his father.

Humayun's first military expedition was directed against the strong fort of Kalanjar in Bundel Khand, then ruled by a pro-Afghan Hindu Raja. But he had to retire, after receiving a large sum of money from the Raja, to deal with the Afghans under Mahmud Lodi, Bahar Khan and Bayezid. They were defeated in the battle of Dourab. Next he laid siege to Chunar, then held by the Afghan chief Sher Khan. But Sher Khan was a clever man. Seeing that he was not strong enough to fight, he submitted and offered the services of his son Qutb Khan to Humayun. Humayun accepted the offer and withdrew because he was now anxious to march against Bahadur Shah of Gujarat.

Bahadur Shah of Gujarat, without serious designs on Delhi and Agra, was nevertheless a menace, for he had recently extended his power by the annexation of the neighbouring kingdom of Malwa. Bahadur next laid siege to the famous Rajput fortress of Chitor. Further, Bahadur Shah had given definite provocation to Humayun by openly giving shelter and help to Alam Khan, uncle of Ibrahim, an old intriguer, and Muhammad Zaman Mirza, a brother-in-law of Humayun demanded the surrender of both these persons from Bahadur Shah, but that Bahadur Shah considered it dishonourable to give up a person who had sought shelter with him. So Humayun marched against Bahadur Shah and conquered both Malwa and Gujarat. Bahadur was driven to seek shelter in Diu. He made his brother, Askari, Viceroy of Gujarat and himself stayed in Malwa to put things in order. In the meantime Bahadur sought the help of the Portuguese and recovered the whole of Gujarat. Even Malwa was lost to Humayun. Thus "one year had seen the rapid conquest of the two great provinces ; the next saw them quickly lost."

Sher Khan's Activities :

Sher Khan's activities roused Humayun from his lethargy. He left Bengal and set out for Agra but Sher Khan intercepted and completley surprised and defeated his army at Chausa near Buxar in 1539 A.D. The emperor fought with great gallantry but he was defeated and barely escaped with his own life to Agra. Sher Khan now assumed the royal title of Sher Shah and ordered *Khutba* to be read and the coins to be struck in his name.

Early next year Humayun tried to recover his fortune. He asked help from his brothers, but none of his brothers was prepared to give him any aid. Humayun was in desperate straits. A decisive battle took place on the bank of Ganges on May 19, 1540 A.D., which is commonly known as the battle of Kanauj. Mirza Haider, the author of the Tarikh-i-Rashidi, who took part in the compaign tells us that"........Sher Khan gained a victory, while the Chaghtais were defeated in the battlefield, where not a man either friend or foe was wounded. Not a gun was fired and the chariots were useless. This statement of Mirza Haider may be an exaggeration but there is no doubt that the battle was not half so bloody as the battle of Panipat and Khanwali. "Thus the work of Babur in India was undone, and the sovereignty of Hindustan once more passed to the Afghans".

Conquest of Sher Shah :

After the flight of Humayun, Sher Shah ascended the throne under the royal style of Fariduddin Abul Muzaffar Shah. He was then the undisputed master of Bengal, Bihar, Jaunpur, Delhi and Agra. He was so strong that Kamran made peace with him by giving up the Punjab. Sher Shah built the fort of Ratho in the Punjab. Sind and Multan were also conquered. Sher Shah returned to Bengal to re-organise the administration of the province. He divided the country into nineteenth Sarkars, and to co-ordinate the work of the Sarkars, appointed Amin-i-Bangala. Affairs in Malwas next claimed Sher Shah's attention and he at once led an expedition there and subjugated it. He laid siege to the strong fortress of Raishin which surrendered after holding out for four months.

The most difficult military operation of Sher Shah was his fight against Maldev, the Rathor chief of Marwar. He was an able General and began to extend his power at the expense of the neighbouring states. In 1544 A.D., Sher Shah marched against him with an army of 80,000 and met the Rajput hosts near Ajmer. The Rajputs had a larger army and fought with reckless bravery, but Sher Shah was a better General. Their ranks broke and fled. It was a great victory and the Rajputs were subdued for a generation.

The next year he sieged the fortress of Kalanjar but he was killed by the explosion of a shell.

Restoration of Humayun :

It has already been pointed out that in Persia, Humayun met with a favourable reception. The Persian king, Shah Tahmasp, decided to help him with 14,000 horsemen on conditions that Humayun should conform to the Shia creed and Qandahar should be given to the Shah after victory. Humayun yielded to the necessity and conquered Kabul and Qandahar in 1545 A.D. with the help of the Persian army and defeated Kamran. So within five years of his defeat at Bilgram at the hands of Sher Shah, Humayun became master of Afghanistan, the country, from where, twenty years before, Banur had left for India. Humayun continued to have troubles with his brothers and his fortunes varied, but he gradually overcame them. He forced Askari to leave for Mecca on a pilgrimage. Hindal died in a skirmish in 1551 A.D. Kamran was captured. Humayun was now free to turn his mind to the reconquest of India. He took possession of Lahore without much opposition, and having defeated Sikandar Shah, one of the claimants to the throne, marched upon Delhi and re-occupied it. But he could not enjoy the royal honour for a long, as he died of a fall from the stair of his palace, in January, 1556 A.D.

AKBAR

(1556-1605 A.D.)

It was while his father, Humayun, was a homeless wanderer when Akbar was born at Amarkot on October 15, 1542 A.D. At the time of Humayun's death, Akbar was in the field under his tutor Bairam Khan, taking part in a campaign against one of Sher Shah's nephews. He, like his grandfather, had started on his military career while still a mere boy. Having been born while his father was a fugitive, he had received no formal education. It is even probable that he could not read or write, but he had a prodigious memory and a passion for knowledge. When the news of his father's death arrived, Bairam Khan hastily arranged for Annar to be crowned as *Padshah*, before rival claimants should have the opportunity of rising. The coronation took place at Kalanaur in the Gurdaspur district, on February 14, 1556 A.D.

Political condition of India in 1556 A.D. :

India in 1556 A.D. "presented a dark as well as a complex picture." The whole country was in a state of disorder and the country round Delhi and Agra was in the horror of a terrible famine. Independent kingdoms in different parts of Sher Shah, Ibrahim Sur and Sikander Sur were contesting for the throne. But the most formidable enemy of Akbar turned out to be Hemu, the Hindu Minister of Adil Shah. He had given up his alligiance to his master and occupied Agra and Delhi from the Mughal Governor Tardi Beg. In the north-west, Mirza Muhammad Hakim, Akbar's half brother, governed Kabul almost independently. Kashmir had also become an independent state under a local Muslim dynasty. Sind and Mutlan had become free from the imperiod control after the death of Sher Shah. Bengal was ruled by kings of Sur Dynasty. Orissa, Malwa and Gujarat and the local chieftains of Goundwana were independent of the control of Delhi. The Muslim Sultanates of Khandesh, Berar, Bidar, Ahmadnagar, Bijapur and Golkunda were ruled by the Sultans who felt little or no interest in northern policies. The Portuguese had established their influence on the western coast by the possession of Goa and Diu. Thus Akbar's task of building up an empire was exceedingly difficult.

Second Battle of Panipat (1556 A.D.) :

It has been discussed above that Akbar's chief rival was Hemu, a clever but unscrupulous Hindu Minister who had done good work under Sher Shah and his nephew Shah Adil. Hemu possessed courage, enterprise and plan. For a time things appeared so serious that Akbar's counsellors thought of retiring to Kabul. But in this crisis Bairam Khan proved a tower of strength to Akbar. He put a bold face on the situation. When Hemu marched against the Mughals after the capture of Delhi and Agra, Bairam Khan met him at the historic field of Panipat in November, 1556 A.D. Hemu was successful in routing the flanks of his enemy's army, and might even have won, when he was struck in the eye by an arrow. His forces, being now leaderless, were at once thrown into confusion and fled. The wounded Hemu was captured and beheaded by Bairam Khan. The defeat of Hemu at the second battle of Panipat marked the final triumph of the Mughals in their contest for supremacy in Indo-Pakistan sub-continent.

The truimph of Babur on the field of Panipat in 1526 A.D. marked the foundation of the Mughal rule in Indo-Pakistan sub-continent. But "the history of India from 1526 to 1556 A.D. is mainly of the story the Mughal-Afghan contest for supremacy in this land." Humayun lost his throne in 1540 A.D. and recovered it in 1555 A.D. He was succeeded by his great son, Akbar. It was Akbar who not only consolidated his father's dominion but also made extensive conquests. After the victory at Panipat, Akbar quickly conquered Agra and Delhi. In the Punjab, Sikandar Sur was compelled to surrender. Then Akbar enlarged his dominion by the conquest of Gwalior, Ajmer and Jaunpur.

Bairam Khan and the Regency :

Bairam Khan, a Turkoman by birth, had accompanied the Persian army sent by Shah Ismail to help Babur. He remained in India and distinguished himself in the service of both Babur and Humayun. He played a very important part in the Bengal expedition of Humayun. After the battle of Kanauj he remained with Humayun and became his chief adviser. As a guardian of Akbar during his minority he had loyally supported the cause of his youthful sovereign and it was chiefly due to his courage and determination that Akbar recovered his lost inheritance. The success of the Mughals in the Second Battle of Panipat was mainly due to him. Thus he had rendered valuable service to the Mughals. He was a man with wonderful qualities. Badauni, who is an orthodox Sunni praises this Shia Minister's upright character, love of learning and devotedness.

The fall of Bairam Khan is one of the most interesting episode in the early history of Akbar's reign. As Akbar now growing into manhood, the Regent's control irked him. Bairam Khan was haughty and arrogant and he had created many enemies by this time by using his power unscrupulously. According to Abul-Fazl, "Bairam's proceedings went beyond all endurance." Hated as a Shia, he made the great mistake of appointing in 1555-59 A.D., Shaikh Gadhai, a Shia, as 'Sadr-us-Sudar', the highest judicial and ecclesiastical position in the empire. The execution of Taradi Beg had offended many Chiefs. Akbar himself was kept short of funds, while Bairam's servants grew rich. A more serious reason for the growing estrangement between Akbar and Bairam was the suspicion that the latter was harbouring the intention to make their youthful sovereign their own instrument. Thus a conspiracy was formed in which the principal partners were the ladies of *Harem*. They induced Akbar to assert himself against his guardian. Early in 1560 A.D., the Emperor publicly announced his intention of taking the reins of the Government into his own hands. He dismissed Bairam Khan and directed him to make a pilgrimage to Mecca.

Akbar, probably at the instance of the ladies, deputed Pir Muhammad Khan, a former servant of Bairam, to follow him and see that he left the imperial dominions without delay. This insult goaded him to rebellion. He was defeated near Jalandhar and captured ; but Akbar pardoned him and sent him off to Mecca. On his way to Mecca, Bairam Khan was murdered by an Afghan (1561 A.D.) whose father had been executed by his order. Bairam's infant son, Abdur Rahim, was brought to the court and educated under Akbar's care and eventually became the first noble in the empire.

Conquests and Annexations :

Akbar was a man of strong imperial instinct. "A monarch," he said, "should he ever intent on conquest, otherwise his neighbour rise in arms against him". "His designs," remarks Dr. V. Smith, "were purely aggressive, his intention being to make himself the unquestioned lord paramount of India, and to suppress the independence of every kingdom within the reach of his arm. He carried out that policy with unflinching tenacity until January, 1601 A.D , when the mighty fortress of Asirgarh, his last acquisition, passed into his hands."

During the Regency of Bairam Khan, Gwalior, Ajmer and Jaunpur were reconquered. Between 1560-61 A.D., the conquest of Malwa was completed. In 1562 A.D., Raja Bihari Mal of Amber (Jaipur) submitted to Akbar without fighting. His son Bhagwan Das and grandson Mann Singh entered Mughal army and both played a leading part in extending consolidation of the Mughal Empire.

Fall of Chitor and surrender of other Rajput chifes (1567-68 A.D.) :

The most famous military feat of Akbar in Rajputana was the storming of the fortress of Chitor (Mewar). Akbar in 1567 A.D. marched against Chitor. At the news of his arrival, Rana Udai Singh flied to hills leaving Chitor in charge of Jaimal and Patta. They offered a stubborn resistance for four months. The siege might have lasted much longer but Jaimal was killed by a lucky shot of Akbar. Patta also fell dead later. The Rajputs, left leaderless, perished fighting bravely.

Struck with terror at the fall of Chitor, the Rajput chiefs of Ranthambhor and Kalinjar surrendered to him. Ranthambhor fell in 1569 A.D. The chief of Kalinjar followed suit in the same year. In 1570 A.D. the ruler of Bikaner and Jaisalmar also submitted to the Mughal Emperor. Some of them gave their daughters in marriage to Akbar.

Conquest of Gujarat (1572-73 A.D.) :

In 1572 A.D., Akbar personally marched against Gujarat. When he reached Ahmadabad, Muzaffar Shah submitted to him. He captured Surat in 1573 A.D. after a siege of one and-a-half month then returned to Fatehpur Sikri. But no sooner had he reached the capital then a fresh insurrection led by the Mirzas broke out in the newly conquered province. He at once fitted out an expedition, and thoroughly vanquished the insurgents in a battle near Ahmadabad (1573 A.D.). Akbar was now complete master of Gujarat and henceforth it became an integral part of his empire.

Conquest of Bengal (1574-76 A.D.) :

With a view to placate Akbar, Sulaiman formally recognised the overlordship of Akbar and maintained friendly relations with him. He transferred his capital from Gaur to Tanda. He also annexed the Hindu kingdom of Orissa. On his death in 1572 A.D., his youngest son Daud became the ruler of Bengal, who according to the author of 'Tabaqat,' "knew nothing of the art of government." Daud fancied himself strong enough to defy the Mughal emperor and to struck coins in his own name. Moreover, he provoked Akbar by attacking the outpost of Zamaina on the eastern frontier of the Empire.

So, in 1574 A.D. Akbar himself marched against the ruler of Bengal and drove him out of Patna and Hajipur. Akbar returned to his capital, leaving the Bengal campaign to be conducted by his General Munim Khan, assisted by Raja Todar Mal. Daud retreated towards Orissa. In March, 1575 A.D., a decisive battle was fought at Tukario in Orissa, in which Daud was defeated. Munim Khan granted him favourable terms. But Daud soon broke his promise and rose in revolt. He was defeated and killed in a battle, near Rajmahal in July, 1576 A.D. Although Bengal formally became a province of the Mughal Empire, but some powerful Bengal chiefs, the most important of whom were Isa Khan of Decca-Mymensingh, Kedar Rai of Vikrampur, Kandarpanarayan of Chandradivpa (Bakarganj) and Pratabditya of Jessore, continued to enjoy practical independence for many years. Orissa was annexed in 1592 A.D.

War with Mewar (1572-97 A.D.) :

Though Chitor was taken, but its Rana Udai Singh did not submit. He, in the mountain fastnesses founded a new capital called Udaipur after his own name. Udai Singh died in 1572 A.D. His son and successor, the valiant Paratap Singh, who embodied in his person the spirit of Rajput freedom, made a vow to recover Chitor and vindicate the honour of the House of Mewar. He kept up the unequal struggle with the Mughal Emperor for nearly a quarter of century. In 1576 A.D., a great fight between the Rana and the Imperial army led by a Rajput chief, Raja Mann Singh of Amber, took place near the pass of Haldighat, in which the Rana's army suffered a severe defeat. After the battle the Rana, was seriously wounded, retired into the distant hills, and all the strong places fell into Mughal hands one after another. But the heroic Pratap, though defeated and dispossessed, continued to hold out till he recovered a large part of Mewar. He died in January, 1597 A.D. "Thus closed the life of a Rajput whose memory" observes Tod, "is even now idolized" by every Rajput.

Rana Paratap was succeeded by his son Amar Singh, in 1597 A.D., who tried to carry the dying behest of his father but was defeated at the hand of Mann Singh in 1599 A.D. Mann Singh could not follow up his victory as he was called to quell the revolt of Usman Khan in Bengal. Akbar contemplated another invasion but could not undertake it owing to illness.

Conquest of Kabul (1581-85 A.D.) :

Muhammad Hakim, Akbar's brother who ruled at Kabul, was encouraged to invade the Punjab by a revolt in Bengal. According to Nazimuddin, Hakim came out from Kabul with the object of conquering Hindustan. At the head of 15,000 cavalry Hakim came as far as Lahore. He was opposed by Mann Singh and compelled to withdraw to Kabul. But Akbar pursueed him. He surrendered to Akbar and therefore was allowed to rule at Kabul as a dependency until 1585 A.D., when he died of excessive drinking. Kabul was annexed then to the Mughal Empire with Mann Singh as its Governor.

Conquest of Kashmir, Sind and Qandahar :

After suppressing the hill tribes, Akbar sent Raja Bhagwan Das and Qasim Khan at the head of 5,000 men to conquer Kashmir. They defeated its Sultan, Yusuf Shah, and his son Yakub, in 1586 A.D. Kashmir was annexed to the Empire and it became the summer residence of the Emperor. Sind and Baluchistan were conquered in 1590-91 A.D. and 1595 A.D. respectively.

The safety of Kabul also required the occupation of Qandahar which was the key to the north-western position. This place occupies a very strategic position between Afghanistan and Persia and was besides an important centre of trade. "The wisemen of ancient times considered Kabul and Qandahar as the twin gates of Hindustan, the one leading to Turkistan, the other to Persia." In an age when Kabul was part of the Delhi Empire, Qandahar was indispensable as first line of defence. The campaign was opened in 1590 A.D., when Akbar proposed to send Abdur Rahim Khan-i-Khanan to attack Qandahar. But the Uzbeg incursion and internal dessensions worsened the position of Husain Mirza's successor Muzaffar

Mirza, who surrendered it to Akbar without fighting in 1594 A.D. Thus all the territories of North-West Frontier were annexed to the Mughal Empire.

Though the genius of Akbar reared up and consolidated the great Mughal Empire, he failed in the upbringing of his own children, whose conduct embittered the last days of his life. Two of his sons, Murad and Danyal, died from the effects of the drink. On his return from the Deccan, he had to deal with the rebellion of his eldest son, Salim, whom he had left in charge of the Government. Salim seems to have resolved to seize the throne. This was grief enough for the affectionate father, but the unworthy son made it worse by secretly bringing about the murder of his father's dearest friend Abul Fazl. Akbar never recovered from the shock and he died in 1605 A.D. Thus ended the career of "one of those illustrious men whom providence sends in the hour of a nation's trouble, to reconduct it into those paths of peace and toleration which alone can assure the happiness of millions."

JAHANGIR

(*1605-1628 A.D.*)

Prince Salim had been indicated by Akbar on his death-bed as his successor, and he now ascended the throne under the title of Nuruddin Muhammad Jehangir Padshah Ghazi. "His liberal education, his natural shrewdness and strong common sense," remarks Dr. I shwari Prasad, "well qualified him to carry on the statemanlike policy of his father." The new monarch began his career by popular acts and he tried "to win the hearts of the people by various measures." He promised to uphold the honour of Islam, to forgive those who had supported the claims of Prince Khusru, and to maintain justice. These undertakings were accompanied by the celebrated twelve ordinances which the Emperor commanded to be observed as rules of conduct (desturul-amal) in his wide dominion. Having secured his position, Jahangir celebrated the first Nauroz of his reign with great splendour in March, 1606 A.D.

The first important event of his reign was the rebellion of Khusru. During the closing years of Akbar's reign a number of prominent nobles like Raja Mann Singh and Aziz Koka had formed a conspiracy against the accession of Salim and actively supported the cause of Khusru. However, the attempt ended in failure and a reconciliation was made between father and son. But this reconciliation was merely on the surface, and Jahangir was compelled to keep Khusru 'in a sort of semi-confinement within the fort of Agra.' Five months after the accession of Jahangir, Khusru escaped from the Agra fort, reached without delay against his son with a large army.

A battle was fought at Bhairowal, and Jahangir was easily victorious. Khusru was captured while attempting to cross the Chenab with a view to proceed to Kabul. His prominent supporters were barbarously put to death. The Sikh Guru Arjan who helped the rebel Prince was executed and the Prince was thrown into prison. Khusru lived till 1622 A.D. and died under awful circumstances.

Subjugation of Bengal :

In 1612 A.D., a rebellion occured in Bengal headed by an Afghan chief Usman Khan. He made a determined attempt to restore Afghan rule in that province but his rebellion was suppressed by Shujat Khan, an officer under Islam Khan, the Governor of the Province. In March, 1612 A.D., Shujat Khan defeated and killed Usman Khan and this was the last Afghan rebellion in Bengal.

Submission of Newar :

Amar Singh, who in 1597 A.D. had succeeded his father Pratap Singh, would not acknowledge the Emperor's supremacy, and Jahangir followed his father's policy of harassing him. In the very first year of his reign, Jahangir sent against Mewar an army of 20,000.

An undecisive battle was fought :

In 1608 A.D., Mahabat Khan conducted a compaign in which he was successful in the field, but was unable to reach the remote fastnesses of the Rajputs who were thus left unsubdued. In 1609 A.D. Mahabat Khan was replaced by Abdullah Khan who managed the campaign very well but had to be transferred to Gujarat and thence to the Deccan.

In 1613 A.D. Jahangir transferred his court to Ajmer, and appointed his third son Khurram to the command of the army assembled for the conquest of Mewar. The operations of the Prince were successful and the proud Rana was compelled to submit (1614 A.D.). He acknowledged the overlordship of the Emperor and agreed to contribute a contingent of 1,000 horses to the imperial army. He allowed him to retain his territory in tact and exempted him from personal attendence at court. The Rana's son, Karan, was appointed to a high military command in the imperial army. Jahangir subsequently placed two life-size marble statutes of the Rana and his son in the garden of his palace of Agra. Dr. Iswari Prasad rightly remarks, "Jahangir's conduct in this affair is wholly worthy of praise. Mewar had given the Mughals no small amounts of troubles but the Emperor forgot the past and adopted a conciliatory policy in dealing with the Rana."

Conquest of Kangra :

Another notable achievement of Jahangir was the conquest of Kangra. The fortress of Kangra is situated in the hill of the north-east Punjab. This fortress had long defied the might of Akbar, and Jahangir occupied it after a long seige of 14 months. But this conquest became temporary and the war-like hillmen continued the struggle till the death of Jahangir.

His Deccan Campaigns :

The Deccan next engaged Jahangir's attention. Following the imperialistic policy of his father, Jahangir wanted to enforce his authority there. But all his efforts ended in failure due partly to the quarrels amongst his own generals and partly to the ability of Malik Ambar, an Abyssinian by birth and a Deccani by adoption. Affairs in the Deccan then were dominated by Malik Ambar. With great administrative capacity, an excellent judgment and considerable military skill he was the central figure in the Deccan history for two decades. He developed the military strength of the Nizamshahi Kingdom.

In 1610 A.D. Ambar had recovered Ahmadnagar and the Mughal force was compelled to retreat to Burhanpur. He transferred his capital to Kharki, and organising guerilla Marátha hands in large numbers continued to offer opposition to the Mughal. He concluded an alliance with Bijapur and Golkonda as the best means of foiling the Mughals. The Mughals assumed the offensive in full vigour in 1611 A.D. but they were forced to retreat. In 1612 A.D. the Khan-i-Khanan was reappointed to the command. He captured and burned Kharki, and to some extent retrieved the disgrace which the imperial arms had suffered earlier. In the autumn of 1616 A.D. Prince Khurram was placed in charge of Deccan affairs. Jahangir moved his court from Ajmer to Mandu, in order to be near the seat of war. Khurram succeeded in detaching Adhil Shah of Bijapur from the Deccan confederacy. Ahmadnagar was recaptured and other strongholds were formally delivered in 1617 A.D. After the conclusion of the treaties, Khurram returned to Mandu. He was then at the height of his fame. He was promoted to the command of 30,000 horses, a rank never before conferred, and received the title of Shan Jahan, or king of the world.

In 1620 A.D. Malik Ambar broke the treaty of 1617 A.D. and renewed his alliance with Bijapur and Golkonda and swept over a considerable portion of Mughal Deccan. He even besieged Burhanpur. Shah Jahan was re-appointed. Malik Ambar was compelled to evacuate all the imperial posts which he had occupied, to retire to Daulatabad and to submit to Shah Jahan. The three kingdoms of the Deccan were obliged to pay *nazarana* amounting to five millions of rupees. In August, 1621 A.D., on receiving the news of his father's illness Shah Jahan returned to the headquarter. After the return of Shah Jahan, Malik Ambar resumed the hositility and continued it till his death in 1626 A.D.

SHAH JAHAN

(*1628-1658 A.D.*)

When Jahangir died Shah Jahan was in Deccan, and Prince Shahariyar declared himself the Emperor of Lahore. But Asaf Khan, father-in-law of Shah Jahan took immediate steps to safegaurd son-in-law's interests. He sent a speedy message to Shah Jahan and in the meantime raised to the throne a son of Khusru, under the title of Dawar Baksh. He used him as a figure-head until he should be able to proclaim Shah Jahan. He then marched on Lahore and defeated Shahariyar who was imprisoned and blinded. In the mean time Shah Jahan reached the capital, deposed Dawar Baksh and ascended the throne on Jaunary, 1628 A.D., with the title of Abul Muzaffar Shahabuddin Muhammad Shan Jahan Padsha Ghazi. The unfortunate Dwar Baksh was permitted to escape to Persia. Nur Jahan was allowed to live in retirement on a sufficiently liberal pension until her death in 1645 A.D. Asaf Khan was made Minister, and retained that office untill his death in 1641 A.D.

Early Rebellions :

There were two more rebellions during the first two years of his accession. In the first year of his reign, Raja Jhujhar Singh Bundela had shown a rebellious and turbulent spirit. He was, however, subsequently chased to death.

In the second year of his reign a formidable rebellion was headed by the Afghan Pir Lodi, entitled Khanjahan, who had for some time been Governor of the southern provinces of the empire. When Shah Jahan left Junnar on his way northwards to assert his claim to the throne, he entered into alliance with the Sultan of Ahmadnagar and gave considerable troubles to the Mughals. Shah Jahan soon sent an army to suppress the rebellion and defeated him at Tel Sehonds, in 1631 A.D. He was then put to death.

War with the Portuguese :

The Portuguese settlers at Hughli in Bengal in the reign of Shah Jahan abused favours so shamelessly that the Emperor was compeled to interfere in their privileges. They offended the Mughal authorities by exacting heavy duties from the local merchants, and they created consternation by kidnapping children whom they converted to Christianity. Furthermore the Portuguese did not shrink from practising piracy. Thereupon Shah Jahan gave orders that they should be expelled. In 1632 A.D. Hughli was besieged and was finally taken.

Shah Jahan's Central Asian Campaigns :

The house of Timur regarded Transoxiana as its ancestral home, and, ever since Babur's explusion from Sarghana, had longed to recover the original domain of its great ancestor. Circumstances had also favoured him. Nazar Muhammad, the incompetent ruler of Balkh and Badakhshan, mismanaged the affairs of the State. Rebellions broke out everywhere. Even his own son Abdul Aziz revolted against him and invited Shah Jahan to help him. In 1646 A.D., Shah Jahan sent a large army under the command of Prince Murad. The campaign was successful and both Balkh and Badakhshan were occupied. But Murad was soon recalled as he behaved in an undisciplined way and Prince Aurangzeb was sent with a large army to consolidate the conquests. But he failed and compelled in 1647 A.D.

Loss of Qandahar :

Qandadar, the great bone of contention between Persia and the Mughals, had been conquered in 1622 A.D. by the Persians but in 1638 A.D. it was surrendered to Shah Jahan by its Governor, Ali Mardan Khan, who joined the Mughal service and was promoted to high rank. The failure of the Mughals in Central Asia encouraged Shah Abbas II of Persia to recapture Qandahar. The Mughal prestige demanded that Qandahar must be won back. Shah Jahan at once sent an expedition under Prince Aurangzeb and Sadullah Khan with an army of 60,000 horses and 10,000 foot (1649 A.D.). But the campaign ended in failure due to the superior military preparations of Persians. A second attempt was made in 1652 A.D. by Prince Aurangzeb and Sadullah Khan but it also ended in failure. A third attempt was made in April, 1653 A.D. under the leadership of Prince Dara Shukoh. He had some success in the beginning but ultimtely failed to re-occupy Qandahar.

The death of a Mughal Emperor was always the signal for the outbreak of intrigues, ending in wars of succession. In September, 1657 A.D. Shah Jahan fell dangerously ill, and all his sons forthwith engaged in fratricidal war for succession.

War of Succession :

Murad crowned himself at Ahmedabad in December, Shuja also proclaimed himself Emperor in Bengal. But Aurangzeb was more cautious and calculative in his proceedings. Shuja was the first to march towards the metropolis of the empire. The imperial army met Shuja's force at Bahadurpur, near Banaras, on February 14, 1658 A.D., and defeated it. Being compelled by the course of events, Aurangzeb decided to march to the north to see his father personally. Aurangzeb had already entered into a solemn treaty with Murad that, in case of success, the latter would get the Punjab, Afghanistan, Kashmir and Sind. Thus the combined troops of Aurangzeb and Murad marched towards the north. Raja Jaswant Singh of Jodhpur and Qasim Khan were sent by Dara to oppose them. The hostile armies met Dharmat on April 15, 1658 A.D., where the imperialists were signally defeated.

Aurangzeb then crossed the Chambal and met an imperial army of 50,000 soldiers under Dara himself. A fierce battle ensued; Aurangzeb and Murad both displayed unexempled courage in fighting, and inflicted heavy losses on Dara's men. No victory was perhaps more complete and no defeat was perhaps more disastrous than this. Filled with despair, Dara fled towards Agra. Aurangzeb entered Agra, imprisoned his father and assumed the reins of Government in his own hand (8th June, 1658 A.D.).

After his victory, Auranzeb restored Bengal and Bihar to Shuja, but the latter could not check his ambition of becoming the Emperor of India. But his hopes were shattered when Aurangzeb signally defeated him at Khajwah, near Allahabad, on the 5th January, 1659 A.D. Mir Jumla chased him to Bengal, and he escaped to Arakan in May, 1660 A.D. Nothing was heard of Shuja again.

Aurangzeb was now the practical master of the empire. But the civil war was not yet over. Murad broke the terms of alliance with Aurangzeb and conspired against his authority, "Flattering courtiers fanned the young prince's jealousy and ambition and prompted him to assert himself......in opposition to Aurangzeb." Aurangzeb imprisoned Murad in the fort of Salimgarh. He was sent later on to the fort of Gwalior, where he was tried for the murder of his Diwan, Ali Naqi, and was executed in 1661 A.D.

Dara once again collected a large army and offered a battle to Aurangzeb. It was a hotty war and Aurangzeb once again defeated him. After this defeat Dara fled to Ahmadabad and then retreated to Sind with a view to fly to Persia. Malik Jiwan, a Baluchi chief of Dara, whose life he had once saved, was approached for shelter. But Malik Jiwan treacherously surrendered him to Aurangzeb. He was executed on a charge of apostacy. Dara's son Sulaiman also met the same fate. Shah Jahan remained confined in the Agra fort until January 22, 1666 A.D., when he died a natural death. Thus ended the prolonged civil war and Aurangzeb emerged victorious.

AURANGZEB

(1658-1707 A.D.)

Aurangzeb, having successfully disposed of all his rivals, was formally crowned in Delhi, with the title of Abul Muzaffar Mohiuddin Mohammad Aurangzeb Alamgir Padshah Ghazi, in May, 1659 A.D. His long reign of fifty years falls into two nearly equal parts. From 1659 to 1681 A.D. he was mostly in northern India, leaving the affairs of the Deccan to his viceroys; from 1681 A.D. to his death he was in the Deccan, engaged in his attempt to subdue the Marathas.

He began his rule by restoring the Muslim lunar calendar and discontinued the Ilahi year of Akbar. To alleviate the distress of his subjects, Aurangzeb abolished many oppressive taxes and cesses. To lower the price of food, the duty on corns was also remitted. With a view to stop corruptions the Governors were transferred from one province to another.

The North-Eastern Frontier :

The Mughal frontier had been pushed in 1622 A.D. to Goalpara and Kamrup in Western Assam. But taking the advantage of the war of succession the Ahoms had violated this frontier, and the Raja of Cooch Bihar had also defied Mughal authority. Mir Jumla was appointed Viceroy of Bengal with orders to punish the Ahoms. In November, 1661 A.D., Mir Jumla started from Dacca, annexed Cooch Bihar and entered Assam. In March, 1662 A.D., the invading army reached Garhgoan, the Ahom capital. The Ahom King, Jayadhwaj Singh, being put to flight, the Mughal fleet compeltely annihilated Ahom naval power. So far the operations of Mir Jumla were successful. But Nature came to the rescue of Ahoms. The rainy season enabled the Ahoms to attack the isolated Mughal outposts. The imperialists suffered terribly from unhealthy climate and lack of provisions and medicine. An epidemic broke out in the Mughal camp. When the rainy season was over, Mir Jumla resumed the offensive attacks and forced the Ahom King to conclude treaty with the Mughals. The Ahom King agreed a pay a heavy war indeminity and an annual tribute and to cede some districts. But this success of Aurangzeb was not permanent. Mir Jumla died on his way to Decca in March, 1663 A.D. After his death the Ahoms recovered the ceded districts and even wrested Kamrup from the Mughals is in 1667 A.D.

After Mir Jumla, the Emperor's maternal uncle, Shaista Khan, was appointed Governor of Bengal. He was engaged in expeditions against Assam and Arakan, and in clearing out the rests of pirates round the deltas of the Ganges, Brahmaputra and at Chittagong. He conquered Chittagong from the King of Arakan in 1666 A.D. Shaista Khan also conquered the island of Sandwip in the Bay of Bengal.

The North-West Frontier :

Operation against the turbulent tribesmen—the Afridis, the Yusufzais, the Khattaks and others of the North Western Frontier were less successful. They gave the Mughals as much trouble as they did the British in later times.

In 1672 A.D. the Afridis rose in revolt against the Mughals under their leader Akmal Khan. He proclaimed himself king and summoned other tribes to join his standard. Akmal Khan defeated the imperial Commander Amin Khan at Ali Kasjid in May, 1672 A.D. Amin Khan and some of the senior officers escaped to Peshawar, but ten thousand Mughal soldiers were slain and more were captured. The situation was worsened by the rising of another tribe named Khattak under their poet chief Khushal Khan. The movement was fast becoming a Pathan national rising against the Mughals. In 1674 A.D. Aurangzeb appointed Shujaat Khan to quell the rebels. Shujaat Khan was killed in action and defeated. Therefore Aurangzeb personally went and crushed the rebles.

Aurangzeb Deccan Policy :

The great ambition of Aurangzeb was to extend the Mughal dominions in the Deccan, where he had once been Viceroy for his father. Edwards and Garret rightly remarked : "He (Aurangzeb) was following the policy of aggressive imperialism, initiated by Akbar in the 16th Century and encouraged by his successors, Jahangir and Shah Jahan." During the first half of Aurangzeb's reign his attention was engrossed with affairs in the north, and the Deccan was left to the Viceroys. But the rapid decline of the Sultanates of Bijapur and Golkonda and the unchecked growth of the Maratha power at their expense created a new political situation in the Deccan. The rise of the Maratha power was a challenge to the Mughal Empire. The situation was further aggravated by the flight of the rebellious Prince Akbar to the Maratha King, Shambhuji. The Deccan policy of Aurangzeb was determined by three factors : the annexation of the Sultanates of Bijapur and Golkonda ; the removal of the danger caused by the presence of his rebel son, Prince Akbar in the court of Shambhuji ; and the suppression of the Maratha power. The Deccan campaigns of Aurangzeb were never guided by religious fanaticism is well-illustrated by the fact that many Shia nobles lived in his court and Mir Jumla, a Shia Muslim, was his most trusted and efficient General. Not religious fanaticism but aggressive imperialism may be said the real cause behind his campaigns in the Deccan.

In 1681 A.D., he directed his arms against Bijapur and Golkonda. Bijapur was besieged in April, 1685 A.D., and captured in September, 1686 A.D. Golkonda was besieged in and captured in 1687 A.D. Thus the Sultanates of Bijapur and Golkonda were annexed to the Mughal Empire. After the fall of the kingdoms of Bijapur and Golkonda, Aurangzeb concentrated his whole energy against the Marathas. Shivaji was succeeded by his eldest son, Shambuji, who had none of the genius of his father. Shambuji took up the cause of the Marathas but was defeated, captured and executed in March, 1689 A.D. His capital Rajgarh fell into the hands of the Mughals. This was the high landmark of Aurangzeb's success against the Marathas. His territory now extended from Kabul to Chittagong and from Kashmir to the Kaveri.

The Marathas stood against Aurangzeb and it was from 1690 A.D., that the tide completely turned against Aurangzeb. Two enterprising Maratha Generals, Santaji Ghorpade and Dhanaji Jadev, made incessant raids. Rebellions broke out in every corner of the empire. Rajaram organised a powerful army and raided the Mughal provinces of the Deccan. The Emperor now personally took charge of operations and showed wonderful energy in capturing several forts—Satara, Parli, Panhala, Khelna, Kondana (Singhgarh), Rajgarh, Torna and Wagingera. Rajaram died in 1700 A.D., and was succeeded by Shivaji III. The Regency was taken up by Rajaram's widow, Tara Bai. She successfully withstood Aurangzeb's final attempt to conquer the Deccan, and it was during her Regency that the Mughal armies were forced to retire into Ahmadabad. Worn out by the indecisive Maratha war, the Emperor fell seriously ill and died on February 20, 1707 A.D. at Ahmadnagar.

Estimate of Aurangzeb :

Aurangzeb was a man of extraordinary character. His resolution, his honesty of purpose, his devotion to duty, his love of Islam, his modesty and his scholarship were acknowledged by all. He was, in fact, one of the enlightened rulers of the Timurid family.

Aurangzeb had a high respect for his office. Painstaking and methodical, he attended to most things himself. He was a very just man and spared neither himself, his sons, nor his subordinates. Foreign travellers as well as the Muslim chroniclers described with admiration his marvellous industry in administration. He personally read all petitions and passed orders on them with his own hand. A learned and competent scholar he was largely responsible for the great digest of Muslim Law made in India bearing his name, *Fatawa-i-Alamgiri*, which has regulated Islamic justice in India ever afterwards. As a General, Aurangzeb had few equals. "Undaunted bravery, grim tenacity of purpose, and ceaseless activity were some of his prominent qualities." He rarely lost a battle.

Thus Aurangzeb had many qualities. He was a brave warrior, a shrewd diplomat, a just and tolerant monarch, and a profound scholar. "He had been by far the most powerful of the line ; he had ruled wider territories and commanded vaster armies than Akbar."......said Lanepoole.

THE OTTOMAN TURKS

Othman, on his deathbed, designated as his successor the younger of his two sons, Orchan, aged forty-two, who had been brought up as a soldier under his father's eye, and had shown capacity in many campaigns, and especially in that resulting in the surrender of Brusa. Alaeddin, the elder brother, was not a soldier. He had led a studious life, devoted to religion and law, both founded on the Qur'an, under the guidance of Idelbali.

ORCHAN

(1326-59 A.D.)

The Turkish historians agree in stating that Orchan was most unwilling to act on his father's wishes and take precedence over his elder brother, and that he proposed to divide the heritage of state between them but that Alaeddin declined that offer. Orchan is then reported to have said: "Since, my brother, thou wilt not take the flocks and herds which I offer thee, be the shepherd of my people. Be my Vizier." Alaedin agreed to this, and devoted himself to the administration of the growing State and to the organisation of the army, under the rule of his brother.

The immediate objects of Orchan's amibition, on his accession, were the Greek cities of Nicaea and Nicomedia, with their surrounding districts, the last important possessions of the Byzantine Empire in Asia. Nicaea was then a great city. It had attained greater importance during the sixty years when the Latins were in occupation of Constantinople and the Greek Emperors were relegated to Asia and made it their capital. It was well fortified. It could only be captured, as Bursa had been, by cutting off its communications with Constantinople, and depriving its people of the means of subsistence. The Greek Emperor, Andronicus III, made an effort to relieve it. He hastily raised an army of mercenaries, in 1326 A.D., and led them across the Bosphorus. He fought a battle against Orchan at Pelecanon, on the north shore of the Gulf of Nicomedia. According to the Greek historians, the Ottomans had much the worst of it, losing a great number of men, while the losses of the Greeks were trivial. However that may have been, Andronicus decided on a retreat. But a scrimmage occurred in the night between his bodyguard and the enemy, in which the Emperor himself was slightly wounded. He thereupon fled precipitately, and was conveyed in a letter to the Bosphorus and thence to Constantinople. His army, dispirited by this abandonment by their Emperor, was defeated and dispersed. As a result, Nicaea surrendered in the following year, 1327 A.D., on favourable terms. The majority of its garrison and citizens followed the example of those of Brusa and adopted Islam. Very few availed themselves of the offer to transfer themselves to Europe. This ill-starred campaign and cowardly flight of Andronicus was the last effort of the Byzantine Emperors to save their possessions in Asia. What remained of them, chiefly, the city of Nicomedia, were left to their own resources, without further aid from Europe. Nicomedia was well fortified and was apparently a tough job for the Ottomans, for it held out till 1337 or possibly 1338 A.D., and eventually surrendered in the same way, and on the same terms, as Brusa and Nicaea.

For this purpose the country districts were divided into fiefs, the holders of which were bound to serve in the event of war, and to come provided with horses and equipment, or to find substitutes in proportion to the extent of their fiefs. It was, in fact, the adoption of the feudal system, then almost universal in Europe, with this marked difference, that the fiefs were small in extent and were not, as a rule, hereditary. They were given for life as rewards for military service, and on the death of their holders were granted to other soldiers, though in some cases hereditary claims were recognised. When new territories were acquired by conquest from non-Muslims, large parts of them were divided into new fiefs, and were granted to the soldiers who had distinguished themselves in the war. Military service, whether in the new infantry or in the feudal cavalry, was strictly confined to Muslims. Christians, who were thus exempted from military duty, were subjected to a heavy capitation tax from which Muslims were free.

He organised the army and divided the districts into fiefs. This new organisation of the army, commenced by Orchan and extended and perfected by his son Murad, who also created the famous corps of Janissaries, converted the nascent Ottoman State into a most powerful engine for war, and gave an immense impetus to the conquest of non-Muslim countries. Most splendid rewards were held out to the Muslim soldiers for victory and bravery.

In has been shown that hitherto in the Ottoman conquests in Asia Minor at the expense of the Byzantine Empire a great proportion of the Christian population embraced Islam ; and it may well have been that the spread of Islam and the conversion of infidels to the true faith were in part the incentives for the expansion of the Ottoman Empire.

In the year 1354 A.D., Orchan, after completing the organisation of his army, turned his attention for the first time to Europe. Thenceforth, till his death in 1359 A.D., his restless ambition was directed against the Byzantine Empire. Advancing age prevented his taking the field himself at the head of his army. But his eldest son, Solyman, who had all the great qualities of his race, and who was the idol of the army, took his place in command of the invading forces.

It may be well to point out here that, at this time the middle of the Fourteenth Century, the Byzantine Empire was already reduced to very insignificant proportions, compared to its ancient grandeur. The territories subject to it, which for centuries had extended to the Danube in Europe, and in Asia over Anatolia and Syria, had been already greatly diminished when the leaders of the fourth Crusade, in 1204 A.D., in one of the most disgraceful episodes in history, turned aside from their avowed object of attacking the Muslims in Palestine and, in lieu thereof, attacked and captured Constantinople, and compelled the Byzantine Emperor to transfer the seat of his Government to Nicaea, in Asia Minor. There followed the brief period of the Latin Empire. But in 1261 A.D. the Byzantine Greeks re-conquered Constantinople, and the ephemeral Latin Empire disappeared from history. The Byzantines were then able to recover a small part only of their old dominions in Europe and Asia. At the time when Orchan, who had driven them from Asia, decided to attack them in Europe, they held there no more than Thrace with Adrinople, a part of Macedonia with Salonika, and the greater part of the Morea in Greece. To the north of them Seriba, under Stephen Dushan, the most eminent of its rulers, had asserted supremacy over the greater half of the Balkan peninsula, was threatening Salonika, and had ambition to possess himself of Constantinople. Bulgaria, though it had lost territory to Serbia, still possessed the smaller half of the Balkans. The Republics of Venice and Genoa owned many commercial ports and islands in the Aegean Sea and Adriatic, and were madly jealous of one another. The position was such as to afford a favourable opportunity to new invaders like the Ottomans, for there was no probability of a combination among these Christian communities to resist them.

On the death of the Greek Emperor Andronicus III in 1338 A.D., the most feeble and incompetent of the long line of Palaeologi, his Grand Chancellor, Cantacuzene, was appointed, under his will, guardian of his son, John Paleologus, and as co-regent with his widow, the Empress Anna. Cantacuzene, not satisfied with this arrangement, and ambitious to secure supreme power in the Empire, had himself proclaimed Emperor at Nicotika in 1343 A.D. This was bitterly resented and opposed by the Empress Anna. Civil war broke out. Both Anna and Cantacuzene appealed to Orchan, their new and powerful neighbour across the Stratits, for aid against the other. Cantacuzene offered his young daughter, Theodore, in marriage to Orchan in return for the aid of six thousand Ottoman troops. Orchan apparently thought this a better offer than that of the Empress Anna, whatever that may have been. He was perhaps flattered by the prospect of a family connection with a Byzantine Emperor. He closed with the offer and sent six thousand soldiers into Europe, in 1345 A.D., in support of Cantacuzene, who made use of them by investing Constantinople of which the Empress had obtained possession. After a year's siege, Cantacuzene effected an entry into the city by the aid of his partisans there, who treacherously opened its gates to him. The Empress was thereupon compelled to come to terms. She agreed that Cantacuzene and his wife should be crowned as Emperor and Empress, together with herself and her son. This union was further cemented by the marriage of the young Emperor John, at the age of sixteen, with another daughter of Cantacuzene. Orchan, in pursuance of his agreement with the new Emperor, was married in 1346 A.D. at the ripe age of sixty-two to the young Theodora, who was to be allowed to remain a Christian.

It may be assumed that the six thousand soldiers lent to Cantacuzene returned to Asia. But the loan of them soon became a precedent for other transactions of the same kind. In 1349 A.D. the Serbians, under Stephen Dushan, were seriously threatening Salonika, and had ultimate designs on Constantinople itself. Orchan was again appealed for aid by the two Emperors, his father-in-law and brother-in-law, and at their instance he sent twenty thousand soldiers into Europe for the relief of Salonika. With their aid Cantacuzene was able to defeat the Serbians, and to extinguish for ever their hope of replacing the Byzantine Empire at Constantinople. On this occasion again, it appears that the Ottoman troops, having effected their purpose, returned to Asia. But four years later another opportunity befell Orchan of sending troops across the Straits, and this time of effecting a permanent lodgment in Europe. Cantacuzene, not satisfied with being only a co-emperor with his son-in-law and the Empress Anna, attempted, in 1353 A.D., to usurp the supreme power in the State. His son-in-law, John Palaeologus, now of full age, strongly opposed this. Civil War again broke out. For a third time Cantacuzene appealed to his son-in-law Orchan for aid. In return for the loan of twenty thousand soldiers he offered to hand over to the Ottomans a fortress on the European side of the Hellespont. Orchan agreed to this. The Ottoman soldiers were sent into Europe, under Solyman, and were employed by Cantacuzene in fighting against his other son-in-law, the co-Emperor John. They were successful in this, and occupied Demotika.

In 1358 A.D. Solyman, who had shown great capacity when in command of the Ottoman army, met with his death by a fall from his horse when engaged in his favourite sport of falcony. His father, Orchan, died in the following year at the age of seventy-two. He had enormously increased the Ottoman dominions. He had achieved the first great object of his ambition, that of driving the Byzantines from their remaining possessions in Asia. He had rounded off his boundaries in the north-west corner of Anatolia by annexing Mysia. He had invaded Europe and had extended Ottoman rule over a part of Thrace. He had reduced the Byzantine Emperor almost to vassalage. These great result had been achieved not so much by force of arms as a General, for he is not credited with any great victory in the field, or by successful assaults on any great fortresses, as by crafty diplomacy and intrigue, backed up by superior force, and by taking advantage of the feebleness and of the Byzantines. He also forged the military weapon by which his son, Murad, was able to effect far greater territorial conquests, both in Europe and Asia.

MURAD I

(1359-89 A.D.)

Murad succeeded his father, Orchan, at the age of forty. He soon proved himself to be eminently qualified to rule by his untiring activity and vigour, his genius for war, and his wise and sane statesmanship. He was illiterate. He could not even sign his name. There is extant in the archives of the city of Ragusa a treaty with its petty republic, which Murad, in 1363 A.D., signed by dipping his hand in ink and impressing it with his finger marks. The 'tughra' thus formed became the official signature of subsequent Sultans of Turkey. Othman and Orchan between them created the Ottoman dynasty and State, but Murad must be credited with having founded the Empire in the sense of imposing Ottoman rule on subject races.

On Murad's accession his territory, though greatly increased by Orchan, was less in extent than some other Turkish Emirates in Anatolia. It consisted of an area on both sides of the Sea of Marmora, two hundred miles in length by about one hundred in depth. It included both shores of the Dardanelles, but only one side of the Bosphorus. Constantinople, on the other side, though nearly hemmed in by the Ottomans, was nominally independent, and its communications with the Greek Province of Thrace were still open. Deducting the area of the Sea of Marmora, the territory under Murad's rule was not of greater area than twenty thousand square miles. Its population probably did not amount to a million in number. It is difficult to understand how Murad from this small territory so enormously increased his Empire in Europe. It may be surmised that large numbers of Turks from other parts of Anatolia flocked to his standard in search of adventure and booty in Europe.

The ownership of both sides of the Dardanelles did not, in days before the invention of gunpoweder, give command of the

Straits, and as Murad was without a navy, the passage of his armies between Asia and Europe was at the mercy of any naval powers. The Genoese, who had important commercial settlements on the shores of the Black Sea and on the Bosphorus at Galata, and who maintained a large naval force in the Aegean Sea, might easily have barred the way of the Ottomans to Europe, but they hated the Greeks and were greedy of money, and they could be relied on to convey Murad's armies across to Straits for a full consideration. It will be seen that Murad, during his reign of thirty years, increased by more than five-fold the Ottoman possessions, and at one point brought them up to the Danube. He compelled other States also, including the Greek Empire itself, to accept the position of tibutaries to his Empire. His fame in Ottoman history must be regarded as on a level with that of Mahomet, the Conqueror of Constantinople, and of Solyman the Magnificent, who raised the Empire to its zenith.

Murad's great extensions of his Empire may more conveniently, than in a chronological order, be treated under three distinct heads :—

1. His conquest of the possessions of the Greek Empire in Thrace and Bulgaria and the reduction of that decadent Empire to the humiliating position of vassalage. 2. His great conquests in Bulgaria, Macedonia, and Serbia. 3. His extensions in Anatolia by the absorption of Turkish Emirates or parts of them.

The conquest of Thrace by the Ottomans and the defeat of the allied Christians at the Maritza were as great blows to the Bulgarians as to the Greek Empire, though they had given no assistance to the allies. The occupation of Adrionople and Philippopolis opened the way to further advance into Bulgaria and Macedonia. It was not, however, till 1366 A.D. that Murad availed himself of this advantage, and commenced the series of attacks which ultimately made him master of Macedonia and of a great part of Bulgaria and Serbia. The position of affairs in the peninsula at this time was very favourable to him. The Bulgarians, Serbians, Bosnians, and Greeks were madly jealous of one another : each of them preferred the extension of the Ottoman rule to that of their rivals. Bulgaria alone, if united, might have successfully resisted Murad. But in 1365 A.D. its Czar, Alexander, died, and his kingdom was divided between his three sons. Sisman, the elder, got the largest share. The other two gave no assistance to their brother when the Ottomans invaded his country. Between 1366 and 1369 A.D., Murad advanced into Bulgaria, and took possession of the Maritza Valley, as far as the Rhodope Mountains. In 1371 A.D. Latashalin encountered an army of Bulgarians and Serbians at Samak of, not far from the city of Sofia, and completely defeated it, with the result the Bulgaria, up to the Balkan range, was annexed to the Ottoman Empire. It remained so far over five hundred years, till its release in our own time.

After this great victory at Samakot, Lalashalin was instructed by Murad not to pursue his conquest of Bulgaria north of the Balkan range, but to proceed westward, and, in concert with Everons, to invade Macedonia as far as the River Vardar. This occupied the two Generals in the years 1371-2 A.D. Kavalla, Druma, and Serres fell into their hands. In 1372 A.D. they crossed the Vardar River and penetrated into Old Serbia, Albania, and Bosnia. The main part of Serbia, however, remained in the hands of Lazar, its prince. But he was compelled to acknowledge the suzerainty of the Sultan. As regards the part of Bulgaria not annexed, its prince, Sisman, was allowed to retain his independence. His daughter entered the *Harem* of Murad, with the understanding that she was not be compelled to adopt the Muslim religion. It was not till 1381 A.D. that a further advance was made by Murad. He then sent his armies across the Vardar River and captured Monastir. He also took possession of Sofia, and in 1386 A.D. of Misch, after fierce struggle with the Serbians.

Between the years 1376 and 1380 A.D. Murad found himself able to turn his attention in the direction of Asia Minor. In the first of these years he induced to the Emir of Kermia, doubtless by threats of war, to give a daughter in marriage to Bayezid, his eldest son. She brought with her as dowry a considerable part of Kermia and the fortress of Kutayia, a position of great strategic importance. In 1371 A.D. he followed this up by inducing the Emir of Hamid to sell a great portion of his Emirate lying between Tekke, Kermia, and Karamania, including the district of Ak-Sheir. The effect of this acquisition was to make his frontier conteminous with that of Karamania. Again, in 1378 A.D., he declared war against the Emir of Tekke, and annexed a part of his territory, leaving to him Adalia.

Murad made no further effort to extend his dominion in Asia till 1387 A.D. when he led a large army against Alaeddin the Emir of Karamania. For this purpose he called upon the Greek Emperor and the princes of Serbia and Bulgaria as vassals of the Empire to send their contingents. His two sons, Bayezid and Yacoub, commanded the wings of this army. With a view to conciliate the peasentry of the district he passed through, and to ensure full supplies of food to his army, he gave strict orders that there was to be no pillage, and that the lives and property of the country people were to be respected. Among his troops were two thousand Serbians, whom the Prince of Serbia was bound by his recent treaty to supply. These men refused to obey Murad's order, and committed attrocious depredations on the route of the army. Murad inflicted severe punishment on them, and directed many of them to be put to death as a warning to the others. The army then marched to meet the Karamanians. A battle again took place on the plain of Angora.

During the twenty-four years of war, in which he led his armies in the field, he never met with a reverse. He extended the Empire for the first time into vast territories inhabited not by Turks or by Byzantines, but sturdy Christian races, such as the Bulgarians, Serbians, and Bosnians. For the first time also the Turks came into conflict with the Hungarians and defeated them. The influence of the Empire was extended practically to the Danube. Some of the intervening territory was not treated as conquered country and added to the Empire, but was allowed to retain the position of tributary or vassal States, as in the case of Serbia. Other parts, such as Thrace, Macedonia, and Bulgaria, were fully incorporated in the dominion of the Sultan.

Murad, when not engaged in war, devoted himself to perfecting the organization of his army on the lines laid down by the father, Orchan. He also created a new standing crops of soldiers, recruited from the Christian population of the provinces conquered in Europe. This was the renowned corps of Jahissaries—the new army.

BAYEZID I

(*1389-1403 A.D.*)

Bayezid succeeded his father, Murad, at the age of thirty-four. He reigned as Sultan for only fourteen years, the last of which was spent in captivity. No one of the Othman race passed through such vicissitudes, with such a brilliant career of victory during nearly the whole of his reign, but ending with overwhelming and crushing defeat. He had all the courage and military capacity of his three predecessors. He excelled them greatly in cruelty and brutality. In his private life he descended to depths of sensuality and unmentionable and degrading view which were unknown to them.

Early in his reign he adopted a much bolder attitude toward the Christian powers of Europe than Murad had thought prudent. To a deputation from Italy asking for a renewal of commercial privileges, he replied that when he had conquered Hungary he intended to ride to Rome, and there give feed to his horse with oats in the altar of St. Perer's. His treatment of his Christian subjects was mhch harsher than that of his predecessors.

Bayezid followed up his father's great victory at Kossova over the Serbians, and compelled Stephen, the successor of

Lazar, to sue for peace. The terms of the treaty then agreed to were very moderate. Instead of being incorporated in the Ottoman Empire as Bulgaira had been, Serbia was to be an autonomous State, under vassalage to the Ottoman Empire paying tribute in money, and bound to provide and maintain a contingent of five thousand soldiers at the disposal of the Sultan. Stephen its prince, also gave his sister, Despine, to the Sultan as an additional wife. He most loyally carried out his promises to Bayezid. In the great battles of Nicopolis against the Hungarians and the crusaders from Western Europe, and Angora against Timur, the Serbian contingent fought with the utmost bravery, and there were no more loyal soldiers in the Ottoman ranks.

In 1393 A.D., Bayezid sent an army, under command of his eldest son, Solyman, to invade the northern part of Bulgaria, which still enjoyed an autonomous existence. Tirnova, its capital, was taken by storm after a siege of three weeks. He then decided to incorporate the northern part of Bulgaria in the Ottoman Empire in the same manner as the southern part had already been treated. This completed the servitude of the Bulgarian people. Sisman, their prince, disappeared from the scene, and the ruling family became extinct. The land was confiscated, except in a few cases where the owners were allowed to become Muslims. It was parcelled out to Turks under a feudal system involving military service, while the cultivators of the soil were reduced to serfdom.

About this time the fortresses of Nicopolis, Widden, and Silistria fell into the hands of the Ottomans and opened the way into Hungary. Bayezid commenced a system of raids into that country, not for the purpose, at that time, of acquiring its territory, but for plunder. His Turkish 'akinjis', or irregulars, spread terror over wide districts, burning and destroying villages and carrying off their inhabitants for sale as slaves, He fitted out ships also with the same object in the newly acquired ports in Asia Minor, and ravaged the islands of Chios and Negropont and districts on the coast of Greece.

Bayezid was now compelled by an outbreak in his recent acquisitions in Asia Minor, formed by the Emir of Karamania, to suspend operations on his northern frontier in Europe and to transfer his army to Asia. He received at Brusa an evoy from his brother-in-law, Alaeddin of Karamania, suing for peace. Bayezid replied that the sword alone could determine the issue between them. He sent an army at once, under Timurtash, against the Karamanians. It encountered Alaeddin on the plain of Ak-Tchai. The Turkish army was completely successful. Alaeddin and his two sons were captured, and without waiting for authority from Bayezid, Timurtash had them hanged. When Bayezid heard of this treatment of his brother-in-law, he affected to be greatly distressed and incensed, but he soon consoled himself by a text from the Qur'an, "The death of a prince is less regretable than the loss of a province," and he gave practical application of the verse by orders to his army to occupy and annex the whole of Karamania. There was no resistance. Koneia and other cities in the eastern part of the State were taken. In spite of this, however, Karamania was not at this time finally incorporated in the Ottoman Empire. After the invasions of Asia Minor by Timur it recovered its independence, and it was not till seventy years later that it was finally subjected and incorporated.

About the some time, 1393-4 A.D., Bayezid made further important conquests in Asia Minor—namely, Samsun, Caesarea, and Sivas, the last of the most important fortresses on the frontier of Aremenia. These great successes both in Europe and Asia were followed by a period of repose, during which Bayezid gave himself up to a life gross debauchery. He was recalled from this by threats of war on the part Sigismund, King of Hungary, and he soon showed that he had lost none of his vigour and dash.

Sigismund had fretted under the constant raids on his kingdom, above referred to, and had for some time part been contemplating war against the Ottomans for the recovery of the fortresses on the Danube, which were so great a menace to him For this purpose he appealed, in 1395 A.D. to the Christian Powers of Europe for assistance. He was backed up by Pope Boniface IX, who preached another crusade against the infidels. Through the efforts of the King of France, Charles VI, a large number of leading nobles of France were induced to band together, under the Comte de Nevers, son of the Duke of Burgundy, a young man of twenty-two years, without any military experience. A thousand horsemen, chevaliers of good birth and position, and six thousand attendants and mercenaries were enrolled in France for this adventure. Other came from England and Scotland, and from Flanders, Lombardy; and Savoy. On their march through Germany to Hungary they were joined by great numbers of German knights, under Count Frederick of Hohenzollern, the Grand Prior of the Teutonic Order, and by a large force of Bavarians, under the Elector Palantine. Later they were reinforced by a number of the knights of St. John of Jerusalem, under the command of de Naillac, their Grand Master. When joined by the Hungarian army, under Sigsmund, and by the contingents from Wallachia and Bosnia, they made up a total force of about sixty thousand men. The expedition was in the nature of a crusade, but was more secular than religious in its aims and methods, and was regarded, it seems, by most of those engaged in it rather as a kind of picnic than as a serious campaign. The composite force collected together at Buda, in Hungary, in the summer of 1396 A.D., and thence marched down the Danube to Nicopolis, capturing Widdin and Sistova on the way. When passing through Serbia they ravaged wide districts inhabited by innocent Christians, and emulated, if they did not exceed the Ottomans in cruel devastation, as though they were in an enemy's country. They established their camp before Nicopolis in September, but for sixteen days they refrained from assaulting the fortress, which was bravely defended by an Ottoman garrison, thus giving time to Bayezid to collect his army and to advance against the allied forces.

The Christian camp was the scene of riotous living and gambling. Large numbers of courtesons had accompanied the crusaders. The whole army was in a state of indiscipline and disorder. The French knights were boastful. They spoke with contempt of the Turkish troops, and could not believe that there was any danger from them. Bayezid, whose army was full of confidence in its superiority, was allowed to appraoch within striking distance, without any attempt to harass his advance. Even then the Christians did not believe there was danger. The Turks suddenly came into contact with them. The knights were compelled to abandon their gaming tables and their women, and to face enemy whom they had so much despised.

The Ottoman army was preceded by large numbers of scouts and irregulars. The leaders of the chivalaries, knowing nothing of the numbers of the Ottomans or of their methods in war, and utterly despising them, most rashly proposed an immediate attack by the whole force of their splendid cavalry. The King of Hungary, who had experience of the Ottomans and who knew their method of masking the main body of their army by irregulars, were more cautious, and advised that the foot soldiers of Hungary and Wallachia should be first employed to meet the attack of the Turkish irregulars, and that the cavalry should be reserved to meet the main body of the Ottomans. The chevaliers were furious at this suggestion. They suspected Sigismund of playing for his own hand, and of wishing to rob them of the glory of a great victory. They insisted on an immediate attack. Sigismund, on hearing of this decision, said, "We shall lose the day through the great pride and folly of these French." And so it turned out.

The chevaliers advanced in splendid array and had no difficulty in dispersing and slaughtering the mob of Turkish irregulars. But this impetuous charge spent their energy and tired their horses. When they were confronted by the main body of the Ottomans, sixty thousand in number, they were powerless to resist. They were surrounded and were compelled to surrender. The main body of Hungarian foot soldiers, when they came in contact with the Ottomans, were not more fortunate. The Wallachians, who formed one of the wings of the army, when they saw how the battle was going, retired from the field without a fight. The centre of the Hungarian army under Sigismund, supported by the Bavarians, made a most gallant fight, and might have been successful if it had not been that the Serbian army, under Prince Stephen, came at a critical time, in support of the Ottomans, and turned the scale in their favour. After a battle of only three hours the Christian allies were completley defeated with great slaughter on both sides. Ten thousand of the Christians, including most of the surviving chevaliers, were taken prisoners. Those who escaped across the Danube suffered terribly in their retreat through Wallachia. They were beaten and maltreated, for whom they had shown no consideration in their advance.

On the morning of the battle of Nicopolis, Bayezid, when told of the heavy losses of his own army, and that in the early part of the battle the chevaliers had massacred a number of Turks who had surrendered on promise of life, was greatly incensed. He gave orders that all the Christian prisoners to the number of ten thousand were to be put to death in his presence. He made an exception only in favour of twenty-four of the knights, including de Nevers, their leader, for whose release a heavy ransom might be expected. But they were compelled to witness the execution of their comrades in arms.

Before their final departure, Bayezid treated these knights to a day's sport on a regal scale ; even thousand falconers, were employed on the occasion, and give thousand men led dogs to pick up the game. The historian does not state what was the bag resulting from this great battle.

Of the twenty-four knights only one, Marshal Boucicaut, took up the parting challenge of Bayezid and returned to the East to make war against him. The others showed no desire to wipe out the disgrace of their defeat.

After this great battle at Nicopolis the Ottoman army made irruptions into Wallachia, Styria, and Hungary. The city of Peterwardein was captured and eighteen thousand of its inhabitants were sold into slavery. Another division invaded Syria, and devastated the country between the Drave and the Danube. The fortresses on the river taken by the crusaders were recaptured. The raid into Wallachia was a failure. The Turks engaged in it were defeated and driven back. Bayezid himself threatened Buda, in Hungary, but his progress was checked by a long and painful fit of gout. Gibbon moralizes on this in the following sentence : "The disorders of the moral are sometimes corrected by those of the physical world ; and on a crimonious humour falling on a single fibre of one man may prevent or suspend the misery of nations." The invasions of Hungary on this occassion was a failure.

After this campaign Bayezid returned to Adrianople, and there occupied himself by inflicting further humiliations on the Greek Empire. He forced Manuel to resign and imposed John, the son of Andronicus, as its Emperor. He then issued forth again with his army, in 1397 A.D., and fell like a thunderbolt on Greece, without any warning or cause of complaint. He marched with his army through Thessaly, capturing on the way Larissa and Pharsalia. He passed through Thermopylae. The mere passage of his army sufficed to subdue Doris and Locris. His two Generals, Yacoub and Evrenos, then pillaged Argos. Its inhabitants, to the number of thirty thousand, were sold as slaves and deported to Asia. Colonies of Turks were planted in the Morea. Theodore Palaeologus, who acted as despot there on behalf of the Greek Empire, agreed to become tributary of the Sultan.

Returning to Adrianople, Bayezid determined to obtain immediate possession of Constantinople. The Greek Empire had been already deprived of nearly all territory outside the walls of its capital. The Sultan opened proceedings against it by sending an envoy to the Emperor with this insulting message :

The citizens of Constantinople, rather than experience the terrible fate which they knew would befall them in the event of a successful assault by the Ottoman army, were willing to come to terms. But the Emperor, who was buoyed up by hope of assistance from the Christian Powers, refused to acquiesce in a pusillanimous surrender. He replied to the ambassador in dignified terms : "Tell your master that, feeble as we are, we know no other power to whom to address ouselves it be not God, Who protects the feeble and humbles the powerful. Let the Sultan do what he pleases."

As this stage, and before he could give effect to his threats, Bayezid was compelled by great events in Asia to raise the siege of Constantinople. Hitherto, in twelve years of incessant war, Bayezid had been uniformly successful. He had annexed the greater part of Asia Minor, Macedonia, Northern Bulgaria, and Thessaly. He had reduced to vassalge the Greek Empire itself and Serbia, Wallachia, Bosnia, and a great part of Greece. He had defeated the feudal chivalry of Europe in the great battle of Nicopolis.

MAHOMET I

(1413-21 A.D.)

On the death of Sultan Bayezid, in captivity, it seemed as though the Ottoman Empire was doomed to extinction, Asia Minor had already passed out of its hand, and was either in possession of the Emirs who had been reinstated in their territories by Timur, and who had sworn allegiance to him, or was still in the occupation of the invading Tartars. It was not to be expected that the Empire in Europe would survive when it could no longer draw support from Asia. The Christian populations of Bulgaria, Bosnia and Wallachi would soon reassert their independence, and the Greek Empire might be expected to recover some of its lost provinces. The Turkish Empire, however, showed a most unexpected vitality. It survived not only the invasion of Timur, but civil war, which after the death of Bayezid broke out between four of his sons. An interregnum of ten years occurred, during which there was interecine war between these claimants to his throne. The Empire emerged from these stupendous difficulties, under the able rule of the youngest of them, Mahomet I, as strong as ever, and without the loss of a single privince

Timur's hosts, after ravaging the whole of Asia Minor, departed like a swarm of locusts which has denuded a district of its produce and then seeks fresh ground they returned to Central Asia. They left nothing behind in Asia Minor of Tartar rule, either of an army or of an administration. The field was left open to the Ottomans to fight among themselves and their former vassals and neighbours for such a settlement as could be achieved by the strongest of them.

Of the six sons of Bayezid, five fought with him at Angora in command of division of his army. One of them, Mustapha, was supposed to be among the slain ; another, Musa, was taken prisoner and shared the captivity of his father. The other three escaped. The eldest of them, Solyman, accompanied by the Grand Vizier, Ali, and Hassan, the Agha of the Janissaries, made his way to Adrianople where, on the death Bayezid himself proclaimed Sultan, and exercised power as such over the European provinces of the Empire. Issa, a younger son, where he also claimed to be successor to his father, and Mahomet, the youngest son, but by far the ablest, retired to Amasia, a small principality in the North-East of Asia Minor. He there assumed authority over the district. After the death of their father these three claimants for succession to his Empire fought it out between themselves and, later on, a forth claimant was added to the list in Musa, who had been set free by Timur, in order that he might convey the dead body of his father for interment at Brusa.

The earliest conflict was between Mahomet and Issa. Mahomet offered to divide between them the Ottoman possessions in Asia. Issa refused and claimed the whole of them. He was defeated and fled to Europe, where he sought the assistance of Solyman, who had firmly established himself in the Ottoman dominons there, and who was now able to lead an army into Asia Minor in support of Issa. Mahomet was hard pressed by Soluman. He sent Musa across the Straits to effect a diversion by raising revolt against Solyman in Europe. This had the desired effect, and Solyman was compelled to return to Adrianople. After his departure Mahomet succeeded in defeating Issa again, and the latter disappeared and was heard of no more.

In Europe, Solyman and Musa were now in deadly conflict. Solyman was much the same type of man as his father—of great vigour and courage in action, but given to orgies of drink and debauchery. The Agha of the Janissaries in vain tried to rouse him from the apathy to which he was often reduced after these bouts. He threatened to shave the Agha's beard with his sword. He was often severe and even cruel to his soldiers, and finally the Janisarries, incensed by his brutal treatment, his dissolute habits, and his inability to rouse himself to action, rebelled against him, at the instance of Hassan, and put him to death. They then took service under Musa, who became master of the position in Europe and assumed the title of Sultan.

After an expedition to Serbia for the purpose of avenging what he considered their treachery to him in supporting Mahomet, and where he committed the most revolting cruelties. Musa returned to Adrianople, and opened a campaign against the Emperor Manuel, who, after the death of Bayezid, had superseded Andronicus on the Greek throne and who supported Mahomet.

The Emperor appealed to Mahomet for assistance. Mahomet, with a Turkish army, supported by the Serbian contingent, crossed the Bosphorus in answer to this appeal, and the strange sight was witnessed of a Turkish army, under the command of one of the Ottoman race, defending Constantinople against another Turkish army.

Musa eventually retreated from his lines in front of Constantinople, and was pursued by Mahomet. When, later the two armies came into close touch on the borders of Serbia, a conflict was avoided by a revolt of Musa's troops. The Agha Hassan, addressed the Janissaries in the very presence of Musa. "Why," he said to them, "do you hesitate to go over to the ranks of the most just and virtuous of the Ottoman princes? Why subject yourselves to be outraged by a man who can take care neither of himself nor of others?"

Musa, on hearing this harangue to his troops, rushed at Hassan and slew him. The companion of Hassan struck at Musa with his sword and wounded him in the hand. The troops, when they saw that their General was seriously wounded, were seized with panic. They deserted him and went over to Mahomet. Musa fled with three attendants, and later, his dead body was found in a marsh.

Mahomet was now in undisputed command of the Empire as Sultan. He reigned as such for only eight years. He showed, during that time, infinite skill and patience, as a Statesman equally as a General, in restoring, consolidating, and maintaning his Empire. He was ardently desirous of peace. To the representatives of Serbia, Wallachia, and Albania he said: "Forget not to tell your masters that I grant peace to all, and that peace I will accept from all. May God be against the breakers of peace!"

He kept on the best of terms with the Greek Emperor, with whom he had made a defensive alliance, and restored to him certain cities on the coast of the Black Sea and in Thessaly. He had frequent causes, however, for the use of his army, and for showing his skill as a General. He compelled the Emirs of Karamania, Kermia, and other principalities in Asia Minor, who had promised allegiance to Timur, to renew their vassalage to the Ottoman Empire. Two or three times the Karamanian price revolted and endeavoured to assert complete independence. As often Mahomet defeated him, but contented himself with asserting supremacy, and did not insist upon the incorporation of his territory with the Empire. He also defeated an attempt of a Turkish upstart to create an independent State at Smyrna and Aldin. He put down a dangerous revolt of Dervishes and extinguished the sect. He came into conflict at sea with the Republic of Venice, and though he was worsted, and his fleet of galleys was destroyed, he succeeded in making an honourable peace.

Mahomet died in 1421 A.D. at the early age of forty-seven. He was buried at Brusa in a mausoleum near the splendid building known as the Green Mosque, which he had himself erected.

MURAD II

(1421-51 A.D.)

Murad II succeeded his father in the Sultanate as second of the name. He reigned for thirty years, including two short periods when he abdicated and retired into private life. But on each occasion he was compelled by the exigencies of the State, and the youth and inexperience of his son and successor, to resume the throne. He much resembled his father in vigour and capacity as a General and in his desire to act justly.

At the very commencement of Murad's reign the Greek Emperor Manuel, by an almost incredible act of folly, hoping to take advantage of Murad's youth and inexperience, let loose from confinement a man who claimed, to be Mustapha, the son of Sultan Bayezid, whether righty or not never clearly established, had disappeared after the battle of Angora. Manuel entered into a treaty with this claimant to the Ottoman throne, by which in the event of his succeeding in establishing his succession, the city of Gallipoli and all the cities on the shores of the Black Sea, taken from the Greek Empire by the Turks, were to be restored to it.

A rival to the Sultan was set up in Asia in another Mustapha, a younger brother of Murad ; who had not been put to death in pursuance of the fratiricidal policy of his family. This new claimant was supported by the Karamanians and Kermians, and with their aid he defeated an Ottoman army in Asia Minor. Murad found it necessary to abandon the siege of Constantinople, and to transfer his main army to Asia Minor for the purupose of dealing with this danger to his throne. He came to close quarters as quickly as possible with Mustapha's army, and defeated it. Mustapha was taken prisoner and hanged at once by his captors, without giving an opportunity to Murad to exercise his elemency in favour of his brother, had he so willed it. Murad then occupied himself by reducing the Karaminian and other Emirs to complete subjection to his Empire.

Meanwhile the Emperor Manuel died, and was succeeded by John Palaelogus. Murad, in lieu of renewing the siege of Constantinople, was content to make another treaty with the new Emperor, imposing on him a heavy tribute and stripping him of almost every possession beyond the walls of his capital. The Empire thus obtained a reprieve for a few brief years.

In the case of Salonika, which had been recently sold by the Greek Emperor to the Republic of Venice, now desirous of effecting a lodgment in Macedonia. Murad refused to recognize the right of the Emperor to transfer to a foreign power a city which at one time had been under Ottoman rule. It had three times in the last hundred years been captured by the Ottomans, and had as often been recaptured by the Greeks. Murad led an army, in 1430 A.D., to attack Salonika, and, after a vigorous resistance by the Venetians, captured it by assault, and finally annexed the city and its district to the Turkish Empire. It was thought that Murad showed great clemency in not allowing his soldiers to indulge in a wholesale massacre. The Greek inhabitants however, were sold into slavery, and their numbers were so great that a good-looking girl was sold for the price of a pair of boots.

The suppression of rebellion in Asia Minor, the subjection of the Greek Emperor to the position of a humble vassal, and the capture of Salonika had occupied Murad for some years. Later he was involved in long struggles with his neighbours, the Hungarians, on the northern boundaries of his Empire. The Ottomans were engaged in constant raids across the Danube, where vast districts were devastated, and thousands of their population were carried off as captives for sale as slaves. There arose about this time in Hungary a national hero, the celebrated Hunyadi, a natural son of the late King Sigismund. He was a born leader of men, not a great General, but almost a valiant fighter. He had gained great distinction in war in other directions. He now became the soul of hostility against the Ottomans. He was known as the White Knight, on account of his silver armour, which always shone in the van of the impetuous charges of his cavalry. He was rightly regarded by his countrymen as a patriot and a national hero. Nonetheless, he was a blood-thirsty ruffian. He made a practice of massacring all the prisoners taken in battle. He found pleasure in having this effected, in his presence, at banguets, where the guests were entertained by the shrieks of the dying men.

Hunyadi for twenty years was a terror to the Ottoman armies. His first encounter with them was at Hermanstadt, north of the Danube, which was invested by an army of eighty thousand Ottomans. He led an army of twenty thousand Hungarians against him, in relief of the fortress, and inflicted a severe defeat on them. Twenty thousand of the Ottomans were killed, including the General. The others were dispersed. Murad sent another army of eighty thousand men against him, under another Pasha. Hunyadi again defeated it with great slaughter at Varsag.

The notable victories roused great enthusiasm in Europe. It was determined to take the offensive against the Ottomans, and to make another effort to drive them out of Europe. A coalition was formed for the purpose between Hungary and Poland, then united under King Ladislaus, and Wallachia and Bosnia. Serbia, which under its king, Stephen Lazariwitch, had been the firm ally of the Ottomans, and had supported them in many campaigns in Asia and Europe, was now induced to abandon this alliance and, under Stephen's successor, George Brancowitch, to join the confederacy against the Ottomans. The Pope, Eugenius, was most active in support of its combination. His legate, Cardinal Julian Cesarini, led an armed force in support of it. Money was raised for the purpose of the war by a great sale of indulgences to the faithful in every part of Europe. A large contingent of French and German knights joined the allied army. It was, in fact, another crusade, prompted by religious zeal on behalf of Christianity against Islam. The allied army was under the nominal command of Ladislaus, but Hunyadi was its real leader.

The Republics of Venice and Genoa gave their support, and as at this time, the Ottomans had naval force, it was hoped that these Powers, by means of their numerous and powerful galleys, would prevent the transfer to Europe of Murad's main army, which was again engaged in conflict with the Karamanians in Asia Minor.

The allied army, under these favourable circumstances, crossed the Danube in 1443 A.D. It defeated an Ottoman army on the banks of the Masova and again at Nisch. It then crossed the Balkan range in winter—an operation of extreme difficulty, which has since only twice been effected, by General Dibitsch and General Gourko—and again defeated the Turks in a battle at the foot of these mountains. Strange to say, instead of marching onwards to Adrianople, as Diebitsch did in 1829 A.D. Hunvadi was content with the laurels already achieved, and returned with his army to Buda, where he displayed his trophies and received a triumph.

Murad, on hearing of the retreat of the Hungarians across the Balkans, determined to come to terms with them, and not to pursue them again across the Danube. With some difficulty, and in spite of the sullen opposition of Cardinal Julian and the French contingent a treaty was agreed to, with Ladislaus, by which Serbin was to be freed from dependence on the Ottoman Empire and Wallachia was to be ceded to Hungary. The treaty was to be in force for ten years. It was solemnly sworn to on the Gospel and the Qur'an by Ladislaus and Murad.

While this treaty was being negotiated, Murad, weary of war, and desirous of spending the remainder of his life in sensual enjoyments which had so long been denied to him, decided to abdicate his throne. He was still in the full vigour of life at the age of forty-one though he was said to be growing rather fat. He did not propose, like the Emperor Charles V, to retire to reastery, but rather, like Diocletian the Roman Emperor, to a luxurious place, surrounded by beautiful gardens, which he had prepared for his retreat at Magnesia. On the ratification of the treaty of Szegeddin, in 1444 A.D., he carried out this purpose, and his son Mahomet, at the age of fourteen, was proclaimed Sultan in his place.

When this became known to the Hungarians a revulsion of opinion took place against the recent treaty with the Turks. The Hungarian Diet determined, at the instance of Cardinal Julian, backed up by the Pope, to break the treaty. News had arrived of a fresh outbreak of the Karamanians. The fleets of Genoa, Venice, and Burgundy were masters of the Hellespont and would, it was believed, prevent the Ottoman army in Asia Minor from crossing into Europe. The opportunity for crushing the Turks and driving them out of Europe seemed to be most favourable.

It was decided to send an army at once against the Ottomans. But it was a much reduced one in comparison with that which had so recently crossed the Balkans. Most of the French and German knights and their attendants had already gone home. Not more than ten thousand remained under Hunvadi. They were joined by five thousand Wallachians. They invaded Bulgaria, and then, instead of crossing the Balkans, descended the Danube to the coast and thence marched to Varna. Meanwhile the Ottomans, in great alarm and fearing the incompetence of the young Mahomet to conduct a great war, induced Murad to emerge again from his retreat. He hastily gathered together an army in Asia Minor. He bribed the Genoese, at the rate of a ducat for each man, to convey it across the Hellespont. He arrived in front of Varna unexpectedly, before the Christian army knew of his intentions. His army greatly outnumbered that of King Ladislaus. In spite of this, the two wings of it were driven back with great slaughter. Murad, in command of the centre of his army, for the moment and for the only time in his life, lost his presence of mind and was disposed to fly. But the Beglerbey of Anatolla laid hold of the bried of his horse and urged him to fight it out. The battle was renewed. The Janissaries stood firm and successfully repulsed the main body of the Christians. Ladislaus was unhorsed and asked for quarter. But he was put to death on the field. His head was stuck upon a lance and was held up by the side of another lance which bore on high a copy of the violated treaty. The Christians, when they saw the head of their dead king in its soldier's helmet thus held aloft, were struck with panic and fled precipitately. Hunvadi escaped with much difficulty. Cardinal Julian expiated by death on the field his sin in advising the breach of the treaty. Two other bishops shared his fate. Never was defeat and disaster more richly deserved. Two-thirds of the Christian army were slain in the battle, and even greater numbers, though a less proportion, of the Ottomans shared their fate.

Murad, having won this great victory, again a second time, abdicated his throne and returned to his retreat at Magnesia, and again the young Mahomet was invested as Sultan. Though history supplies cases of great kings seeking retirement from the cares of office, and of some of them being induced to resume their thrones, it records no other case of a second abdication and a second resumption. Murad was very soon recalled from his abode of pleasure. A serious outbreak of the Janissaries occurred at Adrianople. They ravaged the city and committed great atrocities. The Ministers of the young Sultan were greatly alarmed. They felt that only a strong hand could keep a check on the unruly Janissaries. Murad was again summoned from his retreat. The young Mahomet was induced to go on a hunting expedition. In his absence Murad again made his appearance at Adrianople and resumed power. Mahomet, on his return from hunting, found that his father was again in the saddle. Murad was received by his troops with a great ovation, and even the unruly Janissaries gave in their submission to him. He did not again seek retirement at Magnesia. He reigned for seven more years—another period of almost incessant war. He first made an invasion of the Morea, which the Greek Emperor's brothers had divided between them and Governed as petty princes, or despots, as they were called. Murad had no difficulty in storming and capturing the fortification by which the Corinth was defended. He compelled the two despots to accept the position of vassals under the Empire.

Murad then again turned his attention to Serbia and Hungary. He defeated the combined forces of Hungary, Serbia, and Bosnia, under Hunyade, on the field of Kossava, where in 1389 A.D. Murad I had first subdued the Serbians. As a result of this great battle Serbia lost its independence and was finally incorporated as an integral part of the Ottoman Empire. Bosnia became a tributary State.

Murad was less fortunate in his efforts to subdue the Albanians. These people were under the leadership of George, had been brought up at Murad's Court as a Muslim and had abjured Islam, with a view to leadership of the Albanians. He carried on a guerrilla war against the Ottoman invaders with great success, and Murad was unable to complete the conquest of the State. This was practically the only failure of Murad's adventurous life. His Generals met with many defeats at the hand of Hunyadi, but Murad retrieved them in the two battles in which he came in conflict with the great Hungarian hero. He died of apoplexy in 1451 A.D.

MAHOMET II

(1451-81 A.D.)

Mahomet II, the eldest son of Murad, at the age of fourteen, had been reckoned too feeble to cope with the emergencies of the State. It is very certain that he soon made wonderfully rapid progress. At the age of twenty-one, when he again mounted the throne on the death of his father, he was amply, and almost preconciously, endowed with many of the best, and many also of the worst qualities of an autocrat, and was quite able alone to take command of the State. He was undoubtedly the ablest man that the house of Othman had as yet produced, not only as a General, but as a statesman. He had also great intellectual capacity and literary attainments. He spoke five languages fluently. He was the most proud and ambitious of his race and the most persistent in pursuing his aims. He combined with these high qualities, however, extreme cruelty and sensuality of the grossest and vilest kind. He differed from his predecessors in his craving for absolute power, free from control by his Ministers, and in his reckless disregard of human life. Hitherto, from Othman to Murad II, the Sultans had been in intimate association with their Vizirs and Generals, and had shared their meals with them. They were accessible to their subjects, high and low. Mahomet was very different. He was the true despot after the Oriental fashion. He held himself aloof. He took his meals alone. He made no confidants. He treated his Vizirs and Pashas as though they were his slaves. He had no regard for their lives. Two at least of Mahomet's Grand Vizirs were put to death in this way in his presence without warning. This levelling process was not apparently objected to by his subjects.

On hearing at Magnesia of the death of his father, Mahomet, who was earger to resume power, mounted at once on an Arab horse, and exclaiming, "Let all who love me follow" he rode to the Hellespont, and then crossed to Gallipoli and made his way to Adrianople. He was there again acclaimed as Sultan, not, however, without having to submit to onerous presents to the Janissaries, a bad precedent which was later always followed on the accession of a Sultan. The first act of his reign was to direct that his brother, an infant son of Murad, by his latest wife, a Serbian princess, should be put to death. He feared that the child, when grown up might dispute the throne with him, on the ground that its mother was a legitimate wife of royal descent, while he himself (Mahomet) was only the son of a slave. A high officer of the Court was directed to drown the child in a bath. This was effected at the very moment when the mother was engaged in offering her congratulations to the new Sultan on his accession. The foul deed created a very bad impression, and Mahomet found it expedient to disown the act. He did so by directing the execution of the officer who had carried out his order. He compelled the mother, in spite of her royal rank, to marry a slave, an outrageous insult to the Serbian prince and to the memory of his father.

In the ensuing winter (1452 A.D.) Mahomet made every preparation of Adrianople for a campaign in the next year. Having no means of casting cannons, which at that time were coming into use in European armies, he tempted a Wallachian, who experienced in such work, and who was in the service of the Greeks, to come over to his side for higher pay, and devised with him a cannon of enormous size, firing stone balls of 2½ feet in diameter, and many other smaller, but still large, guns throwing balls of 150 lbs. weight, for use against the walls of Constantinople. Early in the following year (1453 A.D.) he collected in front of the walls of Constantinople an army, estimated at a hundred and fifty thousand men, including twelve thousand Janissaries, and a vast number of irregulars, and camp followers eager for the sack of the great city.

Constantine, on his part, was equally engaged in making preparations for the defence of his capital. He collected supplies of every kind. He did his best to repair and strengthen the walls of the city, which had been neglected and badly repaired by fraudulent Greek contractors. He invited the aid of the Christian princes of Western Europe for the coming struggle. In this view, and in the hope of getting full support from the Pope, he agreed to a scheme of union between the Greek and Latin Churches, in which everything was conceded to the latter. A great service was held at St. Sophia to ratify this union. It was attended by the Emperor and all his Court, clergy and the officers of State. This gave great offence to the main body of the Creek clergy, and to the great majority of the people of Constantinople. There was inplacable hatred between the members of the two Churches, and could induce them to compose their differences. St. Sophia was deserted by its congregation. It was thought to be polluted by the service. The Grand Duke Notaras, the second person in the State after the Emperor, in command of all the forces, was specially offended. He even went saying in public at length that he would rather see the turban of the Turks at Constantinople then the hat of a Cardinal. It resulted that the Greeks were divided into two parties. Priests refused to give the sacrament todying men not of their party. The Churches refused to contribute out of their vast wealth to necessities of the State. Constantine was seriously embarrassed and weakened by the division among his people. Of a total population of the city, reduced as it was, a compared with the past, and estimated at a hundred thousand, not more than six thousand took up arms in support of Constantine against the Turks.

The appeals to the Western Powers resulted in a certain but very insufficient, number of volunteers from Southern Europe giving their services to support the Greek cause in its final struggle with the Muslims. Seven hundred Genocese came under the command of Giustiniani, an able soldier of fortune, who proved to be the main support of Constantine. Others had come with Cardinal Isidore, at the instance of the Pope, and with some small amount of money from the same quarter. There were Catalans and Argonese from Spain, but the number of these recruits from Western Europe did not exceed three thousand. The total force under the command of Constantine for the defence of the city amounted to no more than eight thousand. It is strange that there were no volunteers from France and Germany, or from Hungary and Poland, from whence so many crusaders had volunteered in previous years to drive the Turks out of Europe. Nor was there any valid assistance in men and money from the numerous Greeks in the Levant. The unfortunate Constantine was not only very deficient in men, however, in his service twenty powerful galleys well manned, and three galleys had come from Venice.

Constantinople was protected by a triple line of walls, the two inner of which were very massive, flanked by towers at distances of 170 feet. There was a space of 60 feet between these walls. The third and outer wall was of a width of 60 feet. This powerful line of defence had been devised by the Emperor Theodsius II about a thousand years ago and had protected the city in twenty sieges. Before the invention of cannon it was practically impregnable. There were also fortification extending for about nine miles on the side of the Golden Horn. The eight thousand men were too few even for effective defence of the four miles of walls, which were to be attacked directly by the Ottoman army, to say nothing of the fortifications along the side of the Golden Horn. The defence, however with these limited means, was spirited one. It showed that if the Greek Emperor had been adequately supported by the Western Powers Mahomet might not have been able to capture the city.

The siege was commenced by Mahomet on April 6, 1453 A.D. There were two very interesting incidents in the siege which are worth recording. The one was the breaking of the close blockade of the port by four powerful and well-manned galleys, bringing provisions and stores to the beleaguered city from Chios. They sailed across the Marmora and up the Bosphorus with a strong breeze in their favour. The Sultan sent against them a hundred and forty of his fleet of smaller vessels propelled by oars. They found great difficulty in stemming the heavy sea. The four larger vessels came down on the smaller craft, crashing against them and shivering their oars. Their crews hurled big stones on the Turkish galleys and emitted against others the inextinguishable fire of which the Greeks had the secret. The Turkish boats could make no headway against the superior wieght or the bigger vessels. A large number of them were suck with serious loss of life. When near to the entrance of the harbour the wind died off and the Genoese vessels were in imminent peril, surrounded as they were by the numeous Turkish craft. But at the last moment an evening breeze sprang up. Genoese vessels were able to force their way through. The chain which prevented ingress to the harbour was lowered, and the relieving vessels were admitted.

After seven weeks of siege the bombardment effected breaches in the walls at three points such as to give Mahomet every hope of success in a final assault. The principal breach was at St. Romanus, where the outer of the two main walls was practically levelled for a length of four hundred yards, and four of the flanking towers were destroyed. A part of the broad ditch was filled in by the debris of the wall and a part by fascines. The Sultan decided that the assault should take place on May 29. This became known to the Greeks in the city, and both sides made every preparation supreme effort.

On the 28th, Mahomet ordered a proclamation to be made to his troops, to the effect that when the city was captured it would be given up to them to sack at their will for three days. The Sultan, it said, had sworn by Mahomet, and by his own soul that the whole population of the city, men and women, and children, should be given over to them. This was received by the troops with tumultuous expressions of delight.

On the same day the Sultan reviewed his army in three divisions, each of fifty thousand men, and afterwards received in his tent all the leaders, military and naval. He made a speech to them in which he announced his intention to make a final assault on the city on the next day, explained to them the method of attack, and gave his final orders. He enlarged on his promise to give to the troops to plunder the city.

Very early in the morning of the next fateful day, the 29th May, 1453 A.D., the final assault was delivered by the Turkish army. The scheme of the Sultan was to attack the walls of the city at many points, from both land and sea, but to make the main assault on the part of the wall which had been so much injured by the cannon in the Lycus Valley, near the gate of St. Romanus, and then, by successive waves of his vastly greater army, to overwhelm the defenders, using first his inferior troops, and reserving his best for the last attack, when the enemy would be wearied be long fighting. The first assault was made by an immense horde of irregulars, armed with bows and arrows, and with slings throwing stones and iron balls. Gunpowder, though already used for cannon, was not yet applied to muskets. The men advanced with scaling-ladders for the assault and a cloud of arrows darkened the sky. No more than two thousand Greeks could be spared to defend this part of the long line of fortifications. They were collected in the peribolus between the two walls. The gates in the inner wall were closed, so that these men had no opportunity of shirking the defence and retreating into the city. They had to fight for their very lives between the two walls.

The Sultan directed the great cannon to be brought to the edge of the fosse, and a shot from it broke down the stockade which had been erected in place of the outer wall. Under cover of the dust the Turks made the assault. They were bravely met by the defenders, and were driven back with heavy loss. A second assault was then made by the Anatolian infantry, a very superior force to the irregulars. But they were no more successful. The Sultan, thinking that the Greeks must be exhausted by these two assaults, then personally led a third great body of men to a third assault. It consisted of his Janissaries. He led them to the edge of the foss, and thence directed their attack. The cannon was used again against the stockade, and again under cover of the dust caused by it the janissaries made their assault. Some of them succeeded in getting over the stockade, and a hand-to-hand fight occurred between them and the Greeks. The defenders seemed to have the best of it. But at this crisis a grave misfortune occurred to the Greeks. Giustiniani, who commanded them was severly wounded. Blood flowed freely from his wounds. He decided to leave the field of battle and return to his ship in the harbour, for medical relief. The Emperor Constantine, who was near-by, in vain implored him to remain, pointing out to him the damaging effect of his departure would have on the soldiers who remained. Others thought that the wounds were not very serious and that the General was not justified in leaving the field. But he insisted on doing so, and demanded the key of the gate in the inner wall. With him departed some of his Genoes soldiers. This defection caused dismay and depression among the troops. Their resistance to the Turks slackened.

The Emperor did his utmost to retrive the position. He took upon himself the charge vacated by Giustiniani, and led the defence. Mahomet, on his part, had observed from the other sides of the foss the slackening of the defence. He called out to the Janissaries : "We have the city ! It is ours ! The wall is undefended !" He urged them to final effort. They rushed the stockade and effected an entry into peribolus. Soon great swarms of other followed and overwhelmed the defenders with their vast numbers. The Greeks and Italian soldiers in the peribolus were now completely outnumbered. There was no exist through the inner wall by which they could escape. They were in a trap between the two walls. They were massacred to a man. The Janissaries, having effected this, found no difficulty in making their way through the inner wall, which, as we have explained, was not defended owing to the want of men. All attacks on other part of the city were failures. This one alone succeeded. Victory here was due to the good generalship of Mahomet and to his indomitable persistency, and in part to the ill-fortune of the Greeks in the withdrawal of Guistiniani at the critical moment of the defence.

Bosnia and the Morea, which had become tributary States under previous Sultans, were now again invaded and were compelled to become integral parts of the Empire. Their princess were dethroned and put to death. Wallachia and the Crimea were forced to become vassal States. In Asia, Karamania, was now forcibly annexed, and its Seljukian line of kings was put an end to by death. The great city of Trebizond and its adjoining province of Cappadocia, which had been cut off from the present empire, after the capture of Constantinople by the Crudsaders, and formed into a miniature Empire, under the Comneni dynasty, was invaded and annexed by Mahomet, and at his instance its reigning family was put to death. The possessions of the Genoese on the coasts of the Black Sea were appropriated.

Many islands in the Greek Archipelago, including Lesbos, Lemnos, and Cephalonia, were also attacked and annexed. The same fate be fell Euboea it belonged to the Republic of Venice, which was also deprived of others of its possessions on the coast of the Morea. Besides all these enterprises, Mahomet in several successive years sent armies to ravage parts of Syria and Transylvania. He even sent an army across the frontier of Italy to ravage the region of Friuli, and other districts almost within sight of Venice, whose Republic was completed to enter into an ignominous treaty, binding to assist the Ottomans in other wars with a naval force. The last achievement of the ambitious Sultan was to send to a force to the South of Italy, where it captured Otranto. The only captures which Mahomet attempted without success were those of Belgard, in 1456 A.D., and the island of Rhodes in 1480 A.D. The case of Belgrade was of the greatest importance, for it long barred the way to the invasion of Hungary and Germany. The Sultan himself took command of the army of attack with a hundred and fifty thousand men and three hundred guns. He thought the capture of it should be an easy task after that of Constantinople. But Western Europe, which had rendered so little assistance to the Greek Empire in its extremities, was alarmed at the prospect of the invasion of Germany through the loss of Belgrade. The Pope preached another crusade, and a large body of knights volunteered for the defence of this frontier city.

In all these campaigns Mahomet personally led his armies in the field with the exception of those for the invasion of the Crima, the attack on Rhodes, and the capture of Otranto, where he delegated the task to able Generals, of whom he appears to have had an abundant supply. But there never was a great commander who more completely dominate the Generals under him and maintained his supremacy in the state. He made no confidences as to his intended military operations, or what were his immediate objects of attack. There were no councils of war. His armies were collected, year after year on one side or other of the Bosphorous, without any one knowing their destination. When, on one occasion, one of his Generals asked him what was his next object, he replied that if a single hair of his beard know that his intentions were he would pluck it out and cast it into the fire. He held secrecy and rapidity to be the first elements of success in war, and the rapidity to be the first elements acted on this principle.

Great as Mahomet was as a warrior and General, he was not less conspicuous as an administrator and statesman. The organization and provisioning of his armies in his numerious campaigns were specially worthy of notice. His soldiers were always well fed and were amply equipped with guns and armaments. He was also the sole source of legislation for his Empire. He had supreme power over life and property of all his subjects. More than any of his predecessors and successors, he founded mosques, hospitals, colleges and schools in Constantinople and other cities of his Empire. He fully recognized the importance of science in Education. He cultivated the society of learned men and loved to converse with them. He died at the age of fifty-one, after thirty years of reign. He had collected a great army for another campaign, but no one knew what his aims and intentions were whether for another attack on Rhodes, or for the invasion of Candia, or to follow up his success in Calabria. His secret died with him. He was the first Sultan to be buried at Constantinople, in the famous mosque which he built there.

BAYEZID II

(1481-1512 A.D.)

Mahomet left two sons, of whom the eldest, Bayezid II, succeeded him as Sultan at the age of thirty-five. Von Hammer and other historians, who have founded their narratives on his great work write of Bayezid II in terms of disparagement because, unlike other early Sultans of the Othman race, he did not signalize his reign by any great additions to his Empire. If success as a ruler is only to be measured by territorial expansion, Bayezid II must take rank in history below the other nine Sultans who created the Ottoman below the other nine Sultans who created the Ottoman Empire and raised it to its zenith. A great Empire, however, such as that which the Ottomans had already achieved, may be better served by peace than by way for further conquests. It would certainly have been well for the Ottomans if no attempt had ever been made to Extend their empire northwards beyond the Danube. Bayezid II, so far as we can gather his policy from his actrual deeds, was not favourable expansion of his Empire. If he was engaged for some years in war with Hungary, Venice, and Egypt, he was not the aggressors. He came to terms of peace with these Powers when it was possible to do so. He did not support the army which, under his predecessor, had invaded Italy and captured Otranto. He recalled the very able General, Ahmad Keduk, who commanded it. Khairuddin Pasha, who succeeded in command after mast gallant defence was compelled to capitulate ; and never again was Italy invaded by a Turkish army. It would seem to have been a size decision on the part of Bayezid II not to pursue further the Italian adventure.

As it is not our intention to write a complete history of the Ottoman Sultans, but rather to describe the early expansion of their Empire and its later dismemberment, it will not be necessary to devote more than a very few pages to the comparatively unventful reign of Bayezid II. It may be well, however, briefly to note that he was philosophic temperament, very austere in religion, and without his father's vices. Like many of his race he was devoted to literary studies, and he had a reputation as a poet.

His younger brother Djem, who at the death of Mahomet was only twenty-two years of age, was much more fiery, and ambitious soldier, and of more, attractive personality. He was of a romantic disposition, and had a much greater reputation than Bayezid II as a poet. His poems rank high in Turkish literature. His strange adventures and sad fate from one of the romances of Turkish history, which might well fill many chapters. It must suffice to record of him that, like other brothers of Sultans who were not at once put to death at the commencement of a new reign, he took up arms and claimed the throne against Bayezid II. The latter fortunately was the first to arrive at Constantinople after the death of Mahomet.

The last two years of Bayezid's II fully prosperous reign were obscured by another civil war, this time at the instance of his son and successor, Selim. Selim was the youngest of three surviving sons of Bayezid II. All three had been invested with important posts as Governors of provinces in Asia. Ahmad the second of them was the favourite of his father, who designated him for succession to the throne. But Selim was by far the ablest and most daring of them. He determined to anticipate the death of his father, who was ageing and in feeble health by secrring the throne for himself. Leaving his seat of Government with a large suit, almost amounting to an army, he paid a visit, uninvited, almost to his father at Constantinople, and there fomented intrigues. He was the idol of the Janissaries, who dissatisfied with the long inaction of Sultan Bayezid II, and hoped for new conquests and loot under Selim. Bayezid, however, was supported for the time by a section of his army, and succeeded in defeating his son. Selim then fled to the Crimea, where he raised a new army and, later again made his way to Constantinople by a forced march round the north of the Black Sea. On arriving there he was supported by the full force of the Turkish army.

The Janissaries, at the instance of Selim stormed at the gates of the imperial palace and insisted on the Sultan receiving them in person. Bayezid II gave way and admitted a deputation of them to an audience. Seated on his throne, he asked them what they wanted. "Our Padishah," they said "is old and sickly ; we will that Selim shall be Sultan. Bayezid, II finding that he could not rely on any section of his arm, submitted. "I abdicate", he said, "in favour of my son, Selim. May God grant him a prosperous reign." He only asked as a favour that he might be allowed to retire to the city of Asia Minor where he was born. His son thereupon conducted his father, the ex-Sultan, to the outdeparted on his journey. He died however, three days later, not without grave suspicion of foul play.

An incident worth recording was the first appearance of Russia in the field of Turkish diplomacy. An Ambassador was sent to Bayezid II by Czar Ivan III. He was instructed to refuse to bow his knee to the Sultan or to concede precedence to any other Ambassadors. Bayezid II meekly gave way on these points of etiquette. This was the attitude of Russia which two centuries later threatened the existence of the Turkish Empire.

PERSIA

The Khanate had become a thing of the past. The entire Middle East was divided into small kingdoms. There was no great Muslim power existed at that time in the world. So there was a need of a great warrior and a strong kingdom. In those days in India the sub-continent was divided into minor kingdoms. The same was the position of Africa. By the grace of God a required warrior came to the world known as Timur, a descendent of Chughatai Khan, one of the sons of Chenghis Khan who had inherited Central Asia as his Khanate from the colossal empire of the Great Mongol. Timur became Vizir to the Chughatai Khan. In 1369 A.D., Timur conspired with nobles and overthrew the Chughatai Khan. Now Timur became ruler of Samarqund. After becoming the ruler he conquered the rest of Trans-Oxiania. Timur was very ambitious man and he dreamt of the world empire. Timur desired to make Samarqand as a beautiful city and for this purpose he collected best skilled workmen, artisans, designers and craftsman from all the lands conquered from Delhi to Damascus. Timur had agreed powers great military ability and great force of personality. It is remarkable to note that he never lost a battle. He was a great administrator. He has always kept in mind the honour of Islam.

Conquests of Timur :

Timur conquered Khorasan, Kabul, West India, Persia, Iraq, Syria and Asia Minor. His empire was spread over from Delhi to Sea of Marmara. He conquered Asia Minor due to the provocation of Sultan Bayezid I, the Ottoman. Bayezid I committed blunder of thinking to extent his power in Asia Minor where there were many small principalities of which some were vassals of Timur. Bayezid I was successful in conquering Kamman, Kayseri, Tokat, Sivas and Kastamuni. The ruler of the Vassals rushed up to Timur and sought his help. Timur took this action of the Ottoman king, Bayazid I as his prestige issue. Therefore he ordered his forces to march against him. In 1400 A.D. Timur conquered Sivase, captured Ertughrul, son of Bayezid and killed alongwith him the entire garrison. In 1402 A.D., he defeated Sultan Bayezid and made him prisoner. He died in captivity. He also conquered Syria and Delhi. In 1405 A.D., he decided to conquer China but he died when he reached along with his forces at the borders of China.

SHAH RUKH AND ULUGH BEG

(*1404-1447 A.D.*)

Shah Rukh ruled the empire inherited from Timur for very uccessfully for a period of forty years. Shah Rukh was a worthy successor. He was the man who tried to rebuilt the social and cultural life of Persia and the Middle East. He concentrated his attention for the developments of Khorasan, Merv and Herat. He made prince Ulugh Beg as the Governor of Trans-Oxiania. It is worthy to be noted that he never interfered with that part of the empire during his life. The prince Ulugh Beg proved to be very brilliant and he made Sumarqand as a centre of culture and the sciences. He built in Sumarqand an observatory. It was very renowned observatory. Shah Rukh was a great builder. He raised a mosque at Mashhad which is still the glory of Persian architecture. His court was considered to be the finest and most splendid in Asia at the time. Shah Rukh was also a great fighter. He died in 1447 A.D. He was succeeded by Ulugh Beg. During the kingship of Ulugh Beg the Uzbegs rosed against him and he swept into Trans-Oxiania and also looted Samarqand. This destruction brought such a shock to the Ulugh Beg that he died in 1452 A.D., and was succeeded by his son Abu Said.

ABU SAID

(1452-1467 A.D.)

Abu Said was also a great warrior. He was very capable man. He brought back the great Timur empire from the Indus to the Euphrates. But during the last movements of his reign a new Turkoman tribe rose up in Diyar Bekr. They called themselves to be Turkomen of the White Sheep. This tribe was headed by Amir Uzun Hasan. These Turkomen conquered Kurdistan and Armenia. He tried even to expand towards West but they were defeated by the Ottomans in 1461 A.D. Uzun Hasan now turned towards the east and was successful in conquering Persia. Uzun Hasan also annexed Azerbaijan and Persia. This was a complete breakdown of the Timur with empire. Uzun Hasan was succeeded by his son Yaqub Shah. He was an intelligent ruler and gave peace and prosperity to his territories. His successors were not able persons an ultimately Ismail Safavi overthrew the Turkomen. He founded the great Safavid empire.

It shall not be out of place to mention few words about the great and eminent men produced by the country before the Safavids. During the reign of Monghols there was a very little progress. During this period the Universities had been destroyed, books had been burnt and the men of talent had either been killed or scatterred. During this period the continuity of cultural progress had been broken. Sa'di and Hafiz were born in Shiraz and Asia minor. The country also produced Jalaluddin Rumi a great poet. The father of Jalaluddin Rumi was a very learned man and had found asylum with the Seljuk Ruler of Konya but prince Alauddin made him a Professor at Konya University. Jalaluddin was twenty-three years of age when his father died and he was offered the Professorship. Jalaluddin Rumi was a great learned man and a fine teacher. After the association with Shamsuddin of Tabriz he became a Sufi and wrote a series of narrative poems popularly called as "Masnavi". Mohammad Iqbal the great poet of the East considered Maulana Rumi as his spiritual guide. We also find other great names in the history of writing. Alauddin Juwayni was a Secretary of Hulagu Khan. The collection of his works is known as "Tarikh-Jahan Gusha". This collection tell us the story of the Mongols and their achievements. The another man was Rashiduddin Fadlullah. He was the Minister of Ghazan Mahmud. Rashiduddin wrote a book entitled "Jamiul-Tawarikh". This book is famous for its sober tone and careful treatment. There was another historian named as Mirkhond. He wrote a history about the period of the later Timurids and the Turkomen of the White Sheep. The collection of the work is known as "Raudat-us-safa"—The Garden of Purity.

ISMAIL I

(1501-1524 A.D.)

The Safavids first became prominent under Shaikh Safi al-Din of Ardabil (1252-1334 A.D.). He was a holy man. He founded an order of dervishes which followed the Shiite creed. This institution spread in the north-west of Persia. Shaikh Junaid, was one of the descendants of Shaikh Safi-al-Din, head of the order in the mid-Fifteenth Century. He married with Amir Uzun Hasan's sister. After the Turkomen of the White Sheep overrunning Persia, Shaikh Junaid gained very powerful relatives by this marriage. His son Haider married a daughter of Amir Uzun Hasan. He then started to organize his followers on the lines of the knightly brotherhoods of Europe. These followers wear red caps in order to be distinct from others and so they came to be known as Kizilbashes (Red Caps). Haidar now became the chief of his order. He was very ambitious man. He tried his strength against Yaqub Shah, the Turkoman king, but was defeated.

One of the sons of this Haidar was named Ismail. He was a very enterprising young man. He secretly organised his order on firmer lines, and after Yaqub Shah's death in 1497 he came out and made open arrangements for battle. He was a good Military Commander and had tremendous influence over his followers, and his followers also fought for him with great zeal, so when he led them against the Turkomen of the White Sheep he won the battle of Shurur and took Tabriz, the capital of the Turkoman empire. He started a war of conquest and was soon master of the whole of Persia. He then conquered Iraq, Mosul and Diyar Bekr. As a matter of fact the entire kingdom of the Turkomen of the White Sheep. He then overthrew the Turkomen of the Black Sheep. He next went against the Uzbegs of the north. Ismail had great fervour and his soldiers fought selflessly for him. He defeated Shaybani Khan, the Amir of the Uzbegs. The Amir lost his life in fighting. The Uzbegs were driven back and Ismail became master of upper Khorasan too. He was now supreme ruler over a great empire. He was Persian by birth and a Shiite by faith, he spoke Persian and was therefore accepted as a national hero. He made Shiism the creed of his state and thus founded the first great Shiite Empire. The creed of Persia (Iran) is Shiism even today.

Ismail and the Ottomans :

Ismail was very brave and highly talented. He was a fine millitary commander. The only people against whom he did not prevail entirely were the Ottoman Turks who, under Selim I, opposed the new Shiite power. Selim I was a great fighter and a terror to Christians. He came up with his army against Shah Ismail who met him at the great battle at Chaldibran in 1514 A.D. The Turks were stronger in artillery and broke the Persian ranks. Ismail dashed against the Turks with his cavalry again and again, but could not prevail ; the Turks won and Selim took Tabriz. His army, however, refused to go farther and so Selim retired. He annexed Kurdistan and Diyar Bekr. Due to this incident the Ottomans and Persians fought for the coming three centuries. As a matter of fact these were wars between Shias and Sunnis.

SHAH ABBAS I

(1578-1629 A.D.)

Ismail was succeeded by Shah Tahmasp who fought continually against the Uzbegs of Trans-Oxiania and the Ottomans on the West. He defeated the Uzbegs. He lost a number of battles against the Ottoman Sultan, Sulaiman the Magnificent. It was in Shah Tahmasp's time that Humayun, the exiled Moghul emperor, came to Persia for aid, which was given to him when he became a Shiite. Shah Tahmasp began to rebuild Persia. The new pattern of the Safavids began with him, although it came to flower in the reign of his son. Shah Abbas I, is called as the Great Shah Abbas. He was a man of ideas and of vision. He wanted to bring back the glory of ancient Persia to hi land. Shah Abbas began his work systematically. Finding that Kizilbashes headstrong, he organised another order of fighters, called 'Friends of the Shah' and thus had a new body of men on whom to depend in a crisis. Keeping in view that the Turks had the advantage in the wars in the last two reigns, he reorganised his army with the help of two English adventurers of talent, Anthony and Robert

Shirley. He was now ready for anybody, but his traditional enemies were the Uzbegs and the Turks.

The Turks invaded Persia under the command of General Furhad Pasha in 1587 A.D. The Turks were successful in capturing Tabriz again and annexed the land from Georgia to Luristan. Amir Abudullah II, was a very enterprising man who had conquered the entire area of the two rivers from Faraghana in the east to the Caspian Sea, and to Astrabad and Gilan in the west. The Uzbegs King then captured Herat and Meshhed in Khorasan. He then captured Nishapur, Sabzwar, Isfahan and the whole of Khorasan. In 1597, Shah Abbas took his new army north with such a pray broke their entire military strength and drove them from Khorasan. Shah marched to the north-west, took back Tabriz, and captured Erivan, Shirvan and Kars, and at Lake Urmia defeated the Turks. He took Mosul, Divar Bekr and Mesopotamia, and returned home triumphant. In 1612 A.D. a peace treaty was drawn up which was very favourable to Persia. In 1616 A.D., when the Turks came again with a strong army and besieged Erivan, the Persians fought back and repulsed the attack. In 1618 A.D., the Turks had ventured again and came as far as Baghdad, they achieved little. But afterwards hostilities ceased and there was peace between the two nations.

Shah Abbas was a great ruler. He was also a good administrator and a great warrior. He built caravan series and bridges throughout the land, some of the roads built by him still exist today. He selected Isfahan as his captial and made it garden city. The palaces and other buildings, mosques, madarisahs and religious academies of his time were the marvel of the age.

The Successors of Shah Abbas were not of the sane and the 'Harem rule' began to cast its deadly influence over state affairs. Internal disturbances weakened the power of the Shahs and there was internal strife throughout the empire. The Turks growing unrest in Persia. After Shah Abbas's death, Murad IV, the Ottoman Sultan, invaded Persia, penetrating as far as Hamadan which he sacked. In 1635 A.D. the Turks took Erivan and Tabriz. In 1638 A.D. they took Baghdad. Since then Baghdad remained a part of the Turkish empire and remained so far nearly three hundred years. It was lost along with the rest of their empire, in the First World War. In the Eighteenth Century the last Safavid King went to ear with the Afghans whose ruler Mir Vais, was a staunch Sunni and opposed the extreme views which were prevailing in Persia at that time. Mir Vais refused to pay tribute to the Safavid Shah Husain. The Shah sent an army against him, he dcfeated the Persians easily. The second Afghan ruler after Mir Vais, Mir Mahmud, invaded Persia in 1722 A.D. He after achieving victory at Gulnabad marched towards Isfahan.

THE AFGHANS

Mir Mahmud and Ashraf Shah :

When the Afghans were lords of Persia, Peter the Great was Czar of Russia. He was a great man and a fierce fighter. His one dream was to make Russia great. The best way open to him of achieving his ambition was to attach the Muslims, who were showing signs of weakness everywhere—in the Turkish Empire, as well as the Persian. So he took the excuse of helping the Safavid cause and invaded Persia from the Caucasus. He took Derbent in 1722 A.D., then Resht and Baku. All these towns lay in lower Caucasia which had been in Muslim hands for centuries. Tahmasp II, the Safavid Shah, promised to yield to him Shirvan, Daghestan, Gilan, Mazandaran and even Astrabad, if Peter the Great helped him to drive out the Afghans. The Turks now took action. They took Tiflis in 1723 A.D. There was for some time an alliance between Russia and Turkey. The Turks said they wanted Tabriz, Hamadan and Karmanshah for their efforts against Persia. The Czar agreed and the Turks took these towns (1724-1725 A.D.). The Afghan rulers were themselves having trouble at Isfahan. Then were Sunnis and comparatively uncultured. The Persian nobles were proud of their culture and their past ; they obeyed the new rulers, but always with an air of superiority. The Afghan were short-tempered. They called the airs and graces of the Persians insolence, and punished the people justly as well as unjustly. This made matters worse. Hatred grew on both sides. Things were at this stage when Mir Mahmud died. He was succeeded by Sultan Ashraf Shah, who was a man of more understanding. He tried to meet people halfway, and was tactful, but the Persian nobles were suspicious and did not co-operate. He did not, however, lose heart. When the Turks came in 1727 he defeated them and in the peace treaty which he signed with the Sultan yielded a littled territory, but was acknowledged as Shah of Persia. The following year, however, in 1728 A.D. Tahmasp came back with a powerful ally, Nadir Kuli Khan, the chief of the Afshar tribe of Turks in upper Khorasan. Tahmasp and Nadir Khan began their march, and conquered Meshhed and Herat and then went straight to Isfahan. They defeated Ashraf Shab first near Isfahan, and again two years later in 1730 A.D., near Shiraz. Ashraf Shah left the country, but was killed on the way back to Kandahar and the Safavids came back to power.

THE AFSHARS

Nadir Shah (1734-47 A.D.) :

Nadir Kuli Khan was now the Chief Minister and Commander-in-Chief of the Shah. He married the Shah's sister and became very powerful. Nadir was a greater warrior. Islam had not seen his like for a long time. After defeating the Afghans he turned to the Turks and drove them from Hamadan, Karmanshah and Tabriz. The Abdalis, who had come to power in Kabul, had been given trouble and Nadir marched against them. In his absence, Shah Tahmasp made a foolish attempt to fight the Turks, but was defeated and lost the towns recently conquered by Nadir. Nadir, angered by the loss, returned to the capital and deposed the Shah. He then put the eight-month-old baby, son of Tahmasp, Abbas III, on the throne and himself became Regent. He remained Regent for four years, until the little Shah died. The nobles offered the throne to Nadir. He was a Sunni and accepted the offer, though he made one condition—that the state religion should be changed to Sunni-Islam. The nobles agreed, and during his entire reign Nadir Shah made unsuccessful efforts to bring back the Sunni faith to Persia. He did not, however, fail in other things. He restored the glory of Persia and extended the Persian Empire.

The military campaigns of Nadir Shah read like a romance. Such energy, such military leadership had not been seen in the Islamic world for a long time. He did not forget what Russia or Turkey had taken from Persia during the short Afghan regime. He attacked Russia first, and his campaign was so successful that he recovered Mazandaran, Astrabad and Gilan, but while Nadir was fighting the Russians, the Turks, who had made an alliance with Russia in the previous reign, invaded Persia. Nadir returned to meet them ; in the battle of Kirkuk, which followed, he was defeated. He did not pursue the war at this stage, because there was a rising in Trans-Oxiania, but he made a treaty with Russia. He promised to give the Czar all the Persian areas in Caucasia, such as Baku and Derbent, if the Russians helped him against the Turks. The Czar agreed, and in 1735 A.D. Nadir met the Turks at the battle of Baghawand and defeated them. He now took back Tiflis. Finding himself, for the time, safe in the West he marched into Trans-Oxiania and conquered Balkh. He then went to Kandahar and took it.

Invasion of India :

In 1739 A.D., he captured Kabul, Peshawar and Lahore. Muhammad Shah, the Mughal Emperor of India, sent an army against Nadir, but it was defeated. Nadir then took Delhi, sacked it, and massacred the inhabitants. He emptied the

Imperial Treasury and took the famous Peacock Throne, besides untold wealth. He left behind him a broken Government. The wealth that he took, however, turned his head. He conquered Sind later that year and annexed the treasuries of that province also. He went back, but stopped at Kandahar to display his loot. The jewels and precious stones to say nothing of golden ornaments, thrones and canopies, tents and other material that were spread before his eyes dazzled him. On his return to Persia he had a palace specially built to house his treasures. He spent hours and sometimes days viewing his wealth. It is said that this made him a miser and changed him considerably. Many even go so far as to say that he was never the same man again, though he carried on his wars and his conquests. In 1740 A.D. he conquered Khiva and Bokhara and so extended the boundaries of his empire further.

THE ZANDS

(1750-1779 A.D.)

The Afshar dynasty did not last long after Nadir's death. A grandson, Shah Rukh, lost his throne to a Shiite rival who defeated him and had his eyes put out. The prince escaped, blinded as he was, and making his way to Khorasan, established himself there. He ruled in that province till 1796 A.D. The Abdalis became independent in Afganistan. In Persia two parties contested for power for some time, the Zand party led by Karim Khan, and the Qajar party. Karim Khan succeeded and became the Shah. His strength lay in the south, so he moved his capital to Shiraz. He was a good ruler, kind and yet firm and he brought back prosperity to Persia. He gave certain concessions to the British to open factories at Bushire (1763 A.D.) and Basra (1770 A.D.). After his death, there was same unrest, but after a few short regins Lutf Ali Khan came to the throne in 1789 A.D. He was a fine man and had many kingly virtues. But the Qajars were growing in power, and in 1794 A.D., he had to try his strength with them. The Qajar leader, Agha Muhammad, defeated him and put an end to the Zand dynasty. He then set up the Qadar dynasty, which ruled in Persia till in 1925 A.D.

Part (3)

The Holy Qur'an

CONTAINING

Chapters :

1. ITS REVELATION AND COMPILATION.
2. CERTAIN BASIC PRINCIPLES—
   - ★ Duty towards Allah :—(Submission of His Laws).
   - ★ Duty towards Society :—(Equality, justice and honesty, intellectual as well as financial).
   - ★ Duty towards Nature :—[Understanding (through experimentation), conquest and domination of the forces of nature in the service of Allah].
   - ★ Duty towards self :—(Moral development and purification with an object to serve God's people).
3. CERTAIN INJUNCTIONS—
   - ★ *Wealth.*—The permitted way of earning—illegal gratification—distribution—zakat, inheritance, charity, wakf, interest, giving away of spare wealth.
   - ★ Concept of Love in Islam.
   - ★ *Women.*—Marriage, divorce, polygamy, right to inherit, treatment, education of all, a human necessity. Position of women in Islamic Society.
   - ★ *Administration.*—Power a trust—Selection of an Administrator—efficiency and honesty.

Chapter 1

Its Revelation and Compilation

The Qur'an is admitted by the Muslims as the "Word of God" and therefore the basis of all their law. It is in fact collection of Divine Revelations reaching Prophet Muhammad (Peace be upon him) through the agency of the angel Gabriel. The Qur'an was not revealed as a whole, but came down in fragments as necessity arose during the period of about twenty-three years. Whenever a portion of the Qur'an was revealed to the Holy Prophet he used to order one of his man to take it down. It was also he who prescribed and pointed out the places to which the verse or verses properly belonged ; the verses of the Qur'an were not compiled in chronological order. Obviously they were not witten in the time of the Holy Prophet in book form, but on stray leaves of paper, date leaves, and other handy materials, etc.

The first successor of the Holy Prophet, the Caliph Abu Bakr, in spite of his short term of office (about two years only) arranged a fair copy of the text of the Qur'an and made it in the form of a book (*Mushaf*) ; and keeping the order of the verses as prescribed by the Holy Prophet. The unique copy of the official edition remained with the Caliph ; later his successor, the Caliph Umar, used it after whose murder, it was in the custody of his daughter, Hazrat Hafsah, the widow of the Holy Prophet. It was in the time of the Third Caliph, Hazrat Uthman, that difficulties began to arise in the provinces. The Caliph, therefore, ordered seven copies to be made from the official edition prepared for the First Caliph, these copies were sent to different provincial capitals of the Caliphate, the original being returned to Hazrat Hafsah. The Caliph Uthman gave orders that even the spelling of the official copies must be followed, and that all those private copies that were found to differ from the official edition had to be collected and destroyed.

A new conception of Religion Al-Qur'an came with a new conception of Religion. It gave a new meaning to every article of faith. According to it Religion was neither ceremonialism nor a collection of some moral precepts. It was acode which enabled one to lead a happy life.

Though the Book like other Scriptures makes God and His worship as one of its chief themes, yet it speaks of Him for the benefit of man who has been declared as His vicegerent on the Earth. We needed some guidance to reach the exalted position, and God Himself appeared as our prototype in the Book. He needed no devotion from us. It was conceded that God was transcendental and stood beyond our imagination, but He was given some such Attributes in the Qur'an as could come within our comprehension and imitation. The Holy Names mentioned in the Holy Qur'an cover Attributes like generosity, compassion, intellect and others as worked in Nature long before man ever came into existence. It could not therefore be a man who could fashion the Qur'anic God by himself, but it was the Almighty who made him after His own image, and revealed to him His such characters, so that he may follow Him and act as His vicegerent.

The Book gives God's three special features that would make up human character. Firstly, God is the God of Virtue. Everything in the universe is not without its evil side. The same may be said of these Attributes in their abstract form. Love, compassion and power, for instance, have got their use and abuse. The Holy Qur'an therefore, calls these Divine Attributes as Excellent Name of God. It suggests that these Attributes when spoken as of God should be taken in their good sense and not in the wrong one. Some people think that it would be inconsistent with the Omnipotence of the Lcrd if He should be deemed to be incapable of committing a wrong. The idea gave rise to peculiar. Attributes of God with all their absurdities in an ancient India. It revolted the Buddhistic sense of decency and led some of them either to disbelieve totally in God or in His Attributes. They took him as an impersonal God. The Qur'an however, remedied this defect. The Book secondly describes God as the God of Law. With all His Omnipotence He has been represented in the Qur'an as the first observant of His own Law. All the Holy names in the Qur'an are the source of various laws which work in Nature. The Holy Book wants man to follow his Lord in this respect. For this reason it names *Islam* as His religion, which means obedience to Law. God in the third place has been described by the Book as the God of actions who remains busy all the time. He neither feels tired nor needs any rest. He wants man to do the same. He no doubt has created the night for his rest, but only to refresh him for further exertion.

This conception naturally gives a new import to Muslim devotion. The Qur'an speaks of five methods of Divine worship, named as the five Pillars of *Islam*, Formula of faith, prayers, fasting, alms-giving and pilgrimage to Mecca.

The Qur'an also teaches us certain beliefs, but they are all consistent with reason and can be translated into good actions. The Book never mentions such beliefs that have no practical bearing on our life or demand mutilation of intelligence for their acceptance.

The conception of religion needed a Book that should bring all that man required within its scope. The whole world is the scene of human activities, and contains things beyond our comprehension, although they have been created exclusively for our use. Besides, we alone, out of the whole creation, have special tastes and appetites for them. To make, however, the things in nature purposive, a special and skill knowledge is necessary. The Qur'an declares that the world was full of beauty and utility. It invites our attention to them and opens new avenues for our activities. If the Qur'an had not given these directions and made it clear then the Divine design in creating things would have remained unaccomplished

Man himself is the universe in miniature. His mind stands correlated with everything in the world. There is nothing in it which cannot be utilised by him if his mind is properly cultivated. We have to explore our own mind and work out its capabilities before we can put the things of Nature to their proper use. But our mind remained a barren land until the Qur'an was revealed. Again our nature has got various aspects—spiritual, physical, moral, social, economic, and so forth. They all have to be developed. Ethics, poetry, art and cultivation of various other sciences all come within the scope of human mind and contribute to our pleasure. Our mind is just like a cultivable land that could be converted into a prosperous garden with various avenues and orchard with trees full of fruits and flowers.

Like animals our consciousness is a collection of passions, but they in human frame, are capable of being sublimated into high morality and spirituality. A Book from God should provide for all of tnem. It is not right to crush them, for fear that they may also lead to evil. Divine guidance should come to control them and divert them to virtue. It should bring every human instinct under its salubrious teaching. In fact, a Book from God cannot be complete unless its teachings take account of everytning in the universe including human nature. The Book of Islam meets this demand, though we find other Divine scriptures wanting in this respect. They must have brought all the required knowledge, but time played a havoc with their purity.

Universal Book al-Qur'an is the Book that came to preach a cosmopolitan religion. Every Book before it was sent to a particular country. They worshipped a tribal god and slammed the door of light in the face of all other nations. Previous teachers have been very strict in this respect. The Jewish Patriarchs plumed themselves on being the people chosen for His Message and for this reason they proudly called themselves sons of God. If the old Hindus would dub all others "*Rakhshas*" and "*Malechh*"—the race of devils—Jesus would call the Gentiles and other non-Israelites dogs and swines. He would not even throw to them the children's food. Islam came, on the other hand, with a universal dispensation. It took the whole world as its ambit, and preached its truths to the whole human race. It preached universalism. It declared that all mankind belong to the same family and are one race. The Holy Qur'an demolished all artificial barriers which separated one nation from another. It welded black and white into one harmonious whole, and established universal brotherhood throughout the whole world. The world is on its way to Universalism, but it has much to learn from the Qur'an before the colour and country prejudice is eradicated. Islam is the only religion that gives precepts as well as example for true Universalism and the fraternity of the whole human race. It lays down principles that compel stiff-necked people to respect others as their equals.

The Holy Qur'an says that all religions came from the same Divine source. No religion can claim to bring a universal dispensation of God in religious matters from the beginning. If all of us are His creatures, He will not be guilty of partiality in sending His light to all people. As Universal Father, Her cannot choose any race for His special blessings to the exclusion of others. On the other hand, every nation on earth claims to have its own creed and faith and sent to it by God. A religion with a universal message is therefore bound to have regard for others' faiths. They may have deviated from the original path. The Book in their hands might have lost its purity, but to say that other nations had no guidance from God amounts to an insult to Universal Providence. It is absurd, it is unnatural. Moreover, the whole world will never gather under one universal flag. It has never done so up to now, nor will it ever do so in the future. There ought to be some *via media* between the jarring elements in the world of religion that may create a good understanding and prevent them from disturbing universal peace.

This *via media* gospel, then came to the world through the Qur'an which declared that no nation on God's earth had been left without light from above. If equality in man is the basic principle of the democracy so much desired by all, how can we believe in it if we do not believe in the universal revelation. All nations, says the Qur'an, have had their Prophets from God but their followers became divided among themselves, they quarelled with one another. He has ordered to make no distinction between the various prophets of the world, and directed to pay equal allegiance to all of them. If we cannot live without some religion, nor all of us come together under the same flag (and difference in religion has hitherto created discord and disturbance everywhere), the Qur'anic gospel is clearly needed. It alone can preserve harmony and peace under these circumstances. Sons of the same father live separately from each other, they may become immersed in their respective lives, they are not always antagonistic to each other. We do need some principle of fraternity which we may observe in the religious sphere, and this has been given to us by the last Book.

It is a truism that all religions have drunk from the Divine Fountain, since every one is, as it were, entitled to guidance from God. All Divine Messengers brought and preached the same truth. But the fact did not occur to any Prophet before Islam. The Prophet Muhammad (Peace be on him) has a supreme claim to Prophethood for preaching.

In fact no civilization, religion or philosophy before Islam ever struck such a noble note of liberal-mindedness as did the Qur'an in giving the message of Universal to the whole human race. It was revealed at a time when it was needed the most, for the world was standing at the threshold of bringing the various units into contact with one another. All races were coming in closer touch, and a gospel of general unification was needed. The Qur'an proclaimed it, and it was so successful in its mission that within a decade it could boldly assert to a nucleus of few thousand Muslims at Madina.

> "And remember the favour of Allah on you when you were enemies, then He united your hearts. So by His favour you became brethren, and you were on the brink of a pit of fire, then He saved you from it."

The verse eloquently pictures the condition of Arabia of those days, but within a quarter of a century after this announcement the Qur'an was able to expel the demon of hatred and antagonism from its frontiers. Then it carried its message of universal peace to the other corners of the world and, within a few centuries, successfully established universal brotherhood in a large portion of the globe.

We do need a creed of life like that preached in the Qur'an that teaches us to worship the Lord of all nations, Who maintains and nourishes every one without any partiality and in pursuance one should do the same. Arabia presented the worst example of tribal animosity at the advent of Islam, but the world all over is breathing the same malicious spirit. Islam brought the real panacea to remedy the poison. Had the world not been dazzled with the pomp and grandeur of the Western culture which for a time eclipsed Islam, the World till now had been freed of all racial prejudices.

The Book declares that the whole humanity is a single nation. They are members of God's family, and if they assume different names after the countries of their origin it is only for purposes of identification. It does not give them any distinction. The Book brushes aside all such distinctions as being accidental and makes virtue the only sign of greatness, and declare that it is not exclusive to any one, but is open to all. The Book came at the right time, when human race, like in these days, was divided into cults and creeds, it declared that all religions in their origin came from the same. Divine source God sent His Messengers to guide every class. They all came from His but the people differed from each other afterwards. The Book strongly condemned the practice of making distinction between a Prophet and a Prophet, and asked the Muslims to follow also that which had been revealed before them. They had to accept all Prophets of every country.

The Holy Qur'an says :

> "It is not righteousness that you turn your faces towards the East and the West, but righteousness is this that one should believe in Allah and the Last Day and the Angles and the Book and the Prophets, and give away wealth out of love for Him to the near of kin and the orphans and the needy and the wayfarer and the beggars and for (the emancipation of) the captives, and keep up prayer and pay the poor-rate and the performers of their promise when they make a promise, and the patient in distress and affliction and in time of conflict—these are they who are true (to them selves), and these are they who guard against evil. (*2* : *177*)

The Qur'an not only prohibits speaking ill of others deities, but it admits goodness in other faiths. It does not establish any new faith but comes rather to confirm the old truths, and invites other people to observe their respective good tenets. It repeatedly preaches that belief in God and obedience to Him is the only one eternal faith. It invites others to observe the same and shun differences. It has been very clearly and explicitly asserted in. The Holy Qur'an as follows :

> "Surely those who believe, and those who are Jews and the Christians, and the Sabians, whoever believes in Allah and the Last Day and does good, they shall have their reward from their Lord, and there is no fear for them, nor shall they grieve. (*2* : *6*)

It lays down here another dictum and wipes out the cvil of religious differences. It gives a gospel of universal salvation to every one of any persuasion so long as he observes the three principles mentioned in the above passage.

Though the verse has been breathing the noblest spirit of unity for the last thirteen hundred years, yet ignorance and prejudice blame the Qur'an for narrow-minded teachings. God is the source of all good actions, and our belief in the hereafter can only actuate them. Hence the two beliefs are a necessary adjunct of good action. Can one with his belief in the existence of God take exception to such a religion.

Receive the baptism of Allah, and who is better than Allah in baptizing and Him do we serve.

> Say: Do you dispute with us about Allah, and He is our Lord and your Lord, and we shall have our deeds, and you shall have your deeds and we are sincere to Him. (2 : *138-139*).

This is the gospel of universal peace. If good actions are the only salt of life, how can anyone take exception to it. It shows a largeness of soul not found anywhere else except in Islam.

The Book was couched in a language that is still living, and it remained proof against every change, while other languages in the world have been transformed completely. Words have lost their original shape and meaning, and either new meanings have been given to them or they have become generalized.

There is no change in the Arabic language from the date it existed at the time of the Holy Prophet. Even if other Sacred Books had come to us in their original purity, we could hardly give to their reachings the precise meaning which attached to them in the days of their Revelation. The Qur'an was given to us in a language which is still living and has remained unchanged and is unchangeable, and for this reason its message can be understood even today as conveying the same exact purport, expressed at the time of the first delivery. Arabic can, therefore, claim to be the only language for a Religion from God, since it does not change with the centuries.

Every religion speaks of certain verities, but the words used to signify them do not express the concept intended to be conveyed. Good and Evil, for example, are the chief themes in every religion, but the words used for them do not in themselves express the whole idea. Nothing it itself is either good or bad. If one form of use makes it beneficial, the other form of its use makes it pernicious. The Arabic words for them are eloquent enough to say. *Khair*, the equivalent of good, literally means things elected, while *Sharr*, the word for evil, means anything to be rejected. Again, almost all the words in the Arabic language possess such a wealth of meaning as cannot be found in any other tongue—a fact which renders valuable service to religion in explaining its truths. The words used in the Qur'an are too eloquent to need any commentary on its tenets. All words like *Junah, Ism, Isyan, Udwan*, etc., used in the Qur'an to convey sin, literally mean leaving one's original position and turning aside from it. The language of the Hejaz may or may not be revealed one, but it cannot be denied that it is the proper vehicle to convey the message coming from the Divine mind. It may be asserted that the said language possessed all the characteristics that are commonly found in things in nature. Thus things are unchangeable in their make. They are extraordinarily rich in their inherent qualities which meet all our needs. So is the case with the Qur'anic words in their significations.

But the thing that is most significant in the language and which goes a long way to prove it to be a revealed one, is the philosophy in its component words. Every word contains in it a reason for which it has been selected and does convey a particular idea. There ought to be words to convey these ideas at the very inception of our society. Like all other languages Arabic has got two words: "*Rajul*" and "*Nisa*" conveying the idea of man and woman. The two words are deep in their significance. Men by nature are meant for hard work in life. They have to expose themselves to work which is not meant for females, because the former alone can stand it. For reasons of health we must keep the vital heat within our system. We need some non-conducting material over our body. On the other hand, if the requirements of man demand hardness of constitution in him, and beauty, the necessary assets of a female, requires on the contrary softness of body. Keeping these in view, Divine Economy granted hairy body to men and gave enough of fat to female system, because both materials are the best of non-conductors. Besides, hairy body would have affected female beauty while fat makes body soft. It is admitted that nothing is more non-conducting than hairs. Hairs on body are a visible phenomenon observable by every naked eye, but no one are long knew that the female body did possess a fatty coat next to their skin. It is for this reason that women are less sensitive to cold than men. These are recent discoveries, but the language of Hejas has chosen two words given above that do convey these Truths. If the word "*Rajul*" means hard as well as hairy, the word "*Nisa*" equivalent of woman means soft and fatty. The said words do belong to the most initial society. I may say that they are the first words after mother and father that must be formulated for the respective purposes. Now can an incipient mind in his natural condition could coin such words so rich and eloquent in their meanings to be discovered afterwards. The words must come from the All-knowing Mind. The said two words do signify other meanings which give various characteristics of men and women. These things, besides many other things which the language of the Hejaz possesses, show that the language must have come from God.

If the Revelation from the Almighty came to set man on the right path, it cannot vary in its teachings if it comes again. It may come piecemeal, according to the receptivity of the people to whom it is addressed but it must reiterate its truths, and one day the final message will come. If there cannot be more than one straight line between two points the Revelation that claims to point out the straight path for human guidance, can also claim to be final. The last Book did not come to contradict former Revelations but to confirm them. It preached the same religion as that given to Prophet Noan and the rest of the Prophets. But the Holy Qur'an was to complete it, and herein lies its finality. The ways of God are admittedly infinite, and our knowledge of them can never be complete. It will remain on its increase. But the right way of contemplating them could be shown once and for for all. If knowledge is the only water of life, and God the fountain thereof, the sooner the way to the fountain is shown to humanity the better. So it was from the beginning. If the former Revelations had remained in their original from and could claim authenticity, the Last Book of God would have been of a different character. But almost all the former Books have either disappeared or have suffered from human tampering. The Divine will had to be announced once and for all at the advent of the Holy Prophet, and that announcement was final and free from corruption or interpolation. This appeals as a clinching argument against the attitude of other religions when they hesitate in accepting the Qur'an as a message from the Lord. If the Revelation that came from God to their ancestors had lost its genuine character, a further Revelation must come to us, we have the same claim to Divine guidance as our forefathers had, either the source of knowledge should keep the old message in the form in which He gave it in the olden days or He must send a new one. Such is His method always. The whole of Nature bears conclusive testimony to this truth. Whenever anything necessary for our growth in the universe disappears or is lost, Providence renews it at once, and if He is always observing this principle for our physical subsistence. He will surely do the same for our spiritual nourishment, seeing that the soul is infinitely more valuable than the body. If bygone generations were given some knowledge for guidance from God, we have the same claim to His Providence. There would have come another Book from God for us if the Holy Qur'an had gone the way of the former Books.

It is also very interesting ro note that the Qur'an appeared at a time when the world was in dire need of divine guidance, and every nation looked at the moment for the appearance of the Prophet, seeing that all the old religions had lost their teaching. The prophetic eyes of the former Messengers foresaw that their teachings would suffer in purity, and that coming generations of their followers would naturally need some new Revelation from above. So all the Sacred Teachers spoke of the coming Messenger. No one among them declared that his message was the last. If Moses Prophesied that God would raise up another prophet after him with fiery law in his hands, we cannot look for the fulfilment of the prophecy in the person of Jesus, since he brought no new laws, nor did he depart from the old code in any way. He himself was looking for the spirit of Truth, who was to come to give the whole Truth. Ignorance or prejudice would endeavour to discover the fulfilment of the words of Jesus in the so-called appearance of the Holy Ghost at the Day of Pentecost, when the Miracle of the Tonques occurred. But it is not conclusive. Jesus admittedly could not himself give the whole truth. He looked for one who was to come to do so. The Church that passes under his name cannot claim to do the same, as she has failed to add even a scrap of knowledge to that which the world possessed at the departure of the Nazarene. Moreover, the promised Prophet was to bring the fiery law to complete the old one, as Jesus hoped, but the official Church has totally dispensed with it. The Bible has also prophesied that God would arise from Sinai and appear at Seir, but would shine fully at Mount Paran. If Sinai and Seir refer to the Mosaic and Nazarene dispensations, Mount Paran is not found in any other country except Arabia Mecca being located in its valley. But the Bible is not the only Scripture that speaks of the coming Prophet. Almost all other great Prophets of God including Krishana and Buddha have joyously referred to the illustrious advent of the last Great Prophet.

The Sacred Book has various miraculous features about it which should be borne in mind. It has been admittedly the most successful of all sacred books in its mission. It came first to a people verging on the borders of animality and raised them from thence to the acme of civilization within the shortest period recorded in history for such a transformation. It changed the destinies of the World by bringing the greater portion of its under its healthy influence, while setting the remainder on the right path to civilization. The Book still remains a source of inspiration to the human race, inculcating the noblest of ideals—Monotheism, Universalism and Democracy. It condenses the whole of its teaching into 6,666 verses.

The Qur'an is a miracle for its diction and style. We can sometimes read volumes in a chapter, chapters in a verse, and in a single word perceive a veritable treasure of knowledge, yet it is in no wise dogmatic. It produces logical reasons for each one of its tenets. It appeals to things in Nature for confirmation of its truths. Thus, its opening words are marvellously pregnant with sublime significance. They are as follows :

> "All praise (hand) is for Allah, the *Rabb* (The Creator and Maintainer) of the worlds".

This sentence is not only an epitome of various teachings but it contains the purest of logic to support its assertions. It speaks of the Deity, Whom it calls the *Rabb.*

Science observed many things in Nature before it believe in the existence of the First Intelligent Cause. It saw the whole of Nature bound with the chains of law which, though apparently conflicting in some cases, yet work in harmony as if under a singly controlling hand.

The Book refers to the abovementioned verities among many other things, when speaking of God : but surely it is the wonder of wonders that the very meaning of the word "*Rabb*" should also cover them. The pharse "The Creator of the Worlds" is preceded by the word "*Al-Hamd,*" which first means praise, eulogy and approbation, and secondly our submission to the ways of the Creator ; for by saying "*hamd*" we express our willingness to submit to His laws and the literal interpretation of Islam is "submission". Technically it means Obedience to the Laws of God. Thus the Qur'anic sentence, besides expressing our intelligent belief in the existence of the Deity, refers to our creed of life that is to say our religion, the religion of obedience and commandment. If God has been pleased to base his work of creation of laws, as the word "*Rabb*" denotes our very existence and its proper evolution would command us to observe these laws. Yet, even so, we do not know all the necessary laws and therefore, Revelation must come from God to enlighten us.

Every Prophet of God, as the Qur'an says came with one and the same message. They all taught us to obey Allah or *Rabb.* If Allah is the Source of all laws, and *Rabb* promulgate the ways of creation and sustenance we cannot remain indifferent to such laws. This is the religion of which the Qur'an speaks.

The sentence under discussion, "All praise (or submission) is for Allah, the Creator of the Worlds," refers also to the nature of the religion we have to observe. Science and the Qur'an alike speak of various worlds into which we have passed from the beginning up to the present stage of sojourn which is the final stage of our physical growth. Here we stand at the threshold of a "New Creation". It has been up to now, the world of matter now we enter into that of consciousness. We have found the means of subsistence in every sphere into which we have entered during the journey and, in it, have become prepared for our progress in the sphere immediately following it. We naturally look to our Creator for nourishment in this world as well as for our preparation for the next, if any. We are on the mental plane now, and need intellectual food ; we need knowledge of the ways of progress on the mental and spiritual planes since they are the chief constituents of the present and the coming world ; we need a revelation from God. Thus a single sentence of our Book—*Al-Hamdulillah-i-Rabbil-Alamin*—All submission to *Rabb* of the Worlds—conveys a world of truth in it.

Like everything in creation the Qur'an has baffled all human efforts to produce another book like this in matters of diction and style. But there are other proofs which show that the Book could not emanate from a human brain. Prophecies and their fulfilment, for example, have been spoken of as proof of Divine Messengership in the Book of Deuteronomy. But the prophecy should not be mere guess work, nor couched in oracular terms of mystery. It should be made at a time and under circumstances that make its occurrence an impossibility. Such prophecies are found in the Qur'an.

1. The Qur'an will retain its purity :

It appeared among a most illiterate people. The art of writing was then in its infancy throughout the whole world. Human memory was the only custodian of ancient history, and this affected the purity of such records as there were. For this very same reason almost all Sacred Literature could not remain in its original text. The Qur'an at this period of history, claimed that it would remain free from all corruptions ; and today we find the prophecy fulfilled up to the hilt. It was made in the clearest and most authoritative terms, and it could only have come from one Who possessed the knowledge of coming events and had also the power to create things that would make His words a reality.

2. Islam shall succeed :

Prophet Muhammad, though of noble extraction among the Meccans, was, immediately after his claims to Prophethood, completely deserted by almost all his kith and kin. Most of his uncles and cousins became his mortal enemies, since they were the custodians of the great temple of idols. They owed their income and all honour to idolatry, while the new Prophet was raised to eradicate that form of worship from the earth. He had to work against heavy odds ; not only did he meet discouragement but also every hardship and persecution, and these of a most terrible nature. Every effort was made to put an end to his mission. He had but few followers, but they were all subjected to every kind of oppression and tyranny.

They left their homes for good, as did the Prophet, after 13 years' persecution at a juncture when the enemy decided to murder him and had besieged his house for that purpose ; but he escaped. The Qur'an spoke many a time of the unique success that will :—

> Surely We have revealed the Reminder and We will most surely be its guardian.
>
> And soon will your Lord give you so that you shall be well pleased.

All praise is due to Allah who revealed the Book to His Servant come to the Prophet during the life-time. The prophecy was repeated, especially on those occasions when the hostility of his enemies became more and more bitter. It was prophesied that the whole of Arabia would embrace Islam, and that the enemies of the Prophet would be at his feet, and that the Faith would extend to the four corners of the world with its tenets prevailing over the doctrines of all other religions. The last portion of the prophecy is in the course of its fulfilment today, when Monotheism, Universalism and Democracy with various other Qur'anic tenets vigorously preached for the first time in that Holy Book, are becoming increasingly popular.

3. Total Defeat of the Meccans :

Rightly directing, that he might give warning of severe punishment from Him and give good news to the believers who do good that they shall have a goodly reward.

> Staying in it for ever.
>
> Surely We have given you abundance of good. (*93 : 5 : 18 : 1-3-108 : 1.*)
>
> But what is the matter with those who disbelieve that they hasten on around you.
>
> On the right hand and on the left, in sundry parties.
>
> Does every man of them desire that he should be made to enter the garden of bliss ?
>
> By no means : Surely We have created them of what they know. (*70 : 36-39*).
>
> On that day they shall follow the inviter, there is no crookedness in his and the voices shall be low before the beneficent God so that you shall not hear aught but a soft sound. (*20 : 108*).
>
> He it is Who sent His Apostle with the guidance and the true religion, that He may make it overcome the religions, all of them, though the polytheists may be averse. (*61 : 9*).

> He it is Who sent His Apostle with the guidance and the true religion that He may make it prevail over all the religions ; and Allah is enough for a witness. (*48* : *28*).

And an announcement from Allah and His Apostle to the people on the day of the Greater Pilgrimage that Allah and His Apostle are free from liability to the idolaters ; therefore if you repent, it will be better, for if you turn back, then know that you will not weaken Allah ; and announcement painful chastisement to those who disbelieve. (*9* : *3*).

Prophet Mohammad settled there, but he had hardly time to arrange his affairs in his new place of residence when he heard of his enemy's march against him. With a small band of three hundred and thirteen men, most of whom were inexperienced and under age, he left Madina. At a distance of thirty miles from that city the Muslims saw more than one thousand veteran soldiers, the flowers of Meccan bravery, marching against them. It was a disheartening scene. The Prophet in his tent prostrated himself in prayer to the Almighty, when Hazrat Abu-Bakr, the first Caliph, came to him and reminded him of the Prophetic words that had been revealed years before at Mecca. In fact, that very Prophecy had become a household word with every Muslim before the battle took place. Hazrat Abu Bakr left the tent and recited the Prophetic words to everyone he met. It is a matter of surprise, perhaps, that the small Muslim band, though facing certain death, were in the best of spirits on this occasion. They believed that mighty force come to meet its own destruction in fulfilment of the Prophecy.

There is nothing in history to equal the event at Badr—the scene of the conflict. Though but a small scuffle between one thousand men on one side and some three hundred on the other, it produced far-reaching results in the history of the world.

Gibbon says : "It changed the destinies of the whole human race. Not only did it save Islam but it enabled the Faith to rule the world in the future." The Qur'an has spoken of it as a great witness to the truth of Islam. It says :—

(1) Soon shall the hosts be routed, and they shall turn their backs. (*54* : *45*).

(2) Have you not considered those who are given a portion of the Book : They are invited to the Book of Allah that it might decide between them, then a part of them turn back and they withdraw. (*3* : *22*).

(3) And know that whatever thing you acquire in war, a fifth of it is for Allah and for the Apostle and for the near of kin and the orphans and the needy and the

> wayfarer, if you believe in Allah and in that which We revealed to Our Servant, on the Day of Distinction, the day on which the two parties met ; and Allah has power over all things. (*8 : 41*).

4. The Final Fall of the Enemy :

The Chapter XXVIII of the Holy Qur'an refers to the time when opposition to Islam was approaching its height ; the immediate prospects of the Prophet were of the gloomiest description. At this juncture he received the following words from the Most Right : A mighty host of the Allies shall be here put to flight. It was the fourth year of the *Hijra* when the enemies of the Prophet made their last attempt to uproot Islam. Almost all the tribes of Arabia banded together and marched on Madina. The town was besieged and trenches were dug by the followers of the Prophet to defend it. His force was insignificant in number and powerless before the mighty host which was approaching, but instead of losing heart they rejoiced greatly on account of the said prophecy. The time for its fulfilment, they thought, had arrived. The Holy Book speaks thus of the event : And when the believers saw the Allies, they said. This is what Allah and His Apostle promised us and Allah and his Apostle spoke tbe truth ; and it served but to increase their faith. The Allies refer to the allies of the prophecy and the battle is called the Battle of the Allies. The result was the total overthrow of the Meccans and fulfilment of the mighty prophecy.

5. The Defeat of the Persians by the Romans :

The struggle between these two nations was of long standing. It began in 602 C.E. when Chosroes the Second of Persia set out to avenge the death of Maurice, who had been murdered by Phocas, his armies ravaged Syria and Asia Minor, and in 608 C.E. advanced as far as Chalcedon. In 613 and 614 C.E., Damascus and Jerusalem were taken by General Shahabaraz, and the Holy Cross was carried away in triumph. Soon after, even Egypt was subdued, the Romans being able to offer but little resistance, torn as they were by internal dissensions and hard pressed by Avars and Slavs.

The Meccans rejoiced at the news of the Roman defeat because of their ancient friendship with the Persians. But the following revelation came to the Holy Prophet at the very time when the news of the Roman defeat arrived :

> I am Allah, the Best Knower. The Roman are vanquished in a near land, and they, after being vanquished, shall overcome within a few years. Allah's is the command before and after ; And on that day the believers shall rejoice.

The revelation made in 616 C.E. contained two different prophecies. One was concerned with the overthrow of the Persians by the Romans, who had become utterly powerless by that time and the other foretold the fall and defeat of the Meccans at the hands of but a few Muslims. The time given in the text for the fulfilment of the prophecy in Bid, which literally means a period from three to nine years. The prophecy became, at the time of its revelation, the subject of heated discussion between Muslims and non-Muslims as Mecca: so much so that Abu-Wehl, the arch-enemy of Islam, wagered seventy camels with Hazrat Abu Bakr as to the issue of the prophecy. The events foretold were at that time a sheer impossibility. They could not be a political forecast, seeing that they determined such highly improbable events with exactness and precision, especially when the Greeks were so distressed that there appeared little likelihood of their being able to retrieve their fortune.

Palmer rightly points out, when commenting on these verses in his English Translation of the Qur'an :

> In the year following the revelation, the Persians proceeded to lay siege to Constantinople itself, which showed the hopeless condition of the Romans at that time."

However, in 624 C.E. Heraclius advanced into Northern Media. He destroyed the great fire-temple of Gondzak and routed a large Persian army. The Romans returned victorious, leaving the Persians totally defeated. It was about this time that a handful of persecuted Muslims vanquished the powerful forces of Mecca at Badr, where Abu Jehl who had wagered against the fulfilment of the prophecy, was among the Slain. A foolish critic might, perhaps, describe the revelation as a chance or coincidence, the defeat of a mighty people like the Persians and the Meccans by those of fallen state (the Romans and the Muslims) but how can we explain the synchronizing of the two events of quite different characters especially when the happenings at Badr were a sequel to the flight of the Prophet from Mecca ? No one could have even dreamed of the flight of the time of the prophecy, and what is then to be said of its occurrence in the year 623 of the Christian Era, when the Meccans one year after it would pursue the flying Prophet and fall at Badr in 624 C.E., the year after the Persian defeat by the Romans. It is a most curious event in the history of the world, especially when we find that the event at Badr occurred one year after the flight, as was foretold in the prophecy of the Burden of Arab in the Old Testament as given in the Book of Isaiah, which clearly says that the power of Kedar—the ancestors of the Meccans—would fall just one year after the flight; and so it occurred.

6. The Recovery of Pharaoh's drowned body :

The drowning of Pharaoh with his people in the river Nile was a well-known biblical story at the time of the revelation of the Qur'an. But the old record said that the body of Pharaoh was never found and the river was the grave ; but the Qur'an contradicted the biblical narrative and gave a striking new version of the episode in the following words :

> But We will this day deliver thee with thy body that though mayest be a sign to those after thee.

The Christian critics of the Qur'an declared this Quranic statement to be a fabrication, seeing that the Book of Exodus gave quite a different story. But the last century discovered the body of Rameses, the Pharaoh of Moses, preserved among the mummies of Egypt. The body must have been cast ashore and then embalmed by the Egyptians. No one in the world knew of it, but the Qur'an revealed it some two thousand years after the event.

7. The exalted position of its scribes :

The Book also said that it would see among its scribesmen of very high rank. The prophecy became fulfilled even in this respect, when the Mughal Emperor Aurangzeb, and many other kings, wrote the Qur'an with their own hands.

8. Scientific Predictions :

(*a*) By these predictions it is meant with the relation of certain scientific truths, that have recently been acknowledged, but were mentioned by the Qur'an at a time when no one in the world knew of them, and would have nothing to do with sciences. For example, every little was known of biology in those days, but the Qur'an in the clearest terms, speaks of water as the producer of life. The Book is not a treatise on Science. It merely refers to certain phenomena in Nature for the purpose of elucidating the principles underlying Nature. Since it comes from the Omniscient Lord, it cannot, like the Book of Genesis, impart wrong knowledge.

(*b*) It is, moreover, a recent discovery that everything in the universe has got its mate or supplement for procreative purposes, but the Qur'an disclosed the secret in 51 :49 in the clearest terms.

(*c*) Geology has today confirmed, word for word, everything revealed by the Qur'an as to the earth and its several stages of growth from a fiery mass.

(*d*) The Qur'an speaks of the life germ the seminal :

> Do not those who disbelieve see that the heavens and the earth were closed up, but We have opened them

and We have made of Water everything living ; will they not then believe.

Then He directed Himself to the heaven and it is a vapour, so He said to it and to the earth ; come both, willingly or unwillingly. They both said ; we come willingly. (*41* : *11*).

Fluid—as the essence of earthly matter. It speaks of the various stages through which it passes when in a woman's womb before it evolves into human shape, and the Qur'anic statement has been verified today by physiology.

(*e*) The art of navigation was discovered and brought to a high pitch of perfection by early Muslims. Though everyone before Islam knew well enough that the blowing of the winds did aid the course of the ship on the sea, the Qur'an disclosed a wonderful truth, so helpful to navigation that the winds might be made subservient to human will, and the mighty ocean itself would become the servant of man as soon as he acquired proper knowledge.

(*f*) The world knew something of the heavens in early days, but the Qur'an increased immensely your knowledge of the subject. It inspired the early Muslims to rescue astronomy from the clutches of astrology and place it on a strictly scientific basis, leading to many valuable lumidiscoveries. The Qur'an not only asserted that the luminaries moved in their respective orbits but it revealed that each orbit or sphere consisted of a sort of liquid matter in which it floated ; this again as a recent discovery. The Holy Qur'an enjoins :

(1) "And certainly We created man of an extract of clay."

"Then We made him a small life-germ in a firm resting-place.

"Then We made the life-germ a clot, then We made the clot a lump of flesh, then We made (in) the lump of flesh bones, then We clothed the bones with flesh, then We caused it to grow into another creation, so blessed be Allah, the best of the creators. (*22* : *12-14*).

(2) "Allah is He Who created the heavens and the earth and sent down water from the clouds, then brought forth with it fruits as a sustenance for you, and He had made the ships subservient to you, that they might run their course in the sea by His command, and He has made the rivers subservient to you, and He has made subservient to you the Sun and the Moon pursuing their course, and He made subservient to you the night and the day." (*14* : *32-33*)

"And the Sun runs on to term appointed for it ; that is the ordinance of the Mighty, the Knowing." (*36* : *38*).

(3) "Neither is it allowed to the Sun that it should overtake the Moon, nor can the night outstrip the day; and all float on in a sphere."

(*g*) No one knew of the roundness of the earth in pre-Islamic days, but the Qur'an clearly hints at this when it speaks of numberless Easts and Wests. No one, in those days, could imagine a thing iike that, seeing that they thought of one East and one West. Even certain religious scriptures give ridiculous explanations of the setting of the sun in the West and its rising again from the East. The present division of the hemisphere into East and the West is a man-made barrier. But as in the course of the progress of Islam it had to assume a certain political importance, the Qur'an spoke of many Easts and many Wests. But if the earth be round, every inch of it is a new East and a new West. If, for instance, "B" is at a distance of two hundred miles from "A" which, let us suppose, is situated to the West of "A" the sun will rise there some three minutes before it will rise at "B". Similarly, it will set at "B" three minutes after it has set at "A". If, therefore, we take two places on the hemsiphere two hundred miles apart as rising and setting places for the sun, there will be thousands of Easts and Wests on the earth, thus confirming the truth of the Qur'an.

The Book may be man's handiwork, but if it is, its author must be a person of transcnedental mental calibre, as well as a law-giver, a nation-builder, and a moralist of the loftiest ideals and one fully conversant with the various "elogies," etc., that have been discovered in modern days : geology, botany, biology, physiology, astronomy, geography, etc. This proves that the revelation of the Qur'an is from an All-Knowing being.

Freedom from variations :

Another feature of the Book which is a very strong proof of its Divine origin is its freedom from variations. It makes these claims for itself. It should not be forgotten that the Book that acquired its present shape under Divine Revelation, spread over a period of twenty-three years. Though such a period is long enough to bring changes into the life of every man, yet Prophet Muhammad passed it in exceptional and varied adventurous circumstances. His life was full of vicissitudes. Beginning life as an honourable trader he almost at once became the preacher of a new religion. He was forsaken and persecuted in every possible manner. He fled for his life, and then reappeared as a victorious soldier, he conquered his enemies in many battles and reduced them to complete subjection. Indigence and affluence, adversity and prosperity, he experienced in their most extreme form, and the Holy Book acquired its revelation under circumstances such as these. Had it been a figment of the Prophet's mind his environment must have affected the Book in every way, but in it there is no sign of this. Again, the language of an author, as well as his diction and style, offers aspects of contrast as regards his own writing at different periods of his life.

His early efforts show a certain rawness. Efficiency and ability come to him gradually, but his style is apt to dwindle in its beauty when he approaches old age. We find nothing of this kind in the Qur'an. It is a most wonderful exception to the universal rule. Even the earliest, revelations contained therein are eloquent in the highest degree, and mastery of the art of writing is kept in the background. If Prophet Muhammad had contrived to keep the whole Book from beginning to end a secret, had continued unremittingly to improve it during his lifetime, and then had published it at the end of his life, one might he able to understand the unique and unchangeable character of the Book. But the case is otherwise altogether. Every portion of it was, as it were, broadcast soon after it was revealed. Again, what we find at the beginning of the revelation gets confirmation at the end. The first chapter of the Qur'an is one of the earliest. It was described by the Prophet as the essence of the whole Book. The Qur'an says the same. But we find this truth borne out when the Qur'an became complete. Everything spoken of in the opening chapter was explained at suitable length in the course of the Book. Whatever principles of life were given in the early Meccan days of the revelation were preserved and explained later on. No new principle was ever inculcated to accommodate any unexpected change such as often beset the life of the Prophet.

The claim of the Qur'an, that it would baffle human effort to produce its equal, is based on absolute truth. A Book completed in twenty-three years, dealing with every aspect of human life, and yet remaining free from any kind of discrepancy or even a slight variation, is in itself a miracle.

Chapter 2

Certain Basic Principles

Duty Towards Allah

The primary right of Allah is that man should have faith in Him alone, and a man should acknowledge his authority and associate none with Him (*La ilaha illallah*). Secondly it is the duty of a man to accept His guidance. A man should act upon the Code which the Allah has revealed for man. It is to fulfil the dictates if we believe in the Prophet of Allah and accept His guidance and leadership. It is the third duty of a man that he should obey Allah honestly and unreservedly. It means that a man should act on the injunctions of the Holy Quran and the *Sunnah*. The fourth duty of a man is to worship Him. Maulana Abul Ala Maududi has given a very elaborate discussion on rights and obligation in his book entitled 'Towards Understanding Islam' which runs as follows :

These rights and obligations precede all other rights and as such they are discharged even at the cost of some sacrifice of other rights and duties. For instance, in offering prayers and keeping fasts one has to sacrifice many of one's personal rights. A man has to undergo hardships and offer sacrifices in the proper discharge of these duties to God. He has to get up early in the morning for his prayers and he, therefore, sacrifices his sleep and rest for it. During the day he often puts of many of his important works and gives up his recreations only to worship his Creator. In the month of *Ramadhan* (the month of fast) he faces hunger and inconvenience merely to please his Lord. By paying *Zakat* he loses his wealth and demonstrates that the love of God is over and above everything else and that the love of wealth cannot come in its way. In the Pilgrimage he undergoes sacrifices of wealth and troubles of travel. And in *Jihad* he sacrifices money, material, and all that he has—even his own life.

Similarly, in the discharge of these obligations one has to, more or less, sacrifices some of the ordinary rights of others and thus injure his own interests at large. A servant has to leave his work and attend to the worship of his Lord. A businessman has to stop his business and undertake the Pilgrimage to Mecca. In *Jihad* a man takes away life and gives it away solely in the cause of Allah. In the same way, in rendering Allah's rights one has to sacrifice many of those things which man has in his control, like animals, wealth, etc. But Allah has so formulated the *Shari'ah* that harmony and equilibrium are established in the different fields of life and the sacrifice of others' rights is reduced to the barest minimum. This is achieved by the limits prescribed by Allah. He has allowed us every facility in the fulfilment of the obligation of *Salat*. If you cannot get water for ablution, or you are sick, you can perform *tyammum* (dry ablution). If you are on a journey, you can cut short the *Salat*. If you are ill and cannot stand in the prayer, you can offer it while sitting or lying. Then the recitation in the prayer is so manageable that the prayers can be shortened or enlarged as one may wish : at times of rest and ease we may recite a long chapter of the Qur'an, at busy hours of life we may recite a few verses only. Rather, the instruction is that in the congregational prayers and in those prayers which occur in the business hours, the recitation should be short. Allah is pleased with the optional devotions (*Navafil*), but He disapproves our denying ourselves in sleep and rest and the sacrifice of the rights of our children and of the household. Islam wants us to strike a balance between the various activities of life.

This is also true in the case of fasts. In a year there is only one month for the obligatory fasts. But the women are exempted from fasting when they are pregnant or in their menses or suckling period. It is a must that the fast is to break at the appointed time and any delay in it is disapproved.

Similarly in the case of *Zakat* if any one gives, one fulfils one's duty, but if one spends more in charity, one seeks more and more of Allah's pleasure. Allah does not like us to sacrifice all our belongings in charity or to deny ourselves and our relatives those rights and comforts which they must enjoy.

The same is position as regards Pilgrimage. It is obligatory only for those who can afford money for the journey and who are physically fit to bear its hardships. It is to perform only once in the whole life, in any convenient year. The permission of parents has been made an essential condition, so that the aged parents may not suffer discomfort in your absence. These things clearly show what importance Allah has Himself given to the rights of others *vis-a-vis* His own rights.

In *Jehad* a man sacrifice the most. In it man sacrifices not only his own life and property in His cause but destroys those of others also. One of the Islamic principles is that we should suffer a lesser loss to save ourselves from a greater loss. What comparison can the loss of some lives—even if they are some thousands or more—bear to the calamity that may befall mankind as a result of the victory of evil over good and of aggressive atheism over the religion of Allah.

Duty Towards Society

According to *Shariah* men have to seek their fulfilment in such a way that the rights of other people are not infringed and violated. It has tried to strike a balance in the rights of man and the rights of the society so that no conflict may arise between the two and all must co-operate in establishing the law of Allah.

It had forbidden the telling of a lie in every form and shape, for it sullies the liar, causes harm to other people, and becomes a source of menace to society. Islam has forbidden theft, robbery, bribery, forgery, cheating, interest, usury, for whatever man gains by these means is really obtained by causing loss and injury to others. It also forbids backbiting, tale-bearing and slandering. Islam has prohibited gambling, lottery, speculation, and all games of chance. Islam also prohibited monopoly, hoarding, black marketing, holding of lard from cultivation, and all other forms of individual and social aggrandizement. Islam declares murder, assault and spreading of mischief, disorder and destruction as crimes. It prohibits adultery, fornication, and unnatural sexual indulgence.

These limits and restrictions have been imposed by Islam are to prevent a man from encroaching upon rights of others. A man should not any way violate the rights of others and injure their interests but should positively co-operate with each other and establish such mutual relations and social institutions that contribute towards the welfare of all and the establishment of an ideal human society. Islam has guided us in this respect also. Regarding family life Islam assigns to man the responsibility of earning and providing the necessities of his wife and children and to protect them from all the vicissitudes of life. For woman Islam assigns the duty of managing the household, training and bringing up children in the best possible way, and of providing to her husband and children the greatest possible comfort and contentment. It is the duty of the children to respect and obey their parents, and, when they are grown-up, to serve them and provide for their needs. Maulana Maududi in his book "Understanding Towards Islam" describes the following two measures :

(*a*) The husband has been given the position of the head of the family. No institution can work smoothly unless there is a chief administrator in it. You cannot think of a school without a headmaster or a city without an administrator. If there is nobody to control an institution, nothing but chaos would result. If everybody in the family goes his own way, nothing but confusion would prevail. If the husband goes one way and the wife the other, the future of the children would be ruined. There must be someone as the head of the family so that discipline may be maintained therein and the family becomes an ideal institution of society. Islam gives this position to the husband and in this way makes the family a well-disciplined primary unit of civilisation : a model for the society as a whole.

(*b*) This head of the family has further been burdened with some responsibilities. It is his duty to earn the living, and carry on all those tasks which are performed outside the household. It has freed woman from all the extra household activities and assigned them all on the shoulders of the husband. She has been relieved from the outdoor duties of the house, so that she might devote herself fully to the indoor duties and put all her energies in the maintenance of the household and in the rearing of the children—the future guardians of the nation. The women have been ordered to remain in their houses and discharge the responsibilities assigned to them. Islam does not want to tax them doubly, to rear the children and maintain the household, and to earn a living and do the outdoor jobs also. That would be evidently sheer injustice. Islam, therefore, effects a functional distribution between the sexes.

The *Shari'ah* has provided certain rules of behaviour for wider fraternity as well. According to these rules Muslim to help each other, to bid the good and forbid the evil, and to see that no wrong creeps into their society. The following are the injuctions of Islam :

1. In this regard free mingling of the sexes has been prohibited. It effects a functional distribution between the sexes and set different spheres of activity for both of them. According to Islam it is the duty of both men and women to look after their personal morality and purge their souls of all impurities.

2. Islam has enjoined proper dress should always be worn and no man should expose his body from the knees to the navel, nor should a woman expose any part of her body except her face and hands to any person other than her husband, however, closely related to her he might be.

3. The passtimes, entertainments, and recreation which tend to stimulate sensual passions and vitiate the canons of morality are not approved by Islam. Such things spoil their habit and can have no place in Islamic society.

4. In order to achieve unity and solidarity of the nation and well being of the Muslim community, the believers have been enjoined to avoid mutual hostility, social dissensions, and sectarianism of all hue and colour. They have to settle their differences and disputes in accordance with the principles laid down in the Qur'an and the *Sunnah*.

5. Knowledge and science as the common heritage of mankind and Muslims have full liberty to learn them and their practical uses from whatever quarter they can.

Duty Towards Nature

Allah has bestowed man with authority over His countless creatures. He had been given control on everything. He has been given the power to subdue them and make them serve his objectives. They enjoy the right to use them as they like. But Allah has not given this right as unrestricted. It says that all the creation has certain right upon man. They should not waste them on fruitless ventures nor should unnecessarily hurt them or harm them. When they use them for his service they should cause them the least possible harm. They should employee the best and the least injurious methods of using them.

Maulana Maududi in his book "Towards Understanding Islam" has given the following instances wherein the rights of the creature has been determined : For instance, we are allowed to slaughter animals for food and have been forbidden to kill them merely for fun or sport and deprive them of their lives without necessity. To slaughter them, the method of *zabh* (slaughtering) has been fixed, the best possible method of obtaining meat from the animals. Other methods are either more painful or spoil the meat and deprive it of some of its useful properties. Islam avoids both these difficulties and suggests a method which, on the one hand, is less painful to the animal and on the other preserves all the healthy and useful properties of meat. Similarly, killing an animal by causing continuous pain and injury is considered abominable in Islam. Islam allows the killing of dangerous and venomous animals and of beasts of prey only because it values man's life more than theirs. But here too it does not allow their killing by resort to prolonged painful methods. As regards to the beasts of burden and animals used for riding and transport. Islam distinctly forbids man to keep them hungry, to take hard and intolerable work from them and to beat them cruelly. To catch birds and imprison them in cages without any special purpose is considered abominable. Islam does not approve even of the useless cutting of trees and bushes. Man can use their fruits and other produce, but he has no right to destroy them. Vegetables, after all, possess life, but Islam does not allow the waste of even lifeless things, so much so that it disapproves of the wasteful flow of too much water. Its avowed purpose is to avoid waste in every conceivable form and to make the best use of all resources—living and lifeless.

Duty Towards Self

It is a fact that man is more cruel and unjust to himself than to any other being. It is the greatest weakness of man that when he feels an overpowering desire, he, instead of resisting it, succumbs to it, and in its gratification knowingly causes great harm to himself. For instance if a man takes liquor: he becomes and after it and carries it on at the cost of money, health, reputation, and every thing that he has. Some times a person becomes a slave of his sexual appetites and ruins himself in over-indulgence. On the other hand a person for spiritual elevations: suppresses his genuine desires, refuses to fulfil his physical needs and requirements, controls his appetite, does away with clothes, leaves the home and retires into mountains and jungles. He treats that the world is not meant for him and abhors it in all its forms and manifestations.

The objective of Islam is to establish poise and balance in life. The *Shari'ah* clearly declares that your own self also has certain rights upon you. A fundamental principle of it is that there are rights upon you of your own person.

It forbids the use of all those things which are injurious to man's physical, mental, or moral existence. It also forbids the consumption of blood, intoxicating drugs, flesh of pig, beasts of prey, and poisonous and unclean animals, for all these have undesirable effects upon the physical, moral, intellectual and spiritual life of man. Islam enjoins upon man the use of all clean, healthy, and useful things and asks him not to deprive his body of clean food, for man's body too has right upon him. Islam forbids nudity and orders man to use decent and dignified dress.

Islam does suppress even the sexual desires ; it enjoins man to control and regulate it and seek its fulfilment in marriage. Islam forbids him to resort to self-persecution and total self-denial and permits him, nay, bids him, to enjoy the rightful comforts and pleasures of life and remain pious and steadfast it the midst of life and its problems.

It totally forbids suicide and impresses upon man that life belongs to Allah. The life is a trust which Allah has bestowed upon us for a certain period of time so that we may make the best use of it.

Chapter 3

Certain Injunctions

WEALTH

The permitted way of earning :

The Islamic system of acquiring wealth is based on principle that no person has the right to profit at the cost of any other person and only such transactions are permissible in which both parties are mutually benefitted in a just manner. The Qur'anic injunctions in this regard is as follows :

> "O Ye Muslims ! Do not devour each other's property by illegal methods except that it be by transactions with mutual consent and do not bring ruin upon yourselves. Surely Allah is merciful to you. And whoever behaves aggressively and unjustly. We will soon cast him fire and this is easy to Allah." (*iv* : *29-30*).

It prohibits the hoarding of the money and clearly emphasises upon the circulation of the money. The Qur'anic injunctions in this regard are as follows :

> "Let not those who behave niggardly in that which Allah has granted them out of His grace think that it is good for them. Nay ! it is worse for them." (*iii* : *179*).

> "And as for those who hoard up gold and silver and do not spend it in Allah's way, announce to them a painful chastisement." (*ix* : *34*).

The Holy Qur'an encourages spending the money for the good of others in the way of Allah. The following are the injunctions of the Holy Qur'an in this regard :

> "They ask thee (O Prophet !) as to what they should spend for others. Say : What at all you can spare". (*ii* : *219*).

> "Be good to the parents and to the near of kin and the orphan and the needy and the neighbour of your and the fellow worker and the way-farer and those whom your right hands possess". (*iv* : *36*).

> "And in their property is a portion due to him who begs and to him who is denied (the good of life)." (*ii* : *19*).

The following are the other verses in which the Holy Qur'an impresses that by standing for the good of others wealth does not diminish :—

> "The devil threatens you with poverty and enjoins you to be niggardly and Allah promises you forgiveness from himself and abundance. And Allah is Bountiful and Knowing." (*ii* : *268*).
>
> "And whatever good things you spend for others shall be paid back to you in full measure and you shall not be wronged." (*ii* : *272*).
>
> "Surely they who spend for others out of what We have given them secretly and openly, hope for a gain which will not perish. Allah will pay them back fully their recompense and give them more out of His grace. Surely He is Forgiving, Multiplier of recompenses." (*xxxv* : *29-30*).
>
> "Allah does not bless usury and He causes charitable deeds to bear fruit." (*ii* : *276*).
>
> "And whatever you lay out at usury so that it may bring increase in the property of men, it shall not increase with Allah and whatever you give in charity desiring Allah's pleasure—it is this that increases manifold." (*xxx* : *39*).

Islam insist that a loan should be given to the needy persons and no undue pressure exerted upon the debtor if he is not in a position to pay back the amount rather recommends to relinquish the debt if the debtor is in a hard-pressed circumstances :—

> "And if the debtors is in straitened circumstances then, let there be postponement until he is in ease and that you remit it as alms would be better for you if you only knew." (*ii* : *280*).

The Holy Qur'an emphasises that to give money to the poor once is not to gain publicity but to spend in the way of Allah to seek His goodwill. The verses on the point is as follows :—

> "He who spends his property to be seen of men...his likeness is as the likeness of a man who sows in thin earth which covers a smooth rock. Then a heavy rain washes off the earth upon it leaving the rock bare...... And the likeness of those who spend their property to seek the pleasure of Allah with strong conviction, is as the likeness of a man who lays out a garden in good soil. When a heavy rain does not fall upon it, even light shower is sufficient for its growth and Allah sees what you do". (*ii* : *264-65*).

"If you give alms openly it is well and if you hide it and give it to the poor, it is better for you". (*ii* : *271*).

"They give alms both secretly and openly." (*xiii* : *22*).

"Do not render your charity worthless by laying obligations upon those you have relieved or by reproach or injury." (*ii* : *264*).

"And they give food out of love for Him to the poor and the orphan and the captive, and say : We only feed you for Allah's sake. We wish neither recompense from you nor thanks." (*lxxvi* : *1-9*).

Illegal Gratification :

The Holy Qur'an forbids all the sorts of illegal means of earning. The relevant Qur'anic verses on the point are as follows :—

"O you who believe ! Do not devour your property among yourselves falsely except that it be trading by your mutual consent." (*iv* : *29*).

Consume not each other's property by false pretences, neither make the same a means to approach your officers so that you may consume unjustly a part of the property of others knowing fully well that it is wrong to do so. (*ii* : *188*).

It may be noted that from the above verses it is explicitly clear that Islam prohibits all sorts of bribe and means of earning by illegal gratification.

Distribution :

Islam prohibits the hoarding of money. The relevant Qur'anic verses are as follows :—

1. Let not those who behave niggardly in that which Allah has granted them out of His grace think that it is good for them. Nay ! it is worse for them. (*iii* : *179*).
2. And as for those who hoard up goid and silver and do not spend it in Allah's way, announce to them a painful chastisement. (*ix* : *34*).

Zakat :

No religion of the world prior to Islam had consecrated charity, the support of the widow, the orphan, and the helpless poor, by enrolling its principles among the positive enactments of the system.

The feasts of charity among the early Christians, depended on the will of individuals ; their influence, therefore, could be irregular and spasmodic. It is a matter of history that this very irregularity led to the suppression of the "feasts of charity or love-feasts" only a short time after their introduction.

By the laws of Islam every individual is bound to contribute a certain part of his substance towards the help and assistance of his poor neighbours. This portion is usually one part of forty, or 2½ per cent. on the value of all goods, chattels, on profits of trade, mercantile business, etc. But alms are due only when the property amounts to a certain value, and has been in the possession of a person for one whole year ; nor are any due from cattle employed in agriculture or in the carrying of burdens. Besides, at the end of the month of Ramazan (the month of fasting), and on the day of the *Id-ul-Fitr*, each head of a family has to give away alms, for himself and for every member of his household, and for each guest who breaks his fast and sleeps in his house during the month, a measure of wheat, barley dates, raisins, rice, or any other grain, or the value of the same.

The rightful recipients of the alms, as pointed out by the practice of Prophet Muhammad and his disciples, are : (1) the poor and the indigent ; (2) those who help in the collection and distribution of the obligatory alms ; (3) slaves, who wish to buy their freedom and have not the means for so doing ; (4) debtors, who cannot pay their debts ; (5) travellers and strangers. General charity is inculcated by the Qur'an in the most forcible terms. But the glory of Islam consists in having embodied the beautiful sentiment of Jesus into definite laws.

The Qur'anic injunctions regarding *Zakat* are as follows :—

> Take alms out of their property ; thou wouldst cleanse them and purify them thereby. (*ix* : *103*).

The *Zakat* is placed next after the prayer. The following Qur'anic injuctions are explicitly clear on this point :

> Those who believe in the unseen and keep up prayer and spend (benevolently) out of what We have bestowed upon them. (*ii* : *3*).
>
> Woe to those who worship, who are unmindful of their prayers, who make a show of prayers and with-hold acts of charity. (*cvii* : *4-7*).

The word *Zakat* has been derived from *Zaka* and it meant as "It (a plant) grew" in other words it means the purification from sins. *Zakat* is the basic principle of every religion. We find certain verses in the teaching of every Prophet such as Hazrat Abraham says :

> "And We made them leaders of the people who guided them by Our orders and We inspired into them the urge of doing good and the keeping up of prayer and the giving of *Zakat*." (*xxi* : *73*).

Hazrat Ismail has also spoken a similar commandment from God as follows :

> "And he enjoined on his people prayer and *Zakat* and his Lord was well-pleased with him." (*ix* : *55*).

Hazrat Moses has also prayed as follows :

> "O our Lord ! 'Ordain for us in this world that which is good and in hereafter (that which is good), for, surely we have turned unto thee. He (God) said : I smite with My chastisement whom I please, and My mercy encompasseth all things ; So I will ordain it to for those who guard against evil and pay the *Zakat* and believe in My revelations." (*vii* : *157*).

The Israelite law have depicted the following commandments :

> "And Allah said : Surely I am with you if you keep up prayer and pay the *Zakat* and believe in My Messengers and help them and lend to Allah a goodly loan ; I will certainly remit your sins and I will certainly admit you into gardens in which rivers flow." (*v* : *12*).

Prophet Jesus has also said about a similar commandment which runs as follows :

> "And He hath made me blessed wheresoever I may be and hath enjoined upon me prayer and *Zakat* as long as I remain alive." (*xix* : *31*).

The following are the Qur'anic injunctions regarding the importance of *Zakat* :

1. This Book (the Qur'an) there is no doubt in it shows to live straight in the world to those who (wish to) guard themselves against evil, those who believe in the unseen and keep up prayer and spend benevolently out of what We have given them. (*ii* : *2-3*).
2. And keep up prayer and pay the *Zakat* and bow down with those who bow down. (*ii* : *43*).
3. It is not righteousness that you turn your faces to the East and the West but righteous is he who believeth in Allah and the Last Day and the Angels and the Book and the Prophets and giveth his wealth out of love for Him to his kinsfolk and to the orphan and the needy and the wayfarer and the beggar and for setting the captives free and observeth prayer and payeth *Zakat*. (*ii* : *177*).
4. But if they repent and keep up prayer and pay the *Zakat*, then they are your brethren in faith. (*ix* : *11*).

5. Those who, if We give them power in the land, will keep up prayer and pay the *Zakat* and enjoin good and forbid evil, and the end of all affairs is in the hand of Allah. (*xxii* : *41*).
6. And the believers, both men and women, are protectors one of another ; they enjoin good and forbid evil and keep up prayer and pay the *Zakat* and obey Allah and His Apostle ; Allah will show mercy to them ; surely Allah is Mighty, Wise. (*ix* : *71*).
7. By no means shall you attain to righteousness until you spend (in the way of Allah) out of that which you cherish most. (*iii* : *91*).
8. And those who are saved from their own greed shall be the successful. (*lxiv* : *16*).
9. And let not those of you who possess grace and ease swear against giving to near of kin and to the needy and to the fugitives in Allah' way, and let them forgive and show indulgence. Yearn ye not that Allah may forgive you ? And Allah is Forgiving, Merciful. (*xxiv* : 22).
10. And the given food out of love for Him to the needy the orphan and the captive (saying) we feed you for Allah's sake. We wish neither recompense nor thanks from you. (*lxxvi* : *8-9*).
11. O you who believe ! 'Spend benevolently of the good things which you have earned and of that which We have brought forth for you out of the earth, and seek not the bad (with intent) to spend (in charity) while you would not take it save with disdain and know that Allah is Self-Sufficient, Praiseworthy. (*ii* : *267*).
12. And hasten to forgiveness from your Lord and for a Paradise as wide as are the heavens and the earth prepared for those who guard against evil, those who spend benevolently in ease and in adversity. (*iii* : *132-33*).
13. Whatever good things you spend, it is for your own good, and you should spend only to seek the pleasure of Allah. (*ii* : *272*).
14. O you who believe ! Let not your wealth nor your children distract you from the remembrance of Allah. Those who do so are themselves the losers. (*lxiii* : *9*).

The following are the injunctions of the Holy Qur'an regarding the expenditure of the *Zakat* money :

1. Alms (*Sadaqat*) are only for the poor (*Fuqra*) and the needy (*Masakin*) and those who collect them and those

whose hearts are to be reconciled and the (freeing of) captives and the debtors and for the cause of Allah and for the wayfarer ; an ordinance (*Fariza*) imposed by Allah, and Allah is Knowing, Wise. (*ix* : *60*).

2. And if We had willed We would have raised a warner in every village. So follow not the unbelievers and strive against them a mighty striving (*jihadan kabiran*) with it. (*xxv* : *51-52*).

Inheritance :

During the pre-Islamic Arabia a daughter was not entitled to inherit any thing from the property of her father. A widowed woman has not only any right to inherit but she was treated like a chattel which devolves upon the heirs. The eldest son inherits the whole of the property excluding other sons.

The following are the injunctions regarding the distribution and determination of the shares :

1. Men shall have a portion of what the parents and the near relatives leave, and women shall have a portion of what the parents and the near relatives leave, whether there is little or much of it, a stated portion. (*iv* : *7*).

2. Allah enjoins you concerning your children, the male shall have the equal of the portion of two females... Then if there are two or more than two daughters, they shall have two-thirds of what the deceased has left, and if there is one, he shall have the half. (*iv* : *11*).

3. And as for his parents, each of them shall have the sixth of what he has left if he has issues, but if he has no issue and only his two parents to inherit him, then his mother shall have the third, but if he has brothers (or sisters or both) then his mother shall have the sixth, after the payment of a bequest he may have bequeathed or a debt. (*iv* : *11*).

4. And you shall have half of what your wives leave if they have no child, but if they have a child, then you shall have a fourth of what they leave, after payment of any bequest they may have bequeathed or a debt. (*iv* : *12*).

5. And they (your wives) shall have the fourth of what you leave if you have no child, but if you have a child, then they shall have the eighth of what you leave after payment of a bequest you may have bequeathed or a debt. (*iv* : *12*).

6. If any man or woman who is a *Kalala* (*i.e.*, who has no issues but parents) leaves inheritance, and he (or she) has a brother or a sister, then each of these two shall have the sixth ; but if they are more than that, they shall be sharers in the third, after payment of any bequest that may have been bequeathed or a debt that does not harm others. This is an ordinance from Allah, and Allah is Knowing, Forbearing. (*iv* : *12*).
7. They ask you for a decision of the law. Say Allah gives you a decision concerning a *Kalala*. If a man die without issue and have a sister, she shall have the half of what he shall leave. (And if a woman die) her brother shall be heir to her in case she has no issue. But if there be two sisters, they shall have (between them) two-third parts of what he shall leave ; and if there be several, both brothers and sisters, a male shall have as much as the portion of two females. Allah makes clear to you, lest you err, and Allah knows all things. (*iv* : *177*).

Charity :

Charity does not concern the body, like prayers and fasting, but it includes even the wealth and the property. When the body is subjected to prayers and fasting for the piety of the soul, the belongings of man should be utilised in a greater degree to seek the blessings of the Lord and so the piety of the soul.

According to Alhaj Hafiz Shabbirul Hasan: What man loves most is his body. This love is transferred to the means which maintain body, the money and the personal belongings. If this love of the material is not detached, the soul would get corrupt and debased. In order to elevate and purify soul it is quite essential that the love for the material objects should be transformed for love to spiritual ones. Body and wealth should not be wasted in any way, but they should not be made the interest of life. The interest of life must always centre round the piety of the soul.

Charity means the giving away of a part of wealth in the name of the Lord to the poor and needy. The action of charity should necessarily have two constituents without which charity loses its charm and becomes purely an action of passing away money from one hand to another. Each constituent is important to ensure the virtue of charity and to impress the soul with piety.

It is a must that whatever you give as charity in the name of the Lord and for His sake should be such as you love. You should not give them which is useless for you and which you would like to part. The Holy Qur'an clearly directs "you can never reach virtue, unless you give away out of what you love". Therefore the object of charity should be such as is valuable and is loved by you. It means that your love for the Lord is stronger than for any of your belongings, for charity has for its basis the commandments of the Lord, which you carry out to seek His pleasure and blessing for the piety of your soul.

The next ingredient of the act of charity is the pathos or feeling for the poor whom you help. As a matter of fact the help with a touching heart is the true help. It is to enter into feeling of the poor, whom you extend your hand of help, true sympathy. A charity without fellow-feeling is no charity.

The following words have been used in Qur'anic behests for such voluntary charity :—

1. "*Infaq*".
2. "*Ihsan*".
3. "*Sadaqat*".

Infaq means spending benevolently, *Ihsan* means the doing of good, and *Sadaqat* means a charitable deed. The Qur'anic verses as regards to charity are as follows :

1. The simile of those who spend their wealth in the way of Allah is as the simile of a grain which groweth seven years with a hundred grain in every year, and Allah multiplieth it for whom He pleaseth. (*ii* : *261*).

2. As for those who spend their wealth in the way of Allah, then do not follow up what they have spend with reproach or injury, they shall have their reward from their Lord......kind speech and forgiveness is better than charity followed by injury......O you who believe ! Make not your charity worthless by reproach or injury. (*ii* : *262-64*).

3. If you give alms openly it is well and if you hide it and give it to the poor, it will be better for you and will atone for some of your ill-deeds. Allah is aware of what you do. (*ii* : *271*).

4. Alms are for the poor who are straitened in the cause of Allah, who cannot travel in the land (for trade) the unthinking man takes them to be well-to-do because of their restrain. You can recognise them by their mark ; they do not beg from men importunately ; whatever good thing you spend (for them) Allah will surely know it. (*ii* : *273*).

Wakf :

The Mahomedan Law makes distinction between a gift in *sadaqah* and a wakf and it is necessary to consider the nature of these two transactions and the distinctions underlying them. The Mahomedan, like the Hindu, but unlike the English, Jurisprudence has a wider notion of charity. In Mahomedan Law, as under the Hindu Law, it includes any good act. The words 'piety' and 'charity' have a much wider signification in Muslim Law and religion. Every 'good purpose' (*wajub-ul-Khair*) which God approves, or by which approach (*Kurbut*) is attained to the Deity, is a fitting purpose for a valid and lawful wakf. A provision for one's children, for one's relations and, under the Hanafi Sunni Law, for one's self is as good and pious an act as a dedication for the support of the general body of the poor.

Mr. Justice Amir Ali in *Meer Mahomed Israil Khan* v. *Sashti Churan Ghose* in his dissenting judgment in *Bikani Mia* v. *Shuk Lal Poddu* observes : "The institution of wakfs, in which the endower's family and descendants are the immediate recipients of the benefaction, owes its origin to the direct ordinances of the Prophet. Nor only did he declare that a provision for one's family was the best of alms-giving, but he encouraged members of his household and his companions to create such wakfs, and himself set the example by consecrating create such wakfs, and himself set the example by consecrating certain lands at *Khaibar*. In dealing with the Mahomedan Law, the meaning attached by Muslims to the words 'charitable purposes' has been, unfortunately often lost sight of. Charity has been construed to mean 'charity to the poor' irrespective of the endower and his descendants ; piety and religion to mean such acts as would, in practical Europe, be regarded as pious or religious. This is not the Mahomdan Law" He then quotes in explanation various passages from the Miskkat and two of the precepts of the Holy Prophet as given in Muslim and Bokhari. These precepts are as follows :

(1) The Prophet of God declared that a pious offering to one's family (to provide against their getting into want) is more pious than giving alms to beggars. The most excellent of *Sadaqah* is that which a man bestows upon his family."

(2) "To give money to a free slave, to give alms to the poor, to give to your children and kindred are all *sadaqah*."

In Baillie's Mahomedan Law, a *Sadaqah* is stated to be "a partaker of condition with *hiba* but differs from it in legal effect. It, therefore, comes into the place of *hiba* in respect of *mushaa* and what is not *mushaa* and in requiring possession. But there is no revocation a *sadaqah* after it has been completed and it makes no difference whether it be bestowed on the rich or the poor, for it cannot be revoked in either case. When a man has bestowed a mansion in charity on another, he cannot revoke whether the person in whom it has been bestowed is rich or poor. Gift is not valid without it, on a favourable construction, from a regard to custom. An invalid *sadaqah* is an invalid *hiba*.

So also according to the Shiah law, *sadaqah* (or alms) is stated by Baillie to be : "a contract which requires declaration and acceptance and also delivery of possession. And if the donee should take possession without the assent of the donor, there would be no transfer of property to him. Among its conditions is an intention on the part of the donor of an approach to Almighty God. And after possession has been given it is not lawful to retract the gift, according to the most valid doctrine, for the hire or object in view has been attained, and the gift is like one for which an exchange has been made."

A gift in *sadaqah* is not sufficient to constitute wakf without accompanying circumstances as the words constituting the former gift are susceptible of another interpretation besides wakf. A *sadaqah* operates as a transfer of property while a wakf does not so operate. A *sadaqah* differs from gift. Where it is meant to indicate that the special motive for the gift is the acquisition of religious merit, or 'nearness to Allah' the term *sadaqah* is employed. The motive of the gift determines the question.

Mr. Amir Ali states that in Mahomedan Law *sadaqah* means "an offering or gift made with the object of obtaining the approval of the Almighty, or a reward in the next world." Even in a wakf there is an intention to please Allah and in that respect both wakf and *sadaqah* agree. The difference consists in the fact that in the case of a *sadaqah* there is a transfer of property or ownership to the trustees on behalf of the charity but in the case of a wakf there is only an extinguishment of the proprietary interest of the wakf.

The distinction is well-pointed out by Benson and Abdur Rahim, JJ. in *Ramanadhan Chettiar* v. *Vada Levvai Marakayar*. It was then observed that "Mahomedan Law recognises another form of gift to charity called *sadaqah*, the only important distinction between it and wakf being that by *sadaqah* not only the beneficial interest but also the legal estate is passed to the particular charity to be held by the trustees appointed by the donor. In a wakf the legal estate or 'ownership' is not vested in the *muttawalli* or trustee but is so to speak transferred to God. The trustees or beneficiaries of a wakf, therefore, are not authorised to alienate the wakf property unless especially authorised by the settlor or with the sanction of the Court in cases of necessity, and except in very especial circumstances the corpus of the dedicated property must be left intact and only the income can be devoted to the designed charitable purposes. On the other hand, when property is given by way of *sadaqah* to some charitabie object, the corpus itself or its equivalent, if the trustees find it proper or necessary to sell the property given in *sadaqah* and to convert it into some other form of property and not merely the income is to be devoted to that object."

There can be no doubt, however, that a *sadaqah* or a wakf for one's children and kindred or relations is a charitable and religious act according to the Muslim Law. Indeed, as has already been observed, this is not a peculiar feature of the Muslim Law. Even in the Hindu Law, a gift among others, to poor relations or to near relative is regarded as piece of charity and as producing religious merit. Thus it is stated in the Vyasa Samhita : "By making gifts to one's parents, brothers, father-in-law, wife or children, one is entitled to an eternal residence in heaven. A gift made to one's father is hundred times more meritorious that the one made to an outsider, those made to one's mother and sister being respectively ten times greater than the latter. A gift made to one's brother bears eternal fruit." But there is a vast distinction between a gift made with a charitable or religious motive to specific donees or to private persons and gifts to public objects which are termed in English Law as charitable objects. A gift prompted with a religious or charitable motive and capable of producing religious merit to objects which are private only has to be distinguished from a similar gift to public objects, The fact that a gift is capable, according to a particular religion, of producing religious merit and is regarded as a piece of charity cannot make the objects public and unless the objects are public, they cannot be charitable purposes or come within the definition of 'charity' as understood in the English Law. Wakfs for self and children or for one's kindred or family settlements in wakf can only be regarded as private trusts and not public trusts although there may be an ultimate gift to the poor implied in such cases, *i.e.*, on the extinction of the family or kindred. When the gift to the poor comes into existence then such a gift will be a charitable one but before this, the gift to family must be deemed to only private.

There is a difference in the views of Imam Abu Hanifa and of his two disciples about wakf. Wakf literally means detention. It is constituted by the appropriation or tying up of property in perpetuity so that no proprietary rights can be exercised over the corpus but only over the usufruct. It is a form of alienation by which property passes from the ownership of the person making the disposition without its being transferred to the ownership of any human being. According to Imam Abu Hanifa who was opposed to the legality of such transactions, it is "the detention of a specific thing in the ownership of the appropriator, and the devoting or appropriating of its profits or usufruct in charity on the poor or other good objects, in the manner of an areeat or commodate loan". According to him, however, it is not obligatory so that the wakf may revoke the appropriation or alienate the property. It may, however, be made obligatory in two ways : one, by order of the Judge and the other by using particular words of bequest. According to the two disciples "wakf is the detention of a thing in the implied ownership of Almighty God, in such a manner that its profits may revert to or be applied for the benefit of mankind, and the appropriation is obligatory, so that the thing appropriated can neither be sold, nor given, nor inherited." According to the accepted view of the Sunni schools (which comprise both the followers of Imam Abu Hanifa and Imam Shafie) it is in the very conception of a wakf that all proprietary rights of men should be extinguished in the property dedicated. So that proprietary rights become vested in God inasmuch as He is originally the owner of all created things and it is by His permission that men acquire rights therein so that when men's right ceases in a particular thing it reverts the proprietorship of God. A grant by which mosques and similar institutions are dedicated is known by the name of wakf. Where mosque or other institution is built and consecrated it ceases to be the property of the builder and vest in God" in such a manner as subjects it to the rules of divine property whence the appropriator's right in it is extinguished, and it becomes a property of God by the advantage of it resulting to his creatures."

The following are the essentials of a valid wakf :

(1) capacity of the endower (wakif), (2) a valid dedication or mode of Constitution, (3) property capable of being endowed, and (4) proper object of wakf. As regards the first essential, three conditions are necessary according to the Muslim Law for legal capacity to make a wakf. There must be understanding, puberty and freedom on the part of the appropriator. Thus an appropriation by a boy or a minor or insane person is not valid.

Again, although freedom is an essential condition (*i.e.*, the appropriator must not be a slave) yet Islam is not a condition. Hence a *Zimmee* or *Zimmea* (*i.e.*, a male or female infidel subject of a Muslim state) may make a valid wakf. Thus when a *Zemmee* appropriates his land to his child and his descendants, and ultimately to the poor, the appropriation is lawful, and the produce may lawfully be distributed among poor Muslims and *Zimmees*. If he were to confine the distribution to poor *Zimmees* that also will be lawful and the distribution may be made among Christians, Jews, and Majoosees, unless one particular class be indicated when distribution can be made only to such class. Even though the *Zimmee* should make the wakf to his son and his descendants, and then to the poor, on condition that if any of his children become Muslims they shall be excluded from the charity, the condition will be binding ; and so also, if he should say, "Whoever turns to any other religion, than the Christian is excluded, regard will be paid to the condition. Endowments by *Zimmees* for the benefit of their temples will be good.

The appropriator can only constitute such property as wakf over which he has a disposing power. If he is not the owner of the property, no wakf can attach.

Baillie in his Digest of Muslim Law says: "It is also a condition that the thing appropriated be the appropriator's property at the time of the appropriation ; so that if one were to usurp a piece of land, appropriate and then purchase it from the owner, and pay the price, or compound with him for other property, which is actually delivered up it will not be a wakf. When a man make an appropriation for certain good purposes of land belonging to another, and then becomes the proprietor of it, the wakf is not lawful, though it becomes so if allowed by the proprietor. So also, according to the Shiah Law, "if one should appropriate a thing which is not his own, the wakf will not be valid." But if the real owner should sanction the appropriation that will give it validity according to some of our doctors the sanction being tantamount, in their opinion, to a new appropriation. If the appropriator is owner only of 11 shares out of 16 and purports to make the whole wakf it will be good to the extent of the appropriator's share.

If possession is necessary for the validity of a wakf then some other consequence flow from the condition that a person should own the property which he appropriates as wakf. Thus according to Bailie : "If a bequest were made of land of which the lagatee immediately makes a wakf, after which the testator dies, the land is not wakf ; or if a donee of lands should make an appropriation of it before taking possession, and should then take possession, the wakf will not be valid. Yet if possession were taken of land given by an invalid gift, and it were then made a wakf, it will be lawful, the donee being responsible for its value ; and if one should purchase by an invalid sale, take possession, and then make an appropriation of the subject of sale in favour of the poor, the wakf will be lawful, subject to the like responsibility for its value to the seller ; but if the appropriation were made before taking possession, it will not be lawful. When a man buys land by a lawful sale, and make an appropriation of it before taking possession and paying the price, the matter is in suspense until he pays the price and takes possession, when the wakf is lawful ; but if he dies without leaving any property, the land is to be sold, and the wakf is void. And if a right is established in the property by a Shoofee under his right of pre-emption after the purchase has been made, the wakf is void." The principle deducible from the above is that a wakf of property before the full proprietory right in it have vested in the person appropriating it, is generally and subject to certain exceptions, invalid.

Again, the wakf must not, at the time of constituting property a wakf, be suffering from a mortal illness. If the wakif only intends it as a testamentary devise, it will be effective as regards one-third of his estate unless assented to by the heirs when it will take effect in its entirety. Such a testamentary devise is revocable at any time before death. But the wakf of a person made during illness from which he eventually recovers is valid with respect to the whole.

As regards the second essential, *viz.*, the mode of constituting a wakf it may be observed that in order that here may be a valid appropriation under the Muslim Law it is not necessary to use the term wakf. The appropriation may be made orally or by deed *inter vivos* or by will. In the case of bequests and death-bed gifts the wakf is not valid beyond a third of the net assets unless the heirs consent.

The appropriation becomes complete when there is a dedication. If the term wakf is used that is no doubt sufficient to constitute a valid permanent dedication (of itself, even though no object is expressed specifically to the poor) for that is its express meaning, so that the poor are beneficiaries in all such cases but as already stated the use of this term is not necessary. It is also not necessary that any set form of words should be used. There are several words which are express in their meaning and the use of which will clearly constitute a wakf (as conveying a permanent dedication) such as "*wakafto*" (I have dedicated) "*haramto*" (I have consecrated) "*habasto*" (I have tied up) "*sabalto*" (I have given the way, *i.e.*, of god), etc. The use of such terms will clearly constitute wakf.

Interest :

In order to understand Islamic view regarding the interest it is better to go through the Holy Qur'anic injunctions and following are the Holy Qur'anic behests in this regard :—

1. Those who (in charity) spend of their goods by night and by day. In secret and in public, Have their reward with their Lord : On them shall be no fear, Nor shall they grieve. (*v. 274*).
2. Those who devour usury will not stand except as stands one whom the Evil One by his touch hath driven to

madness. That is because they say: "Trade is like Usury". But God hath permitted trade and forbidden usury. Those who after receiving Direction from their Lord, desist, shall be pardoned for the past; their case is for God (to judge); But those who repeat are companions of the fire: they will abide therein. (*v. 275*).

3. God will deprive usury of all blessing, but will give increase. For deeds of charity: For He loveth not Creatures ungrateful and wicked. (*v. 276*).
4. Those who believe and do deeds of righteousness, and establish regular prayer and regular charity will have their reward with their Lord. (*v. 276*).
5. On them shall be not fear nor shall they grve. O ye who believe! Fear God, and give up what remains of your demand for usury, if ye are indeed believers. (*v. 278*).
6. If ye do it not, take notice of war from God and His Apostle; But if ye turn back, Ye shall have your capital sums: Deal not unjustly and ye shall not be dealt with unjustly. (*v. 279*).

Now the question arises what is meant by interest. Sir Sayyed has translated the word "*riba*" as usury and proceeded to differentiate it from interest. He says that Usury, refers to the primitive form of money-lending when money was advanced for consumptional purposes. It is indeed cruel, that money advanced to men who need it for their day-to-day expenses should be made a basis of profit. Holy Qur'an prohibits usury. Interest, on the other hand, is a reasonable charge for the use of money employed in productive processes—industry or trade. The borrower uses the money and gets some profit. It is reasonable for him to pay some interest to the lender whose advance enabled him to make that profit. He concluded interest, therefore, is not prohibited by the Holy Qur'an.

Shiekh Mahmud Ahmad differs from Sir Sayyed and says in rebuttal as follows :—

Even in the days of the Holy Prophet the Jews of Medina advanced money not only for consumptional purposes but also for trade. Similarly, modern banks advance money not only for productive purposes but also for consumptional purposes. In fact, the essential difference between primitive and modern banking is one of degree and development, not of kind. The most important thing is that this bearing of banking on commerce was known to the Arabs even during the Prophet's days. Indeed, it greatly surprised them that the Holy Qur'an should permit trade and prohibit interest; but the Holy Qur'an in spite of knowing the strength of their argument and let us add that of Sir Sayyed and men of his school-repeated : Yes, trade is permitted and interest is prohibited. Let us read the relevant verse again :

> Those who devour usury will not stand except as stands one whom the Evil One by his touch hath driven to madness. That is because they say, "Trade is like usury". But God hath permitted trade and forbidden usury.

Mark the last four lines. The Holy Qur'an foresees the bearing of interest on trade. Yet in its own glorious way it insists on permitting trade and prohibiting interest. So far as the alleged difference between usury and interest is concerned, there is nothing in the verses of the Holy Qur'an to justify it. As already pointed out, the word in the original is "*riba*" which means excess or addition and therefore it covers both interest and usury.

Another question arises what does not come in purview of interest. The clue to the solution of this question is provided in the following verses of the Holy Qur'an :—

> They say "Trade is like usury," but God had permitted trade and forbidden usury.

Why Holy Qur'an permits trade and forbids usury? Capital invested in trade brings an excess called profit, and capital invested in banking brings interest. Whether there is any difference when God prohibits one excess and permits another. According to Mahmud Ahmad the difference is that profits are the result of initiative, enterprise and efficiency. They result after a definite value—creating process. Not so with interest. It may even retard a value—creating or productive process and too often does, as we shall soon see. A still more fundamental difference is that interest is fixed, profit fluctuates. In the case of interest you know your return and can be sure of it. In the case of profit you have to work to ensure it. If a banking structure could be evolved in which the return for the use of money would fluctuate according to the actual profits made from it, Islam would have no objection to it. That would be a developed form of *shirakat* which is already recognized in Islamic jurisprudence. What Holy Qur'an prohibits is a fixed return for the use of money irrespective of the profit gained or loss incurred by the borrower. So "*riba*" or interest means : Fixed return for the use of money. It is always prohibited whether it results from the "loans of gold and silver" or "economic credit, the creature of modern banking and finance."

But Professor Smith includes even land rent in interest. To quote him : 'It is hardly necessary to add that these religious proponents not only have never put forward the arguments, but cannot even understand, that the prohibition of interest, if taken seriously, would include the prohibition of land rent and of the whole landlord system would mean precisely the socialization of agriculture in the interests of those who labour on land".

But Smith has not explained as to how he includes land rent in interest.

Giving away of Spare Wealth :

Islam encourages spending money for the good of others in the way of Allah. The following are the Qur'anic injunctions regarding spending of spare wealth :

1. They ask thee (O Prophet !) as to what they should spend for others. Say : What all you can spare. (*ii : 219*).

2. Be good to the parents and to the near of kin and the orphan and the needy and the neighbour of your kin and the fellow worker and the way-farer and those whom your right hands possess. (*iv : 36*).

3. And in their property is a portion due to him who begs and to him who is denied (the good of life). (*ii : 19*).

4. The devil threatens you with poverty and enjoins you to be niggardly and Allah promises you forgiveness from Himself and abundance. And Allah is Bountiful and Knowing. (*ii : 268*).

5. And whatever good things you spend for others shall be paid back to you in full measure and you shall not be wronged. (*ii : 272*).

6. Surely they who spend for others out of what we have given them secretly and openly, hope for a gain which will not perish. Allah will pay them back fully their recompense and give them more out of His grace. Surely He is Forgiving, Multiplier of recompenses. (*xxxv : 29-30*).

7. Allah does not bless usury and He causes charitable deeds to bear fruit. (*ii : 276*).

8. And whatever you lay out at usury so that it may bring increase in the property of men, it shall not increase with Allah and whatever you give in charity desiring Allah's pleasure—it is this that increases manifold. (*xxx : 39*).

It may be noted that Islam not only enjoins its followers to give loan to the needy but also insists that no undue pressure should be exerted upon the debtor if he is not in a position to pay back with ease and even recommends to relinquish the debt if the debtor is in straitened circumstances. Which is quite clear from the following Qur'anic verses :—

> And if the debtor is in straitened circumstances then, let there be postponement until he is in ease and that you remit it as alms would be better for you if you only knew. (*ii* : *280*).

This giving away of spare wealth should not be for the purpose of aggrandizement or goodwill but it should only be spent in the way to seek Allah's pleasure. The Holy Qur'an enjoins as follows :—

> He who spends his property to be seen of men......his likeness is as the likeness of a man who sows in thin earth which covers a smooth rock. Then a heavy rain washes off the earth upon it leaving the rock bare...... And the likeness of those who spend their property to seek the pleasure of Allah with strong conviction, is as the likeness of a man who lays out a garden in good soil. When a heavy rain falls upon it, produces fruit two-fold, but if heavy rain does not fall upon it, even light shower is sufficient for its growth and Allah sees what you do. (*ii* : *264-65*).

The direction of Allah for the manner in which spare wealth should be given to the needy is that it is better to give hidingly than giving openly. The relevant Qur'anic behest are as follows :—

1. If you give alms openly it is well and if you hide it and give it to the poor, it is better for you. (*ii* : *271*).
2. They give alms both secretly and openly. (*xiii* : *22*).
3. Do not render your charity worthless by laying obligations upon those you have relieved or by reproach or injury. (*ii* : *264*).
4. And they give food out of love for Him to the poor and the orphan and the captive, and say : We only feed you for Allah's sake. We wish neither recompense from you not thanks. (*lxxvi* : *1-9*).

Concept of Love in Islam

The Prophet Mohammad has exalted the status of woman and assigned her true and natural place in the society. The Holy Prophet recognised her as an independent individual in her own being and not other shadow of her hushand to be absorbed in his essence after death as in Hinduism. Prophet Mohammad in respect and honour of woman has said :

1. The best among you are those who are best to their

wives and children.

2. Paradise lies under the feet of mothers.
3. Three things has Allah created most precious : they are perfumes, woman and prayer.
4. One of the greatest blessings of Allah on earth is a virtuous wife.
5. The women are garments for you and you are garments for them.
6. And one of His signs is, that He created that you may find comfort and peace in them and He put between you love and compassion most surely there are signs in this for those who reflect.

Durrani interprets the above verses in the following manners :

Certainly, it is a most glorious sign of the existence of God and His mercy. Peace and comfort and quiet and calmness of mind, love and compassion. Note the two sentiments 'love and compassion' mentioned together. A truer conception cannot be imagined of the mutual relations of a loving husband and a loving wife—a husband and a wife who have chastened themselves and have purified their hearts of the ugliness of baser passions, and not the common animals who mate together from sheer animal necessity and call themselves husbands and wives. Such is the exalted conception of married life in Islam, a description as well as an ideal for every Muslim to strive for. What a distance between the new Testament and the Qur'an, the former holding connection with woman to be defiling and the latter to be so purifying.

In fact the Holy Prophet believed that the love of man and woman was necessary to the moral purification and spiritual advancement of the two. There was a young man at Medina, Jabir bin Abdullah by name, in whom the Prophet saw much good. The young man and lost his father in the battle of Ohud, and in view of his orphaned state and of his personal excellence the Holy Prophet took keen interest in his doings and personally attended to the strengthening up of his affairs after his father's death. On one occasion, when they were returning from an expedition, Jabir's camel would not walk fast enough, the Holy Prophet offered to drive it for him. The Holy Prophet was great in his own self and could enter into such easy familiarity with any one and do any humble labour without falling in dignity. So he took a stick and drove the animal, while the young man rode its back. As they rode side by side, the Holy Prophet offered to purchase the camal. The young man accepted the offer, the price was agreed upon and payment and delivery was postponed till their arrival at Medina. Presently the Prophet said, "I hear, my son, you have married." "Yes, your Majesty, I have," the young man replied. "Was it a widow or a maiden ?" the Prophet asked. "A widow, your Majesty." "Why, you ought to have married a maiden. She would have played with you and you would have played with her." Remember it was not a common man of the streets, but a teacher of the purest morals and highest virtues who was speaking. He said so, because the play of a loving young man and a loving young woman has something holy and elevating in it, which is known only to the clean and the pure-minded.

The Holy Prophet had his own ideal of female beauty which is indicated by the expression the white-eyed beauties of paradise. The Holy Qur'an paints glorious pictures of the pleasures and joys of paradise, but they are drawn in such a pure manner that only a very lewd person will see anything offensive in them. Also, it is not a small complement to womanhood that beautiful women should be set up as the highest reward of human endeavour, as something that men should battle and strive for.

Now one of the blessings of paradise, with which the righteous are to be rewarded, is the company of woman who are described in the Qur'an as white-eyed beauties, pure as pearls (*lvi : 23*), 'who restrain their eyes' (*lv : 56*).

Mr. F. K. Khan Durrani in his book entitled "Muhammad the Prophet" narrated the concept of Prophetic love as follows :

The Holy Prophet had his own notions about love too. The story is about Moses. After killing an Egyptian he fled to Median which he reached safely. There he saw some men watering their cattle at a well. He also saw two young maidens holding their cattle back at some distance. Youth and chivalry took him to the girls and he asked them what they were waiting for? They said, their father was a very old man and they had come to water his cattle for him, but could not do so until the men were gone. Moses gallantly offered to water their cattle for them. After he had finished, he went back to the shade of a tree and prayed : "My Lord, surely I stood in need of what good Thou hast sent me." Presently, one of the girls returned "walking bashfully," took him along with her to her father and pleaded on his behalf : "O my father, employ him surely the best of those whom you can employ is the strong man, the faithful one" (*xxxviii : 23-26*). Note the words of praise the woman bestows upon the object of her affections. 'Strong and trusty' the two things which a true woman loves most in a man, and these two things embrace almost the whole of manhood.

Mr. Durrani without being afraid from the Maulvis's criticism on the point have further said :

'But I must adhere to the text. What was he praying for : For safety ? He was safe already. For bread ? What a thing to pray for ? Besides, there is no mention of bread anywhere near.

And why did she walk bashfully ? They were not very bashful when Moses spoke to the girls first. In fact, country girls who roam about with their flocks never are bashful and speak to strangers with perfect freedom. She was bashful because she had become self-conscious, because she was in love and was going to meet her lover, her 'strong man and true', for the first time after awakening had come.

But it is to Moses' declaration of love that I desire to draw the reader's attention. Those who have had the experience will remember how deeply humble one feels at the time, humble not to move the lady to compassion and acceptance of your proposal but from the sheer holiness of that rare and wonderful experience. One feels the thing to be altogether too vast to be contained in one single breast and too sweet to be true. Moses was a mighty man, who could hurl a fellow into eternity with one blow of his fist. But with the sudden and sweet awakening of love he realized that something had been lacking to complete his manhood. That something had come and his spirit bowed down in deep obeisance before the Giver of all good. He suddenly finds several hollows and caverns in his heart, of which he was not aware before, but which he now finds filled with a blaze of light, the light of love which was necessary to complete his manhood, and he bows down before the Almighty to return thanks for this great mercy. A nobler or a holier confession of love I have not met with anywhere else.

Such was Prophet Muhammad's conception of womanhood and of love for woman. Peace and the blessings of Allah be upon him.

But the Holy Prophet was not a weak sentimentalist as some modern feminists happen to be, who would exalt woman to such an ethereal height as to make her wholly useless for the race. Woman's sphere of life is limited. Nature herself has delimited it. She can be either a wife or a mother. A third vocation nature has not allotted her. In these two positions she rules supreme. In every other walk of life man can beat her any day. A prodigy of a woman here and a prodigy there only proves the case against her. Woman is entirely a being of love, whereas love occupies but a small part in man's life ; he has a multitude of other interests. Woman bears the race, whereas man is the bearer of the tradition of the race. He carries the tradition of art, technique, science and civilization as a whole from one generation to another. He is the builder, whereas woman only ministers to the comfort and well-being of the builder. He is the hard-headed thinker and organizer and designer, while she inspires him only with the beauty of the design. "The happiness of man is : I will. The happiness of woman is : He will. Behold, even now has the world become perfect !—Thus thinketh every woman when she with all her love obeyeth."

Man is the master, while woman prefers to sink her personality into that of her husband, because it is in that only that she finds her greatest happiness and bliss. Therefore, the Holy Qur'an plainly recognizes the superiority of man over woman and gives him authority over her. (*iv : 34*). And the Holy Prophet said that if worship of another than God had been lawful in Islam, he would have commanded women to worship their husbands.

WOMEN

Marriage :

Islam had recognized woman as a free and responsible member of the society and has assigned an important position to her.

Qur'an says about women in these words :

> 'They (the wives) are a garment for you and you are a garment for them.'

It has been interpreted to mean that just as a garment hides one's nakedness, the husband and wife, by entering into marriage relation, secure each other's chastity. Similarly, the Holy Prophet has defined the object of marriage, in the first place, as a safeguard against lewdness and incontinence; and, in the second place, as a means of procreation. It is on these grounds that he always encouraged a married life in preference to a life of celibacy, and laid so much stress on the piety and fruitfulness of women. The law of marriage are so framed by the Holy Prophet that they ensure the permanence of marriage relations, without impairing individual freedom.

The wife has an individual personality of her own and retains her distinct individuality. She never assumes her husband's name. In this connection, Pierre Grabites, an American Judge, observes :

> "A Muslim girl may marry ten times, but her individuality is not absorbed by that of her various husbands. She is not a moon that shines through reflected light. She is a solar planet, with a name and legal personality of her own."

Coverture has no place in the Muslim marriage. The woman is regarded as an entity in herself. Even after marriage she does not ceases to be a separate member of the society, and her existence does not merge in that of her husband. She retains her own property. She is empowered to alienate and dispose of her property herself, to enter into contracts and agreements on her own account, and to sue her debtors in the open court without the necessity of joining a next friend or under cover of her husband's name.

Considered juristically a Muslim marriage is a civil contract and not a sacrement. It follows that there can be no marriage without consent. Secondly, it can be dissolved by the will of the parties or by operation of law.

Muslim Law recognises the consent of women as on indispensable incident of a valid marriage. Muslim jurists agree in holding that a marriage without consent is void and a marriage with consent under compulsion is invalid. Thus, a woman, who is *sui juris*, cannot be married to any person without her own express consent.

Sometimes, the woman can be given in marriage by a guardian. But in that case also the consent of the woman is material so much so that on attaining puberty she can exercise the right known as 'option of puberty' and repudiate the marriage. There are also traditions to the effect that on various occasions, the Holy Prophet either annulled the marriage or gave option to the girl if the marriage was without consent.

> (1) "Khans-bin-Khejan reported that her father gave her in marriage, after she became a widow. She disliked it and came to the Holy Prophet. He annulled the marriage."
>
> (2) "Ibne-Abbas reported that a virgin grown up girl came to the Holy Prophet of Allah and narrated that her father had given her in marriage to a person whom she disliked. The Holy Prophet gave her option."

According to the Hanafi School the wife can exercise her option of puberty only if she is given in marriage by a guardian other than her father or grandfather. The marriage of a minor under consent of father or grandfather is held to be good on the assumption that a marriage thus contracted is in the best interest of the child and therefore she cannot repudiate it on attaining puberty unless there be good ground for such a step.

It would not be out of place to mention that in Indo-Pakistan, the provisions of Hanafi Law on the point have been modified by Dissolution of Muslim Marriages Act, 1939. Section 2, Clause VII shows still greater concern for the minor's consent. It provides that a girl can repudiate the marriage even if she is given in marriage by the father or grandfather. If she is married before attaining the age of 15 years, and the marriage is not consummated, right of repudiation can be exercised till she attains the age of 18 years. The repudiation has to be confirmed by the Court. There is also a provision to the advantage of the girl. Even after repudiation the marriage is deemed to subsist till the decree of the Court is passed, and if the husband dies in the meantime she is entitled to inherit from him.

According to Shafei and Maliki Schools of Law a maiden cannot personally contract her marriage, without the intervention of a *Wali*. Ameer Ali suggests that this is due to the presumed incapacity of the woman of the marriage contract, to settle the term and other matters of similar import, and to guard the girl from being victimized by an unscrupulous adventurer or from marrying a person morally or socially unfit for her.

Under Shia law "A woman who is adult and ôf sound mind, may be married by virtue of her own consent although the contract may not have been made or acceded to by her guardians and this, whether she be a virgin or Saibbah." But the girl who has not attained puberty is incompetent to contract herself in marriage without the consent of the father or grandfather.

Another incident of marriage which determines the status of a Muslim woman is dower.

During pre-Islamic Arabia dower was more or less a purchase price given to the father or the guardian of the woman. Moreover, the husbands used to resort to devices to avoid the liability for the payment of dower.

Islam made it obligatory to pay the dower to the wife and not to the guardian. The Quranic precept in this regard is :

> "And give unto women their dowers as a gift and if or themselves they give up thereof unto you, then eat in pleasure and profit."

If was also ordained in Qur'an that a gift once made could not be taken back :

> "And if ye intend to replace a wife by another, and he have given the one of them a talent, take not back aught therefrom, would ye take it back by slander and manifest sin."

The true nature of dower is well described by Abdur Rahim in these words : "It is not a consideration proceeding from the husband to the wife for the contract of marriage but it is an obligation imposed by the law on the husband as a mark of respect for the wife as is evident from the fact that the non-specification of dower at the time of marriage does not affect the validity of marriage."

The author of "Hedaya" also holds that the "payment of dower is enjoined by the law merely as a token of respect" for the woman. Even where no dower is expressly fixed or mentioned at the marriage ceremony, or marriage is contracted on the special condition that there would be no dower, the law confers the right of dower upon the wife. In such cases she is entitled to *Mahrul-mith*, or proper dower, which is fixed with reference to the social position of the bride's father's family.

Dower is, thus, a real settlement in favour of the wife, it is a provision for the rainy day. It strengthens the financial status of the woman so that she is not prevented from defending her rights for lack of money.

The dower also serves as a check on the capricious exercise by the husband of his unlimited power of divorce. The amount of dower to be fixed is quite in the discretion of the parties and it varies according to their status. The higher the dower agreed upon, the greater is the financial burden for the husband. Eventually the husband would think twice before pronouncing divorce, when he knows that upon divorce the whole of the dower would be payable immediately.

The wife is entitled to two types of dower—prompt and deferred. Prompt dower is payable at the time of marriage contract. The payment of prompt dower is essential to such an extent that if the husband fails to pay it, the guardian of a minor wife can refuse to allow her to be sent to her husband's house ; and similarly the wife can refuse the husband his conjugal rights, provided no consummation has taken place. The wife is entitled to maintenance (even) after refusing to have sexual intercourse with her husband, and she can go out of her husband's house for her necessities and to visit her relatives, without husband's permission, so long she is not paid her prompt dower. If the husband files a suit for restitution of conjugal rights before cohabitation, the wife can plead the non-payment of prompt dower, as a defence.

The deferred dower is payable on the dissolution of marriage by death or divorce. Wife has been given the right of deferred dower so that she may not pass the monetarily handicapped life after dissolution of marriage.

The widow's rights in respect of her dower are far-reaching. The dower ranks as a debt and the widow is treated as an unsecured creditor along with other creditors of the deceased husband. If she has obtained possession of the property of her husband in lieu of her dower "lawfully or without force of fraud", she is entitled to retain possession until dower debt is satisfied. There are conflicting opinions of various High Courts, whether the possession obtained lawfully and without force should also be "with consent—expressed or implied of the husband or his heirs. There are also conflicting opinions, whether the right of retention by widow of husband property in lieu of her dower is heritable or transferable.

It should be noted that the right of retention does not give any title to the property. She has only right to retain possession and if she is dispossessed she can sue for recovery. The title to the property is in the heirs including herself. Thus, the woman has the right to the property of the deceased husband in two capacities. In the first place she is entitled to her dower debt as a creditor along with other creditors of the deceased husband. In the second place she is an their of the deceased husband and inherits her share along with other heirs.

The wife is entitled to maintenance from her husband, even if she may have the means to maintain herself, and her husband may be without means. The wife is also entitled to maintenance even if she is in the house of her father, provided the husband did not ask her to move. Besides maintenance, she may also be entitled to a special allowance under stipulation in the marriage contract. Such allowance are called Kharcha Pandan, Guzara or Mewa Khori.

If the husband refuses to pay maintenance, the wife is entitled to sue for it. Her right may be based on the substantive law or she may sue under Sec. 488, Cr.P.C. Her right to maintenance ceases, immediately, on the death of her husband. But in case of divorce she is entitled to maintenance during *iddat* also. In case the wife is pregnant at the time of divorce is entitled to maintenance for 2 years counting from the date of divorce.

Under Sec. 2 (*ii*) of the Dissolution of Muslim Marriages Act, 1939, the wife is entitled to dissolution if the husband has failed or neglected to provide maintenance for a period of 2 years.

If the husband refuses to pay special allowance under stipulation in the marriage contract, the wife is entitled to sue for it also.

In *Khwaja Muhammad Khan* v. *Hussaini Begum* there was a contract between the father of the bridegroom and the father of the bride that in case the proposed marriage was performed the father of the bridegroom would pay the Kharcha Pandan to the bride every month. After marriage when the father of the bridegroom stopped paying the Kharcha Pandan, the bride sued him for its recovery and she was held entitled even though she was stranger to the contract.

This shows that the law has shown great regard for the wife in respect of her right to dower and maintenance and the amount of stipulated dower, maintenance and Kharcha Pandan are usually in accordance with the status of women.

Divorce :

The critics of Islam consider it a weakness of the Islamic system when it gives a right to the husband to divorce his wife even without assigning reasons therefor. Anderson remarks : "It is Islamic Law of Divorce—not polygamy—which is the major cause if suffering to Muslim women. The Muslim wife indeed has always lived, so far as the law is concerned, under theev er-present shadow of divorce, a shadow mitigated only in comparatively rare cases by certain pre-cautionery devises."

The critics, however, ignore the statistics of divorce in the Muslim world as compared with other countries which could be a clue to the understanding of the spirit and purpose of this provision of the law. However, a close examination of the institution of divorce would reveal that a Muslim is not free to exercise the right of divorce on the slightest disgust. The law in fact has put many limitations on the exercise of this power.

First of all, the teachings of the Qur'an and the traditions have rendered divorce most repellent to the Muslim world. A Muslim is permitted to pronounce divorce when there is ample justification for such an extreme measure. The Holy Qur'an enjoins a man not to seek pretext for divorcing his wife so long she is faithful to him.

> If they (namely, women) obey you, then do not seek a way against them.

The Qur'an enjoins forbearance even with a wife one does not like :

> Associate with the wives not goodness, and if ye dislike them, it may be that ye dislike a thing and God may put in abundant good in it.

The Holy Prophet of Islam has also expressed his abhorrence of divorce on various occasions. There is a tradition reported by Abn-i-Daud : "Talak is to be the most desetable before God of all permitted things."

A tradition narrated (in the Collection Dartutni) by Maaz bin Jabl is : "God has not created anything on earth which He likes better than emancipation of slaves, nor He has created anything which He dislikes more than divorce."

Other traditions in this regard are :

> "Marry but do not divorce, because God does not like men and women who relish variety in sexual intercourse. The curse of God rests on him who repudiates his wife capriciously."

Thus Islam discourages divorce in principle and permit only when it is altogether impossible for the parties to live together in peace and harmony. It avoids the greaten evil by choosing a lesser one.

Before the parties are driven to the extremity of divorce for unvoidable reasons, the Qur'an enjoins all lawful means to be adopted for avoiding a breach.

In respect of the adoption of courses that tend to make reconciliation possible. Holy Qur'an says :

> Virtuous women are obedient, careful during the husband's absence, because God hath cf them been careful. But those for whose refractoriness he have cause to fear, chide, remove them into beds apart ; and chastise them but if they are obedient to you, then seek not occasion against them : Verily God is High and Great. And if ye fear a breach between husband and wife, send a Judge out of his family, and a judge out of her family ; if they are desirous of agreement, God will effect a reconciliation between them ; for God is Knowing and Apprised of all.

The Holy Prophet of Islam is reported to have said, "Feed thy wife as thou feedest thyself. Clothe her as thou clothest thyself, strike not on her face, separate not from her except within the house but if she persists in her refractoriness...being with admonitions, and awaken in her the fear of God the Most High ; if she does not submit, banish her from thy bed, and converse not with her three days, if still she refuses to mend her manners, beat her but not so as to leave any mark on her person, as would be the case of a rod were used, for the object is to correct her ; and not to destroy her. Should this course fail to amend matters, let the case be referred to two Muslim arbitrators, free and just, one chosen from the family of each of the parties ; and they shall see whether in the particular case reconciliation or separation is desirable ; and their decision shall be binding upon them both."

The provision for mediation is only made in the case where the wife, without cause furnished by her husband, becomes intolerant of his authority and refuses to her marital obligations. There is no such provision in the case where the wife fears unjust treatment, or hatred, avoidance or shunning amounting to detention, on the part of her husband. The omission cannot be without significance. Where the wife is an injured party, there is first an injunction that an attempt at reconciliation should be made by the parties, having cleared their hearts of selfishness, and acting solely with a desire to do good and to avoid evil. On the other hand, where the wife's determined disobedience and non performance of her marital obligations is the cause of estrangement, there being no fault in the husband, he can very well deal with the case under his unilateral power of divorce, but it is enjoined that there should be first a reference to arbitrators. This would ensure not only the sanctity and preservation of marriages against the danger that divorce may be given too lightly, but also that marriages are not reduced to contracts of unwilling slavery for the wife. The need of reference to the judicial authority of the state does not arise, for there is available the powerful influence of the elders to ensure that everything is done by the parties, which is necessary to bring about a proper and complete resolution of the difficulty. Delegation of the husband's power of divorcing his wife to the elders can likewise be ensured if it should prove necessary.

The drift and the tone of the Qur'anic injunction and the traditions point to the desirability of exercising the power of correction in three degrees. In the event of failure of all these expedients and resort to arbitrators, divorce is permitted as a last recourse.

Before discussing divorce at the instance of husband and separation at the instance of wife under Muslim Law it would be interesting to examine by the comparative study and to evaluate in brief the status of Hindu women are regards to divorce under Hindu textual law.

The institution of divorce was unknown to ancient Hindus. Manu declares, 'Neither by sale nor by desertion can a wife be released from her husband. Let mutual fidelity continue till death. The Hindu marriage was treated as a sacrament, and hence indissoluble. The husband in case of disagreement with the wife, could at the most supersede her by a second wife, but could not divorce the first one. The wife, however, under no circumstance, could obtain divorce or separation. The ideal patiwarta not merely implied fidelity to the husband but made the service to the husband the only duty of the wife and her only purpose in life. As a river merging itself in the ocean loses its identity, so a wife was supposed to merge her individuality with that of her husband.

There was no question of raising a word against him even when he was found to be ill-tempered, vicious, or a drunkard. Though the institution of divorce was unknown in the ancient Hindu society yet we find instances where a woman was given a right to obtain divorce. As indicated by some of the commentators and Smriti writers such as Narada. Madhova Ragunandan and Prthshastrya of Kautilya mentioned certain circumstances under which a wife could obtain such divorce.

The wife was attached to the husband not only during his life-time, but even after his death. Naturally, on the death of the husband the wife accompanied him to the other world by immolating herself on the pyre of her husband. This custom of *Sati* had become deep-rooted in the Hindu Society. Raja Ram Mohan Roy and Lord Wiiliam Bentinck tried to stop this practice in 1829 A.D. by passing an Act. Moreover, widow was denied the right to remarriage. There were pitiable instances where a woman in a quite young age became widow and during the rest of her life she was compelled to remain a widow.

Now, let us examine the position of Muslim women as regards to divorce at the instance of husband and separation at the instance of wife, separately.

Divorce by husband : When it comes to divorce as a last resort even then the prescribed form of divorce is a powerful check on the injudicious and arbitrary use of divorce and affords many opportunities to the parties for an amicable agreement if desired. Of the several forms of divorce approved by the Holy Prophet and recognized by law is *Talaq-i-Ahsan*. In such form of *Talaq* the following conditions have to be observed :—

1. The husband must pronounce only on *Talaq*.
2. The *Talaq* must be pronounced when the wife is in the state of purity or *tuhr*.
3. The husband must abstain from the exercise of conjugal rights after pronouncing *talaq* for the period of three *tuhrs*.

In *talaq-i-hasan* the husband is required to declare the *talaq* three times during the three successive periods of *tuhrs*. In this case when the last pronouncement is made there shall be final separation, otherwise the *talaq* shall be presumed as withdrawn.

The object of one pronouncement in *talaq-i-ahsan* or three pronouncements in *talaq-i-hasan* is to prevent permanent breach. After the first pronouncement the husband may subsequently, when better sense prevails, revoke the *talaq*, if he has pronounced if from the caprice or in a moment of excitement.

Similarly, there are two reasons regarding the condition of the pronouncement of *talaq* during *tuhr*. Firstly, the physical disability during menstruation leads her sometimes to act and behave in a manner which she disapproves on becoming clean. Secondly, that the normal sexual relations between the husband and wife are suspended for the time she undergoes her monthly course and sexual relations are commonly the basis of love and amity between husband and wife. It is possible that the couple may resume their normal attitude to each other and forget their quarrels when their sexual relations are restored after the period of menstruation, is over. This would be in conformity with nature.

There is a Qur'anic precept enjoining Muslim to divorce their wives during the period of *tuhr* :

> "O Prophet when ye do divorce women, divorce them at their special times."

"There are also some traditions to this effect : Abdullah bin Omar divorced his wife when she was having her monthly period. His father reported the matter to the Holy Prophet who became very angry and ordered that Abdullah should revoke his divorce and wait until his wife is clean, after which he is free to do as he like.

On another occasion the Prophet is reported to have said: "You should wait for '*tuhr*' (period of cleanliness), then pronounce divorce during one '*tuhr*' and another during the second. During the third '*tuhr*' you should decide finally and either retain your wife or finally divorce her."

Commentators point out that the purpose of the Qur'anic behests and tradition is to avoid rash and hasty decisions on the part of the husband to pronounce *talaq*. By fixing a long period of abstinence, the husband has been given an opportunity to reconsider his decision about the divorce ; he may repent ; will have the chance to exercise the right of return before the expiry of the term.

If, however, the parties fail to take advantage of the prescribed procedure aimed at postponement of separation and the husband pronounces the divorce for the third time the marriage is dissolved definitely. The divorced wife is forthwith rendered unlawful to the husband, and he cannot remarry her unless a particular procedure is adopted. The procedure laid down in the Holy Qur'an is as follows :

> If the busband divorces her a third time, it is not lawful for him to take her again, until she shall have married another husband ; and if he also divorce her then shall no blame attach to them if they return to each other, thinking that they can keep within the bounds fixed of God.

In accordance with the above verse the woman who is divorced after observing *Iddat* should remarry another person. The second husband should divorce her after consummation of the marriage. Thereupon the wife should again observe the period of *Iddat* and only to remarry her first husband. This serves as a very potent check or divorcing the woman simply on whims and momentary anger, and then withdrawing the divorce at their pleasure. Tyabji observes that this rule "did away with a great engine of oppression in the hands of husbands in the pre-Islamic Arabia who could keep their wives in species of perpetual bondage, pretending to take them back after repeated divorce, merely for the purpose of preventing the wives from remarrying and from seeking the then much needed protection of husband." Ameer Ali is also of the view "that this rule was framed with the object of restraining of the frequency of divorce in Arabia."

As a matter of fact even in our socially advanced world, no man would like to marry a girl again who had been consummated by someone else also. Therefore, before giving a *talaq* a man has to consider the pros and cons of his action. In fact, this provision serves a detterent and penalty for the husbands who are prone to act rashly without considering the consequences of their action.

The wife is protected against the capricious use of *talaq* by the husband to a great extent. If the husband divorces the wife irrevocably during *marzul maut* (death illness) and dies during the period of *iddat* of the wife, the wife is entitled to inherit from him. The rationale behind the rule seems to be that the husband cannot divorce the wife capriciously merely to deprive her of the right of inheritance.

Thus it can be concluded by saying, that in the first instance Islam had discouraged divorce in principle and permitted it only when it becomes altogether impossible for the parties to live together. The exercise of the right of divorce is subject to so many restrictions and limitations that it cannot be used capriciously and intensively.

It is suggested that the rule of Hanafi Law allowing divorce under the influence of intoxication and intimidation is quite unjust and should be abolished. It is suggested by Ameer Ali and Abdur Rahim that in such cases the Court should, on grounds of equity, apply the Shafi and not their own law when the parties happen to be Hanafis. The right course is to abolish it through statute as it is done in Middle East countries. In the Ottoman Law of Family Rights that the formulas of repudiation uttered under the influence of intoxication or compulsion is no longer given any legal effect. Similarly, other Muslim countries like Syria and Morocco abolished this unjust rule through legislative enactments.

The Syrians have introduced a provision that where wife is divorced without adequate cause and shows that she will suffer damage and poverty as a result, the Court may order her husband to pay her limited sum (in addition to the maintenance to which she is entitled in Hanafi Law for the duration of her *iddat*) by way of compensation. The Tunisians have gone still futher by providing, that the divorce will be recognized only if effected in a Court of Law, which always orders financial compensation where either party unilaterally insists on ending the marriage without such justification as the Code allows. It is suggested that in Pakistan, a Muslim divorced woman should be allowed maintenance till she remarries as a matter of compensation. The quantum of allowance should be fixed as the Court deems fit in accordance with the financial conditions of the parties.

The Pakistan Government through an Ordinance has trammelled and curtailed the arbitrary power of the husband to divorce his wife to a great extent. It has abolished the practice of disapproved form of *talaq*. Moreover, it has been made mandatory that the notice of *talaq* should be given in writing to the Chairman of Union Council. The *talaq* shall be effected only if the efforts of reconciliation finally fails.

Repudiation by wife : In view of the husband's wide power of divorce, sale, an eminent scholar has raised the issue of inequality of two parties in regard of obtaining a divorce. This inequality is more seeming than real.

We have already discussed the rights given to the husband for securing a release from the marriage bond and the conditions attached thereto. Similar rights have been given by Islam to the wife to enable her to get rid of an unpleasant husband and to select another husband of agreeable nature. Islam does not force on the spouses a life devoid of harmony and happiness and if the parties cannot live together as they should, it permits separation. The wife can demand divorce in different ways, such as by *Khula*, under Dissolution of Mulsim Marriages Act, 1939, and *Tafwiz*.

(*i*) *KHULA* : *Khula is* a repudiation with consent and at the instance of the wife in which she agrees to give a consideration to the husband for her release from the marital tie. The Qur'anic behest in this regard is :

(1) Divorcement is twice : thereafter either retaining her reputably, or letting her off kindly. And it is not allowed unto you to take away what ye have given them, except the twain fear that they may not observe the bonds of Allah, then no blame is on the twain for that wherewith she ransometh herself. There are the bonds of Allah, then verily they are the wrongdoer.

(2) It is not proper that you should take back what you have bestowed on your women. But when both are afraid that they will not be able to observe the limits prescribed by God Almighty, no sin is imputed to the wife or husband respecting the matter on him of which she has released herself.

There is also a tradition on the point : The wife of Thabit-abne-Qais came to the Holy Prophet and said, 'O Messenger of God, I am angry with Thabit of his temper not religion, on which account I wish to be separated from.' The Holy Prophet said, 'Will you give back to Thabit the garden which he gave to you as your settlement ?' She said 'yes'. Then the Holy Prophet said to Thabit, 'Take your garden and divorce her at once.'

On the basis of the above behests and traditions the principle is laid down by the Fatwa-i-Alamgiri, the Raddul Mukhtar and other eminent commentaries on Muslim Law to the effect that when married parties disagree and are apprehensive that they cannot observe the bounds prescribed by the divine law the woman can release herself from the tie by giving up some property in return in consideration of which the husband is to give her a *Khula* and when they have done this a *talaqul-bain* takes place. In Sunni Law, a *Khula* obtained under compulsion is valid. Similarly, *Khula* obtained under the influence of drink is valid provided there was knowledge of what was being done.

Thus in *Vadabe-Vitel Ismail* v. *Obadael Beyabuth Umal* a woman claimed divorce on grounds which she failed to establish but the husband at the suggestion of the Court reluctantly agreed to a *Khula* divorce on terms to be settled by the Qazi. It was held that the *Khula* was valid though under compulsion.

On the other hand if a woman is compelled or forced to accept *Khula*, a *talaq* takes place without the wife having to pay anything. In a case decided by the Qazi in Algeria reported by Ameer Ali, the wife was so cruelly treated that she was compelled to release herself from the marriage by paying her husband 400 francs. In fact, the husband forced her to take a *Khula*. After the divorce she sued the husband for 400 francs which she had been compelled to pay him. The Qazi, on the facts being proved as stated above upheld the divorce and ordered the husband to pay back 400 francs to his wife. In accordance with Qur'anic behests this right is extended to woman due to the aversion being on the part of the wife, and not on that of the husband, it would be abominable in him to take anything from her, because the Holy Qur'an says :

> If ye be desirous of changing (that is, repudiating one wife and marrying another), take not from her anything.

As regards the question of consideration, there are conflicting opinions amongst the jurists. The Egyptian Code of Hanafi Law, Art. 275 lays down : "A *Khula* repudiation can validly take place before or after consummation of the marriage, and without payment of compensation by the wife.

A Full Bench of the Lahore High Court has held that a woman can claim *Khula* as a matter of right provided that she is ready to restore of what she has received in consideration of marriage. If the dissolution is due to some fault on the part of the husband, there is no need of any restitution. If the husband is not in any way at fault, there has to be restoration of property received by the wife and ordinarily it will be of the whole of the property but the judge may take into consideration reciprocal benefits received by the husband and continuous living together also may be a benefit received. The jurisdiction of the Qazi do dissolve marriage in cases of *Shiqaq* is limited only by what is stated in the Qur'an, *i.e.*, "if you fear a breach" which means that there is real discord between the parties and in case of *Khula* by the words "if you fear that they will not observe the limits of God" while effecting separation, the Qazi adjusts the financial matters so as to direct a partial restoration of the benefits recieved by the wife.

(*ii*) *DISSOLUTION OF MUSLIM MARRIAGES ACT, 1939:* In India and Pakistan the wife is entitled to dissolution of marriage under the Dissolution of Muslim Marriages Act, VIII of 1939. It may be noted that the grounds for dissolutions of marriage incorporated in this Act have been adopted with a slight adaptation from the Maliki School.

Section 2 of the Act extends certain grounds to obtain divorce from the husband through Court. The Act provides fairly complete list of the grounds upon which a Muslim wife may obtain a judicial separation.

The grounds under which a woman can seek divorce under the Act are as follows:

(*i*) that the whereabouts of the husband have not been known for a period of four years;

(*ii*) that husband has neglected or has failed to provide for her maintenance for a period of two years;

(*iii*) that the husband has been sentenced to imprisonment for a period of seven years or upwards;

(*iv*) that the husband has failed to perform without reasonable cause, his marital obligations for a period of three years;

(*v*) that the husband was impotent at the time of marriage and continued to be so;

(*vi*) that the husband has been insane for a period of two years or is suffering from leprosy or a virulent venereal disease;

(*vii*) that she, having been given in marriage by her father or other guardian before she attained the age of fifteen years (now sixteen years in Pakistan) repudiated the marriage before attaining the age of eighteen years:

Provided that the marriage has not been consummated;

(*viii*) That the husband treats her cruelty, that is to say:

(*a*) habitually assaults her or makes her life miserable by cruelty of conduct even if such conduct does not amount to physical ill-treatment, or

(*b*) associates with woman of evil repute or leads an infamous life, or

(*c*) attempts to force her to lead an immoral life; or

(*d*) disposes of her property or prevents her exercising legal rights over it; or

(*e*) obstructs her in the observance of her religious possession or practice; or (*f*) If he has more wives than one, does not treat her equitably in accordance with the injunctions of the Qur'an ;

(*ix*) on any other ground which is recognized as valid for the dissolution of marriage under Muslim Law.

In Clause (*ii*) the word 'neglect' implies the existence of a right and a duty, the right of the wife to maintenance and the duty cast on the husband to provide her maintenance. Where-ever there are rights there are obligations also. If it is the right of the wife to obtain maintenance from the huband she is also under obligation to submit herself to the husband, to live with him and to obey his lawful orders.

Muslim Law recognizes the consent of a woman as an indispensable incident of a valid marriage. Without consent a marriage is void and a marriage with consent under compulsion is voidable. Thus a woman, who is *sui juris*, cannot be married to any person without her own express consent. Sometimes, the woman can be given in marriage by a guardian. But in that case also the consent of the woman is material so much so that on attaining puberty she can exercise the right known as 'option of puberty' and repudiate the marriage. There are also traditions to the effect that on various occasions, the Holy Prophet either annulled the marriage or gave option to the girl if the marriage was contracted without her consent.

Khaus-bin-Khejan reported that her father gave her in marriage, after she became a widow. She disliked it and came to the Holy Prophet. He annulled the marriage. Ibne-Abbas reported that a virgin grown-up girl came to the Holy Prophet of Allah and narrated that her father had given her in marriage to a person whom she disliked. The Holy Prophet gave her option.

According to Hanafi School the wife can exercise her option of puberty only if she is given in marriage by a guardian other than her father or grandfather. The marriage of a minor under consent of a father or grandfather is held to be good on the assumption that a marriage thus contracted is in the best interest of the child and therefore she cannot repudiate it on attaining puberty unless there be good ground for such a step.

In Pakistan, the provisions of Hanafi Law on the above point have been modified by Dissolution of Muslim Marriages Act, 1939, Section 2, Clause VII, which shows still greater concern for the minor's consent. It provides that a girl can repudiate the marriage even if she is given in marriage by the father or grandfather. If she is married before attaining the age of 16 years, and the marriage is not consummated, right of repudiation can be exercised till she attains the age of 18 years.

The option of puberty may be exercised at any time before the age of 18 years by the girls withholding of her consent to the marriage. The withholding of consent may be expressed in different ways : indication by the institution of a suit for the dissolution of marriage ; re-marriage with another husband ; by serving a notice on the husband through an attorney or publishing a notice in the newspaper that the option of puberty has been exercised. It may be manifested by the mere institution of a suit for dissolution of marriage which eventually be dismissed in default under Order IX, rule 3, C.P.C. or by making categorical averment that option of puberty has been exercised.

It is immaterial whether she was given in marriage by her uncle or grandfather. Since according to the prevalent law where a minor has been given in marriage by her father or other guardian may repudiate her marriage before she attained the age of 18 years provided the marriage has not been consummated. If the consummation is by force or before she reached the age of 16, then the wife is entitled to exercise the right of option of puberty.

Muslim Law prescribes no limitation for obtaining a judicial decree on the ground of option of puberty.

Cruelty is another ground for obtaining dissolution. In a case where the husband is living with another wife in the same house, and does not share the bed of the (applicant) wife, Chief Justice Murshid held, that the relationship between husband and wife (applicant) is such as would amount to cruelty to the wife to continue the martial tie. If the marriage is not dissolved it would be impossible for the wife to live within the limits of *Shariat*. Islam does not ignore the prepensities of human nature. Although actual habitual cruetly may not be established, dissolution can be granted when considering the circumstances it would be cruel to the wife to continue the marriage.

If the husband levels a false charge of adultery, the wife is entitled to obtain dissolution. It is not the right of the husband to defeat a claim for dissolution based on a false charge of adultery by just saying that he would withdraw the charge. A retraction, in order that it may be effective, has in the first place, to be sincere. In the second place, the husband has to satisfy the Court that he brought the charge *bona fide* and not carelessly. A retraction can be of no help to the husband if his sole object is to defeat the suit of the wife. A true and effective retraction takes place when a husband comes to the Court and says, "I brought this charge because I was misled by certain circumstances. The circumstances were such that one would reasonably come to the conclusion that my wife was guilty. I have found now that, in fact, she is altogether innocent. I am very sorry. I withdraw the charge." In such case, the Court allows the retraction because the husband has not behaved in an improper manner at all and it was simply a case of *bona fide* misapprehension.

(*iii*) *TAFWIZ* : The third way for the wife to demand divorce is through *talaq-i-tafwiz*. As the marriage is a civil contract under Muslim Law, the wife is entitled to dictate the terms and conditions, the wife would pronounce divorce upon herself has been held to be valid, provided first, that the option is not absolute and unconditional and secondly, that the conditions are reasonable and not opposed to public policy.

An ante-nuptial agreement by a Muslim husband that he would pay separate maintenance to his wife in case of disagreement and that the wife should have the power to divorce in case of failure to pay maintenance for a certain period is not opposed to public policy and is enforceable. Where in the course of two years the husband did not regularly pay the wife her maintenance but remitted in all a sum of rupees 46 only, it cannot be said that there was sufficient compliance of the terms of *Kabirnama* which stipulated monthly maintenance charges of rupees 15 and, therefore, the wife was entitled to divorce her husband by exercising the right of *talaq-i-tafwiz* given to her by the terms of *kabirnama*.

In case it is stipulated in the *kabirnama* that if the husband does not pay the prompt dower to the wife, the latter will have the option of exercising her right of divorce delegated by the husband. It was held, that the wife can validly exercise this power on failure of the husband to pay the prompt dower.

Even an agreement by which the husband authorizes the wife to divorce herself from him in the event of marrying a second wife without her consent has been repeatedly held to be both valid and irrevocable. A clause in the marriage contract, that should the husband marry another wife, the first will *ipso facto* become void, is valid provided it is so worded as to be capable of being interpreted as a contingent divorce. In *Mohd Amin* v. *Amina Bibi*, the agreement ran "I shall not marry another woman in the presence of Mst. Amina Bibi and if I do so she is to be held to have been divorced by me on account of second marriage, simultaneously with that second marriage, she will be *qatai haram* to my person and this very divorce by me in her favour would be valid and legal." It was held that on the husband marrying second wife the first wife was validly divorced. It was also held by Justice Addison that an agreement made before and after the marriage by which it is provided that the wife should be at liberty to divorce herself under certain specified conditions is valid if the conditions are of a reasonable nature and not opposed to the policy of Muslim Law.

In *Moharram Ali* v. *Ayesha Khatun*, the learned Judges held that the contention that the wife could divorce the husband on a second marriage was valid and was unaffected by S. 26, Contract Act. Tyabji says that such a conditional option is different from an agreement prohibiting the husband to marry another wife : the latter would be void according to Sharayal Islam. Ameer Ali on the other hand considers such a condition valid and says, 'even in Persia where Shia doctrines are chiefly in force, this condition is frequently imposed. Malik Shah being the first to impose it on Caliph Muhtadi to whom he gave his daughter in marriage.

The original purpose of such stipulation as observed by Schacht was to inculcate monogamy and to check indirectly the polygamy prevalent in the then Arabia. Thus, this form of delegated power to divorce was the most potent weapon in the hand of a Muslim wife to obtain her freedom without the intervention of any Court.

These are the three ways in which a wife can see dissolution of marriage at her instance. But she is not at liberty, like the husband, to get herself released by any outright declaration of divorce. In case her husband refuses to release her from marriage bond, she has to go to the Court of Law and obtain a decree in her favour. This may seem to place her at a disadvantageous position in contradistinction to her husband and may be asserted that this implies inequality of right as between husband and wife. Actually the intervention of the Court in the matter of divorce is for a fuller protection of her rights. It is possible due to certain inherent weaknesses in the women that the husband may, if he so desires, place many impediments in her way. If the state does not protect the interest of the women, then she may find herself handicapped in many ways, despite all they can be provided for the equality of man and woman. It is, therefore, in her own interest to seek the support of authority in defending and exercising her rights.

Another reason for man's superiority over woman in general is explained by Abdur Rahim in these words : "The relations between the members of the opposite sexes which marriages legalize are, however, so subtle and delicate and require such a constant adjustment involving the fate and well-being of the future generations, that in their regulation the law considers it expedient to allow the voice of one partner more or less predominance over that of the other."

It may be mentioned that if the divorce is due to a cause imputable to the husband he has to make over to her all her property and pay off the dower that may be settled upon her. But if the divorce is at the instance of the wife without any justifiable cause, she has simply to abandon her claim to the dower. "The wife thus occupies" observes Ameer Ali, "a decidedly more advantageous position than the husband."

Polygamy :

It would not be out of place to mention the institution of polygamy which has an important impact on the status of women. It has been said that by permitting polygamy, Islam has degraded the status of women. A close examination of the institution of polygamy will make the critics realise that it is not so in fact.

At the advent of Islam, the Arabs generally used to have eight or ten wives and they have often treated them badly. The Holy Qur'an ordained that a man could keep up to four wives at a time :

> "And if ye apprehend that ye may not deal justly with the orphan girls, then marry such as please you, of other women, by twos, threes or fours."

Though, polygamy was permissible by Islam, it was tolerated on the ground of necessity and was permitted under certain conditions. It became necessary to permit polygamy, "in order to provide for the many whose husbands (or prospective husbands) had died fighting for Islam.

To commentators indicate that the Qur'anic injunction permitting polygamy was revealed to guide the Muslims under the conditions which followed the battle of Uhud. In that battle out of 700 hundred Muslims 70 men had been slain. The number of males was likely to suffer a still greater diminution in the battles which had yet to be fought while the number of women would be increased with the addition of the prisoners of war.

If under such circumstances one woman was married to one man there would be surplus of women. Consequently, three alternative were left :—

(*i*) These surplus women would have to live single with consequent physical and mental ailments, or

(*ii*) To satisfy their sexual needs and economical requirements they would have to take the profession of prostitution, or

(*iii*) Every man should be allowed to marry more than one woman. In this way women could satisfy their sexual needs within the bounds of law. They could be supported economically and helped in the increase of population.

It is obvious that only the last alternative was helpful in such state of affairs. Hence, polygamy was a temporary measure in order to control the situation from much frightening evil.

Secondly, the permission of polygamy was subject to condition that one could keep four wives only when he could do full justice to them and treat them equally. The Qur'anic injuction in this regard is :

> "If you cannot deal equitably and justly with all, you shall marry only one."

Muslim doctors point out that equality signifies not merely equality of treatment in the matter of lodging, clothing and other requisites, but also complete equality in love, affection and esteem. At the same time it is also realised that due to personal likes and dislikes, prejudices and pre-dispositions complete equality in love, affection and esteem is almost impossible.

The fraility of man as such is well assessed in Qur'anic behest as :

> "Certainly you have not in your power to treat your wives with equal justice even though you fain would do so."

On the basis of the above Qur'anic behests, it is argued that the Holy Qur'an after having permitted polygamy has virtually abrogated it by providing almost an impossible condition of dealing equitably with all the wives, and at the same time declaring the man's inability to fulfil it.

This position was taken as early as the 3rd Century of *Hijrah* in the reign of Al-Mamun. The first Mutazalite doctors even held that the developed Qur'anic laws inculcated monogamy.

The Egyptian thinker, Muhammad Abduh (1849-1905 A.D.) also declared that Islam did not permit polygamy. He based his aversions against polygamy on the assumption that the Holy Prophet himself had shown preference for monogamy by his demand for equal treatment of all spouses. The provision was understood to imply both economic and emotional equality. Considering the near impossibility to achieve that impartiality, the Holy Prophet was thought to have indicated his dislike of polygamy without prohibiting it outright.

Recently this trend of thinking has found an expression in a judicial pronouncement. In *Itwari* v. *Asghari* while interpreting the Qur'anic verses, Justice Dhawan remarked that Muslim Law permitted polygamy but did not encourage it, and the Qur'anic injunction shows that in practice perfect equality of treatment on the part of the husband was for all practical purposes impossible of achievement. Hence, Muslim Law as enforced in India has considered polygamy as an institution to be tolerated but not encouraged.

It may, therefore, be concluded that Islam has tolerated polygamy on ground of necessity and permitted it only subject to certain conditions. The condition is so difficult to fulfil that it has led the Muslim doctors to observe, that polygamy is virtually abrogated by the text. And despite the recognition of polygamy as valid, there is general aversion to it in all the Muslim communities at present.

The institution of polygamy is also whittled down in almost all countries either by legal prohibition or disuse. Even in the Middle East Mutazalites by conviction are monogamous. According to them the law forbids the second union during the subsistence of prior contract.

In Turkey, Polygamy was abolished with the introduction of the Swiss Civil Code in 1926 A.D. In 1953 A.D., the Syrian Law of Personal Status provided that "the Court may withhold permission for a man who is already married to marry a second wife where it is established that he is not in a position to support them both." This was mild, however, by comparison with the Tunisian Law of Personal Status, 1957 which tersely enacted that "polygamy is prohibited."

In Pakistan polygamy has been restricted through an Ordinance. Section 6 (I) of the Muslim Family Laws Ordinance, 1961 makes it mandatory to refer the case to the Arbitration Council if any person wishes to contract second marriage during the continuance of first marriage. Clause 2 of the said section makes obligatory that the application should contain the reasons for contracting the second marriage alongwith the consent of the existing wife or wives. In case the second marriage is contracted without the permission of the Council then the persons shall be liable for imprisonment extending for a period of one year and fine up to Rs. 5,000/- or both.

Inheritance :

A woman is entitled to share in the inheritance of her parents along with her brothers, and though the proportion is different, the distinction is founded on the relative position of brother and sister. She also gets her share of inheritance from husband, offspring and other near relatives. An ante-nuptial settlement by the husband in favour of the wife is a necessary condition, and on his failure to make a settlement the law presumes one in accordance with the social position of the wife. A Muslim marriage is a civil act, needing no priest, requiring no ceremonial. The contract of marriage gives the man no power over the woman's person, beyond what the law defines, and none whatever upon her goods and property. Her rights as a mother do not depend for their recognition upon the idiosyncrasies of individual judges. Her earnings acquired by her own exertion cannot be wasted by a prodigal husband, nor can she be ill-treated with impunity by one who is brutal. She acts, if juris, in all matters which relate to herself and her property in her own individual right, without the intervention of husband or father. She can sue her debtors in the open Courts, without the necessity of joining a next friend, or under cover of her husband's name. She continues to exercise, after she has passed from her father's house into her husband's home, all the rights which the law gives to men.

Treatment with Women :

In order to understand the exact reforms introduced by Islam to elevate the position of woman, it is better to study with the background of pre-Islamic Arabia. The status of women was at an extremely low ebb. The birth of a daughter was considered as a great misfortune. Female infanticide was rampant in the Arab society. The woman was not a free-agent on contracting marriage. It was the privilege and the right of her father, brother, or other male guardian to give her in marriage to whomsoever he chose. Among the pagan Arabs a woman was considered a mere chattel ; she formed an integral part of the estate of her husband or her father, and the widows of a man descended to his son or sons by right of inheritance, as any other portion of his patrimony. There was no restriction as to the number of wives an Arab could marry. Besides unlimited number of wives, an Arab also had a number of slave girls which he could possess.

Ameer Ali says, "Among all Eastern nations of antiquity polygamy was a recognized institution. Its practice by royalty, which everywhere bore the insignia of divinity, sanctified its observance to the people". Westermarck observed, "Polygamy was permitted by most of the ancient people with whom history acquaints us, and is, in our day, permitted by several civilized nations and the bulk of the savage tribe. Among Athenians, the most civilized and most cultured of all the nations of antiquity, the wife was a mere chattel, marketable, and transferable to others, and subject of testamentary disposition. An Athenian was allowed to have any number of wives, and Demonsthenes gloried in the possession by his people of three classes of women, two of which furnished were the legal and semi legal wives".

Maulana Maududi points out that in the Hinduism, the woman stood debarred from being educated in the *Vedas*. Buddhism did not recognize salvation for the one having sex relations with woman. Christianity and Judaism looked upon woman as the source of all evil committed by man in the world. In Greece, the housewives were neither entitled to receive any education, nor training in culture, nor social rights. Only the prostitute was entitled to all these blessings. The condition in Rome, Iran, China, Egypt and other centres of human civilization was not any different. Centuries of inhuman treatment and universal contempt meted out to the woman had disgraced her in her own eyes. She herself had developed the mentality that she had no right and was not entitled to any place of honour in the world. The man considered himself to be perfectly within his right to treat her harshly, and she endured all this as part of her natural obligations. She had become slavish and prided herself on being called the "maid" of her husband ; her religion was to extol and worship him as her god and lord.

It is Islam which revolutionized this state of affairs not only legally and practically but also intellectually. Islam had indeed changed the mentalities of both the man and the woman. The concept of giving the woman her rights and a place of honour in society has in fact been created in man's mind by Islam.

The Qur'anic verses regarding the treatment with woman are as follows :

1. "Allah created you of a single soul, and from the same soul created his mate." (*4 : 1*).
2. "Allah does not distinguish between the man and the woman : What they have earned and the women according to what they earned." (*4 : 32*).
3. "Their Lord answered their prayer (and said) : 'I never let go to waste the labour of any one that works among you, whether male or female, for in My sight all of you are alike." (*3 : 195*).
4. "And those who do good works, whether men or women, provided that they are Believers, will enter into Paradise and they will not be deprived in the least of their rightful rewards." (*4 : 124*).
5. "Wives have the same rights as the husbands have on them in accordance with the well-known principles." (*2 : 228*).
6. "The man who brought up two daughters, so that they attained maturity, will appear at my side on the Day of Judgment as are my two adjacent fingers." (*Muslim*).
7. "A man of whom only daughters are born, and he brings them up properly, the same daughters will become a covering for him against Hell." (*Muslim*).

8. "The best blessing among the blessings of the world to a man is a virtuous wife." (*Nasa'i*).
9. "Two things in the world please me the most : the woman and the perfume ; and in *salat* is the solace of my eyes". (*Nasa'i*).
10. "Nothing among the choicest blessings of this world is better than a virtuous wife." (*Ibn-i-Majah*).

The Holy Prophet of Islam taught the son that the one who most deserved his respect, veneration and kind treatment after Allah and His Prophet, was his mother :

1. "A man asked : 'O Holy Prophet of Allah, who deserver to be treated well by me most of all ? The Holy Prophet said : 'Your mother'. He asked : 'Who then' ? The Holy Prophet said : 'Your mother'. He asked : 'Who then ?' The Holy Prophet said : 'Your mother'. He asked : 'Who then ?' The Holy Prophet said : 'Then your father." (*Al-Bukhari*).
2. "The woman is like a rib. If you try to straighten her, you would break her. But if you employed her usefully, you will benefit from her in spite of her crookedness." (*Al-Bukhari*).
3. "Allah has forbidden you to disobey your mothers and deprive them of their rights". (*Al-Bukhari*).

Abdullah bin 'Umar has reported that during the lifetime of the Holy Prophet the Companions treated their wives most politely for fear that a commandment concerning them might be sent down, and not until he had passed away they began talking with them freely.

The Holy Prophet had forbidden maltreatment of women. Maulana Maudoodi reports regarding a status. Once Hazrat 'Umar complained that the women had grown insolvent and sought permission to have resort to beating to set them right. The Holy Prophet granted the permission. The same day seventy women were beaten in their houses by the husbands who had long been awaiting such a permission. The next day all the women thronged the Holy Prophet's house with bitter complaints. The Holy Prophet called the people together and addressed them thus :

> "Today seventy women have visited Muhammad's house complaining against the harsh treatment of their husbands. The men who have misbehaved in that manner are certainly not the best among you."

Maulana Maududi in his book "Pardah and the Status of Woman in Islam" opined that the Islamic civilization segregates men and women and employs them respectively for the purposes Nature has created them for, affording them equai opportunities of attaining success and honour and progress in their own natural spheres. It regards both womanhood and manhood as two equally necessary components of humanity. Both are equally important for the development of civilization.

Education :

Woman is allowed to obtain education in religious and mundane branches of knowledge. Their education and cultural training has been considered as important as that of men. Maulana Maududi says that women also used to take lessons in religion and morality from the Holy Prophet along with men, though they had separate arrangements for the purpose. The wives of the Holy Prophet, especially Hazrat Alishah, not only taught women, they taught men also. Many an illustrious Companion and follower of the Companions learnt the Qur'an, *Hadith* and Islamic Jurisprudence from Hazrat Aishah. Besides educating free men and nobility, the Holy Prophet that enjoined the Muslims educate their slave-girls, too. A Tradition says :

> "If a person has a slave-girl, then he educates her liberally and trains her in the best manner and culture, then sets her free and marries her, he has a double reward (from his Lord)". (*Al-Bukhari*).

Therefore according to Islam for purposes of education there is no distinction between man and woman. But Maulana Maududi in his book entitled "Towards Understanding Islam" points out the distinction in the nature of education between man and woman as follows :

From the Islamic point of view, the right sort of education for woman is that which prepares her to become a good wife, good mother and good housekeeper. Her sphere of activity is the home. Therefore, she should be retained primarily in those branches of knowledge which make her more useful in that sphere. Besides, she needs to be educated also in those sciences which help her become a good human being, morally as well as culturally, and which widen her outlook. Thus it is obligatory for every Muslim woman to acquire knowledge and cultural training. If, however, a woman possesses extraordinary abilities of the intellect, and is desirous of acquiring higher education in the other branches of knowledge as well, Islam does not stand in her way, provided that she does not transgress the limits for her by the *Shariah*.

Woman a Human Necessity :

Allah has said :

> "All things We made in pairs". (*Al-Our'an, 51 : 49*).

It means all the parts of this great machine have been created in pairs, and all that one can see in this world is indeed the result of the mutual interaction of these pairs.

Man and woman are not only physical entities but they are living organisms also. The following verses of the Holy Qur'an depict the natural object of the sexual pair :

> "He has given wives from among yourselves to multiply you, and cattle male and female". (*ii* : *42*).
>
> "Your wives are your farms". (*2* : *223*).

As we have pointed out above, animal nature is like the base and foundation on which the superstructure of humanity has been built.

Maulana Maududi substantiate the Qur'anic injunctions on the point as follows :

1. The kind of mutual relationship, with which partners of the human pair have been endowed, has been stated as follows :

> "He created for you mates from among yourselves that you may find rest and joy in them, and created between you love and mercy". (*30* : *21*).
>
> "They are (like) a garment to you and you are (like) a garment to them". (*2* : *187*).

The verse which mentions together the creation of the pairs of man and animal also states the object of the creation of sex as propagation, but in the above verse, a higher function of sex in man has been indicted. That is, the mutual relation of a human pair should not only be of sexual nature : it should also be a relation of love and sympathy and a relation of the inclination of the heart and soul. The two partners should be the real partners with each other, who can share each other's grief and joy. They should have such a close fellow feeling and abiding companionship between them as exists between the dress and the body. This relation between the sexes is the bedrock on which the human civilization is built. The words "that you may find rest and joy in them" allude to the fact that woman is the source of peace and comfort for man and that the natural function of the woman is to provide for the man a place of peace and comfort in this world, which is ridden with struggle, toil and hardship. This is the home life of man whose significance and importance has been overlooked by the Westerners in pursuit of material gains. The fact, however, is that this aspect of life is as important and necessary as any other aspect of civilization for the well-being of the social and community life of man.

2. This sex relation not only demands mutual love between the male and the female but also it demands that they should

have a deep spiritual relation with their offspring, the direct result of their sex relationship. The Divine Will has endowed man, and especially the woman, with such a physical structure and natural course of pregnancy and suckling that the love of offspring becomes her very nature. The Holy Qur'an says :

> "His mother bears him with much pain and he is not weaned before he is two years of age." (*31* : *14*).

> "With much pain his mother bears him, and with much pain she brings him into the world. He is born and weaned in thirty months." (*46* : *15*).

The man also loves his offspring though his love is not as intense as of the mother.

> "Men are tempted by the lure of women and offspring." (*3* : *14*).

This natural love helps to establish blood and marital relations. From these relations then spring up families and clans and nations whose inter-relations give birth to civilization.

> "It was He Who created man from water and gave him kindred of blood and or marriage." (*25* : *54*).

> "Man" We have created you from a male and a female and divided you into nations and clans that you may be able to recognise one another." (*49* : *13*).

Thus the ties of blood and the relations of descent and marriage provide indeed the very basic and natural foundation for the human society. And the strength of these relations depends on the certainty and indubitability of parentage and purity of descent.

3. Another demand of the human nature is that if a person leaves something behind him from the fruits of his lifelong labours and toil, he wishes it to go to his offspring and near relations with whom he is bound in ties of blood all his life.

> "......according to the Book of Allah, those who are bound by ties of blood are nearest to one another (in the matter of inheritance)". (*8* : *75*).

> "Allah does not regard your adopted sons as your own sons." (*33* : *4*).

This shows how important the purity of descent is for the purpose of the division of inheritance.

Position of Woman in Islamic Society :

Before the advent of Islam the status of woman was at an extremely low ebb : even the birth of a daughter was frowned upon as a great misfortune. Female infanticide was rampant in the Arab society and it was notoriously common practice to bury a female child as soon as it was born. This inhuman custom was most prevalent among the tribes of Koraish and Kendah.

The woman was not a free-agent in contracting marriage. This was under the complete dominion of her male relations. It was the privilege and the right of her father, brother, or other male guardian to give her in marriage to whomsoever he chose. Even the guardian of the bride used to take the dower himself, and in this sense the contract of marriage virtually amounted to a sale. To quote Ameer Ali, "Among the pagan Arabs, a woman was considered a mere chattel ; she formed an integral part of the estate of her husband or her father, and the widows of a man descended to his son or sons by right of inheritance, as any other portion of his partimony."

There was even a practice of marrying women by force. This often happened on the death of a man leaving widows. His sons or other heir would immediately cast a sheet of cloth on each of the widows (excepting her natural mother), and this was a symbol that he had annexed them to himself. This custom was described as the inheriting of a deceased man's widows by his heirs, who, in such cases, would divide them among themselves like goods.

Mahmudullah Jung mentions three peculiar forms of marriages prevalent in the pre-Islamic Arabia. He cites three traditions of the Holy Prophet in this regard :

1. "A number of men, not more than ten, used to cohabit with a woman. When she conceived and delivered a child, then she would sent for all these men, who were bound to attend. She told them, 'you remember our agreement, now I have brought forth a child and I am of opinion that this child is so and so's issue' the named father had to recognize the paternity.'
2. "Many men used to have sexual intercourse with a woman, who would not refuse any visitors. When such a woman had issue born to her, then her 'frequent' visitors would assemble, and by physiognomistic test used to decide, who was the father of the child."
3. "A custom was that a husband would say to his wife after the termination of her monthly courses, send for such a man and have intercourse with him and the husband would keep away from her, until she had conceived by that man, and thereafter would return to her. This was done with a view to obtain a noble seed."

Abdul Rahim has also referred to some customs in the pre-Islamic Arabia relating to matrimonial ties and determination of paternity of children born as a result of such relations. Basing his classification on the authority of Kashful-Ghumma, as has mentioned four types of marriages. Out of these form of marriage, one is the type that is sanctioned by Islam, where man asks another for the hand of the latter's word or daughter, and then marries her with dower.

Muta or temporary marriage was also a common practice. As stated in the Fathul-Qadir, "When a man came to a village and he had no acquaintance there (to take care of his house), he would marry a woman for as long as he thought he would stay so that she would be partner in bed and take care of his house." A similar report in Al-Timrizi says, "*Muta* was only in the beginning of Islam. A man would come to a town in which he had no acquaintances, then he would keep (marry) a woman for the time that he would stay there, and she would look after him and cook his food for him." This form of 'Legalized prostitution' was tolerated by the Holy Prophet in the earlier days of Islam. But later on he prohibited it.

There was no restriction as to the number of wives an Arab could marry. Besides unlimited number of wives, an Arab also had a number of slave-girls which he could possess.

An Arab was absolutely free to release himself from marital tie. The husband could pronounce *talak* without assigning any reason or without any particular procedure. Some other forms of divorce were *Ila, Zihar* and *Khula*. *Illa* was common custom among the pagan Arabs; under which the husband took a vow of abstinence that he would have nothing to do with his wife. The wife had no voice in the matter. Custom recognized no right on her part to question her husband's faculty to divorce her in this manner.

Zihar was also a popular practice with pagan Arabs to divorce their wives. They called their wives like the back of their mothers or sisters. The calling of these words immediately disconnected their marital tie and had the effect of an irrevocable divorce. While describing this practice Ameer Ali remarks, "The frequency of repudiations by injurious assimilations had assumed a mischievious magnitude at the time of the Holy Prophet's appearance and had tended to degrade the morality of the Arab tribes beyond any other custom.

Islam has recognized woman as a free and responsible member of the society and has assigned an important position to her. Qur'an has spoken about women in these words :

> "They (the wives) are a garment for you and you are a garment for them".

It has been interpreted to mean that just as a garment hides one's nakedness, the husband and wife, by entering into marriage relation, secure each other's chastity.

The husband has been instructed to use the authority granted him over the wife with discretion in a large hearted and magnanimous manner. The Qur'an says :

> "Treat your women kindly" and "Forget not magnanimity in your mutual dealing".

The Holy Prophet said : "The best among you are those who are good to their wives and kind to their people".

Islam does hot give only moral instructions. If the husband abuses his authority the wife reserves every right to have recourse to the law. The laws of marriage are so framed by the Holy Prophet that they ensure the permanence of marriage relations, without impairing individual freedom. The wife has an individual personality of her own and retains her distinct individuality. She never assumes her husband's name. Coverture has no place in the Muslim marriage. The woman is regarded as an entity in herself. Even after marriage she does not cease to be a separate member of the society, and her existence does not merge in that of her husband. She retains her own property. She is empowered to alienate and dispose of her property herself, to enter into contracts and agreements on her own account, and to sue her debtors in the open Court without the necessity of joining a next friend or under cover of her husband's name.

Muslim Law recognises the consent of women as an indispensable incident of a valid marriage. Muslim jurists agree in holding that a marriage without consent is void and a marriage with consent under compulsion is invalid. Thus, a woman, who is *sui juris*, cannot be married to any person without her own express consent. Sometimes, the woman can be given in marriage by a guardian. But in that case also the consent of the woman is material so much so that on attaining puberty she can exercise the right known as 'option of puberty' and repudiate the marriage. There are also traditions to the effect that on various occasions, the Holy Prophet either annulled the marriage or gave option to the girl if the marriage was contracted without her consent. Islam made it obligatory to pay the dower to the wife and not to the guardian. The Qur'anic precept in this regard is : "And give unto women their dowers as a gift and if of themselves they give up sought thereof unto you, then eat in pleasure and profit." The true nature of dower is well described by Abdur

Rahim in these words: "It is not a consideration proceeding from the husband to the wife for the contract of marriage but It is an obligation imposed by the law on the husband as a mark of respect for the wife as is evident from the fact that the non-specification of dower at the time of marriage does not effect the validity of marriage.

The wife is entitled to maintenance from her husband, even if she may have the means to maintain herself, and her husband may be without means. The wife is also entitled to maintenance even if she is in the house of her father, provided the husband did not ask her to move.

In the laws which the Arabian Prophet promulgated he strictly prohibited the custom of conditional marriages, and though at first temporary marriages were tacitly allowed, in the third year of the *Hejira* even these were forbidden. Prophet Mohammad secured to women, in his system, rights which they had not before possessed; he allowed them privileges the value of which will be more fully appreciated as time advances. He placed them on a footing of perfect equality with men in the exercise of all legal powers and functions. He restrained polygamy by limiting the maximum number of contemporaneous marriages, and by making absolute equity towards all obligatory on the man. It is worthy of note that the clause in the Qur'an which contains the permission to contract four contemporaneous marriages, is immediately followed by a sentence which cuts down the significance of the preceding passage to its normal and legitimate dismensions. The passage runs thus, "You may marry two, three, or four wives, but not more." The subsequent lines declare, "but if you cannot deal equitable and justly with all, you shall marry only one." The extreme importance of this proviso, bearing especially in mind the meaning which is attached to the word "quity" (*adl*) in the Qur'anic teachings, has not been lost sight of the great thinkers of the Muslim world *Adl* signifies not merely equality of treatment in the matter of lodgment, clothing and other domestic requisites, but also complete equity in love, affection and esteem. As absolute justice in matters of feeling is impossible, the Qur'anic prescription amounted in reality to a prohibition. This view was propounded as early as the Third Century of the *Hejira.* In the reign of al-Mamun, the first Mu'tazilite doctors taught that the developed Qur'anic laws inculcated monogamy. And though the cruel persecution of the mad bigot, Mutawakkil, prevented the general diffusion of their teachings, the conviction is gradually forcing itself on all sides, in all advanced Muslim communities, that polygamy is as much opposed to the teachings of Prophet Mohammad as it is to the general progress of civilised and true culture.

Maulana Maududi in his book 'Purdah and the Status of Woman in Islam' have said that it was the Holy Prophet of Islam who first taught the world that woman is as much a human being as man.

The high places of honour and distinction that man can attain by virtue of his faith and righteous deeds are also attainable by woman. If a man can become Ibrahim bin Adham, nothing can prevent a woman from becoming Rabi'ah Basriah.

1. "Their Lord answered their prayer (and said) : 'I never let go to waste the labour of any one that works among you, whether male or female, for in My sight all of you are alike". (*3* : *195*).

2. "And those who do good works, whether men or women, provided that they are Believers, will enter into Paradise and they will not be deprived in the least of their rightful rewards". (*4* : *124*).

Then it was the Holy Prophet of Islam who warned the man and infused the feeling in the woman that she had the same rights on him as he had upon her.

"Wives have the same rights as the husbands have on them in accordance with the well-known principle. (*2* : *228*).

Again it was the Holy Prophet of Islam who raised the woman from disgrace and shame to the place of honour and dignity. He told the father that the birth of a daughter did not bring him any shame ; bringing her up and educating her was rather a means of his salvation.

1. "The man who brought up two daughters, so that they attained maturity, will appear at my side on the Day of Judgment as are my two adjacent fingers". (*Muslim*).

2. "A man of whom only daughters are born, and he brings them up properly, the same daughters will become a covering up him against Hell". (*Muslim*).

3. "The best blessing among the blessings of the world to a man is a virtuous wife". (*Nasai*).

4. "Two things in the world please me the most : the woman and the perfume ; and in *salat* is the solace of my eyes". (*Nasa'i*).

5. "Nothing among the choicest blessings of this world is better than a virtuous wife". (*Ibn-i-Majah*).

ADMINISTRATION

Power a Trust :

It is one of the most important basic principles of the Islamic State that man takes every thing in trust for Allah in Whom all dominion rests, and that he was merely the usufructuary of all he possessed. The Holy Qur'an on many occasions lays down that it is Allah Who is the dispenser of authority and He could therefore change possession and hand over authority to whoever He likes. Man is simply a beneficiary and whatever he holds he does so in favour of the Divine Being, in effect, in favour of the whole community. It is due to the very reason that Prophet Muhammad was the spiritual lord of the whole of Arabia but he continued to live as the most lowly. He preferred coarse bread to rich vainds which some of those around him could relish, would dress in patched clothes and would ask his daughter Hazrat Fatima to be content with a stone grinder, a bucket and a piece of rope as her marriage portion. The Prophet has said in unambiguous words that he was merely the treasurer and distributor and it was Allah alone who dispensed gifts of any kind. The man who was master of the whole of Arabia left "neither a dinar nor a dirham nor a camel nor a slave, male or female" as his legacy, and when he died even his coat of mail was found to be mortgaged with a Jew for thirty dirhams ! It is impossible to understand why the Prophet wore the coarsest of garments, ate the coarsest of food and lived the life of the commonest man even when he exercised supreme authority over the whole Peninsula such as no one has ever done since, except when we realised his belief that every thing he possessed really belonged to Allah and that he was a mere trustee.

According to Mr. H. K. Sherwani : This makes it quite clear that the Islamic ruler in the mundane sense is different from the 'Sovereign' as evolved later by European politicians and political scientists, for according to the Islamic doctrine no person can be an autocrat The very basis of political power in this sense is delegation, *wilayah,* and this obviously entails responsibility. Moreover the idea of absolute property either in political or personal sense in foreign to the Islamic spirit for every thing is owned by God and therefore by the community in the practical sense, and is held in trust by the person using it. This applies to all those who exercise political power.

When all the lands from Egypt to Iran and even beyond that were under the control of Caliph Hazrat Umar, he lived the life, not of the ruler of a vast Empire but as a true servant of Allah and of His people.

Selection of an Administrator :

Allah does not exercise His authority directly in political matters but delegates it to human beings. As a matter of fact the concept of the supremacy of Allah and the vicegerency of man rests on the principle that Allah exercises his powers and authority through human exercises agency and that there should be uniformity in the behaviour for the vicegerents as have faith and are prone to do good deeds, for without this even an attempt at obedience to the Universal Laws of Nature would not be possible. The Holy Qur'an enjoins : "Allah has promised such of you as believe and do good that He will surely make them to succeed (the present rulers) on the earth." Therefore it is quite evident that the process of vicegerency is not a make believe but Allah has promised that He would delegate His powers of earthly sovereignty to those who believe in the Universal Law of Nature and who do good deeds. It means that the totality of earthly power is to be exercised by those who have proved by their ways that this would not go against the basic principles of universal conduct such as equality of man, humanitarianism, centralization, discipline, humility, self-sacrifice and a number of other qualities spread throughout the Holy Qur'an. It is not that Holy Qur'an completely rules out certain standards prescribed for the ruler. We find best example of such delegation of power when the first Caliph Hazrat Abu Bakar who declared on his death-bed that he had been appointed a *wali* of the community, and which is quite a community with the famous formula of obedience as enunciated in the Holy Qur'an, "Obey Allah and obey the Holy Prophet and those from among you who possess authority" entails delegation. It follows that the selection of the ruler can only be made through the agency of the community which is empowered to elect its chief.

Part (4)

The Application of Islamic Teachings to Socio-Economic Development in the 20th Century

The economic problem which we are facing nowadays has become the centre of our intellectual life which had never before come to so much prominence or assumed the importance it does today. According to Maulana Maududi who in his address delivered in the Muslim Universrsity, Aligarh on 20th October, 1941 said that the main reason for the difficulty encountered in understanding and correctly solving the economic problem of man is that some people look at this problem from the point of view of economics alone ; others exaggerate its importance and declare it to be the whole problem of life, still others wish to build a complete philosophy of life and the whole system of morality, culture, and society on economic foundations only and in this manner they have reduced man's position in this world to that of a free grass-eater in a pasture, for if economics alone were to be the foundation of human life, then the idea for which man exists is no better than that for which a bullock exists, namely, to fatten himself merrily on the green grass. Likewise, if the economic stand-point predominates in the spheres of moral, spiritual, rational, sociological, phychological and other sciences, it will lead to a very great disequilibrium, because in these spheres of life, economics has no application whatsoever. Applied to these spheres economics will convert morality and spirituality into selfishness and materialism, transform the rational sciences into the culinary arts, infuse business motives aad commercial ideas in social conduct and lead psychology to study man as merely an economic animal. Can there be a greater injustice to humanity ?

Professor M. N. Huda in his Article 'Islam and Economics' has given his experts opinion regarding the contribution of Islam as follows :

The contribution of Islam to this many-sided problem of development is yet to be found out, and expressed in clear and unequivocal language. But, even as it is understood today Islam's insistence on Man living within his means and being frugal in expenditure, and its abhorrence of excesses, showing off, and luxuries, are good indications of encouraging private savings, Islam's injunction on *Zakat*, which is compulsory levy on all forms of wealth is a clear recognition of the principle of tax revenue for community purposes, which include development today. It must be remembered that these ideas, encouraging Man to save, and compelling him to pay a part of his income for community expenses were mooted by Islam think or hear of these. These ideas have been further explored, expanded, modified and ramified by subsequent thinking, both by Muslims and by non-Muslims.

Islam also visualised the need for institutional mobilisation of savings for investment in community projects in its concept of '*Baitul-Mal*'. Again, it is the principle that Islam promulgated ; which principle has only been worked in details, and ramified and refined by subsequent generations into the mighty banking system of today. But why deny Islam what is its due credit namely, the first enunciation of the principles of savings and of taxation and of institutional pooling of resources and financing of development (as distinguished from details) ?

We shall examine the application of Islamic teachings to socio-economic development in the 20th Century under the following headings :

1. Justice and benevolence.
2. Landed Property and Ownership.
3. Economic Activities and purpose of enterprise.
4. Interest.
5. *Zakat*.
6. Banking.
7. Insurance.

1. Justice and Benevolence :

In this chapter we will discuss the attitude of a Muslim businessman towards his fellow businessmen and towards the consumers, etc. The impact of the Islamic approach on the organization of production, on price policy, on competition and on other relevant institutions, also be looked into. Mohammad Nejatullah Siddiqi have pointed out that the entire ethos of economic enterprise can be summed up as consisting of a sincere devotion to the two values of Justice and Benevolence. Ibne Qaiem states :

"Allah has classified human conduct in economic affairs in the concluding paragraphs of *sura Al-Baqara*. They are of three types : Just, Offensive and Benevolent. Therefore Justice and benevolence are the basic values which offer guidance in almost every walk of life. In the course of the proper economic conduct, they unite and harmonise economics with the political and the social conduct. It is the nature of the Islamic System."

Therefore it is necessary to interpret the meaning of the terms according to the spirit of Islam.

Justice: The Holy Qur'an ordains us to observe the principle of justice throughout our lives, particularly social life. There are not only various means to the ends we seek to achieve, but also just means and unjust. An individual faces not only the problem of choice between alternative means but also the choice between just means and unjust means. The Holy Qur'an has very clear injunctions on the point as follows:—

> "Lo! Allah enjoineth justice and benevolence, and giving to kinsfolk, and forbiddeth lewdness and abomination and offence." (*xv*: *90*).
>
> "Allah commandeth you that you restore the trusted deposits to their deserving owners, and, if you judge between mankind that you judge justly."
>
> "O ye who believe! Be staunch in justice witnesses for kindred .... So follow not passion lest you lapse (from truth) ...." (*iv*: *135*).
>
> "Give full measure and full weight in justice." (*vi*: *153*).
>
> "Say: Allah, verily, enjoineth not lewdness. Tell ye concerning Allah, that which ye know Not? Say: My Lord enjoineth justice." (*vii*: *29*)
>
> "We verily sent our messengers with clear proofs, and revealed with them the Scripture and the Balance, that mankind may abide by justice (and righteousness)." (*lvii*: *25*).
>
> "O man, what hath made thee careless concerning thy Lord, the Bountiful, who created thee, then fashioned, then proportioned thee?"

From the above verses it is quite evident that justice is a very comprehensive concept and is concerned with almost all the aspects of our life, social, economic, political and even spiritual.

Justice also implies balance, proportionality and harmony as much as it implies legal justice and "rendering to each what is his due", *i.e.*, rights. It prescribes the balanced and righteous way of life as "abidance by justice."

The Holy verse says :—

> "It will be judged between them fairly and they will not be wronged."

It may be noted that justice is clearly narrated in the Qur'anic verses as folllows :

> "Say : I believe in whatever scripture Allah hath sent down, and I am commanded to be just among you." (*xlii* : *15*)
>
> "Give full measure and full weight in justice." (*vi* : *153*).

In view that Social Equality, as a value complementary to social justice has been by the Qur'an and *Sunnah.* Hazrat Umar has elaborated it as follows : "The low and the respectable, all are equal in the religion of Allah."

Maulana Maududi as quoted by Mohammad Nejatullah Siddiqi observes as follows :—

"This concept is composed of two elements. First that a sort of balance and proportion should be maintained between the people with respect to their rights. Secondly that every one's due share should be conscientiously rendered to him . . . . What justice really demands is balance and proportion and not equality. In certain cases, justice undeniably requires equality between all the members of a society, *e.g.*, equality in the rights of citizenship. But in certain other respects equality is quite contrary to justice, *e.g.*, moral and social equality between parents and their children, and equality of remuneration between those doing higher services and those not so eminently engaged. So what Allah has ordained is not equality of right but proportion and balance in them, and this order requires that to every person should be rendered all his moral, social, economic, legal, political, and civic rights honestly."

The following principles are to be observed in order to meet the above ends.

No Injury : If taken negatively Justice requires that we would not cause any injury to any body, unless required by justice itself.

Allah has given direct commandments in this regard as follows :—

1. "Verily the oppressors shall not prosper." (*xxxii* : *37*).
2. "Allah loveth not aggressors." (*vii* : *55*).
3. "And eat not up your property among yourselves in vanity."

4. "A mother should not be made to suffer because of her child nor should he to whom the child is born (be made to suffer)."
5. "No injury, and no inflicting of injury."
6. "Whosoever injures, Allah will injure him and whosoever tyrannises, Allah shall tyrannise over him."

In case an individual business-policy involves some injurious effect Mohammed Nejatallah Siddiqi makes the following considerations necessary before deciding whether it should be carried out or not :

1. Is the impact of the injury general, or, does it affect only a small group of persons ?

2. Is the injurious effect sure to occur, or, is it only slightly probable ?

3. Is it large and substantial, or, small and negligible.

4. Is it intended by the individual, being a part of the motive behind his policy ?

5. If he does not intend to inflict any injury, is the individual conscious of the fact that his policy involves some injurious effect, or not ?

6. Is the injury accompanied by some greater general good, if so, is that general good itself very important ; so that it must be achieved ; or is the case otherwise, and it can easily be foregone ?

7. What is the importance of the gainful side of the policy to the individual's own economy ? Can he stand its loss, or not ?

8. Are there any other alternatives open for the same end, which involve no injury, or lesser injury, in comparison to this policy ?

Therefore, it is only after a careful consideration of all these points that a sincere enterpreneur can be sure whether it is advisable to launch upon the injury—involving policy or not.

Honesty and truthfulness : It strictly prohibited of these values : Fraud, deception, exploiting the innocence and ignorance of the other party, or false statements. A tradition narrated by Abu Horaira that the Prophet (peace be upon him) passed by a stock of wheat in the market. He put his hand into it whereupon his fingers got wet.

"What is this O wheat seller ?" he enquired. The man replied, "It has got wet in the rain." The Prophet said, "Why did not you put the wet stock at the top of the heap, so that the buyers may notice it ? He who deceives is not from amongst us."

On many other occasions the Holy Prophet said :

1. "Fraud leads to hell, andwhosoever starts some practice which is not in accord with our ways is condemned."

2. "To exploit the person who confides (in you) is akin to usury."

3. "One Muslim is the brother of another Muslim. It is not permissible for a Muslim to sell a commodity to an other, in which there is some defect, and not to state that defect."

It means the Prophet has directed both the buyer and the seller are at liberty to cancel the transaction until they depart from one another. If they act honestly and truthfully their transaction will bring them good. If they conceal and tell lies the good of the contract is thereupon destroyed.

Dubious and Vague Transactions : Uncertain, ambiguous, and dubious transactions are also prohibited. The following are the traditions regarding such transactions :

"The Prophet (peace be upon him) prohibited purchase by means of (random selection done by) throwing a stone (to select the object it hit as the commodity purchased), and he prohibit-all dubious transactions."

"The Prophet prohibited deals effected through touch or throwing of an object (which was thus selected as the commodity transacted. There was no close inspection or observation of it)."

"The Prophet prohibited the sale and purchase of animals not yet born, or even conceived by the female."

Hazrat Omar have said : "Do not sell or purchase fish which is still in water for it is a dubious deal."

It simply means Islam as a principle requires fair dealing, with the object of trade clearly determined, so as both the parties to a transaction may be able to weight their advantages. Ibne Hazam has stated the principle in these terms : "Sale of a thing whose particulars are not known to the seller is not allowed even if they be known to the buyer similar the commodity about which the buyer is in the dark though the seller is informed. And also transaction of such commodities is disallowed of which both of them known not the particulars of."

Ibne Qaiem has said "That the sale of non-existent things is not allowed is to be found nowhere in the Book of Allah, or traditions of the Prophet, or sayings of the Companions. It is stated neither in general terms nor with a universal meaning. The traditions do prohibit the sale of certain non-existent goods as they have prohibited dealings in certain existing commodities. The reason behind prohibition in either case is neither non-existence nor existence. The thing which the *Sunnah* disallows is ambiguous and dubious dealings and it is to be defined as the sale of things which the seller is unable to deliver, whether it exists or not.

Benevolence : Dr. Nejatullah Siddiqi gives the following meaning to *Ihsan* :

"*Ihsan* mean good behaviour, generous dealing, sympathetic attitude, tolerance, humane and kind approach, mutual consideration, regard of one another's interests ; rendering to others even something more than their due right, contenting oneself with even something less than one's own due right. It is something more than justice and its importance in social life is even more than of justice. If justice is the cornerstone of society, benevolence is its beauty and perfection. If justice saves society from undesirable things and bitterness ; benevolence makes life sweet and pleasent. No society can stand as one whole if each one of its individuals is always keen in obtaining the correct measure of his own rights at all costs, conceding to other strictly what is their due, and never more. Such a rigid society may well be free of strain and strife but it is bound to remain deprived of the (higher) values of love, gratitude, large-heartedness, sacrifice, sincerity and altruism, which alone can give to life its sweetness and beauty, and make the good in social life grown and flourish.

The following are the injunctions regarding benevolence :

1. "Allah enjoineth justice and benevolence, and giving to kinsfolk........." (*xv* : *90*).
2. "And forget not generosity among yourselves." (*ii* : *237*).
3. "Spend your wealth for the cause of Allah and be not cast by your own hands to ruin, and do good, Lo ! Allah, loveth the beneficent ." (*ii* : *195*).
4. Divorce must be pronounced twice and then (a woman) must be retained in honour or released in kindness." (*ii* : *229*).
5. "Provide for them (the divorced women), the rich according to his means and the straitened according to his means, a fair provision. (This is) a bounden duty for those who do good." (*ii* : *236*).
6. "And for him who is forgiven somewhat by his injured brother, prosecution according to usage and payment unto him in kindness." (*ii* : *178*).
7. "Is the reward of goodness aught save goodness." (*lv* : *60*).
8. "The good deed and the evil deed are not alike. Repel the evil deed with one which is better, then Lo !

he, between whom and there was enmity, will become as though he was a bosom friend." (*xli* : *34*).

9. "And be thou kind as Allah hath been kind to thee, and seek not corruption in the earth." (*xxvii* : *78*).

It is reported that Holy Prophet has said :

1. "No pity is taken upon a person who does not take pity on other people."

2. "He who is bereft of kindness is deprived of good itself."

3. "Allah is kind and likes kindness......"

4. "May Allah show mercy upon people who are polite and considerate when they sell, purchase or demand back their debts."

5. "When you weigh tilt the scale (in favour of the other party)."

6. "The Holy Prophet said to a person weighing something, weigh, and tilt the scale (in favour of the buyer).

2. Landed Property and ownership :

The system of ownership in Islam is based on the principle that no person shall possess an object except he who has control over it and who can utilize it. It is Allah alone Who owns every thing. The Holy Qur'an says :

> Say : "To whom belong the earth and all beings therein ? (say) if ye know : " They will say, "To God" ; Say : "Yet, will ye not receive admonition" ....Say : "Who is it in whose hands is the governance of all things —, Who protects (all), but is not protected (of only) ? (Say) if ye know." They will say, "(it belongs) to God". Say : "Then, how are you deluded"?

Syed Abdul Hamid Al-Khatib interprets the above verse as follows :

As Allah is the Creator of all humanity. He is their Master and their Lord. He has assumed the responsibility of providing them with their needs and has ordered them to try to discover the place where He has treasured provisions for them in this world, according to His Law. Should they then possess and utilize these treasures of provision at their will ? This is what logic and reason do not agree with. The opinion of the real owner must be known about the extent to which man is allowed to use these treasures, whether it is on a permanent basis or temporary, to what extent and for how long ?

As for permanent ownership, it is not acceptable to reason on the ground what life itself is not permanent. Permanent ownership is, therefore, reserved for Allah alone, Who says:

> "It is We who will inherit the earth and all beings thereon: To Us will they all be returned."

Therefore the temporary ownership is an individual's personal possession which he enjoys during his life-time and exercises no power over it thereafter. Holy Prophet had pointed when he said: The son of Adam says, "My wealth, my wealth": and do you possess, O, son of Adam! any wealth except that which you ate and destroyed that which you put on and have worn out or that which you spent in charity and have preserved.

A man has no right to spend the wealth except in the way he has been ordered by the original owner. If he transgresses the prescribed limits he shall be reckoned among transgressor deserving admonition. The Holy Qur'an says:

> "And ye certainly know already the first form of creation: why then do ye not celebrate His praises? See ye seed that ye sow in the ground? Is it ye that cause it to grow or are We the cause? Were it Our Will, We could crumble it to dry powder and ye would be left in wonderment (saying) "We are indeed left with debts (for nothing): Indeed we are shut out (of the fruits of our labour)". See ye the water which ye drink? Do ye bring it down (in rain) from the cloud or do We? Were it Our Will, We could make it salty (and unpalatable): then why do ye not give thanks? See ye the fire which ye kindle? Is it ye who grow the tree which feeds the fire or do We grow it? We have made it a memorial (of our handiwork), and an article of comfort and convenience for the denizens of deserts. Then celebrate with praises the name of thy Lord, the Supreme".

Regarding the ownership Holy Qur'an says:

1. Moses said to his people: "Pray for help from God, and (wait) in patience and constancy, for the earth is God's to give as a heritage to such of his servants as He pleaseth".
2. Before this We wrote in the Psalms, after the message (given to Moses): "My servants, the righteous, shall inherit the earth."

Syed Abdul Hamid Al-Khatib makes the following observations regarding landed property: The term *salihoon* meaning righteous, able, fit, mean those who are able to enliven the earth, develop it and extract its treasures, not those who are fit for worship, for every individual is fit for worship. As for enlivening and developing the earth, none but experts are fit for it to the extent they are capable of deriving benefit from it, Nisai and Abu Dawood narrate from Urwah who narrates from the Holy Prophet who said: One who enlivens a deed piece of land becomes its owner and the progeny of the oppressor has no right. One who develops a land which belongs to no one has more right to it than anyone else.

Two men came quarrelling to the Holy Prophet, one of whom had planted a date palm on the cultivated land of the other. The Holy Prophet decided that the land and men both belong to Allah. He who enlivens a dead land has more right to it than anyone else. He then ordered the owner of the field to retain his land and the owner of the date palm to remove it. It was cut down with axes and was removed. The Holy Prophet ordered this ownership to continue and go down to the heirs and legalised its renting so long as it continued to be productive and taxes were paid on it. But if the owners should neglect it and turn it into an unproductive piece of land so that no benefit is extracted from it, the owners should have no right to rent it. Jabir and Abu Hurairah narrate from the Holy Prophet, "A man must cultivate his land ; if he is not able to do that he may present it to his Maslim brother and not rent it, but if he fail to do so his land may be confiscated."

The 'Sihah' (acknowledged books of Hadith) agree on the point that the Holy Prophet had prohibited '*Muhakalah*', which they explain, means renting of land. Malik in his "Muatta" says it means renting against wheat. Rafi says that renting of land against gold and paper was unknown in those days, hence the Holy Prophet did not mention it. In such case the owner may transfer right of enlivening the land by sale or renting it to one who can cultivate it, and take compensation for what he had spent in the course of developing it. If he fails to do so, his right to it is nullified ; and if another person comes and develop it, it becomes his property. Said bin Zubair narrates from the Holy Prophet: One who develops a land when its owner had neglected it, becomes its owner.

This means that Allah has ordained the land to be a common property for all and that He has made it unlawful that one should possess it exclusively except in case one has developed it and brought forth its fruit for the common welfare. When one desists from developing and cultivating it one's right to it is cancelled and the land becomes a common property again.

By making cultivation and development of land a condition for ownership and by prohibiting its renting, the Holy

Prophet has aimed at establishing the sublime principle which was taught by Islam, *i.e.*, collective ownership and equality in rights and duties, so that each may be free to work in his own sphere of activity resulting in ampler production. This will also result in preventing one group from enforcing its superiority over the other, materially, and also in preventing a man from being a burden on the society. This will give each one an opportunity to co-operate with others in the common purpose. Qur'an say : "Man shall not get but what he labours for and the result of his labour he shall forthwith see. There he shall be rewarded amply."

Renting of land against cash payment for cultivation is equal undoubtedly, and illegal acquisition of wealth. For land belongs to Allah and is a common property and the one who cultivates has a greater right to it. The person who rents the land may be regarded as an usurper and no payment is lawful to him. His character is similar to that of the person who stands on the road to interfere in people's performance of their duties in order to force them into payment of money so that they may be allowed to proceed. This is not allowed in Islam and this is why the Holy Prophet has prohibited renting of land against cash payment. Ibn Abbas narrates from the Holy Prophet : "That a man should present his land to his brother is better for him than taking on it a fixed rent.

3. Economic Activities and Purpose of Enterprise :

According to the Holy Qur'an all the human activity should be directed towards the achievements of *Falah*—a comprehensive term denoting all sided welfare of this life as well as that of the Hereafter. Welfare means earthly existence and crowning success is the fruit of a definite cultural pattern.

It is, therefore, essential that a man should cultivate and develop all the desirable attributes in his personality and eliminate all the undersirable traits of character. The Holy Qur'an enjoins :

> "They are sure to prosper who purify themselves and manage to grow (devleop)." (*lxxxxvii* : *14*).

2. "Truly he succeeds who purifies it and causeth it grow." (*xci* : *8*).

The Qur'an has not confined itself merely to giving a list of desirable moral values but has also shown us their tangible and concrete bearing upon the various aspects of life : economic, political and social. Therefore we acquire a set of values designedly competent to function as a norm for the social sciences and for the whole art of life. These can be referred to ethical values of both with the individual and the society. Dr. Muhammad Nejatullah Siddiqi has rightly pointed out these values being the desirable ends of human achievement all life activities, individual or collective must strive towards their attainment. Economic, political, social and spiritual objectives and ideals are legitimate in so far as they contribute to the achievement of this ultimate goal. Economic activity, end economic ends are also conceived as means to this life end. The economic subtends must be consistent with the ultimate end, *Falah.* The economic policies should aim at furthering the all sided welfare denoted by the Qur'anic conception of *Falah.* This principle directly relates the economic policies with the moral values.

The Holy Qur'an has made very clear directives in this regard :—

1. "Then withdraw (O Muhammad) from him who flees from our remembrance and desires but the worldly life. (*liii : 29*).
2. "Whoso desires the harvest of the world, We give him thereof, and he has no position in the Hereafter." (*xlii : 20*).
3. "Rivalry in worldly increase has made you indifferent (to everything else) until you come to the graves. Nay, but you will come to know (the reality of things)...... You will behold the Fire." (*cii : 1-6*).
4. "And those who disbelieve indulge (in the worldly life) and eat even as the cattle eat, and Fire is their habitation." (*xlvii : 12*).
5. "Know that the worldly life is only play, and idle talk, and pagenatry, and boasting among you and rivalry in respect of wealth and children." (*lvii : 20*).

The Prophet says :

1. "Worldly craving is the source of all evil."
2. "Perish the slave of Dinar ; the slave of Dirham ; the slave of (fine) cloth......"

But it may be noted that poverty is no desirable state in the eyes of Islam. The Holy Qur'an says :—

> "By Allah I do not apprehend poverty that may befall you ; I fear abundance of wealth and of your rivalling amongst yourselves as it happened with your forerunners, and that this should distract you (from the right conduct) as it did with those that have preceded you."

Abdul Qasid narrates a tradition as cited by Dr. Muhammad Nejatullah Siddiqi as follows :—

"A man happened to pass by the Holy Prophet (peace be upon him). The Holy Prophet's Companions liked his vigour and exclaimed ; "O Prophet, had this activity been in the cause of Allah (it would have been better)." The Holy Prophet said : "If he is striving (to earn) for his small children, he is (striving) in the cause of Allah. If he is striving (to earn) for his old parents, he is in the cause of Allah. (Even) if he is striving for maintaining himself, he is in the cause of Allah. If he is striving for his wife, he is in the cause of Allah. But if he is striving to amass wealth and take pride into it and boast of it, he is (striving) in the cause of *Satan*."

The Holy Prophet once prayed : "Allah I ask thy refuge from apostasy and poverty" thereupon a person enquired : Are the two similar ?' The Prophet said "Yes".

"Allah, I ask thy refuge from poverty, scarcity and ignominy". 'Allah, I ask thy refuge from hunger for it is the worst bed fellow."

It clearly shows that Islam abhors the state of abject poverty in view of the hundred and one evils that accompany such a state of body and mind. The Holy Qur'an enjoins :

> "If you fear poverty Allah shall preserve you of His bounty, if He will." (*ix* : *8*).
>
> "Allah coineth a similitude : (on the one hand) a (mere) chattel slave, who hath control of nothing, and (on the other hand) one on whom we have bestowed a fair provision from us, and he spendeth thereof secretly and openly. Are they equal ? (*xvi* : *75*).

The Holy Prophet has streassed to earn a livelihood :

1. "The strive to earn a livelihood through right means is an obligation after the main duty (prayer)."

2. "Bread earned by one's own labour is the best of all earnings."

3. "Wealth is regarded a positive asset for a good man of the right conduct. The Holy Prophet has said : "Wealth rightly acquired is a good thing for the righteous man."

4. "Good is the righteous wealth for the righteous man."

It is also been stressed by the Holy Qur'an all the natural resources which have been created by Allah are for man's use. The Qur'anic injunctions in this regard are as follows :—

1. "And We have given you (mankind) power in the earth and appointed for you therein a livelihood." (*vii* : *10*).
2. "He it is Who has made earth subservient unto you, so walk in the paths thereof and eat of His providence." (*lxvii* : *15*).
3. "And We have appointed the day for livelihood." (*lxxvii* : *11*).

4. "And when the prayer is ended, then disperse in the land and seek of Allah's bounty". (*lxii* : *10*).
5. "And others travel in the land in search of Allah's bounty." (*lxxiv* : *20*).

4. Interest :

We have discussed this topic very elaborately in part 3, Chapter 1 of this book. Here we shall only add to our previous discussion making a special reference to the application of Islamic teachings to Socio-Economic Development in the 20th Century.

Prof. M. N. Huda in his article "Islam and Economics" regarding interest opines that the modern economy is an important challenge to Islam, namely, interest, is also increasingly losing the ground under its feet. It is well-known that Islam prohibits interest, as a pre-determined payment on borrowed funds, irrespective of the purpose, or the results of use, of such funds ; it encourages, instead, a sharing of post-determined profits, between the borrower and the lender. It has been alleged that a modern developing economy cannot work except through interest, for encouraging savings, mobilising them into banks, and allocating and channelising them into investments ; if so, interest is the basis of Economics, and of economic planning. But the question is : Is it really so ? Is Interest playing such an important role in any of these activities ? Interest might have been freely determined, and might have been a powerful influence, in the hey-days of free enterprise ; but these hey-days have long ceased to exist, ever since the establishment of the first Central Bank in the world, which influenced, and later on controlled, the rate of interest. Even when interest influenced mobilisation and allocation of resources, it was controlled, severely, and even made ineffective, by deliberate policies of the Central Bank. And now that we have a planning economy, everywhere in the world, the allocation of resources presents a problem, not of interest but of choice. Once this very important choice of investments is made, interest, as well as other policies of the Government, are made to serve the only purpose of implementing those decisions, and inducing, and if necessary compelling, these investments. In the planned economy of today, interest has thus already been relegated to a negligible position.

Interest is regarded as the price of funds, borrowed by the banker from the saver, and by the investor from the banker ; and this price, as any other price, is alleged to have an influence on the supply of funds at both ends. It is true that interest works as the price for borrowed funds ; today this price is pre-determined and fixed ; this is said to ensure enough borrowed funds. If this price is made indeterminate, and is fixed *adhoc* as a share of profits and losses, actually made at the end of a business year, it is alleged that the price will be uncertain, and therefore, the supply of borrowed funds will be fluctuating. This uncertainty will be there, even if the share of profits and losses, as between borrowers and lenders, is pre-determined, on the basis of the share of 'stake', taken by respective parties in business. Therefore, so it is said, the replacement of Interest by Profit and-Loss-Sharing is bound to affect a modern economy adversely, in its problem of mobilising adequate savings into proper investments.

But, do we have knowledge enough, to be dogmatic about this predominant role attributed to interest, in channelising savings into investments ? Have we searched, adequately or at all, the minds of the saver, the banker, and the investor, so as to know how they will react to a sharing of profits and losses, in place of the present interest ? How will they respond to a pre-determined share of post-determined not profits, as against a pre-determined interest irrespective of profits or losses ? This search, not research, into the hearts of the saver, the banker, and the investor, is yet to be made : and that being so, should we not keep our minds open, and not hazard a dogmatic proposition, either this way or that, till an intensive search is made to know the reactions of the of groups involved ?

Mr. S. A. Irshad in his article "Economic System for Interest Free Islamic Society" while discussing Economy based on interest made the following observations and submitted the reasons for introducing the Interest-Free Economy System as follows :—

Interest has been forbidden in the Holy Scriptures of Jews as well as of Christians. The limits of interest imposed by the Old Testament were not adhered by Jews and the Roman Catholic Church prohibited interest as long as it remained in power. The Scripture of Islam, the Holy Qur'an, has forbidden interest very strictly. The Muslims adhered to the limits of the Holy Qur'an religiously and politically as long as they remained powerful in the world. During the Feudal System the State Rulers used to need funds to wage wars against other States and private money-lenders started lending money to these State Rulers on interest. It was during the reign of Henry VIII that interest was recognized by Law. After the control of the Imperialistic Powers in Europe the public banks were established and the application of interest was legally recognized and practised around the world wherever this modern banking system prevailed.

Interest has been responsible for the destruction of many powers and cause of misery of many societies. The collapse of Wall Street Finance Market in the early 30s in U.S.A.

brought an earthquake in the economic structure of the West. The economy of the world was shaken and shattered and many thinkers began to wonder about the soundness of such an economy based on interest. This followed the control of credit and interest by the Central Bank in almost all the countries of the world. Since then the Central Banks are fighting with the rate of interest whereas the problems of inflation, deflation and trade crisis continue and the bankers as well as the economists are facing a new problem every day all over the world.

When we look at the two main existing economic systems of the world the Capitalism and the Communism we find that Communism allows no free enterprise and almost all trade and industry is owned by the State. In the Capitalism, the power and wealth is concentrated in few hands and the interest constitutes one of the foundation stones on which the edifice of modern economy based. Can we look forward to a time when these defects are eliminated from the society and by working on economic plans establish an economy of golden means eliminating the application of interest which is the real cause of the economic ills of the world and thus evolving an Interest-Free Economy in this world, as conceived of by Islam.

The Interest-Free Economy has aroused interest not only in Islamic World but also in the Christian World from time to time. It is interesting to note that eminent Western economists regard the abolition of interest as the only way to save the Capitalism from disaster. For example Lord J. W. Keynes, a well-known economist, believed that interest is in the nature of unearned income, it both initiates and aggravates crisis and it could be dispensed with by bringing about the necessary institutional change.

5. *Zakat* :

This topic we have already discussed in detail in Part 3, Chapter I of this book. Here we shall only add to our previous discussion by making a special reference to the application of Islamic teachings to Socio-Economic Development in the 20th Century.

Mr. S. A. Irshad regarding *Zakat* opines that the main objective of the Institution of *Zakat* is the eradication of poverty from the society. The greatest evil of money is when it is accumulated in few hands whereas there exists poverty and distress in the society. The *Zakat* is a duty laid by Allah on the well-to-do people of the Society for the benefit of the poor and the distressed. The institution of *Zakat* should, therefore, be organized and the funds collected and utilized for the purpose of eradication of poverty from the society. There is no other economic system in the world which has solved the problems of hoarded idle money which remain unproductive and denies all the benefits for the welfare of the society. Moreover, it is the most effective method to eradicate poverty from the society.

Mr. Shujat Ali Siddiqi in his article entitled "Islamic Economics with special reference to *Zakat*" while dealing with the *Zakat* observe that the operation of this ideal tax can bring about a gradual re-distribution of wealth and also help considerably in fighting inflationary tendencies whenever they appear in a country. Apart from the undue increase in the currency of a country, shortage of goods and "velocity" there is one important factor which keeps the market uneasy and it is the wrong distribution of wealth. The aftermath of the last World War had been an unduly excessive issue of currency notes which enriched a small percentage of the population everywhere but improvished the rest. This situation was further aggravated by the circumstances which paved the way for the earning of easy money by a number of persons, the decline in the purchasing power of the middle classes and the impoverishment of the bulk of the population. The correct operation of this tax can gradually restore the equilibrium. The imposition of 2½% on the savings as well as the assets will in 5 to 10 years time redistribute the wealth more equitably, considerably increase the purchasing power of the masses, and also import stability to the market by indirectly influencing general and the under-developed countries in particular and the obvious remedy is to gradually curtail the flow of easy money and reduce the purchasing power of the favoured few in the larger interest of the Community. This tax is therefore, not a mere tax but a complete scheme which can gradually bring about a sociological revolution, a steady but sure economic change and a moral awakening wherever it is tried with all its attendant requirements.

The attendant requirements are as already mentioned a belief in God and the life Hereafter. Can it be imagined that the threatening Anti-God Forces can be fought with an open profession of allegiance to Mammon and with the culture of Capitalist and Corporative economy? Can the onslaught of Communism be stopped with industrialisation and the gradual raising of the standard of living unaccompanied by a moral and religious awakening in the masses? Will not the continuous stream of propaganda raising hopes of a higher and a still higher standard of living create more hopes than can be fulfilled and generate frustration and envy even where it does not exist at present? So let the economic and moral forces work together instead of working against each other and see how a change can be brought about by this remedy, a tax in name but really the most potent cure of our ills. This tax is no other than "*Zakat*" and constitutes one of the five obligations of a Muslim.

The Qur'anic injunction "So that the wealth shall not circulate only among the rich from among you sums up the guiding spirit of the Islamic State. It does not believe in class war nor dies it undertake a complete socialisation of the basic instruments of production and distribution. It allows individuals to acquire private property and the right to pass it in inheritance but it does not allow the concentration of wealth into few hands in order to perpetuate Capitalism in its naked form.

The Islamic State is a welfare State which guarantees full employment along with equality of opportunities. The leavy of *Zakat*, a tax of 2½% on the capital and savings, produce of the land and articles of trade and cattle, is intended to distribute wealth in the society. The amount collected must be spent on the specific objects mentioned in the Holy Qur'an (which says) :—

> "The alms are only for the poor and the needy and those who collect them and those whose hearts are to be reconciled, and to free the captives and the debtors and for the cause of Allah, and for the wayfarers, a duty imposed by Allah ; Allah is Knowing and Wise."

The taxable limit is kept very low and consists of the possession of 52 tolas of silver or 8 tolas of gold, which means that the mere possession of a little saving in gold or silver turn a man into a "bourgeois" and conduces to a wider distribution of wealth.

Thus the society in an Islamic State becomes a class free and contended entity where the basic requirements of each individual are provided for by the State if he fails to get them through his own efforts. If, however, the operation of the *Zakat* tax fails to provide basic requirements (*i.e.*, food, clothing and shelter) the State is bound to levy additional takes (*Zariabs*) on the well-to-do members of the population to enable the State to meet its obligations. Even the non-Muslims are the State's responsibility if they are poor or cripple. This is illustrated by one of the clauses of the treaty entered into by Khalid bin Walid, the well-known conqueror, with the Christians in the time of the First Caliph :—

"*Jazia* will be leviable but the State will support the non-believer and his dependents if he is old and has become incapacitated or cripple or when a rich man becomes poor."

6. Banking :

Mr. S. A. Irshad while making assertions in his article "Economic System for Interest-Free Islamic Society" and while discussing about the feasibility of the interest-free economic society regarding the banking system based on the abovementioned theory discusses the implementation of the principle of *Mudarabah* as follows :

One of the very important things, the Interest-Free Economic System can do, is to establish institutions on the basis of *Mudarabah*, where capital and labour can be combined together as partners for work and can share the profit and loss of the enterprises equitably. It will, therefore, be a great service to the human race if the differences of the capital and the labour can be reconciled once for all in the theory and practice of *Mudarabah*. In this way labour and capital can work together smoothly and whole-heartedly in co-operation to bring about a better understanding against the labour strikes in the national field and the economic cold wars in the international sphere. Agriculture, Industry and Business can be developed on this principle. This will serve as a good device for the mobilization of capital and utilization of labour and this can prove one of the most effective methods for full employment in the country to provide basic needs to every citizen of the State and to eradicate poverty from the society.

Dr. Nejetullah Siddiqi in his book entitled "Banking without Interest" discusses the feasibility of the functioning as follows :

The bank would be established on the principles of joint stock companies. A number of persons would provide share capital, so that with this joint investment some enterprises may be financed and services rendered for earning profit and receiving remunerations, on the basis of partnership or *Mudarabat*. The people who would thus provide capital investment would hereafter he called "shareholders". The minimum number of shareholders would be two. But no maximum number has been fixed as a rule, although for the sake of operational convenience and for other considerations it is appropriate to fix a ceiling, which would vary from place to place and from time to time. The number of shareholders would not be very large and if considered in their best interest may be lowest, but would always be more than two. The amount of capital provided by each shareholder may be equal or may vary. It may, however, be an ideal proposition to fix the value of one share at Rs. one lac, and every shareholder may be allowed to secure as many shares as he may like. The minimum and maximum limits of the subscribed capital may also be specified. Eventually, each shareholder would become the owner of the bank, proportionately according to the position on his assets in the total investment.

As regards Interest-free World Bank Mr. S. A. Irshad in

his article entitled "Economic System for Interest-Free Islamic Society" has made the following suggestions :

When any country decides to eliminate interest within the country and intends to carry on international trade with other countries on zero rate of interest, it will find many friendly countries to co-operate and thus they will extend all necessary economic facilities for the common cause. Where there is will, there is way. They will find several alternatives to eliminate interest in their trade transactions between the respective countries. One of the methods will be to do international trade on barter system, exchanging the commodities between the various countries. It can be further modified to balance if any, on either side will be dealt with on zero rate of interest. Foreign loans, if necessary, should be secured on the basis of profit sharing investments. In this way the interest cannot only be eliminated inside the country but it can also be dispensed with in the International Field. For this purpose, all the Muslim countries of the world can have their own Interest-Free World Bank to take care of the International Trade and Foreign Loans between the member countries. Any other country believing in the concept of Interest-Free Economy can also become the member of this Bank. The working of the Interest-Free World Bank will be in the following manner :

1. All the countries of the world believing in the concept of Interest-Free Economy will become the members of this Bank. The share capital will be subscribed by all the member countries and the Bank will be governed by a Board of Directors elected by the member countries.

2. All the international trade between the member countries as well as outside the member countries will be routed through this Bank and it will be transacted free of interest as mentioned above.

3. The surplus resources of the member countries will make the Investment Pool at the disposal of the Bank to help financially the under-developed member countries by way of interest-free loans or investment on profit sharing basis, as the case may be.

4. The Bank will make a Code of Economic Ethics and the working of the Bank will be so designed as to meet the social and economic requirements of the Interest-Free Society.

7. Insurance :

As regards the status of modern contract of Insurance under the Islamic. Law Dr. Mohammad Muslehuddin observed as follows :—

The basic notions of the Shari'a or Islamic Law relating to transactions are ethical in character. Unjustified enrichment and risk (gharar) are both forbidden, vague expressions and delays in delivery rejected. In short all such factors as lead to disputes are condemned. Uncertainty as to obligations undertaken by the parties is considered to be a risk. 'Starting from the Qur'anic prohibition of a certain game of hazard, Islamic Law insists that there must be no doubt concerning the obligations undertaken by the parties to a contract. The object of the contract, in particular, must be determined (*ma'lum*, 'known'; opposite *majhul*, unknown'). This requirement is particularly strict as regards objects which can be measured or weighed, which are subject to prohibition of *riba*; no undermined quantity (*juzaf*) is permissible here, not even if the price of a unit of weight or measure be stated. For this reason it is forbidden to sell dates which are still unripe, to be delivered when they have ripened, because it is unknown whether they will ripen at all.'

Among other causes which go to vitiate a contract unjustified enrichment and risk are the most conspicuous. Clearly, the contract of insurance could not be valid in Islamic law unless it were free from these. The Modernists contend that it is in fact a contract of indemnity providing for the genuine loss of the insured with no unlawful enrichment to either of the parties. If their contention were correct then the contract would be unobjectionable. We must, therefore, examine whether it does in fact correspond, at least in its outward form, to the contract of indemnity called *Kafala* (bailment or suretyship).

Kafala, according to the Islamic law, is of two sorts, *Kafala* for the person which is termed as *Kafala al-Nafs* and *Kafala* for property which is termed as *Kalafat al-Mal*. It is the latter with which we are here concerned. The word '*at-Kafala*' is derived from '*al-Kifl*' which means junction or addition. In the language of the law it signifies the junction of one person to another in relation to a claim. The *Kafala* is so named because it implies the adding by one person of his responsibility to that of another in respect of a demand for something. The peculiarity of this contract is that 'the creditor or obligee can call upon either the original debtor or the surety to perform the obligation, and a demand from one would not affect his right of demand from the other if the obligation remains unfulfilled. So that if the agreement be that the original debtor should be released from his obligation, it would not be a contract of suretyship (bailment), but of *Hawala* or transfer of an obligation.'

Mr. S. A. Irshad in his article "Economic System for Interest-Free Islamic Society" has made the following assertions regarding Insurance :

The main purpose of Insurance in Islam is to divide the financial loss of a person among the majority of the people of the society so that the burden of a particular person who becomes the victim of an unfortunate happening should be shared by other fortunate persons of the community to keep economic equilibrium in the society. Its mechanism is based on the principles of co-operation and mutual help for the welfare of the society. The Interest-Free Insurance in the country will, therefore, eliminate all the chances of gambling and speculation and will insure all genuine and normal risks of the members of the society to provide moral and material protection of the people in lieu of payment of reasonable premium. The surplus funds of the Insurance Companies will be utilized for investment in business and industry for the economic development of the society on the profit-sharing basis either through the Banks or through Public Investment Fund or direct by the Insurance Companies.

To make it more useful for Interest-Free Economy, Insurance Companies will work in close co-operation with the Interest-Free Banks. They will insure that the losses in the Bank's business are written off for the investors and the depositors. The Insurance Companies will also insure the repayment of loans to the banks and will insure the investments of the people with the banks.

THE END